The Relationship between Human Security Discourse and International Law

The concept of human security has emerged in international relations and policy as an idea which not only seeks to relocate the focus of international society on the individual, but also challenges the current priorities of the international community. In particular, it places emphasis on promoting and facilitating a nexus between security, development and human rights. It is potentially a paradigm in the making, gaining considerable momentum within the UN, international relations scholarship and regional bodies. And yet by and large it continues to be unexplored by the international legal community, despite the success of a number of international treaties being attributed to the discourse.

This book seeks to address this gap, and establish the nature of the relationship between human security discourse and international law, determining whether human security can meaningfully contribute to the international legal framework. To determine this, the book analyses the core principles of human security discourse and examines the degree to which they find parallels in the existing normative structure of international law. The book examines how the broad–narrow debate that dominates human security discourse has played out in international law-making. It goes on to consider the processes for the creation of so-called 'human security' treaties in order to determine a blueprint for future development of international human security treaty law. In concluding, Shireen Daft sets out a structured principled approach through which international legal scholarship can engage with human security, highlighting the ways in which engagement between the two fields can be sustained.

Shireen Daft is an Associate Lecturer at Macquarie University in Sydney, Australia.

Routledge Research in International Law

For a full list of titles in this series, visit https://www.routledge.com/Routledge-Research-in-International-Law/book-series/INTNLLAW

Available:

The Rule of Law in the United Nations Security Council Decision-Making Process
Turning the Focus Inwards
Sherif Elgebeily

Universal Jurisdiction in International Criminal Law
The Debate and the Battle for Hegemony
Aisling O'Sullivan

The Right to Democracy in International Law
Between Procedure, Substance and the Philosophy of John Rawls
Khalifa A Alfadhel

Latin America and the International Court of Justice
Contributions to International Law
Edited by Paula Wojcikiewicz Almeida and Jean-Marc Sorel

Fragmentation vs the Constitutionalisation of International Law
A Practical Inquiry
Edited by Andrzej Jakubowski and Karolina Wierczyńska

Legal Accountability and Britain's Wars 2000–2015
Peter Rowe

Means of Transportation and Registration of Nationality
Transportation Registered by International Organizations
Vincent P. Cogliati-Bantz

Regionalism in International Law
Ján Klučka

The Relationship between Human Security Discourse and International Law

A Principled Approach

Shireen Daft

Routledge
Taylor & Francis Group
LONDON AND NEW YORK

First published 2018 by Routledge

2 Park Square, Milton Park, Abingdon, Oxfordshire OX14 4RN
52 Vanderbilt Avenue, New York, NY 10017

Routledge is an imprint of the Taylor & Francis Group, an informa business

First issued in paperback 2019

British Library Cataloguing in Publication Data
A catalogue record for this book is available from the British Library

Library of Congress Cataloging in Publication Data
A catalog record for this book has been requested

ISBN: 978-1-138-24391-0 (hbk)
ISBN: 978-0-367-88438-3 (pbk)

Typeset in Galliard
by Taylor & Francis Books

Contents

List of abbreviations

AFRICOM	United States Africa Command
ANSA	Armed Non-State Actor
APEC	Asia-Pacific Economic Cooperation
APMs	Anti-Personnel Mines
ASEAN	Association of Southeast Asian Nations
ASP	Assembly of State Parties
ATT	Arms Trade Treaty
AU	African Union
CCM	Convention on Cluster Munitions
CCMs	Country Coordinating Mechanisms
CFSP	Common Foreign and Security Policy
CCW	Convention on Certain Conventional Weapons
CD	Conference on Disarmament
CHS	Commission on Human Security
CICC	Coalition for the International Criminal Court
CROC	Convention on the Rights of the Child
CSDP	Common Security and Defence Policy
DRC	Democratic Republic of the Congo
ECOSOC	Economic, Social and Cultural Council
ECOWAS	Economic Community of West African States
ESS	European Security Strategy
EU	European Union
FHS	Friends of Human Security
GATT	General Agreement on Tariffs and Trade
HDR	Human Development Report
HRW	Human Rights Watch
HSN	Human Security Network
HSU	UN Human Security Unit
IANSA	International Action Network on Small Arms
ICBL	International Campaign to Ban Landmines
ICC	International Criminal Court
ICCPR	International Covenant on Civil and Political Rights
ICESCR	International Covenant on Economic, Social and Cultural Rights

ICISS	International Commission on Intervention and State Sovereignty
ICJ	International Court of Justice
ICRC	International Committee of the Red Cross/Crescent
ICTR	International Criminal Tribunal for Rwanda
ICTY	International Criminal Tribunal for Former Yugoslavia
ILC	International Law Commission
ILM	International Law Materials
IR	International Relations
JICA	Japan International Cooperation Agency
KPCS	Kimberley Process Certification Scheme
LDCs	Least Developed Countries
LRA	Lord's Resistance Army
MDGs	Millennium Development Goals
MNC	Multinational Corporation
MOFA	Ministry of Foreign Affairs (Japan)
MSF	Médecins Sans Frontières
MSI	Multi-Stakeholder Initiative
NGO	Non-Governmental Organisation
NSA	Non-State Actor
OAU	Organisation of African Unity
OCHA	United Nations Office for the Coordination of Humanitarian Affairs
ODA	Official Development Assistance
OECD	Organisation for Economic Cooperation and Development
OSCE	Organisation for Security and Cooperation in Europe
PAC	Partnership Africa Canada
PCIJ	Permanent Court of International Justice
PPPs	Public–Private Partnerships
R2P	Responsibility to Protect
RBM	Roll Back Malaria
ROC	Republic of Congo
RUF	Revolutionary United Front
TICAD	Tokyo International Conference on African Development
TWAIL	Third World Approaches to International Law
UDHR	Universal Declaration on Human Rights
UN	United Nations
UNAIDS	Joint United Nations Programme on HIV/AIDS
UNAMID	African Union–United Nations Mission in Darfur
UNDP	United Nations Development Programme
UNFCC	United Nations Framework Convention on Climate Change
UNGA	United Nations General Assembly
UNITA	National Union for the Total Independence of Angola
UNMEER	United Nations Mission for Ebola Emergency Response
UNSC	United Nations Security Council

UNSG	United Nations Secretary-General
UNTS	United Nations Treaty Series
VCLT	Vienna Convention on the Law of Treaties
WHO	World Health Organisation
WTO	World Trade Organisation

Acknowledgments

This book has been a labour of love and perseverance, and only possible through the support, encouragement and guidance of those around me.

First and foremost, my sincerest appreciation must go out to my mentors and colleagues at Macquarie Law School, where this book first came to fruition in the form of my PhD dissertation. Particular acknowledgment must go to my principal supervisor, Shawkat Alam. He has been a steadfast pillar of support and a source of inspiration throughout the process, and the final product would not have been possible without his diligence and encouragement. Also my thanks to the former dean of the Law School, Natalie Klein, who was a constant source of insightful advice and an inspiration, and more generally to my colleagues at Macquarie Law School, who have been sources of encouragement and insight throughout the process.

I would like to thank my friends, and in particular my fellow doctoral candidates, who have been a source of shared experience, unique understanding and encouragement. Last but not least, I want to thank my family for their enduring love, patience and support throughout this endeavour. This book is dedicated to the memory of my father. He may not have truly understood his bookish, scholastically minded daughter, but he had an unwavering faith in my ability to achieve whatever I set my mind to do. And that has made all the difference.

The relationship between human security discourse and international law

An introduction

> *And what is the argument for the other side? Only this: that no case has been found in which it has been done before. That argument does not appeal to me in the least. If we never do anything, which has not been done before, we shall never get anywhere. The law will stand still while the rest of the world goes on and that will be bad for both.* – Lord Denning[1]

I Introduction

While it is accurate to state that international law has traditionally had the primary goal of regulating the relationships between states, this is not the whole story. From the inception of the United Nations a human-centred focus has been present,[2] and this focus has become increasingly entrenched in the international legal system, especially, though not exclusively, as a result of international human rights law, international refugee law and international humanitarian law. This is well encapsulated in a seminal decision of the International Criminal Tribunal for Former Yugoslavia:

> … a state-sovereignty-orientated approach has been gradually supplanted by a human-being-oriented approach. Gradually the maxim of Roman law *hominum causa omne jus constitutum est* (all law is created for the benefit of human beings) has gained a firm foothold in the international community as well.[3]

The duty of states to protect their citizenry against abuse is one of the fundamental principles of the international human rights regime and has been firmly enshrined as such.[4]

1 *Packer* v *Packer* [1953] 2 AER 127, 129 (Lord Denning).
2 Indeed, it can be said to pre-date the United Nations, in the likes of the earliest architects of international law, such as Grotius and de Vattel, who will be discussed later.
3 *Prosecutor v Tadíc (Interlocutory Appeal)* (International Criminal Tribunal for Former Yugoslavia, Appeals Chamber, Case No 94-1, 2 October 1995) [97].
4 Most notably in Article 2(1) of both the *International Covenant on Civil and Political Rights,* opened for signature 16 December 1966, 999 UNTS 171 (entered into force

Beyond human rights, international humanitarian law is another reflection of international law that seeks to protect individuals. A number of norms emerging out of international humanitarian law, such as the humane treatment required by Common Article 3 of the *Geneva Conventions*,[5] have attained the status of customary international law, and consequently form the bedrock of international norms and principles.[6]

People-centred concerns are also increasingly influencing the perception of the role of the international community in international peace and security. In an article written in 1999, Kofi Annan pointed out that '[w]hen we read the [UN] Charter today, we are more than ever conscious that its aim is to protect individual human beings, not to protect those who abuse them'.[7] Currently, the Security Council is charged with the maintenance of international peace and security.[8] The Security Council has been vested with considerable political and legal authority to discharge this responsibility, and under the auspices of Chapter VII of the UN Charter has the unique ability to make decisions that are binding on all Member States. It has been increasingly recognised in the past two decades that large-scale human suffering is both a consequence of and contributing factor to conflict and instability, and thus that massive human rights violations constitute a direct threat to international peace and security.[9] A very early example of human rights considerations influencing the work of the Security Council was the imposition of the mandatory sanctions regime on South Africa from 1977 to 1994, demonstrating a universal consensus on the unacceptability of the practice of Apartheid.[10] In recent years the Security Council has recognised an increasingly broad range of threats as

3 January 1976) ('ICCPR') and the *International Covenant on Economic, Social and Cultural Rights*, opened for signature 16 December 1966, 993 UNTS 3 (entered into force 3 November 1976) ('ICESCR').

5 *Geneva Convention for the Amelioration of the Condition of the Wounded and Sick in Armed Forces in the Field (First Geneva Convention)* opened for signature 12 August 1949, 75 UNTS 31 (entered into force 21 October 1950); *Geneva Convention for the Amelioration of the Condition of Wounded, Sick and Shipwrecked Members of Armed Forces at Sea (Second Geneva Convention)* opened for signature 12 August 1949, 75 UNTS 85 (entered into force 21 October 1950); *Geneva Convention Relative to the Treatment of Prisoners of War (Third Geneva Convention)* opened for signature 12 August 1949, 75 UNTS 135; *Geneva Convention Relative to the Protection of Civilian Persons in Time of War (Fourth Geneva Convention)* opened for signature 12 August 1949, 75 UNTS 287 (entered into force 21 October 1950) Common Article 3.

6 See, eg, Jean-Marie Henckaerts and Louise Doswald-Beck, *Customary International Humanitarian Law* (ICRC and Cambridge, 2005) vol I: Rules.

7 Kofi Annan, 'Two Concepts of Sovereignty', *The Economist* (London), 18 September 1999 <http://www.un.org/News/ossg/sg/stories/kaecon.html>.

8 *Charter of the United Nations*, art 24.

9 See, eg, Kofi Annan, *In Larger Freedom: Towards development, security and human rights for all*, UN GAOR, Fifty-ninth sess, Agenda Item 45 and 55, UN Doc A/59/2005/Add.3 (26 May 2005); United Nations General Assembly, *United Nations Millennium Declaration*, 55/2, UN GA Res, Fifty-fifth sess, Agenda Item 60(b), UN Doc A/RES/55/2 (18 September 2000).

10 Security Council Resolution 418 (1977), UN SCOR, UN Doc S/RES/418 (4 November 1977) [2]–[5].

part of its mandate, such as viewing the spread of HIV/AIDS as a security threat,[11] and has demonstrated an increasingly people-oriented focus, reflected in resolutions relating to civilians in armed conflict, threats to children in armed conflict, and the role of women in peace and security.[12] These developments have, however, occurred in a piecemeal and inconsistent fashion, without a clear normative framework.

These comprise just a few examples of how a 'humanisation of international law'[13] is evident in existing international law. It is in light of this movement in international law that a shift away from the traditional paradigm of security to a focus on 'human security' is considered. Human security is not a concept that (necessarily) requires fundamental change of the international legal system, but rather one that builds on its existing precepts. What it offers, however, is cohesion, and a clear normative framework through which to perceive the role of international law. As security is one of the central values of any legal system,[14] it is vitally important that we understand the purpose and depth of the concept, and its surrounding discourse.

II Human security

Human security emerged in the wake of the Cold War and the rise of globalisation. Human security discourse has since permeated much of the discussion of international peace and security.[15] First introduced in 1994 by the United Nations Development Programme (UNDP) in its annual Human Development Report, human security is a people-centred approach that challenges the current security paradigm and its focus on the state.[16] The Commission on Human Security[17] defines human security as a concept 'to protect the vital core of all human lives in ways that enhance human freedoms and human fulfilment. Human security means protecting fundamental freedoms – freedoms that are the essence of life. It means protecting people from critical (severe) and pervasive (widespread) threats and situations.'[18]

11 Security Council Resolution 1308 (2000), UN SCOR, UN Doc S/RES/1308 (17 July 2000).
12 See, eg, Security Council Resolution 1674 (2006) on the Protection of Civilians in Armed Conflict, UN SCOR, UN Doc S/2006/1674 (28 April 2006); Security Council Resolution 2143 (2014) on Children Affected by Armed Conflict, UN SCOR, UN Doc S/2014/2143 (7 March 2014).
13 Using the phrasing of Theodor Meron, *The Humanization of International Law* (Martinus Nijhoff, 2006).
14 Jeremy Bentham, *The Theory of Legislation* (Elibron Classics, Reprint, 1896) I, 307.
15 Mary Martin and Taylor Owen, 'The Second Generation of Human Security: lessons from the UN and EU experience' (2010) 86(1) *International Affairs* 211, 212.
16 United Nations Development Programme (UNDP), *Human Development Report 1994* (UNDP, 1994).
17 Commissioned by the UN with the express purpose of defining human security and determining its scope, the Commission was chaired by Amartya Sen and Sadato Ogata.
18 Commission on Human Security (CHS), *Human Security Now* (UN, 2003) 4.

The UNDP described human security as having four essential characteristics.[19] The first of these, and the least disputed, is the notion that human security is *people-centred*. In other words, human security requires a shift in the security paradigm away from the state as the referent of security to the individual as the object to be protected. This approach refocuses security on the survival, livelihood and dignity of individuals.[20] Secondly, the UNDP emphasised that human security is a *universal* concern.[21] This was a response to the interconnected and transnational nature of threats on the modern global stage. Thirdly, human security is easier to ensure through the pursuit of *prevention* strategies than later intervention.[22] And finally the UNDP described the components of human security as *interdependent*.[23] Human security, according to the UNDP, could be broken up into seven components: economic, food, health, environmental, personal, community and political security.[24] These components, and their related threats are closely interconnected, and it is only by recognising the linkages that effective strategies to achieve human security can be sought.

III Why human security?

Human security was not the only 'new' model of security to emerge in recent years in response to the developing threats and altered security environment. Alongside human security, other alternative conceptions of security have included constructivist, feminist and post-structuralist security studies, the Copenhagen School of securitisation, and critical security studies, which promotes intellectual pluralism on the issue of security generally.[25] A number of these theories support a shift in focus towards the interests of individuals. However, none places the individual as squarely at the centre of the conception of security in the way that human security does. Nor do the other theories offer the holistic approach of addressing a multitude of threats in an integrated way as the best means to protect security. Finally, no other has had the widespread acceptance outside of the academic sphere of security studies that human security has experienced.

Human security not only complements but potentially unifies the overarching principles and goals established in the UN Charter. The Preamble to the UN Charter establishes the goals of the UN to promote and protect international peace and security; to promote economic and social progress and improve standards of living; and to promote justice, respect human dignity and reaffirm universal human rights.[26] Human security discourse considers these goals to be interconnected

19 UNDP, *Human Development Report 1994* (UNDP, 1994) 22–3.

20 *Follow-up to Paragraph 143 on Human Security of the 2005 World Summit Outcome*, GA Res 66/290, Sixty-sixth sess, Agenda Item 14 and 117, UN Doc A/RES/66/290 (25 October 2012) [3].

21 UNDP, *Human Development Report 1994* (UNDP, 1994) 22.

22 Ibid.

23 Ibid 23.

24 Ibid 138.

25 These various schools will be examined in detail in Chapter One.

26 *Charter of the United Nations*, Preamble. See also the purposes of the United Nations as outlined in Article 1.

and mutually reinforcing, and seeks to protect the core of these principles – to establish a safe and stable environment in which these goals can be fully realised.[27] In promoting integrated policy action for addressing threats, human security may offer the best possible opportunity for developing a sustainable strategy for international peace and security.

IV Human security and international law

Human security remains a highly contested concept, both in terms of its conceptual definition and its practical utility, but it is also a concept and discourse receiving increased attention in UN forum policy-making, and the subject of a continuing body of debate and discussion in academic circles. However, while human security has been, if not embraced, at least increasingly discussed by a range of disciplines, legal scholars have largely remained silent on the issue, though a small body of dedicated work has recently started to emerge.[28] What discussion there has been has mainly focused on the perceived challenges of human security to state sovereignty, or its operationalisation in controversial areas of international law. But rarely have the analyses of human security given concentrated attention to the multifaceted dimensions of human security, generally concerning themselves solely with the shift in focus from state to the individual.

Bringing international law into the discussion of human security is vital for a number of reasons. Law is the major framework through which security is pursued. As von Tigerstrom points out, 'the provision of security is one of the central purposes of legal systems'.[29] The referent of human security is the individual, and as such justice is an important aspect to be considered and is a contributing factor to both security and development, along with accountability and the rule of law central to promoting good governance, peace and stability. As a number of discussions and definitions of human security point out, the rule of law, legal accountability, good governance and respect for international legal norms are essential to human security strategies.[30] It is also essential that human security is embraced by international law to give the concept greater legitimacy and authority, and it is equally

27 These issues will be explored in more detail in Chapter Four.

28 See, eg, Barbara von Tigerstrom, *Human Security and International Law: Prospects and Problems* (Hart Publishing, 2007); Gerd Oberleitner, 'Human Security: A Challenge to International Law?' (2005) 11 *Global Governance* 185; Cedric Ryngaert and Math Noortmann (ed), *Human Security and International Law: The Challenge of Non-State Actors* (Intersentia, 2014); Matthias C Kettemann, 'The Conceptual Debate on Human Security and its Relevance for the Development of International Law' (2006) 1(3) *Human Security Perspectives* 39; Andrej Zwitter, *Human Security, Law and the Prevention of Terrorism* (Routledge, 2011); Alice Edwards and Carla Ferstman (eds), *Human Security and Non-Citizens: Law, Policy and International Affairs* (Cambridge University Press, 2010).

29 Tigerstrom, above n 28, 3.

30 See, eg, Kofi Annan, 'Towards a Culture of Peace' (2001) UNESCO <http://www.unesco.org/opi2/lettres/TextAnglais/AnnanE.html>; UN Human Rights Council, *Report of the Human Rights Council Advisory Committee on the Right of Peoples to*

important that international law not impede the pursuit of human security, or be an instrument in itself for producing human insecurity.

Despite the potential, there are obstacles that will need to be overcome for human security and international law to achieve a harmonious, mutually supportive relationship. The dynamics between human security, the role of the state, and state sovereignty need to be carefully considered. The notion of sovereignty as responsibility will be relevant in this respect. 'State sovereignty implies responsibility, and the primary responsibility for the protection of its people lies with the state itself.'[31] Moreover, the fragmented nature of international law presents challenges to a concept founded in the notions of interconnected threats and interconnected solutions. Perhaps most significantly, however, the broad, often nebulous nature of human security makes it particularly challenging for international law and international legal scholarship.

Despite the potential importance of this relationship, there remains only limited engagement between human security discourse and international legal thought. This book seeks to plug that gap, and indeed explore why such a gap exists in the first place. Application of human security discourse exposes the existing trends in both international relations and international law to privilege this narrow construction (focused on traditional notions of security in the form of conflict) over a broader conceptualisation of human security, more inclusive of a wider range of threats (eg pandemics, climate change and poverty). It analyses the scope for human security discourse to be employed as a framework for the development of multilateral, integrative and rights-based approaches to human insecurity. Engagement with human security allows a light to be shone on the interrelated dimensions of issues of pressing concern to humanity, places special emphasis on the vulnerable and promotes a dual strategy of protection and empowerment. The book will examine the degree to which international law has developed constructions of international peace and security in line with human security, and serves as a conceptual framework for the interaction of international law and human security. Beyond all else the aim of the book is to emphasise the need for greater interdisciplinary engagement with human security, and the need for international legal scholarship not to embrace human security but to acknowledge and explore the discourse.

V Structure of the book

Chapter One: The emergence of human security: the broadening and deepening of the security paradigm

This chapter examines the core concept of 'security' and the arguments in favour of moving towards a new paradigm of security and beyond reliance on the

Peace, UN GAOR, Twentieth sess, Agenda Item 5, UN Doc A/HRC/20/31 (16 April 2012) Draft Declaration on the Right to Peace, Article 2.

31 International Commission on Intervention and State Sovereignty (ICISS), *The Responsibility to Protect* (International Development Research Centre, December 2001), Synopsis, Basic Principles.

traditional conceptualisations of state security and sovereignty that continue to dominate international legal discourse. Chapter One will introduce the concept of human security, exploring its origins and growth, and analysing the contested nature of its definition. It will examine how the concept has been employed by academics and policy-makers, and discuss the ongoing debates as to its utility and scope.

Chapter Two: The security problematique *and the transformative potential of human security discourse*

This chapter builds on those origins and examines the critical questions about the nature of security and how human security should be defined. It starts from the position that security is an essentially contested concept, and explores why human security can be best utilised as a discourse. It explores the transformative potential of human security with a view to the influence it might exert on international law if properly harnessed.

Chapter Three: The resistance of international legal scholarship to human security discourse: an examination

Chapter Three identifies and explores the reasons why international legal scholarship has failed to engage with human security discourse. It highlights the need for international legal scholarship to engage with the discourse for the benefit of both, and demonstrates that while there may be sound grounds for international legal scholarship to be critical of human security, there is little justification for ignoring the discourse entirely.

Chapter Four: The intersection of human security discourse and international law: in search of principles

Chapter Four explores the existing principles of human security discourse, discussing the ways in which these principles operate as a lens to evaluate existing international law. This chapter then examines the normative framework of human security and identifies the commonalities that exist between human security and international law. The chapter also examines the differences between broad and narrow approaches to human security and the impact of this debate on international law.

Chapter Five: Human security discourse – an 'authoritative interpretation' of the UN Charter?

This chapter examines whether human security could appropriately be considered an authoritative interpretation of 'international peace and security' within the UN Charter. It begins by examining the UN Charter through the lens of human security discourse and through an analysis of how 'security' is used in the Charter.

It then broadens this discussion by examining how security has been approached in other significant documents from the UN and the degree to which human security principles can be identified within those documents. Given that the Security Council is entrusted with the primary responsibility for the maintenance of international peace and security, focus is placed in this chapter on the broadening interpretation by the Security Council of its mandate through an analysis of Security Council Resolutions and its decision-making processes.

Chapter Six: International law-making and a human security template

Chapter Six examines the processes leading to the creation of the so-called human security treaties, to determine a blueprint for future development of international human security treaty law. It examines ways in which international norm production has moved beyond the traditional constraints of state-centric law development, and how these processes aid (or hinder) human security. It discusses the crucial role of coalition building for the development of the human security treaties discussed in Chapter Seven, and the involvement of non-state actors, specifically NGOs, in these processes. Secondly, it moves beyond the scope of traditional international law development into the field of soft law and quasi-legislative measures, examining the degree to which human security has been facilitated through the development of multi-stakeholder initiatives.

Chapter Seven: 'Human security treaties' so-called: an examination of the content of human security discourse in international treaties

A series of treaties have sometimes been labelled 'human security treaties', since these treaties, their content and success have been credited to the influence of human security discourse. This chapter examines how the principles of human security discourse manifest within these treaties, and the trends that become apparent as a result of the influence of human security. It examines the degree to which human security discourse has actually penetrated the language and structure of international treaties.

Chapter Eight: Conclusion – the relationship between human security discourse and international law: the time for engagement

This chapter concludes the book, drawing together the common threads observed across the chapters that govern the current relationship between human security discourse and international law, and the degree to which constructions of security have evolved. It highlights the pressing need for human security to be taken up by international law scholars and practitioners, and for a genuine dialogue to commence.

VI Conclusion

This study seeks to address the general lack of engagement that international legal scholarship has currently displayed towards human security discourse. It will fill this gap by identifying the core conceptual framework for the relationship between human security and international law, and examining the current influence of human security on international law constructions of security. It highlights the need for international law not to give in to the desire to narrow the scope of human security, and suggests instead that a broad approach can be functionalised by identifying core principles, and using these principles as a normative framework for the future development of international law.

1 The emergence of human security

The broadening and deepening of the security paradigm

Securitatem nunc appello vacuitatem aegritudinis, in qua vita beata posita est. – Cicero[1]

I Introduction

'Security' is a notion that lies at the heart of international relations, the role of the state and the role of law. It is also a concept that is more easily instinctively understood than capable of being encapsulated neatly by an academic definition. The word security is derived from the Latin *securitas* which means literally 'without care'.[2] This provides only a limited answer, however, to what security in fact is, and opens the door to a series of further questions: freedom from care for whom? What sort of cares? Security by what means, and at what cost? These questions form the structure of the security *problematique.*

Despite this range of questions that need to be addressed, it is only since the 1980s that the concept of security has been problematised. Before that time, security was treated, as Booth points out, as 'one of those common-sense, pre-defined terms in international relations orthodoxy that appear unproblematic until examined with a critical eye.'[3] The dominance of realism as a school of thought in international relations was so prominent during the Cold War that not only did it form the orthodoxy of security studies, but ontological questions about security went largely ignored between the 1940s and the 1990s.[4] Der Derian summarises the issue well:

> we have inherited an ontotheology of security, that is, an *a priori* argument that proves the existence and necessity of only one form of security because there currently happens to be a widespread, metaphysical belief in it.[5]

1 'Security is the absence of anxiety upon which the fulfilled life depends', Cicero, *Tusculanae,* Liber V Caput XIV, 42.
2 'Se' meaning without and 'curitas' from cura meaning care.
3 Ken Booth, *Theory of World Security* (Cambridge, 2007) 96.
4 See, eg, Peter Hough, *Understanding Global Security* (Routledge, 2nd edn, 2008) 6.
5 James Der Derian, cited in Annick TR Wibben, 'Human Security: Towards an Opening' (2008) 39 *Security Dialogue* 455, 457.

This chapter will explore the development of the concept of security as framed in international relations and security studies, and establish the context in which human security has emerged and been utilised. It will explore what 'security' means and how human security fits into this broader ontological discussion. It is important to appreciate human security within the context of security studies, and realism in particular, for a number of reasons. One, the transformative potential of human security and the need for a shifting paradigm can only be appreciated by analysis of the failings and fallacies existent in the traditional paradigm. Further, while realism no longer holds the same level of hegemony over security discourse that it once did, it remains the dominant school of thought in international relations, and as such this must be taken into account when examining the critiques of human security. This chapter traces the emergence of human security within the broader enterprises of security studies, and within the scope of international legal and policy documents.

II Traditional conceptions of security

According to realist thought,[6] security is a state-centric concept that rests on a state taking any action necessary to ensure its survival, power and political influence when confronted by external threats, specifically military threats from other states.[7] This realist view of security of course presupposes the backdrop of the realist perception of international relations in general. According to Mearsheimer, realism rests on five assumptions about how the world works.[8] The first is the anarchy of the international system, resulting from the lack of central supra-national authority and the exclusivity of sovereignty to states. The second assumption is a focus on the military power of states, based on the belief that they are inherently dangerous to each other. Furthermore, in realist theory war is treated as a legitimate instrument of international politics, in the tradition of Clausewitz.[9] Thirdly, there is inevitable uncertainty in the international system as states cannot trust each other and their intentions. Even where intentions are good, they can change swiftly and so uncertainty must be ever-present. Fourth, the basic motivating factor of all states is

6 It should be noted of course that while there are key points of commonalities among realist scholars, thus allowing for categorisation as a school of thought, there is also vast diversity within this school – for example the disparate views of Hans Morgenthau and Kenneth Waltz, two of the foremost realist thinkers. For discussion see John J Mearsheimer, 'Realism, the Real World and the Academy' in Michael Brecher and Frank P Harvey (eds), *Realism and Institutionalism in International Studies* (The University of Michigan Press, 2002) 23–33.

7 See, eg, Kenneth Waltz, *Theory of International Politics* (McGraw-Hill, 1979) *inter alia*, 91–92; Stephen Walt, 'The Renaissance of Security Studies' (1991) 35 *International Studies Quarterly* 211, 212.

8 John J Mearsheimer, 'The False Promise of International Institutions' (1994) 19(3) *International Security* 5, 10.

9 'We see therefore, that War is not merely a political act, but also a real political instrument, a continuation of political commerce, a carrying out of the same by other means': Karl von Clausewitz, *On War* (Col JJ Graham trans, Kegan Paul, Trench, Trubner & C, 1918) vol 1, Chapter I, [24].

survival. Finally, all activities of a state taken in the international realm are strategically oriented and concerned with ensuring the state's survival. Thus the security paradigm that emerges from realist thought is an idea that is centred firmly on states as the referent object of security, and one that presumes the legitimacy and perpetual threat of war and insecurity. Security becomes largely synonymous with power.

International security (or insecurity) then is largely defined by the 'security dilemma' that emerges as a result of states ensuring their own security.[10] The security dilemma refers to the paradox that emerges from this traditional conceptualisation of security. When states protect themselves via the accumulation of power this inevitably places them in perpetual competition with each other. One state's security, therefore, comes at the cost of the security of other states – 'each state must guarantee its own survival since no other will provide its security'.[11] The previously mentioned anarchical situation of states maximising their power at the expense of others is averted only by a balance of power, that is, the mutual interest of the most powerful states in maintaining the status quo. The bipolar power structure witnessed during the Cold War is thus deemed to provide relative stability, and a more sustainable sense of peace and security, one that rests on international cooperation, is viewed as unrealistic and unachievable. International cooperation, while not impossible, is thought under this model to have distinct limits, as international relations are 'constrained by the dominating logic of security competition, which no amount of cooperation can eliminate.'[12]

There are a number of implications that emerge from the realist paradigm of security. The first is that 'security' essentially becomes a negative value. Rather than being something meaningful in itself, security under this paradigm is essentially merely the absence of insecurity.[13] Thus under the realist approach, '[a] nation has security when it does not have to sacrifice its legitimate interests to avoid war and is able, if challenged, to maintain them by war.'[14] With its strong focus on military threats, the realist construction of security ignores other threats to the security of people within the state. By ignoring other forms of threat, this narrow view of security, as Ullman correctly points out, ultimately reduces the total security of the state.[15] He takes this a step further and asserts that this framework also increases global insecurity, as it leads to ever-increasing militarisation of

10 The term 'security dilemma' was first coined by John Herz in the 1950s – for a discussion see Hans Günter Brauch, 'From a Security towards a Survival Dilemma' in Hans Günter Brauch et al (eds), *Globalization and Environmental Challenges* (Springer Berlin Heidelberg, 2008) vol 3, 537.

11 John J Mearsheimer, 'Back to the Future: Instability in Europe After the Cold War' (1990) 15(4) *International Security* 5, 12.

12 John J Mearsheimer, 'The False Promise of International Institutions' (1994) 19(3) *International Security* 5, 9.

13 Arnold Wolfers, 'National Security as an Ambiguous Symbol' (1962) republished in Christopher W Hughes and Lai Yew Meng (eds) *Security Studies: A Reader* (Routledge, 2011) 5, 7.

14 Lippman, cited in Peter Hough, *Understanding Global Security* (Routledge, 2nd edn, 2008), 11.

15 Richard Ullman, 'Redefining Security' (1983) 8(1) *International Security* 129, 129.

international relations which is inevitably harmful to the global community in the long run.[16]

This traditional notion of security is almost entirely dependent on the endurance of the Westphalian state system, and as Burgess points out, rests on the idea of states providing unconditional protection to their citizenry, presupposing a 'rarefied, even idealised, notion of the state'.[17] Wyn-Jones goes further, arguing that a 'fetishization of the state'[18] lies at the root of traditional approaches to security. Such a fetishisation privileges the state as the object to be protected and presumes the intrinsic value of the state. However, focus on national security in a way that idealises the state and ignores the citizens within discounts the philosophical construction of the state itself. As Surin Pitsuwan, Secretary-General of ASEAN observes, the classic social contract theories were based on the idea that people give up their autonomy to join the collectivity of the state for the express purpose of their protection or, put another way, their individual security.[19] Burke describes the solemn pledge between citizens and political leaders to the effect that 'their people's security is "the first duty", the overriding goal of domestic and international policy making.'[20] Thus while the construction of human security as it exists today is innovative and potentially transformative, it is rooted in older, fundamental ideas of human interaction and the role of the state.

The fetishised national security approach is clearly closely aligned to a Hobbesian view of the world, the state and sovereignty. The justification of the realist view of the state is made clear in the work of Hans Morgenthau, one of the leading figures of the realist movement:

The nation state is to a higher degree than ever before the predominant source of the individual's moral and legal valuations and the ultimate point of reference for his secular loyalties. Consequently, its power among the other nations and the preservation of its sovereignty are the individual's foremost concern in international affairs.[21]

Given the centrality of the state to people's lives, according to Morgenthau, the interests of the state should be prioritised by the individuals within that state. Nef finds irony in this realist world view, with its over-attention to the state, as this results in the actual threats to individuals being eclipsed and ignored.[22] Hayden

16 Ibid.

17 J Peter Burgess, 'The Ethical Challenges of Human Security in the Age of Globalisation' in Moufida Goucha and John Crowley (eds), *Rethinking Human Security* (Wiley-Blackwell, 2008) 49, 52.

18 Wyn-Jones, cited in Peter Hough, *Understanding Global Security* (Routledge, 2nd edn, 2008) 9.

19 Surin Pitsuwan, 'Keynote Address on Regional Cooperation for Human Security', International Development Studies Conference on Mainstreaming Human Security: The Asian Contribution (10 October 2007) (Bangkok, Thailand).

20 Anthony Burke, 'Aporias of Security' (2002) 27 *Alternatives: Global, Local, Political* 1, 1.

21 Hans Morgenthau, *Politics Among Nations* (A Knopf, 5th edn, 1972) 32.

22 Jorge Nef, 'Human Security, Mutual Vulnerability and Sustainable Development: A Critical View' (2006) 7 *Whitehead Journal of Diplomacy and International Relations* 55, 58.

frames the issue slightly differently, stating that the history of state security demonstrates a prioritisation of this traditional conception of security over the concept of peace.[23] From an international legal perspective, it is easy to trace this same dichotomy and emphasis on state sovereignty.

For Hobbes, the great champion for the cause of state sovereignty, the role of sovereignty is tied to the ability of the sovereign to protect his or her people, with 'the safety of the people as the supreme law'.[24] State sovereignty could only be justified by the continuing protection of the people:

> The obligations of subjects to the sovereign, is understood to last as long, and no longer, than the power lasteth, by which he is able to protect them.[25]

Thus, even for Hobbes, sovereignty is to be equated with responsibility rather than privilege or intrinsic value in and of itself. As Wæver puts it, '[t]he right of the individual to self-preservation is the starting point of Hobbes' Leviathan argument. The ultimate meaning and measure of security is individual security, but it is procured through vesting authority in the state.'[26] The notion of sovereignty as responsibility[27] rests on premises of moral legitimacy for authority and the operation of law and politics, and is found in a diverse range of scholars' (including jurists') reasoning, from Grotius to Hobbes to Lon Fuller, to name but a few. Grotius, writing in 1625, placed an automatic limit on sovereignty:

> The kingdom is forfeited if a king sets out with a truly hostile intent to destroy a whole people … for the will to govern and the will to destroy cannot coexist in the same person.[28]

The reliance on an over-simplified Hobbesian construction of the state and security in realist thought also ignores the role of liberalism in political and legal philosophy in the years since Hobbes wrote the *Leviathan*. Kant's pursuit for 'Perpetual Peace' in particular has a resonance that rejects realism's account and is consistent with the idea of human security.[29] Kant's definitive articles for this

23 Patrick Hayden, 'Constraining War: Human Security and the Human Right to Peace' (2004) (October–December 2004) 6(1) *Human Rights Review* 35, 46.

24 Thomas Hobbes, *Leviathan or the Matter, Forme & Power of a Common-Wealth Ecclesiastical and Civil* (Oxford Classics, republished 1998, originally published 1651) 143.

25 Ibid 208.

26 Ole Wæver, 'Peace and Security: Two Evolving Concepts and Their Changing Relationship' in Hans Günter Brauch et al (eds), *Globalization and Environmental Challenges* (Springer Berlin Heidelberg, 2008) vol 3, 99, 102.

27 As will be discussed in Chapter Five.

28 Grotius, cited in Larry May, *Crimes Against Humanity: A Normative Account* (Cambridge University Press, 2005) 10.

29 Immanuel Kant, *Perpetual Peace,* 1795 republished in *Kant's Political Writings* (HB Nisbet trans, Cambridge University Press, 1970). See, also, Bruce Russett, 'A Neo-Kantian Perspective: Democracy, Interdependence, and International Organizations in

peace comprised of representative governments, interdependence and pacific cooperation between states, and respect for international law. The concept of responsible sovereignty has also found modern relevance in the form of the Responsibility to Protect (R2P) doctrine, a notion closely linked to that of human security, and which will be briefly discussed in Chapter Four.

Despite these limitations and challenges, the realist vision of security endured as orthodoxy throughout the Cold War and continues to be the dominant school of thought today in both security studies and international relations more generally.[30] However, the conclusion of the Cold War brought a definite, discernible shift in how the notion of security was perceived and discussed.

III Shifting paradigms

A The need for a shift

The abrupt end of the Cold War, and the disappearance of the polarity and power struggles that defined that era, further opened the notion of security to critical assessment. The modern global security climate has urged a rethink of the traditional principles over the past two decades, with a number of factors altering both the nature and perception of threats to security:

> Geopolitical patterns, economic trends, technological change and other developments are severely straining the system of collective security that has been in place for the past 60 years. Today's threats – familiar ones with added potency and some entirely new dangers – are borderless, highly connected and capable of crippling, and even destroying societies everywhere.[31]

Since the conclusion of the Cold War there has also been a discernible shift in the nature of conflict, with conflicts increasingly being internal rather than international in character.[32] Mary Kaldor's work has been significant in this respect, in the form of her seminal work, *New and Old Wars.*[33] She argues that a shift has

Building Security Communities' in Emanuel Adler and Michael Barnett (eds), *Security Communities* (Cambridge University Press, 1998).

30 See, eg, Stefano Guzzini, *Realism in International Relations and International Political Economy: The Continuing Story of a Death Foretold* (Routledge, 2013); Daniel H Deudney, 'Regrounding Realism: Anarchy, security, and changing material contexts' (2000) 10 *Security Studies* 1.

31 Kofi Annan, 'Managing Risk', *Global Agenda: The Magazine of World Economic Forum Annual Meeting*, 2005 edition, cited in Shahrbanou Tadjbakhsh and Anuradha M Chenoy, *Human Security: Concepts and Implications* (Routledge, 2007) 11.

32 See, eg, Human Security Report Project, *Human Security Report 2009–2010* (Simon Fraser University, 2010), Part I: The Causes of Peace.

33 Mary Kaldor, *New and Old Wars: Organised Violence in a Global Era* (Cambridge Polity Press, 1999).

occurred in the field of armed violence. Where once organised violence came in the form of states, militaries and interstate wars, violence in the global era is characterised by a blurring between war, organised crime and wide-scale violations of human rights. It has also become increasingly clear that states are often potential threats to rather than protectors of their own people.[34] As Mack notes, 'in the last one hundred years, far more people have died at the hands of their own governments than have been killed by foreign armies'.[35]

Emerging alongside the end of the Cold War was the increasing influence of globalisation. Globalisation and the related increased interdependence of states and people have a potentially profound effect on people's security. '[T]oday's global flow of goods, finance and people increases the risks and uncertainties confronting the international community.'[36] These threats include increased trafficking of drugs, people, arms and natural resources across borders. Globalisation has also led to an increase in inequalities within and between societies, increasing tensions and heightening the possibilities of conflict.[37] The interdependence of people and states challenges constructions of the world that focus on state sovereignty, especially territorial sovereignty, as borders are rendered increasingly meaningless. Hayden, for example, posits that 'what is required is a new global outlook: an approach that recognises the highly interdependent nature of human life across political and territorial boundaries and the growing irrelevance of the traditional conception of state sovereignty as an end in itself.'[38]

There is also increased awareness of the multitude of threats to people's survival, livelihoods and dignity, and increased analysis of the interconnections of these types of threats.[39] For example, there are increasing academic insights into the correlation of poverty and conflict, and analysis of how these two phenomena interact.[40]

34 United Nations Development Programme (UNDP), *Human Development Report 1994* (UNDP, 1994) 4. See also UN Commission on Human Security, *Human Security Now* (United Nations, 2003) 129.
35 Andrew Mack, 'A Signifier of Shared Values' (2004) 35 *Security Dialogue* 366, 366.
36 United Nations General Assembly, *Report of the Secretary-General on Human Security*, UN GAOR, Sixty-fourth sess, Agenda Item 48 and 114, UN Doc A/64/701 (8 March 2010) [10].
37 See, eg, World Commission on the Social Dimension of Globalization, *A Fair Globalization: Creating Opportunities for All* (International Labour Organization, February 2004); United Nations Department of Economic and Social Affairs (DESA), *The Inequality Predicament: Report on the World Social Situation 2005* (United Nations, 2005).
38 Patrick Hayden, 'Constraining War: Human Security and the Human Right to Peace' (2004) October–December 2004 *Human Rights Review* 35, 35.
39 Amartya Sen, 'Why Human Security?' (Speech delivered at the International Symposium on Human Security, Toyko, Japan, 28 July 2000). Sabine Alkire, 'A Conceptual Framework for Human Security' (Working Paper No 2, Centre for Research on Inequality, Human Security and Ethnicity (CRISE) 2003).
40 See, eg, Maria Stern and Joakim Öjendal, 'Mapping the Security – Development Nexus: Conflict, Complexity, Cacophony, Convergence?' (2010) 41 *Security Dialogue* 5; Brian-Vincent Ikejiaku, 'Poverty–Conflict Nexus: The Contentious Issue Revisited' (2012) 1(2) *European Journal of Sustainable Development* 127; Frances Stewart,

Thus it is not just the threats themselves that have altered, but also our collective understanding and analysis of those threats.[41]

Not only have potential threats increased and evolved over time, the capacity to respond to such threats has also increased and become increasingly sophisticated. Of particular note are the expanding role, influence and capacity of international institutions, and the emergence of coordination between institutions, though admittedly they have much further to go in this respect.[42] Nobel Laureate Amartya Sen has pointed out that 'there is an enhanced possibility in the contemporary world to put our efforts and understanding together to achieve a better coordinated resistance to the forces that make human survival so insecure'.[43] While the peace dividend that was anticipated following the Cold War has failed to materialise,[44] the unparalleled connectivity of the globe today offers opportunities that were previously improbable and inconceivable.

Along with the interconnected nature of the world, and the need for global responses to transboundary challenges, Renner observes three other trends that render traditional approaches to security inadequate.[45] Firstly, he observes that 'weapons do not necessarily provide security',[46] and that the proliferation of military technologies is a threat to global security, not a solution. This challenges traditional thinking on security, as well as the close ties of securitisation with militarisation. Secondly, '[t]he traditional focus on state (or regime) security is inadequate and needs to encompass safety and well-being for those living there. If individuals and communities are insecure, state security itself can be extremely fragile.'[47] And finally Renner notes the important influence of non-military dimensions to security and instability.[48] Taking this a step further, the concurrent increasing importance of non-military actors as securitising actors should also be

'Development and Security' (Working Paper No 3, Centre for Research on Inequality, Human Security and Ethnicity [CRISE] 2003) David Chandler, 'Rethinking the Conflict–Poverty Nexus: From Securitising Intervention to Resilience' (2015) 4 *Stability: International Journal of Security and Development* 13.

41 Sabine Alkire, 'A Conceptual Framework for Human Security' (2003) 11–12.

42 See, eg, Dennis Dijkzeul, *The Management of Multilateral Organizations* (Kluwer Law International, 1997); Burcu Balcik et al, 'Coordination in Humanitarian Relief Chains: Practices, Challenges and Opportunities' (2010) 126 *International Journal of Production Economics* 22; Roland Paris, 'Understanding the "Coordination Problem" in Postwar Statebuilding' in Roland Paris and Timothy D Sisk (eds) *The Dilemmas of Statebuilding: Confronting the Contradictions of Postwar Peace Operations* (Routledge 2009) 53.

43 Amartya Sen, 'Why Human Security?' (Speech delivered at the International Symposium on Human Security, Toyko, Japan, 28 July 2000).

44 United Nations Development Programme (UNDP), *Human Development Report 1994* (UNDP, 1994)

45 Michael Renner, 'State of the World 2005: Redefining Security' in M Mwagiru (ed), *Rethinking Global Security: An African Perspective?* (Heinrich Böll Foundation, 2006) 1, 2.

46 Ibid.

47 Ibid.

48 Ibid 3.

noted, and beyond this, the role of non-state actors in the promotion (and endangerment) of security.

The combination of these various factors has had a profound effect on the field of security studies, and the very idea of 'security' is now considered by many to be an essentially contested concept.[49]

B The development of security studies and the notion of 'security'

The first major challenge to realism and its construction of security, and the beginnings of the shift in security studies generally, are usually credited to Barry Buzan's work in 1983, *People, States and Fear: The National Security Problem in International Relations.* While there had been isolated challenges to the realist conceptualisation of security prior to this,[50] Buzan's effort led to the development of the Copenhagen School (discussed below), and a challenge to realism's hegemony as a school of thought in security studies. Buzan's work not only challenged realism's narrow view of security, arguing for a broadening and deepening of the notion, but also paved the way for 'security' to be explored, examined and problematised in a way that had not occurred in the decades prior. Thus human security's emergence in the field of international relations came at a time when 'security' was receiving attention the likes of which it had never seen before. The enlargement of security studies that began with Buzan and the Copenhagen School has since become 'something of a cottage industry'.[51]

It was Krause and Williams who first referred to the broadening and deepening of security.[52] By 'broadening', they meant the identification of a wider range of potential threats to be addressed by the notion. 'Deepening' on the other hand refers to moving the notion of security down to the level of the individual and/or up to the level of global security. Wibben adds a third layer to this with the 'opening' of security, that is, the opening of the examination of the deeper meanings of the term 'security'.[53]

49 See, eg, Mely Callabero-Anthony and Rolf Emmers, 'Understanding the Dynamics of Securitising Non-Traditional Security' in Mely Callabero-Anthony, Rolf Emmers and Amitav Acharya (eds), *Non-Traditional Security in Asia: Dilemmas in Securitisation* (Ashgate, 2006) 1, 1. See also, Ramesh Thakur, *The United Nations, Peace and Security: From Collective Security to the Responsibility to Protect* (Cambridge University Press, 2006) 72.

50 Most notably by Arnold Wolfers, 'National Security as an Ambiguous Symbol' (1962) republished in Christopher W Hughes and Lai Yew Meng (eds) *Security Studies: A Reader* (Routledge, 2011) 5, and Richard Ullman, 'Redefining Security' (1983) 8(1) *International Security* 129.

51 David A Baldwin, 'The Concept of Security' (1997) 23 *Review of International Studies* 5, 5.

52 Keith Krause and Michael C Williams, 'Broadening the Agenda of Security Studies: Politics and Methods' (1996) 40 *Mershon International Studies Review* 229.

53 Annick T R Wibben, 'Human Security: Towards Opening' (2008) 39 *Security Dialogue* 455, 456.

(i) New schools for security studies

(A) THE COPENHAGEN SCHOOL

The Copenhagen School was founded by the collective minds of Buzan, Wæver and de Wilde and encapsulated by their seminal work *Security: A New Framework for Analysis:*

> Threats and vulnerabilities can arise in many different areas, military and non-military, but to count as security issues they have to meet strictly defined criteria that distinguish them from the normal run of the merely political. They have to be staged as existential threats to a referent object by a securitizing actor who thereby generates endorsement of emergency measures beyond rules that would otherwise bind.[54]

This approach focuses on the notion of 'securitisation' of threats, the classification of a threat as such by what they refer to as a 'speech act'.[55] This traditionally involves the invocation of the language of security, and a call for extraordinary counter-measures to be adopted.[56] This school of thought is widely thought of as a subset of the broader school in international relations of Social Constructivists.[57] Hough, however, labels the Copenhagen School as neo-realists, on the ground that while they broaden the threats and the possible referent objects of security, the so-called 'securitizing actor' remains the state, as the agent which determines what matters are attributed the requisite sense of urgency.[58] This is not necessarily true, as the theoretical framework was left deliberately broad, and proponents of securitisation theory argue that the 'securitising actor' can include the international media, NGOs and, most interesting from an international law perspective, the UN and the Security Council in relation to Chapter VII of the UN Charter.[59] However, they have also acknowledged that in the practical reality of modern society, the state is the key actor in the securitisation process at the international level.[60] The nature of the 'securitising actor' generally remains an underdeveloped aspect of securitisation theory.[61]

54 Barry Buzan, Ole Wæver and Jaap de Wilde, *Security: A New Framework for Analysis* (Lynne Rienner Publications, 1998) 5.
55 Ibid 26–28.
56 Ibid.
57 See, eg, Hans Günter Brauch, 'Conceptual Quartet: Security and its Linkages with Peace, Development, and Environment' in Hans Günter Brauch et al (eds), *Globalization and Environmental Challenges* (Springer Berlin Heidelberg, 2008) vol 3, 65, 65.
58 Peter Hough, *Understanding Global Security* (Routledge, 2nd edn, 2008) 9.
59 Barry Buzan, Ole Wæver and Jaap de Wilde, *Security: A New Framework for Analysis* (Lynne Rienner Publications, 1998), 26.
60 See, eg, Barry Buzan, *People, States and Fear: An Agenda for International Security Studies in the Post-Cold War Era* (Harvester Wheatsheaf, 2nd edn, 1991) 35.
61 For critiques, see, eg, Monica Barthwal-Datta, 'Securitising Threats without the State: A Case Study of Misgovernance as a Security Threat in Bangladesh' (2009) 35(02) *Review of International Studies* 277. Javier Fabra Mata, 'Who Can Make Security?

The Copenhagen School, while broadening the approach to security, is ultimately critical of the process of securitisation. For them, the mobilisation of resources for securitised issues can be disproportionate or have negative effects, and can further entrench conflict and other social ills.[62] This negative outlook towards security is in contrast to views of the so-called 'Welsh School' a sub-set of critical security studies discussed below that takes a positive approach to security, and which shares many traits and values with human security discourse.[63]

The three core elements of securitisation, as outlined in the quote above, are that there are a) existential threats to a referent object; b) emergency measures pursued; and c) effects on inter-unit relations as a result of breaking free from the rules.[64] The first thing to note is that this theory places no express limit on the nature of threats, or the referent object, which can potentially be humanity or the individual, as in the case of human security. That said, one of its chief proponents, Wæver, has firmly asserted that 'as concepts, neither individual nor international security exist ... there is no literature, no philosophy, no tradition of security in non-state terms ... the *concept* of security refers to the state.'[65] What causes a further breach between securitisation and human security discourses is that emergency measures are widely deemed to be those that operate as 'exceptional or outside the normal bounds of political procedure.'[66] Securitisation theory thus firmly maintains a focus on a negative construction of security, and equates it with areas of crisis, rather than prevention. In a comparison of the Copenhagen School and human security, Floyd argues that while the Copenhagen School has more analytical utility than human security, human security has more normative utility and thus more value in terms of producing results.[67] This is not surprising since, as shall be seen, human security emerged in the context of policy development and not within the sanctified halls of academia.

Competition over Securitisation between the State and Non-state Actors in Colombia' (2008) 4 *Journal of Human Security* 37.

62 Barry Buzan, Ole Wæver and Jaap de Wilde, *Security: A New Framework for Analysis* (Lynne Rienner Publications, 1998) 32.

63 For a comparison of the Welsh and Copenhagen Schools in the context of human security, see Edward Newman, 'Critical Human Security Studies' (2010) 36 *Review of International Studies* 77, 85.

64 Barry Buzan, Ole Wæver and Jaap de Wilde, *Security: A New Framework for Analysis* (Lynne Rienner PublicationsPublications, 1998) 26.

65 Ole Wæver, *Securitization and Desecuritization* (Centre for Peace and Conflict Research, 1993) 48–9.

66 Barry Buzan, Ole Wæver and Jaap de Wilde, *Security: A New Framework for Analysis* (Lynne Rienner Publications), 1998, 26. For critical analysis see, eg, Scott Watson, 'The "Human" as Referent Object? Humanitarianism as Securitization' (2011) 42 *Security Dialogue* 3, 6–8; Thierry Balzacq (ed) *Understanding Securitization Theory: How Security Problems Emerge and Dissolve* (Routledge, 2010); Rita Floyd, 'Can Securitization Theory Be Used in Normative Analysis? Towards a Just Securitization Theory' (2011) 42 *Security Dialogue* 427.

67 Rita Floyd, 'Human Security and the Copenhagen School's Securitization Approach: Conceptualizing Human Security as a Securitizing Move' (2007) 5 *Human Security Journal* 38.

(B) SOCIAL CONSTRUCTIVISTS

Social constructivists entered the security debate with a focus on security as a social construct rather than an inherently objective concept, and place an emphasis on the cultural dimensions of security related decision-making.[68] Constructivists argue that the traditional approaches to security ignore the normative elements of the notion of security and they assert that the claim that the traditional paradigm is 'value-free' in fact disguises the power and social relationships underlying the norms and institutions that make up international relations.[69] It is the normative focus of social constructivism and the willingness of this movement to deviate from the traditional state-centric approach to security that has enabled human security to develop.

(C) FEMINIST SECURITY STUDIES AND DEVELOPING COUNTRY PERSPECTIVES

In terms of feminist thought, Tickner points out that women have little role to play in traditional notions of security and are 'seldom ... recognised by the security literature'.[70] This is despite the fact that women and girls make up the majority of the casualties and displaced in armed conflict, and the use of rape as a traditional weapon of war.[71] Likewise, others have emphasised the fact that insecurity is experienced differently according to gender, especially in the form of structural violence.[72] Thus feminist challenges to traditional security are, as Tigerstrom notes, closely related to human security approaches.[73] Indeed, human security can be greatly benefitted by an alignment with and appreciation of the feminist approach. There is a small but growing fellowship of gendered approaches to human security emerging.[74] Feminist security studies also problematised security

68 See, eg, John Baylis, 'The Concept of Security in International Relations' in Hans Günter Brauch et al (eds), *Globalization and Environmental Challenges* (Springer Berlin Heidelberg, 2008) vol 3, 495, 499–500.
69 See, eg, Alexander Wendt, 'Anarchy Is What States Make of It: The Social Construction of Power Politics (Spring 1992) 46(2) *International Organization* 391.
70 See, generally, J Ann Tickner, *Gender in International Relations: Feminist Perspectives on Achieving Global Security* (Columbia University Press, 1992).
71 See, eg, Security Council Resolution 1325 (2000) UN SCOR, UN Doc S/RES/1325 (31 October 2000).
72 J Steans cited in Barbara von Tigerstrom, *Human Security and International Law: Prospects and Problems* (Hart Publishing, 2007) 13. Structural violence, as originally conceived by Galtung, is briefly explained below.
73 Ibid 12–13.
74 See, eg, Heidi Hudson, '"Doing" Security As Though Humans Matter: A Feminist Perspective on Gender and the Politics of Human Security' (2005) 36 *Security Dialogue* 155; Aili Mari Tripp, Myra Marx Ferree and Christina Ewig (eds), *Gender, Violence and Human Security: Critical Feminist Perspectives* (New York University Press, 2013); Gunhild Hoogensen and Kirsti Stuvøy, 'Gender, Resistance and Human Security' (2006) 37(2) *Security Dialogue* 207; Ghada Moussa, 'Gender Aspects of Human Security' (2008) 59 *International Social Science Journal* 81; Asha Hans and Betty A Reardon, *The Gender Imperative: Human Security vs State Security* (Routledge, 2012).

in many ways that were essential for the development of human security, by questioning the underlying values and presumptions in realist thought that aligned security with militarism, and broadening the scope of threats to consider other constructions of violence beyond armed conflict.[75]

Likewise, developing country perspectives also need to play a key role in the development of human security, such as the work of Ayoob, who emphasised that it is internal threats, rather than external ones, that are the principal security concern of most Least Developed Countries ('LDCs').[76] These sorts of considerations are recognised by some human security scholarship, but need to be developed further. Thomas, for example, argues that insecurity results 'directly from existing power structures that determine who enjoys the entitlement to security and who does not.'[77]

(D) THE WELSH SCHOOL

The Welsh School, led by Jones and Booth in particular, is a strongly normative school within critical security studies, which equates security with emancipation, 'freeing people, as individuals and collectivities, from contingent and structural oppressions.'[78] Critical security studies are interested in transforming the current paradigm of security, challenging existing structures and power relations, and as such, it is not uncommon to see theorists place human security within this school of thought. While critical security studies focuses on altering existing hegemonic structures of security, human security discourse goes further by articulating the need for the shift to notions of human dignity and rights, and focusing on the policy reform necessary to produce the needed results.[79] Some of those within the critical security studies authorship, however, find human security superfluous, feeling that critical security studies has already made the points made by human security discourse, and they are 'suspicious of human security as a hegemonic discourse [co-opted by the state]'.[80] Human security, while critical of the focus of the state in the definition

75 See, eg, Aili Mari Tripp, 'Toward a Gender Perspective on Human Security' in Aili Mari Tripp, Myra Marx Ferree and Christina Ewig (eds), *Gender, Violence and Human Security: Critical Feminist Perspectives* (New York University Press, 2013) 11, 18–20.

76 See, eg, Ayoob, cited in Peter Hough, *Understanding Global Security* (Routledge, 2nd edn, 2008), 7.

77 Caroline Thomas, 'Global Governance, Development and Human Security: Exploring the Links' (2001) 22(2) *Third World Quarterly* 150. This point is also raised in Edward Newman, 'Critical Human Security Studies' (2010) 36 *Review of International Studies* 77, 81.

78 Ken Booth, cited in Edward Newman, 'Critical Human Security Studies' (2010) 36 *Review of International Studies* 77, 86.

79 See, eg, Des Gasper, 'Human Security: From Definitions to Investigating a Discourse' in Mary Martin and Taylor Owen (eds), *Routledge Handbook of Human Security* (Routledge, 2014) 28.

80 Edward Newman, 'Critical Human Security Studies' (2010) 36 *Review of International Studies* 77, 87.

of security, widely embraces the role of the state in promoting and protecting human security, taking a pragmatic policy-driven approach to security.[81]

C The emergence of human security

Human security, like the other non-traditional approaches to security discussed, seeks to challenge the orthodoxy of traditional, state-centric security. Human security represented a radical and fundamental shift in the conceptualisation of security that went beyond the progressive broadening and deepening of the notion prior to its introduction. It challenged the roots of realism's construction – people, not states, were the focus and purpose of security:

> … from the highly abstract imaginary of the nation-state to the immediate corporeal distress of the human; a human which, in that distress, activates a call for difference that simultaneously undermines the illusory unity of a body politic that would subsume all differences beneath a common imagination of home.[82]

Proponents of human security highlight two central points. The first is that the state can pose a greater threat to people than any external adversary, returning to Mack's point that more people have died as a result of their own government than foreign armies. The second is that threats to people extend far beyond those issues classed as 'high politics'.[83] Human security seeks to challenge the privileging of so-called high politics, and stresses that human insecurity extends to experiences of deprivation, disaster and beyond. Threats to security can thus include internal conflict and violence, disease, hunger, environmental threats and natural as well as man-made disasters.[84]

While, like the other theories that have emerged, human security developed in response to the perceived failing of the traditional paradigm of security, in many ways its emergence and development is unique. Human security did not develop out of a particular school of thought, or within the academic field of security studies, or even international relations. Instead, human security was produced initially entirely in the field of policy development, and more remarkably, in the field of human development, as opposed to security policy.

81 This is not surprisingly most notably in the UN's approach to human security; see, eg, General Assembly, *Report of the Secretary-General: Follow-up to General Assembly Resolution 66/290 on Human Security*, Sixty-eighth sess, Agenda Item 14 and 118, UN Doc A/68/685 (23 December 2013).

82 Anthony Burke, 'Aporias of Security' (2002) 27 *Alternatives: Global, Local, Political* 1, 4.

83 The relationship between 'high politics' (ie those situations deemed of strategic importance according to realist thought) and 'low politics' (everything else) is explored in, *inter alia*, Norrin M Ripsman, 'The Political Economy of Security: A Research and Teaching Agenda' (2009) 3(1) *Journal of Military and Strategic Studies* 1.

84 Note, however, that there is a split in human security scholarship on how widely the term should be interpreted. This will be discussed in Chapter Three.

First introduced in 1994 by the UNDP in its annual Human Development Report,[85] human security is a people-centred approach that challenges the traditional paradigm and its focus on the state:

> The concept of security has for too long been interpreted narrowly: as security of territory from external aggression, or as protection of national interests in foreign policy, or as global security from the threat of nuclear holocaust … Forgotten were the legitimate concerns of ordinary people who sought security in their daily lives. For many of them, security symbolised protection from the threat of disease, hunger, unemployment, crime, social conflict, political repression and environmental hazards. With the dark shadows of the Cold War receding, one can see that many conflicts are within nations rather than between nations.[86]

While the term had appeared before,[87] the concept was fleshed out for the first time in this report, engineered by Mahbub al Haq. The concept drew heavily on the concepts of 'Freedom from Fear' and 'Freedom from Want' adopted from Franklin D Roosevelt's famous 'Four Freedoms' Speech in 1941.[88] The idea behind raising human security in this context and at this time was to capture the peace dividend following the Cold War, and refocus the priorities of the world, now that the perpetual state of emergency created by the Cold War had passed.[89]

The UNDP described human security as having four essential characteristics.[90] The first of these, and the least disputed, is the notion that human security is *people-centred*. In other words, human security requires a shift in the security paradigm away from the state as the referent object of security to the individual, or person,[91] as the object to be protected. It refocuses security on the survival, livelihood and dignity of individuals.[92] Secondly, the UNDP emphasised that human security was a *universal concern*. This was a response to the interconnected and transnational nature of threats on the modern global stage. Thirdly, human

85 At least as we understand the concept today. The term 'human security' does however predate the UNDP Report.
86 United Nations Development Programme (UNDP), *Human Development Report 1994* (UNDP, 1994) 22–3.
87 Its first known usage in the context of the United Nations was made by Boutros Boutros-Ghali in *An Agenda for Peace* (United Nations, 1992) [16].
88 Franklin D Roosevelt, 'State of the Union Address ("Four Freedoms Speech")' (Speech delivered at the Joint Session of Congress, Washington, DC, United States of America, 6 January 1941) <http://www.fdrlibrary.marist.edu/pdfs/fftext.pdf>.
89 Ibid. See also, Mahbub Al Haq, *Reflections on Human Development* (Oxford University Press, 2nd edn, 1999) 136.
90 UNDP, *Human Development Report 1994* (UNDP, 1994) 25.
91 See Chapter Two for a discussion of this distinction.
92 *Report of the Secretary-General on Human Security*, UN GAOR, Sixty-fourth sess, Agenda Item 48 and 114, UN Doc A/64/701 (8 March 2010) [26]. Reaffirmed by UN General Assembly, *Follow-up to Paragraph 143 on Human Security of the 2005 World Summit Outcome*, GA Res 66/290, Sixty-sixth sess, Agenda Item 14 and 117, UN Doc A/RES/66/290 (25 October 2012).

security is easier to ensure through the pursuit of *prevention strategies* than through later intervention. And finally, the UNDP described the components of human security as *interdependent.* Human security, according to the UNDP, could be broken up into seven components: economic, food, health, environmental, personal, community and political security. These components and their threats are closely interconnected, and it is only by recognising the linkages that effective strategies for achieving human security can be sought. The breaking up of human security into subdivisions was not necessarily meant to be comprehensive, but rather to make the concept more analytically accessible.

The United Nations set up a Commission on Human Security to define and analyse the concept of human security and determine how it could be practically implemented by the UN. The Commission was chaired by Sadako Ogata and Amartya Sen and produced its final report in 2003.[93] The Commission on Human Security defines human security as a concept 'to protect the vital core of all human lives in ways that enhance human freedoms and human fulfilment. Human security means protecting fundamental freedoms – freedoms that are the essence of life. It means protecting people from critical (severe) and pervasive (widespread) threats and situations.'[94] This is the definition now employed by UN institutions when discussing human security.

The United Nations has since embraced the concept in a variety of ways, including the establishment of the United Nations Trust Fund for Human Security (which was initially financed by the government of Japan) and the initiation of a series of human security projects by a range of UN institutions since 1999.[95] These projects are undertaken under the management of the Human Security Unit which was established within the UN Office for the Coordination of Humanitarian Affairs. There have been a series of thematic debates within the UN and the publication of a Report by the Secretary-General in 2010 as a result of the discussion of human security at the 2005 World Summit. It was expressly recognised in the 2005 World Summit Outcome document that 'all individuals, in particular, vulnerable people, are entitled to freedom from fear and freedom from want, with an equal opportunity to enjoy all their rights and fully develop their human potential.'[96] In 2010 the United Nations General Assembly also adopted a Resolution, for the first time formally recognising the concept of human security, discussed below.[97]

93 UN Commission on Human Security, *Human Security Now* (United Nations, 2003).

94 Ibid 4.

95 For list of projects and institutions involved, see *Report of the Secretary-General on Human Security*, UN GAOR, Sixty-fourth sess, Agenda Item 48 and 114, UN Doc A/64/701 (8 March 2010).

96 *World Summit Outcome Document*, GA Res 60/1, UN GAOR, Sixtieth sess, Agenda Item 46 and 120, UN Doc A/RES/60/1 (24 October 2005) [143].

97 *Follow-up to Paragraph 143 on Human Security of the 2005 World Summit Outcome*, GA Res 66/290, Sixty-sixth sess, Agenda Item 14 and 117, UN Doc A/RES/66/290 ('Human Security Resolution').

(i) State practice

There is a plethora of state practice from the two decades of human security's existence. A brief survey of some of the more notable examples is offered below. In particular there are a number of trends regionally endorsing human security, although not without significant caveats in each case. The following discussion traces these trends, to demonstrate how human security has been approached by governments around the world.

(A) EUROPE

In relation to Europe, the work of the Organisation for Security and Cooperation in Europe (OSCE) is of particular significance. The European approach to security, as promoted through this organisation, is one of 'comprehensive security', with a human dimension as one of its pillars

> The OSCE was created as a security organization. However, it does not deal exclusively with issues of military security, disarmament or border issues. Based on a broad concept of security, it deals equally with human rights.
>
> The OSCE considers security more than merely the absence of war. Instead, it was the intention of the OSCE participating States to create a comprehensive framework for peace and stability in Europe.[98]

In addition, the European Union's shared security policies, including the European Security Strategy (ESS) of 2003 and the development of both the Common Foreign and Security Policy (CFSP)[99] and the Common Security and Defence Policy (CSDP),[100] have all been influenced by commissioned reports on the role of human security in European security architecture.[101] The European Security Strategy emphasises the relationship between security and development. It acknowledges both that '[s]ecurity is a precondition of development,' and that 'poverty and disease cause untold suffering and give rise to pressing security concerns.'[102] It also emphasises a rules-based multilateral security policy, with an

98 Organisation for Security and Cooperation in Europe (OSCE), *Human Dimension Commitments: Volume 1, Thematic Compilation* (OSCE, 3rd edn, 2012).

99 Information about the CFSP can be located at <http://www.eeas.europa.eu/cfsp/index_en.htm>.

100 For information about the CSDP see <http://www.eeas.europa.eu/csdp/about-csdp/index_en.htm>.

101 *Barcelona Report of the Study Group on Europe's Security Capabilities: A Human Security Doctrine for Europe,* presented to EU High Representative for Common Foreign and Security Policy (15 September 2004); Human Security Study Group, 'A European Way of Security' (The Madrid Report of the Human Security Study Group comprising a Proposal and Background Report 8th November 2007); EU–Russia Human Security Study Group, 'Helsinki Plus: Towards a Human Security Architecture for Europe' (First Report May 2010).

102 *European Security Strategy, A Secure Europe in a Better World*, Brussels (12 December 2003).

emphasis on prevention.[103] All of this is in keeping with human security. Moreover, the emphasis on multilateralism, international law and regional focus present in the strategy reflects principles advocated in the Barcelona Report, commissioned during the development of the strategy.[104] On the other hand, however, other principles emphasised by the Report, most notably those emphasising a rights-based approach and bottom-up strategies – aspects essential to human security – were omitted. Likewise, as will also be seen with the treaties that are the subject of Chapter Seven, despite the explicit influence of human security discourse, the term 'human security' is not to be found in any part of the ESS.

In 2008 the EU published a report on the implementation of the ESS.[105] This document is significant in itself, as it is the first official usage of human security expressly made by the Council of Europe. Likewise, it acts as a catalogue of European practice promoting human security, noting activities such as post-tsunami peacebuilding in Aceh and refugee protection in Chad.[106] It also draws on the centrality of human rights and good governance for the realisation of human security, filling in some of the human security gaps of the ESS itself. European security practices under the CFSP have also seen an increase in the merging of military and civilian activity.[107] In terms of state practice implementing these policies, it must be noted, however, that inconsistent responses have been observed, and commentators have noted that it is difficult to find examples of European action that have not had underlying self-interest guiding the way, rather than being actions taken for directly humanitarian reasons.[108] Nonetheless, as Solana points out, the EU 'was breaking new ground in combining different aspects of security.'[109]

103 Ibid.

104 *Barcelona Report of the Study Group on Europe's Security Capabilities: A Human Security Doctrine for Europe,* presented to EU High Representative for Common Foreign and Security Policy (15 September 2004).

105 Council of the EU, Report on the Implementation of the European Security Strategy – Providing Security in a Changing World, Brussels, EU Doc S407/08 (11 December 2008).

106 Ibid 2.

107 For discussion, see, eg, Nicoletta Pirozzi and Sammi Sandawi, 'Military and Civilian ESDP Missions: Ever Growing and Effective' (2009) *Istituto Affari Internazionali* 1; Måns Hanssen, 'Civil–Military Interaction in the European Union: Applying a Comprehensive Approach to CSDP Operations' (Working Paper FOI, 2010); Per Martin Norheim-Martinsen, 'Managing the Civil–Military Interface in the EU: Creating an Organisation Fit for Purpose' (2010) 14(10) *European Integration online Papers (EIoP)*; Per Martin Norheim-Martinsen, 'Matching Ambition with Institutional Innovation: The EU's Comprehensive Approach and Civil–Military Organisation' (Report for the Norwegian Defence Research Establishment (FFI), 3 July 2009); Björn Olav Knutsen, 'The EU's Security and Defense Policy (ESDP) and the Challenges of Civil–Military Coordination (CMCO): The Case of the Democratic Republic of Congo (DRC)' (2009) 18(4) *European Security* 441.

108 Lorenzo Fioramonti, 'Human Security? The Weaknesses of the EU's Involvement in Human Rights Crises' EU-Grasp Policy Brief (March 2012).

109 Javier Solana, 'The European Union and Human Security' in Mary Martin and Taylor Owen (eds), *The Routledge Handbook of Human Security* (Routledge, 2014) 251, 254.

(B) ASIA

In Asia, the picture not only varies compared to other regions of the world, but internally too, there are limits to how far a common understanding of human security has been found.[110] However, the strongest commonality among Asian states in terms of their deliberations and practices regarding security is a commitment to the principles of state sovereignty and non-intervention in their traditional form, a commitment generally considered inimical to the cosmopolitan mindset of human security discourse.[111] In regional fora such as the Association of Southeast Asian Nations (ASEAN), the Asia Pacific Economic Cooperation forum (APEC), and the East Asia Study Group, the term has been used (but not expressly endorsed) sporadically, but with no agreed-upon definition applied.[112]

However, Japan has proven the world's strongest state advocate of a broad approach to human security, something it has continued to pursue even as its fellow human security advocates have time and again reverted to narrower approaches to the concept. Japan is responsible for the establishment of the UN Trust Fund for Human Security and the Commission on Human Security, and human security is core to the work of the Japan International Cooperation Agency (JICA). Furthermore, the entirety of Japan's ODA programme is built around the concept.[113] It has also been noted that Japan is the only nation in the world that has dedicated an ambassador exclusively to the issue of human security.[114] Japan has also championed human security on the world stage, and

110 On the different views of human security among Asian countries, see Arabinda Acharya and Amitav Acharya, Human Security in Asia: Conceptual Ambiguities and Common Understanding, 12–18 (February 12 2001). <www.yorku.ca/drache/talks/pdf/acharya_delhi.pdf>. See also, Tan Hsien-Li, 'Not Just Global Rhetoric: Japan's Substantive Actualization of Its Human Security Foreign Policy' (2010) 10 *International Relations of the Asia-Pacific* 159.

111 See, eg, Sung Won Kim, 'Human Security with an Asian Face?' (2010) 17 *Indiana Journal of Global Legal Studies* 83. See also, Li Dongyan, 'China's Approach to Non-Traditional Security (NTS)' (conference report, Institute of East Asian Studies, Berkeley, 8 March 2007): Chinese human security proponents do not exclude sovereignty security and the principle of non-intervention. Even the most active advocates of human security believe that judgments about the human security situation should be based on domestic judgments, not on judgments by people or governments outside the state. Therefore, human security should not become an excuse for foreign interference in domestic affairs (manuscript available at <http://ieas.berkeley.edu/events/pdf/2007.03.08LiDongyan.pdf>).

112 See, eg, Paul Evans, 'Human Security and East Asia' in Mary Martin and Taylor Owen (eds), *The Routledge Handbook of Human Security* (Routledge, 2014) 272.

113 This policy is outlined by the Japanese Ministry of Foreign Affairs, <http://www.mofa.go.jp/policy/human_secu/index.html>. For evaluation of this work see Tan Hsien-Li, 'Not Just Global Rhetoric: Japan's Substantive Actualization of its Human Security Foreign Policy' (2010) 10 *International Relations of the Asia-Pacific* 159.

114 Yukio Takasu, 'Japan and Networked Human Security' in Mary Martin and Taylor Owen (eds), *The Routledge Handbook of Human Security* (Routledge, 2014) 239. It should be noted that the aforementioned author, Yukio Takasu, is Japan's current ambassador with this function.

particularly regionally, including in fora such as APEC and ASEAN. Human security is said to fit into the 'psyche of the Japanese'[115] as expressed in the 1945 Constitution of Japan:

> We, the Japanese people, desire to occupy an honoured place in an international society striving for the preservation of peace, and the banishment of tyranny and slavery, oppression and intolerance – from the earth. We recognise that all peoples of the world have the right to live in peace, free from fear and want. – We pledge our national honour to accomplish these high ideals and purposes with all our resources.[116]

However, Japanese practice in relation to human security has not been without criticism. Some have noted that despite the embrace of human security, Japanese practice remains rooted in upholding state sovereignty at the cost of more active engagement in its pursuit.[117] It has also been noted that while the Japanese model of human security emphasises poverty reduction and human empowerment, it has pursued human security in a way almost entirely detached from any consideration of human rights.[118] A failure to engage with NGOs has also been an aspect of Japanese policy generally, and this stands in the way of an effective and comprehensive human security framework committed to empowerment and bottom-up approaches.[119] A final criticism made of Japan's approach – a common criticism of human security policy – is that it is outward-looking. Japan has largely failed to mobilise the approach internally, despite lessons learnt from the 2011 tsunami, the Fukushima nuclear power plant disaster, and other local challenges in protecting the vulnerable.[120]

(C) AFRICA

One aspect of Japan's commitment to human security is a regular symposium on human security during its annual Tokyo International Conference on African Development (TICAD). This event is regularly attended by high-level panellists within the African Union and African states.[121] Regionally, human security has been widely embraced within African policy development, and finds expression in a number of regionally significant legal instruments. Africa collectively has long

115 Ibid 245.
116 Translated version cited ibid, 245–6.
117 Satomi Ho, 'Japan's Human Security Policy: A Critical Review of its Limits and Failures' (2008) 28(1) *Japanese Studies* 101.
118 Ibid. See also, Mieko Fujioka, 'Japan's Human Rights Policy at Domestic and International Levels: Disconnecting Human Rights from Human Security' (2003) 15(2) *Japan Forum* 287.
119 Ibid 292.
120 Ibid. See, also, Yukio Takasu, 'Japan and Networked Human Security' in Mary Martin and Taylor Owen (eds), *The Routledge Handbook of Human Security* (Routledge, 2014) 239, 248–9.
121 See, eg, panellists at the 2013 TICAD V: <http://www.mofa.go.jp/policy/page11e_000003.html>.

held security to be an issue of regional rather than national significance and responsibility, and it has developed a range of instruments to respond to concerns of human security. An example of this is the Economic Community of West African States (ECOWAS) Protocol Relating to the Mechanism for Conflict Prevention, Management, Resolution, Peacekeeping and Security, signed by sixteen member states in December 1999. The East African Community has likewise emphasised the need for common efforts to respond to the root causes of conflict and to promote good governance and respect for human (and peoples') rights. In 1991, predating the emergence of UNDP approach to human security, the Organisation of African Unity (OAU) adopted the Kampala Document, which asserts that security

> embraces all aspects of the society including economic, political and social dimensions of individual, family, community, local and national life. The security of a nation must be construed in terms of the security of the individual citizen to live in peace with access to the basic necessities of life while fully participating in the affairs of his/her society in freedom and enjoying all fundamental human rights.[122]

The African Union's Non-Aggression and Common Defence Pact goes a step further, by explicitly employing and endorsing the term 'human security':

> Human security means the security of the individual in terms of satisfaction of his/her basic needs. It also includes the creation of the social, economic, political, environmental and cultural conditions necessary for the survival and dignity of the individual, the protection and respect for human rights, good governance and the guarantee for each individual of the opportunities and choices for his/her full development.[123]

The expansive nature of this description must be noted. It is a rare formalised recognition of the rights-based nature of human security,[124] expressly notes the comprehensive nature of human security and its interconnected dimensions, and associates human security closely with issues of good governance, demonstrating an appreciation of the preventive nature of human security. The AU president reconfirmed the Union's commitment to human security at the recent High-Level Event on Human Security conducted by the UN.[125]

122 OAU, 'The Kampala Document: Towards a Conference on Security, Stability, Development and Co-operation in Africa' adopted at the Kampala Summit, 19–22 May 1991.

123 *African Union Non-Aggression and Common Defence Pact*, 2005. See more generally <http://www.peaceau.org/en/resource>.

124 For a discussion see, eg, Ademola Abass, 'African Peace and Security Architecture and Protection of Human Security' in Ademola Abass (ed), *Protecting Human Security in Africa* (Oxford, 2010) 247, 258.

125 Antonio Tete on behalf of Ramtane Lamamra Commissioner for Peace and Security of the African Union, 'Relevance and Added Value of Human Security: Regional Perspective' (Speech delivered at the High-Level Event on Human Security, United

(IV) THE HUMAN SECURITY NETWORK AND FRIENDS OF HUMAN SECURITY

Approaches to human security have not only manifested themselves under regional lines. The Human Security Network (HSN) represents a small coalition of states with diverse membership. The network was established in 1998 with the Lysøen Agreement signed by Norway and Canada to establish a policy agenda and theoretical framework for human security. The HSN currently consists of 12 member states from a diverse range of backgrounds: Austria, Chile, Costa Rica, Greece, Ireland, Jordan, Mali, Norway, Panama, Slovenia, Switzerland and Thailand. South Africa is also a part of the Network with observer status.[126] The HSN has played an integral part in the establishment of the treaties discussed in Chapter Seven. While the membership of the HSN is relatively small, it has been accompanied in recent years by the establishment of the 'Friends of Human Security' (FHS) – an initiative co-founded and co-chaired by Japan and Mexico. The FHS is an open and informal forum for Member States and UN organizations to discuss human security issues. The 6th meeting of the FHS in 2009 saw the highest number of participants, with representatives of 96 states and 20 UN organisations attending.[127]

While it is arguable that the HSN and its activities, and especially the increasing involvement of states in the activities of the FHS, are a significant indicator of state practice, it is also a cautionary tale in terms of consistency in state practice. As noted above and elsewhere in this study, Canada was a founding member of the HSN and one of the strongest advocates of human security, especially during the tenure of Lloyd Axworthy as Canada's Minister of Foreign Affairs (1996–2000). During this time Canada commissioned the International Commission on Intervention and State Sovereignty (ICISS) in its development of the R2P, and actively promoted a humanitarian agenda of foreign policy (not uncontroversially, as this included NATO's intervention in the Balkans). However, following changes in political leadership, Canada withdrew from the HSN, and not only discontinued any pursuit of the concept internationally, but has gone so far as to blacklist the term in governmental documents.[128] Likewise, the HSN has lost much of its earlier vision and drive, with the meetings now largely cursory, and no longer attracting high level officials, as was common in the past. Martin and Owen note that the HSN is now largely used as a vehicle for the pet projects of whichever state is currently the chair of the coalition.[129]

Nations, New York, 8 May 2013) <https://docs.unocha.org/sites/dms/HSU/Statement%20by%20Amb%20Antonio%20Tete,%20African%20Union.pdf>.

126 Information obtained from Slovenian foreign policy website: <http://www.mzz.gov.si/en/foreign_policy/human_security_network_hsn/>.

127 OCHA, Sixth Meeting of the Friends of Human Security (2009) <http://ochaonline.un.org/SixthMeetingoftheFriendsofHumanSecurity/tabid/5709/language/en-US/Default.aspx>.

128 The leaked internal memorandum is noted in Mary Martin and Taylor Owen, 'The Second Generation of Human Security: Lessons from the UN and EU Experience' (2010) 86(1) *International Affairs* 211.

129 Ibid 213.

Such activities show that human security is still widely subject to the vicissitudes of political influence, making it difficult to demonstrate the consistency necessary for acceptance as international custom. It also demonstrates a divided focus between what have been referred to as the 'Canadian' (freedom from fear focused) and the 'Japanese' (freedom from want oriented) approaches. This reflects a broader conceptual divide in the concept, which will be examined in more depth in Chapter Four.

(ii) The legal character of human security

The International Court of Justice (ICJ) has twice used the term 'human security'. The first instance was in the *Armed Activities* case by Judge Koroma. Human security was raised in relation to a discussion of the provisional measures the Court can order under Article 41 of the *Statute of the International Court of Justice.* In this discussion he referred to such measures as intended to be taken in relation to the 'Court's role in maintaining international peace and security, including human security and the right to life.'[130] The second usage was by Judge Cançado Trindade in the Court's Advisory Opinion on the Unilateral Declaration of Independence issued by Kosovo. Here, human security was invoked to justify a continuing UN presence in Kosovo, 'for the sake of human security, and the preservation of international peace and security in the region.'[131] These are two extremely isolated uses of the term, and no context or discussion of what precisely was meant by 'human security' was provided in either case. In both cases, however, it is worth noting that human security was contextualised directly in relation to the maintenance of international peace and security. Also as discussed below, the ICJ has increasingly addressed and recognised the intersection of international human rights law and international humanitarian law, an important connection to be made in relation to human security.

Also relevant are the resolutions and the informal thematic debates that the General Assembly has engaged in over the concept of human security. While not binding international law in themselves, the ICJ has noted, in the Advisory Opinion on the Legality of the Prohibition of Nuclear Weapons, that

> resolutions, even if they are not binding, may sometimes have normative value. They can, in certain circumstances, provide evidence important for establishing the existence of a rule or the emergence of an *opinio juris.* To establish whether this is true of a given General Assembly resolution, it is necessary to look at its content and the conditions of its adoption; it is also necessary to see whether an *opinio juris* exists as to its normative character. Or

130 *Armed Activities (Democratic Republic of Congo v Uganda) (Judgment)* [2005] ICJ Rep 116, 307 (Judge Koroma).

131 *Accordance with International Law of the Unilateral Declaration of Independence in Respect of Kosovo (Advisory Opinion)* [2010] ICJ Rep 150, 216 (Judge Cançado Trindade).

> a series of resolutions may show the gradual evolution of the *opinio juris* required for the establishment of a new rule.

There is not yet a series of resolutions specifically to point to such a normative character. The first expression of human security in General Assembly resolutions was in 2005, calling for further discussion of the concept.[132] Far more significant is the 2012 resolution, expressly endorsing and outlining the concept of human security.[133] This Resolution was adopted without vote, by consensus by the General Assembly on 10 September 2012. While much of state practice still reflects a narrower view of human security, it must be noted that the Resolution adopts a broad definition of the concept. Moreover, while there has not been a series of Resolutions, there has been a steady stream of informal thematic debates within the General Assembly on an annual basis on the topic of human security.[134] The debates in themselves have, however, reflected continuing confusion and hesitancy from some member states over the years they have been conducted, since 2008. At the same time, they also manifest a common understanding, culminating in the 2012 Resolution, of what human security entails and its relevance and universality.

Problematically for arguments in relation to the impact of human security discourse on international law, an issue recurring in the debates was the argument that human security should not bring with it legal obligations. This argument ultimately found expression in the 2012 Resolution:

> (*h*) Human security must be implemented with full respect for the purposes and principles enshrined in the Charter of the United Nations, including full respect for the sovereignty of States, territorial integrity and non-interference in matters that are essentially within the domestic jurisdiction of States. *Human security does not entail additional legal obligations on the part of States...*[135]

It is worth noting, however, that this statement is not necessarily fatal to the legal development of human security. It states that no new legal obligations should emerge. However, as shall be discussed throughout this book, much of the human security discourse develops from existing obligations and precepts. Human security is more concerned with producing a synthesised overarching framework for the expression of those principles. Thus, while this reluctance to produce legal norms

132 *Follow-up to Paragraph 143 on Human Security of the 2005 World Summit Outcome*, GA Res 64/291, UN GAOR, Sixty-fourth sess, Agenda Item 48 and 114, UN Doc A/RES/64/291 (27 July 2010).

133 *Follow-up to Paragraph 143 on Human Security of the 2005 World Summit Outcome*, GA Res 66/290, Sixty-sixth sess, Agenda Item 14 and 117, UN Doc A/RES/66/290 (25 October 2012) ('Human Security Resolution').

134 The debates can be collectively located at UN Human Security Unit, Publications and Resources, <http://unocha.org/humansecurity/humansecurity/resources/publications-and-products/Human-Security-At-The-General-Assembly>.

135 *Human Security Resolution*, UN Doc A/RES/66/290 [3], emphasis added.

directly in relation to human security is damaging, human security still has the capacity to gain a legally normative status, and at present it is the inconsistencies between state practice and rhetoric, and the variations in interpretation of the discourse that remain the more immediate obstacles to this realisation.

IV Conclusion

Human security, while emerging in the late twentieth century, is an idea that has its roots in the traditional constructions of sovereignty, liberalism and security. Human security emerged at a time of significant upheaval in the international sphere and in particular in the arena of global politics. It was created as a response to a perceived urgent need in the international community to respond to emerging threats, and to capitalise on a changed security environment. Human security is about the transformation, within the international community, of state-centric security to a sense of security grounded in people and the threats that they face in whatever form those threats may take. It is also about addressing vulnerability, because the way people experience threats will differ according to their place in society. Human security, then, is different from traditional security, which is about security for the elite: human security is security for all. It is also about acknowledging that there is an ethical dimension to security, one that must be fostered and heeded for genuine, and sustainable, security to exist. This chapter has shown how human security emerged within the framework of security studies scholarship. While human security has also seen an increasing foothold in the activities of states, at present it is far too inconsistent to provide any clarity to what the legal content and influence of human security should be. The next chapter explores the contours of what security actually means in the context of human security discourse.

2 The security *problematique* and the transformative potential of human security discourse

A reconceptualisation of security is one of the contributions the academic community can make to shaking up the complacency of the globally powerful in these critical times[1]

I Introduction

The previous chapter traced the history of the emergence of human security, and placed it into the broader framework of security studies. This chapter builds on those origins and examines the critical questions about the nature of security and how human security should be defined. It starts from the position that security is an essentially contested concept, and explores why human security can be best utilised as a discourse. It explores the transformative potential of human security with a view to the influence it might exert on international law if properly harnessed.

It is important to address the fundamental questions related to security since human security scholarship is often accused of neglecting the theoretical underpinnings of the concept.[2] As a discourse that seeks to challenge and reform traditional understandings of security, it is vital that human security can position itself within the field of theory in a coherent manner. As the definition of human security is deliberately kept broad (and arguably vague),[3] it is essential that human security discourse has a clear perspective on what, precisely, it is trying to achieve and why. This can only be done through an understanding of the meaning of 'security' itself, and an examination of the security *problematique.*

II Essentially contested concept? What security actually means

Buzan suggests that 'the nature of security defies pursuit of an agreed definition'.[4] Many now argue that security, when exposed to examination, proves itself to be

1 Ken Booth, *Theory of World Security* (Cambridge, 2007) 97.
2 See, eg, Edward Newman, 'Critical Human Security Studies' (2010) 36 *Review of International Studies* 77.
3 A topic that will be the subject of discussion in Chapter Three.
4 Barry Buzan, *People, States and Fear: An Agenda for International Security Studies in the Post-Cold War Era* (Harvester Wheatsheaf, 2nd edn, 1991) 16.

an essentially contested concept.[5] However, both Baldwin and Booth argue that security is more accurately characterised as a neglected concept. Booth thus concludes that it is too early to determine if it is essentially contested, and that it is only the shift of examining a concept that has remained uncontested for so long that leads to the assumption of it being essentially contested. He argues that '[t]he problem of security is not in the meaning of the concept, but in the politics of the meaning'.[6] Baldwin, on the other hand, contends that current efforts at redefining security are generally too focused on shifting policy agendas, and therefore neglect the conceptualisation of security itself.[7] In part, this may be an issue about how security is framed. Security (and human security) has been variously framed as a concept, a discourse,[8] a condition,[9] an aim or destination,[10] a guiding principle,[11] a political rallying cry or leitmotif,[12] a value or normative orientation,[13] a process,[14] a collective good,[15] and a fundamental human need.[16]

Wæver argues that while the definition of security may be disputed, at least one element is common among writers on the topic; 'it is something good. In other words, the very term "security" is positively value-loaded.'[17] Indeed, for some authors security seems to be the *ultimate* good:

5 See, eg, Ramesh Thakur cited in David Roberts, 'Empowering the Human Security Debate: Making It Coherent and Meaningful' (2005) XXII(4) *International Journal on World Peace* 3, 5.
6 Ken Booth, *Theory of World Security* (Cambridge, 2007) 96.
7 David A Baldwin, 'The Concept of Security' (1997) 23 *Review of International Studies* 5, 5.
8 Laura J Shepherd and Jutta Weldes, 'Security: The State (of) Being Free From Danger?' in Hans Günter Brauch et al (eds), *Globalization and Environmental Challenges* (Springer Berlin Heidelberg, 2008) vol 3, 529, 532–6.
9 'Security is a condition, like health or status, which defies easy definition or analysis': Patrick Morgan, cited in Ken Booth, *Theory of World Security* (Cambridge, 2007) 96, 97.
10 Berma Klein Goldewijk, '"New Wars" and the State: The Nexus Religion-Human Security' in Georg Frerks and Berma Klein Goldewijk (eds), *Human Security and International Insecurity* (Wageningen Academic, 2007) 65, 65.
11 Symposium, Ministry of Foreign Affairs (Japan) ('MOFA'), *Summary Conclusion of the Symposium on Human Security*, 15 July 2010, Okuma Auditorium, Waseda University <http://www.mofa.go.jp/policy/human_secu/pdfs/sympo1007_con.pdf>.
12 See, eg, Claudia F. Fuentes Julio and Hans Günter Brauch, 'The Human Security Network: A Global North–South Coalition' in Hans Günter Brauch et al (eds), *Facing Global Environmental Change* (Springer Berlin Heidelberg, 2009) vol 4, 991, 991.
13 Berma Klein Goldewijk, '"New Wars" and the State: The Nexus Religion-Human Security' in Georg Frerks and Berma Klein Goldewijk (eds), *Human Security and International Insecurity* (Wageningen Academic, 2007) 65, 66.
14 Peter Uvin, 'A Field of Overlaps and Interactions' (2004) 35 *Security Dialogue* 352.
15 P H Liotta and Taylor Owen, 'Why Human Security' (2006) 7 *Whitehead Journal of Diplomacy and International Relations* 37, 40.
16 Anthony Burke, 'Aporias of Security' (2002) 27 *Alternatives: Global, Local, Political* 1, 1.
17 Ole Wæver, 'Peace and Security: Two Evolving Concepts and Their Changing Relationship' in Hans Günter Brauch et al (eds), *Globalization and Environmental Challenges* (Springer Berlin Heidelberg, 2008) vol 3, 99.

> In both its realist and humanist guises, security takes the form and promise of a *metaphysical* discourse: an overarching political goal and practice that guarantees existence itself, that makes the possibility of the world possible.[18]

Bain makes a similar point:

> ... For without security all that is beneficial in individual and collective life, all art, industry, all commerce, and all science, is condemned to a precarious, if not fleeting, existence.[19]

He argues that international relations are interpreted more with reference to 'security' than to any other idea or value.[20] This point is also one raised by Tickner.[21] It is not surprising, then, that Burke frames security as 'one of modernity's most stubborn and enduring dreams'.[22] While some thus argue that security is a universal good, others treat security as a relative concept.[23] The UNDP took this approach when it posited that 'most people instinctively understand what security means', and emphasised the importance of feeling secure, whatever that might mean for the particular individual or community.[24]

The reason it is so important to grasp what security means, and to broaden it from its limited military associations, is that the word 'security' is in itself extremely powerful. This is recognised by the Copenhagen School in their discussion of securitisation. The consequence of securitising an issue is resort to 'extraordinary measures' in the traditional framework of security.[25] For Booth, '[o]nce the security label has been attached to an issue, it changes from being a problem to a priority for society'.[26] Prioritisation is at the core of the use of security in political and legal discourse. 'Security' creates a sense of urgency, magnifying the severity of the problem, demanding attention and resources, and emphasising the necessity of a response. Baldwin is critical of the building of urgency into the discussion of security, arguing that it prejudges the values,[27] but despite his concerns, it seems

18 Anthony Burke, 'Aporias of Security' (2002) 27 *Alternatives: Global, Local, Political* 1, 3.
19 William Bain, *The Empire of Safety and the Safety of the People* (Routledge, 2006) 8.
20 Ibid.
21 '[T]he achievement of security has always been central to the normative concerns of international relations': J Ann Tickner, *Gender in International Relations: Feminist Perspectives on Achieving Global Security* (Columbia University Press, 1992), 22–3.
22 Anthony Burke, 'Aporias of Security' (2002) 27 *Alternatives: Global, Local, Political* 1, 1.
23 Ken Booth, *Theory of World Security* (Cambridge, 2007) 105.
24 United Nations Development Programme (UNDP), *Human Development Report 1994*, 23.
25 See Barry Buzan, Ole Wæver and Jaap de Wilde, *Security: A New Framework for Analysis* (Lynne Rienner Publications, 1998). A critique of this argument, however, will be made in Chapter Four.
26 Ken Booth, *Theory of World Security* (Cambridge, 2007) 109.
27 David A Baldwin, 'The Concept of Security' (1997) 23 *Review of International Studies* 5, 21.

clear that urgency remains an inherent element of security, at least in the context of international relations.

But the question remains, what does the term 'security' in fact mean?

A Security

Beyond its ancient roots and dictionary definitions, the starting point in the search for a definition of security usually begins with the work of Wolfers. For Wolfers,

> Security is a value, then, of which a nation can have more or less and which it can aspire to have in greater or lesser measure ... Security, in an objective sense, measures the absence of threats to acquired values, in a subjective sense, the absence of fear that such values will be attacked.[28]

Clearly there remains a focus on national security in this definition, not surprisingly, as it was written in 1962. However, there is no reason why this definition cannot be applied to different referent objects, such as the individual. This definition remains one of the most widely used constructions of security. It does not, however, explain what constitutes a threat, nor what should be encompassed by 'acquired values'. Baldwin is critical of approaches that appeal to 'core values' or 'vital interests', as this brings inherently normative judgments into the discussion.[29] Certainly, however, conceptualisations of security are normative by their very nature, perhaps none more so than the idea of human security. Security is not an apolitical condition with an objective reality, or part of the natural order of things. Security is what humans in a community make it to be, for themselves and for others – a human artifice.

Ullman, for whom security is not merely a goal but a consequence, finds it more meaningful to define security by the threats which challenge it. Ullman, who like Wolfers maintains a focus on national security, defines a threat as 'an action or series of events that (1) threatens drastically and over a relatively brief span of time to degrade the quality of life for the inhabitants of a state, or (2) threatens significantly to narrow the range of policy choices available to the government of a state or to private, nongovernmental entities within the state.'[30] While this is a useful definition in many ways, threats and their determination are always going to be fundamentally interpretative rather than objective, a point made by Shepherd and Weldes.[31] They use the example of immigration, which can simultaneously be

28 Arnold Wolfers, 'National Security as an Ambiguous Symbol' (1962) republished in Christopher W Hughes and Lai Yew Meng (eds) *Security Studies: A Reader* (Routledge, 2011) 6.

29 David A Baldwin, 'The Concept of Security' (1997) 23 *Review of International Studies* 5, 14.

30 Richard Ullman, 'Redefining Security' (1983) 8(1) *International Security* 129, 132.

31 Laura J Shepherd and Jutta Weldes, 'Security: The State (of) Being Free From Danger?' in Hans Günter Brauch et al (eds), *Globalization and Environmental Challenges* (Springer Berlin Heidelberg, 2008) vol 3, 529.

viewed as a threat or boon to a state.[32] They thus see it as more meaningful to construct and understand security as a discourse rather than view it as a rooted, neutral concept. While it is debatable whether security in itself is better constituted as a concept, discourse, or some other phenomenon, a number of authors make a strong case for treating *human security* as discourse.[33]

A discourse, as described by Frerks, is the way in which we perceive and talk about the world around us, and give meaning to it. Put another way, and in the context of human security,

> [a] discourse is more than a concept. Through the concept, attention is directed to a widened, yet prioritised, set of key aspects, and to stability. The discourse involves further normative claims that what matters is the content of individuals' lives, including a reasonable degree of stability; and the predictive/explanatory hypotheses that a broad set of aspects not conventionally connected in theory are often importantly connected in reality.[34]

Given the integrative nature of human security – a point that will be highlighted in Chapter Four and be a recurring theme throughout this book – this is a particularly powerful argument. The Madrid Report, written for the Organization for Security and Cooperation in Europe (OSCE),[35] terms it a 'narrative' but makes a similar point. This report describes human security as 'more than just another security concept or label. It can be seen as a narrative that encapsulates the goals and methods of a highly diverse … policy system'.[36]

One point that can be taken from Ullman and applied to people-centred security, especially in relation to his second example of a threat, is an interest in choices, a defining element of Booth's influential approach to security. Booth rejects the Copenhagen School's focus on survival as the determinant of security.[37] As Booth points out, survival is merely existential, literally the continuance of

32 Ibid 532.

33 For human security as a discourse, see, eg, Des Gasper, 'Securing Humanity: Situating "Human Security" as Concept and Discourse' (2005) 6(2) *Journal of Human Development* 221; Georg Frerks, 'Human Security as a Discourse and Counter-Discourse' (2008) 19(1) *Security & Human Rights* 8; Des Gasper, 'Human Security: From Definitions to Investigating a Discourse' in Mary Martin and Taylor Owen (eds), *Routledge Handbook of Human Security* (Routledge, 2014) 28. The role of human security as a discourse does not, however, preclude it from being applied in other forms.

34 Des Gasper, 'Securing Humanity: Situating "Human Security" as Concept and Discourse' (2005) 6(2) *Journal of Human Development* 221, 228.

35 Human Security Study Group, 'A European Way of Security' (The Madrid Report of the Human Security Study Group comprising a Proposal and Background Report, 8 November 2007).

36 Ibid 8.

37 The Copenhagen School's focus on survival can be found within Barry Buzan, Ole Wæver, Jaap de Wilde, *Security: A New Framework for Analysis* (Lynne Rienner Publications, 1998) 21. For Booth's discussion see Ken Booth, *Theory of World Security* (Cambridge, 2007) 102–4.

existing. Security, on the other hand, he describes as 'survival-plus'. By this he means that security concerns more than just the quantity of life, but also its quality; not just being alive but living, and having the 'space to make choices'.[38] This argument is supported by the work of Hobbes, who also saw security as a broader concept than mere survival:

> But by safety here is not meant a bare preservation, but also other contentments of life, which every man by lawful industry, without danger or hurt to the Commonwealth, shall acquire to himself.[39]

Refugees, for example, are survivors, but their lives could hardly be classified as secure. Booth convincingly argues that the 'insecure life, for groups and individuals, is a determined life'.[40] Thus human security should not be seen solely as freedom from fear and freedom from want, but also the freedom to live with human dignity.[41]

While security is generally accepted as a universal good as discussed above, it is worth highlighting that complete security can, and has, been seen as a negative. In Roman literature and philosophy, the notion of *securitas* had both positive and negative connotations. As mentioned, *securitas* can be defined literally as 'freedom from care'. On the one hand, this could mean freedom from danger, a sense of safety. But it could also be used to mean carelessness or negligence.[42] This point is relevant in the modern context, as outlined by Burgess. He points out that security in this secondary context can be equated with lassitude.[43] This can be carelessness not only in our own lives but towards others, with security associated with 'a lack of need to be aware of our environment, those close by us and ourselves'.[44] He thus highlights the moral dimension of security. This is an important point for human security discourse, which must include an awareness of the ethical dimensions of security and the actions associated with it.[45] The ethical dimension

38 Ibid.
39 Thomas Hobbes, *Leviathan or the Matter, Forme & Power of a Common-Wealth Ecclesiastical and Civil* (Oxford Classics, republished 1998, originally published 1651) 143.
40 Ken Booth, *Theory of World Security* (Cambridge, 2007) 103.
41 Such is the approach taken by the UN; see, eg, General Assembly, *Report of the Secretary-General: Follow-up to General Assembly Resolution 66/290 on Human Security*, Sixty-eighth sess, Agenda Item 14 and 118, UN Doc A/68/685 (23 December 2013) [4].
42 For discussion see J Frederik M Arends, 'From Homer to Hobbes and Beyond – Aspects of "security" in the European Tradition' in Hans Günter Brauch et al (eds), *Globalization and Environmental Challenges* (Springer Berlin Heidelberg, 2008) vol 3, 263.
43 Peter J Burgess, 'The Ethical Challenges of Human Security in the Age of Globalisation' in Moufida Goucha and John Crowley (eds), Rethinking Human Security (Wiley-Blackwell, 2008) 49, 53.
44 Ibid.
45 This is a point taken up by P H Liotta and James F Miskel, 'Towards an Ethical Framework for Security' in Hans Günter Brauch et al (eds), *Globalization and Environmental Challenges* (Springer Berlin Heidelberg, 2008) vol 3, 879.

of security is also reflected in the ways in which security is tied to political legitimacy; '[w]e feel safe if we trust our institutions, and we trust our institutions if we see that they act effectively in crises'.[46]

Vulnerability is sometimes used as an alternative or complement to threats in defining security. As will be seen in later chapters, vulnerability is becoming an increasingly emphasised component of human security, perhaps the most essential principle. Suhrke sees the core of human insecurity as extreme vulnerability.[47] Human security then becomes a matter of ensuring the immediate protection of vulnerable individuals and communities so that the longer-term measures to improve conditions (eg, sustainable development)[48] can have an opportunity to work. He draws on Tawney's famous depiction of extreme vulnerability among peasants in rural China in 1931:

> There are districts in which the position of the rural population is that of a man standing permanently up to the neck in the water, so that even a ripple is sufficient to drown him.

This is different from a focus on threats, as it tries to address those that will be most affected by a threat, and produces a preventative focus to the idea of security that is significantly lacking in most accounts, but is central to the conceptualisation of human security.

Perhaps the most meaningful way to analyse security (and more specifically human security's place in this framework) is to apply Baldwin's set of questions, which for him makes up the security *problematique*.[49] Baldwin considers Wolfers' definition of security to be the most conceptually sound approach to date. From it he draws two base questions – (i) security for whom? and (ii) security for which values? – and says these form the basis of any meaningful discussion of security. He then draws from this a series of secondary and largely self-explanatory issues that also contribute to the discussion of security. One of these is (iii) how much security? This is a question of degree – more specifically, how much security is enough? Other issues are (iv) from what threats? and (v) by what means? (A related question that should be added to Baldwin's construction is: security provided by whom?) Further issues are (vi) at what cost? and (vii) in what time period?

46 Mary Kaldor, Mary Martin and Sabine Selchow, 'Human Security: A New Strategic Narrative for Europe' (2007) 83(2) *International Affairs* 273, 282.

47 Astri Suhrke, 'Human Security and the Interests of States' (1999) 30(3) *Security Dialogue* 265, 271.

48 Conceived as addressing the needs of future generations; see, eg, World Commission on Environment and Development, *Our Common Future*, (Oxford University Press, 1987).

49 David A Baldwin, 'The Concept of Security' (1997) 23 *Review of International Studies* 5.

B Human security and the security problematique

(i) Security for whom?

On the surface, this might seem to be the easiest question for human security discourse to answer. After all, the fact that human security is about *people-centred* security is the one issue undisputed within human security scholarship. But what is meant by 'people'? At one end of the spectrum it could imply the individual, or the communities to which individuals belong, while at the other end 'people' might refer to humanity as a whole, as a collective entity. Yet neither of these two subjects seems sufficient to provide a meaningful construction of security that is responsive to the *actual* needs of people.

There is certainly an argument to be made for human security referring to humanity as a whole. As Kofi Annan has pointed out, '[h]umanity, after all, is indivisible'.[50] There would be value in defining the referent object of human security as humanity, thus emphasising the mutual vulnerabilities of the people of the world.[51] Likewise, such an approach emphasises the universality that is embedded in the human security discourse.[52] However, humanity is arguably highly diverse, and the concept of humanity itself is extremely abstract, so there is a risk here of losing the policy value that is a defining trait of human security.

But limiting human security to the individual, and not giving weight to communities and communal identities, seems an equally risky enterprise. The priority of the individual over social groups is arguably an iconically Western approach, and risks lessening the meaning of human security for some cultures and societies. Shani, for example, argues that conventional discourse on human security reproduces 'the modernist conception of the individual, found in its most extreme form in the concentration camps, as "mute and absolutely alone". Stripped of membership of the cultural communities through which individuals find meaning, dignity and "identity" …'.[53] Understandings of identity, and local context, were of primary concern for the UNDP when they first conceived human security.[54]

So who is, or should be, the intended referent object of human security? Booth has opined that

> [a] critical theory of security seeks to denaturalize and historicize all human-made political referents, recognizing only the primordial entity of the *socially*

50 Kofi Annan, 'Two Concepts of Sovereignty', *The Economist,* (London), 18 September 1999 <http://www.un.org/News/ossg/sg/stories/kaecon.html>.
51 As discussed in Chapter Five.
52 As one of the four components identified by the United Nations Development Programme (UNDP), *Human Development Report 1994* (UNDP, 1994) 23.
53 Giorgio Shani, 'Securitising "Bare Life": Critical Perspectives on Human Security Discourse' in David Chandler and Nik Hynek (eds), *Critical Perspectives on Human Security: Rethinking Emancipation and Power in International Relations* (Routledge, 2011) 56, 61.
54 United Nations Development Programme (UNDP), *Human Development Report 1994* (UNDP, 1994) 34.

> *embedded* individual … The only transhistorical and permanent fixture in human society is the individual physical being, and so this must naturally be the ultimate referent in the security *problematique.*[55]

The socially embedded individual is not the isolated individual of Shani's concern. This individual draws identity from a group, meaning the notion of security, while geared to the individual, has to be flexible enough to accommodate notions of group identity and politics to truly safeguard *human* security. If human security abstracts individuals from the communities from which they draw meaning, identity and indeed security, then it ceases to function as a useful discourse. Allowing flexibility in the way 'people-centric' security is understood addresses the criticism of McDonald, who argues that human security effectively abstracts individuals. Using the example of the Kurdish population in Turkey, who are threatened as members of a group rather than as individuals, McDonald argues that '[t]reating individuals as the referent object of security does not always represent the best means of understanding a particular situation of insecurity, or redressing it'.[56] Therefore it is important that while the individual is the best, and most logical, referent object for human security, it is acknowledged that human security is *not* to be equated with individual security, and that the personhood of the individual is not abstracted from cultural and other contextual factors.

At least as important, for human security to have real value and transformative potential, is that it must be sufficiently gendered. As Enarson points out, gender was only 'tangentially included' in initial constructions of human security,[57] despite the fact that '[h]istory has shown that women's experience of insecurity is fundamentally different than that of men'.[58] In particular, for human security to effectively serve as a discourse, gender perspectives are essential, and as noted above, feminist scholarship has had a long history critically examining the normative assumptions and hegemonic constructs that have traditionally made up security and security studies. Hudson notes the positive impact of feminist human security analysis, in making the discourse both more critical and practically relevant: 'it has made the discipline self-aware and forced – although with obliqueness at times – the discourse outside the confines of mere problem-solving and into the realm of engaging with power.'[59] A fully gendered approach to human security

55 Ken Booth, 'Beyond Critical Security Studies' in Ken Booth (ed), *Critical Security Studies and World Politics* (Lynne Rienner, 2005) 264, 268, emphasis added.
56 Matt McDonald, 'Human Security and the Construction of Security' (2002) 16 *Global Society* 277, 281.
57 Elaine Enarson, 'Human Security and Disasters: What a Gender Lens Offers' in Christopher Hobson, Paul Bacon and Robin Cameron (eds), *Human Security and Natural Disasters* (Routledge, 2014) 37, 38.
58 R Jolly and DB Ray, *The Human Security Framework and National Human Development Report: A Review of Experiences and Current Debates* (2008) <http://hdr.undp.org/docs/nhdr/thematic_reviews/Human_Security_Guidance_Note.pdf>.
59 Heidi Hudson, '"Doing" Security As Though Humans Matter: A Feminist Perspective on Gender and the Politics of Human Security' (2005) 36 *Security Dialogue* 155, 171.

also makes the discourse more inclusive, participatory and empowering when actualised through policy and law.

Largely, though, the 'human' in human security discourse has been unexamined. One useful, recent contribution has encapsulated the issues raised in this section. Gasper has noted:

> Humans are not only individual choosers, but are 'encumbered subjects' who have each a body, gender, emotions, life-cycle, identity and social bonds, including memberships of (multiple) groups and of a common species. Normative priorities for being human include a sense of meaning and identification, and recognition of and respect for others. The vision of humans is as both vulnerable and capable.[60]

(ii) Security for which values?

According to the Commission on Human Security (CHS) definition, human security protects 'the vital core of all human lives', or put in other words, it protects 'the fundamental freedoms – freedoms that are the essence of life'.[61] As noted previously, Baldwin disapproves of approaches that appeal to a 'vital interest', arguing that it prejudges the notion of security as a policy objective (among many).[62] Certainly, conceptualisations of security, however, are normative by their very nature as discussed above, and none more so than the idea of human security. The CHS definition was left intentionally broad, to be adaptable to different people in different situations with different priorities. There are a number of approaches, however, that could be taken to pin down the values under consideration.

One place to start would be with the ideas of 'freedom from fear', 'freedom from want' and 'freedom to live in dignity'.[63] The UNDP sought to delineate the dimensions of human security into seven components: economic, food, health, environmental, personal, community and political security. Human rights are another source that inquiries into human security must have recourse to when determining the values to be protected. Human security is distinctively a rights-based approach to security. This, however, may not be sufficient, as it then raises questions of whether human security meaningfully adds anything to the pre-existing rights discourse, a concern addressed in Chapter Three.

See also Charlotte Bunch, 'Feminism, Peace, Human Rights and Human Security' (2003) 22(2) *Canadian Woman Studies* 6.

60 Des Gasper, 'Human Security: From Definitions to Investigating Discourse' in Mary Martin and Taylor Owen (eds), *Routledge Handbook of Human Security* (Routledge, 2014) 28, 34.

61 UN Commission on Human Security, *Human Security Now* (United Nations, 2003) 4.

62 David A Baldwin, 'The Concept of Security' (1997) 23 *Review of International Studies* 5, 14.

63 This is the current general approach of the United Nations. See, eg, United Nations General Assembly, *Report of the Secretary-General on Human Security*, UN GAOR, Sixty-fourth sess, Agenda Item 48 and 114, UN Doc A/64/701 (8 March 2010) [19].

Alternatively, Thakur provides one of the most cogent approaches, arguing that 'human security refers to the quality of life of the people of a society or polity. Anything which degrades their quality of life – demographic pressures, diminished access to or stock of resources, and so on – is a security threat.'[64] A complementary approach, and one that seems to have influenced Alkire in the construction of the CHS definition, is the capabilities approach of both Sen and Nussbaum.[65] For Sen, capabilities allow people 'to lead the kind of lives they value – and have reason to value'.[66] This includes things such as political freedom, social opportunities and economic facilities. Nussbaum takes a slightly different but related approach, stating that capabilities 'are so central that they seem definitive of a life that is truly human.'[67] They represent a human social minimum, and she argues that they are all implied by the concept of human dignity.[68] She relies on human dignity being a largely intuitive idea that does not need detailed explication. From a legal standpoint, the invocation of human dignity again leads us back to a rights-based approach.[69]

These approaches help locate the values relevant to human security, but clearly do not offer a tangible, measurable list of issues that can be drawn on. This indicates a need for human security literature to move beyond the debates about the scope of the concept, and to spend more time on developing a set of principles through which human security can be pursued. This is where international law could meaningfully enter the discourse of human security. Human dignity, however, seems to be a common thread that runs throughout the different approaches to value, and may be the core value that human security seeks to protect.

(iii) How much security?

This is a question not easily answered by the human security literature. However, it is worth emphasising that absolute security is both impossible and undesirable:

> ... people do not really want 'absolute' security, if such a state is imaginable, 'optimum' security would probably still leave an area of challenge, risk, doubt, danger, hazard and anxiety. Men [sic] are not lotus-eaters.[70]

64 Ramesh Thakur, 'From National Security to Human Security', in Stuart Harris and Andrew Mack (eds) *Asia-Pacific Security: The Economics–Politics Nexus* (Allen & Unwin, 1997) 52.

65 See Sabine Alkire, 'A Conceptual Framework for Human Security' (Working Paper No 2, Centre for Research on Inequality, Human Security and Ethnicity (CRISE) 2003) 3.

66 Amartya Sen, *Development as Freedom* (Oxford University Press, 1999) 18.

67 Martha C Nussbaum, *Frontiers of Justice: Disability, Nationality, Species Membership* (The Belknap Press, 2006) 70.

68 Ibid.

69 See, eg, *Universal Declaration of Human Rights*, GA Res 217A (III), UN GAOR, Third sess, 183rd plen mtg, UN Doc A/810 (10 December 1948) Preamble; art 1.

70 Dahl and Lindblom, cited in David A Baldwin, 'The Concept of Security' (1997) 23 *Review of International Studies* 5, 19.

Ramphele points out that total security is an unwelcome value: '[j]ust like a being that is immortal, a being not vulnerable is not human.'[71] This reaffirms the value of Booth's approach to security as emancipation or choice. Individuals, then, generally have the ability to elect the dangers they are exposed to, and the concept of security remains concerned with those threats the individual has no control over. This, then, rejects the argument put forward by Buzan that security is an inherently absolute condition:

> The word itself implies an absolute condition – something is either secure or insecure – and does not lend itself to the idea of a graded spectrum like that which fills the space between hot and cold.[72]

The question 'How much security?' does however reveal what for many is a central tenet of human security – that is, the idea of addressing vulnerabilities to threats, most specifically disproportionate and preventable vulnerability. This is closely tied to the argument for including structural violence as a form of threat to human security. The term 'structural violence', first coined by noted peace researcher Johan Galtung, refers to violence where there may not be an obvious actor directly harming another, but rather where harm is built into the structures of a society in the form of, *inter alia*, unequal power producing unequal life chances.[73] This is also reflected in the work of Rawls, who has pointed out that 'unjust social arrangements are themselves a kind of extortion, even violence'.[74] This approach again highlights the importance of vulnerability in issues of human (in)security. It also ties human security closely to values of social justice. Both Thomas and James draw on the examples of natural catastrophes to demonstrate how people experience crises differently, based on their vulnerability.[75] As Thomas argues, 'human insecurity results directly from existing structures of power that determine who enjoys the entitlement to security and who does not'.[76] For Thomas, human security has both quantitative (material sufficiency) and qualitative (human dignity) elements. The question of how much security then becomes closely tied to questions of the transformative potential of human security, discussed below.

For human security discourse, the issue of how much security is enough must be closely tied to the nexus between human security, human development and human rights. Human security represents the necessary minimum conditions for

71 Cited in Des Gasper, 'Securing Humanity: Situating "Human Security" as Concept and Discourse' (2005) 6(2) *Journal of Human Development* 221, 241.

72 Barry Buzan, *People, States and Fear: An Agenda for International Studies in the Post-Cold War Era* (Harvester Wheatsheaf, 2nd edn, 1991) 18.

73 Johan Galtung, 'Violence, Peace and Peace Research' (1969) 6 *Journal of Peace Research* 170.

74 John Rawls, *A Theory of Justice* (Harvard University Press, 1971) 302.

75 Stephen James, 'Human Security: Key Drivers, Antecedents and Conceptualisation' (Working Paper No 1, Institute for Human Security, La Trobe University, 2010).

76 Caroline Thomas, 'Global Governance, Development and Human Security: Exploring the Links' (2001) 22(2) *Third World Quarterly* 150, 160.

the realisation of the other two.[77] It has also been established that security is a relative value, and that these minimum conditions will change over time, based on the context of those whose security is in question.

(iv) Against what threats?

This is the question that lies at the heart of the schism that has occurred within human security scholarship, and will be addressed in Chapter Four in more detail. If nothing else, human security scholarship as a whole recognises that threats have a broader focus than a concern merely with external military threats. Instead, it highlights the fact that threats may also emerge from within the state, and that these should be treated with the same attention accorded to external threats.[78] Going beyond this, it can also be argued that an identification of what these threats are is ultimately unhelpful for human security discourse, and that this is in fact a counter-productive question. Rather than focusing concern on the nature of the threats, a dominant thread in human security discourse emphasises that rather than limiting the notion of human security by introducing criteria regarding the nature of the threats, it is better to focus instead on a threshold approach – on the seriousness of threats and their potential impact.

Taylor Owen has been a significant player in producing such an approach, and describes the value of the approach thus:

> A threshold-based conceptualization, one that limits threats by their severity rather than their cause, allows all possible harms to be considered, but selectively limits those that at any time are prioritized with the security level.[79]

It might be possible to draw here on Ullman's definition of threats, to reach some conclusions on what will reach such a threshold. For Ullman, as will be remembered, a threat is

> an action or series of events that (1) threatens drastically and over a relatively brief span of time to degrade the quality of life for the inhabitants of a state, or (2) threatens significantly to narrow the range of policy choices available to the government of a state or to private, nongovernmental entities within the state.[80]

77 Amartya Sen, 'Birth of a Discourse' in Mary Martin and Taylor Owen (eds), *Routledge Handbook of Human Security* (Routledge, 2014) 17. See also *Follow-up to Paragraph 143 on Human Security of the 2005 World Summit Outcome*, GA Res 66/290, Sixty-sixth sess, Agenda Item 14 and 117, UN Doc A/RES/66/290 (25 October 2012).

78 See, eg, S Neil MacFarlane and Yuen Foong Khong, *Human Security and the UN: A Critical History* (Indiana University Press, 2006) 245–7.

79 Taylor Owen, 'Human Security – Conflict, Critique and Consensus: Colloquium Remarks and a Proposal for a Threshold-Based Definition' (2004) 35(3) *Security Dialogue* 373, 384.

80 Richard Ullman, 'Redefining Security' (1983) 8(1) *International Security* 129, 133.

Sabina Alkire helped produce the definition of human security supplied by the Commission for Human Security highlighted previously, namely,

> to protect the vital core of all human lives in ways that enhance human freedoms and human fulfilment. Human security means protecting fundamental freedoms – freedoms that are the essence of life. It means protecting people from critical (severe) and pervasive (widespread) threats and situations.[81]

This approach also draws on thresholds, in this case 'critical' and 'pervasive'. Alkire states that threats become critical if 'they threaten to cut into the core activities and functions of human lives'.[82] She emphatically argues that, contrary to what Ullman's definition implies, a critical threat need not be sudden – it is to be assessed on its impact, not its suddenness. Pervasive threats, on the other hand, are threats that are either large-scale or where the threat forms a pattern of recurrent behaviour.[83]

Other academics have also taken up the threshold approach and offer possible determinants for when a threat becomes a human security issue. Renner argues that the test is 'whether the well-being and integrity of society are so compromised that they lead to possibly prolonged periods of instability and mass suffering.'[84] Thakur and Newman, on the other hand, argue that issues become security concerns when they 'undermine and diminish the survival chances' of a large number of people, or, as Renner argues, when the stability and integrity of the society is threatened.[85] That approach is severely limited, however, to a rather narrow vision of security. A focus on survival ignores threats to the quality of life as a security issue, attending merely to quantity, in contrast to Booth's definition of security addressed above. Ullman's treatment of threats as limits to policy choices seems more useful for human security, and Alkire's model, while arguably too broad, can also be a useful gauge of where the threshold of human security lies.

(v) By what means? And provided by whom?

The means of providing human security are intentionally not circumscribed in human security literature. Certainly, the idea of military means being central to security has become outdated and is largely inappropriate when considering the issue of human security. As Kaldor, Martin and Selchow point out, human security moves beyond the construction of military oriented operations; 'it is about an

81 UN Commission on Human Security, *Human Security Now* (United Nations, 2003) 4.
82 Sabine Alkire, 'A Conceptual Framework for Human Security' (Working Paper No 2, Centre for Research on Inequality, Human Security and Ethnicity (CRISE) 2003) 4.
83 Ibid.
84 Michael Renner, 'Security Redefined' in Michael Renner (ed), *The State of the World 2005: Redefining Global Security* (Worldwatch Institute, 2005) 3, 5.
85 Ramesh Thakur and Edward Newman, 'Introduction: Non-Traditional Security in Asia' in Ramesh Thakur and Edward Newman (eds), *Broadening Asia's Security Discourse and Agenda: Political, Social and Environmental Perspectives* (United Nations University Press 2004) 1, 3.

entirely new way of functioning in crises that is best described by a new language of human security.'[86] Human security, instead, is norm- and process-oriented security. It aims to address human insecurity in a systematic and integrated way, and is interested in preventative and rule-oriented security, not stop gap measures, or the extra-political (and extra-legal) strategies that have often entered the international stage in the name of traditional security.

One important feature of human security must be emphasised in relation to means: human security is not only about protection but about empowerment. '[H]uman security starts from the recognition that people are the most active participants in determining their well-being'.[87] People, thus empowered, the CHS goes on to argue, can demand respect for their dignity when it is violated, and create new opportunities for local solutions to local problems.[88] Human security is best framed as a participatory approach.[89] This does present a challenge to international decision-making bodies and institutions, which remain noticeably state-oriented. While the factor of participation does also make human security a more difficult discourse to operationalise, without it human security will remain incapable of existing in a desirable form, and it will not be possible to cash in on its transformative potential.

The relevant agents of human security are then by necessity far broader than the agents of traditional security (ie, states). Human security is commonly framed as a global problem requiring a global solution. Contrary to what critical security studies suggest, the role of the state in securing people cannot not to be dismissed by human security, given its problem-solving orientation.[90] But the state is not the only source of action. Global civil society, non-governmental organisations, international institutions, multinational corporations and, not least, people themselves, comprise the actors who have a role to play in providing human security. Human security discourse aims to reflect the current situation, whereby security is truly within the hands of a wide range of actors, and circumscribing this list seems counter-productive. It is for this reason that Chapter Six discusses the relationship between human security, international law and non-state actors in the context of international law-making and norm generation.

(vi) At what cost?

Traditional constructions of security have been conspicuously silent on the question of the costs of security. But these costs are just one of the ethical dimensions

86 Mary Kaldor, Mary Martin and Sabine Selchow, 'Human Security: A New Strategic Narrative for Europe' (2007) 83(2) *International Affairs* 273, 280.

87 UN Commission on Human Security, *Human Security Now* (United Nations, 2003) 4.

88 Ibid 11.

89 Georg Frerks and Berma Klein Goldewijk, 'Human Security and International Insecurity: The Quest for Humane Global Governance' in Georg Frerks and Berma Klein Goldewijk (eds), *Human Security and International Insecurity*. (Wageningen Academic Publishers, 2007) 21, 27.

90 The delicate balance that human security discourse pursues between critical and problem-solving approaches is discussed in more detail below.

of the discourse which human security seeks to address. From a human security perspective, the notion of costs is in large part incorporated by the integrative dimension of human security, as discussed in Chapter Three. Issues are weighed together collectively, with the effects of one issue assessed by its impact on other issues. Likewise, the preventative focus of human security gives more weight to the allocation of resources to developmental issues, in the interest of producing sustainable security results.[91] This does not mean, however, that costs are an uncomplicated issue in the context of human security. For example, the line separating the allocation of resources to human security and to human development projects will not always be clear. But what human security does is provide a framework for assessing issues, and their short- and long- term consequences, and pursuing coordination between stakeholders and relevant institutions in reaching such conclusions.

(vii) In what timeframe?

This is primarily a question of whether the security pursued is in the short term or the long term. The difference can be significant, especially as it is widely accepted that short-term protection of security can have negative impacts on the long-term realisation of security.[92] Security is more typically framed, at least in policy terms, as having a short-term-oriented focus. The sense of urgency built into the term 'security' promotes a framing of security issues as immediate responses to exigent circumstances.[93] Human security, while seeking to address urgent and immediate problems, also seeks to promote sustainable security.[94] This is demonstrated by its preventative focus. Human security can only be successful, then, if it balances the short and long term interests of its referents.

The dual interest of human security in relation to long- and short-term threats and vulnerabilities is reflected in the approach of the UNDP:

> [Human security] means, first, safety from such chronic threats as hunger, disease and repression. And second, it means protection from sudden and hurtful disruptions in the patterns of daily life – whether in homes, in jobs, or in communities.[95]

91 See, eg, UN Commission on Human Security, *Human Security Now* (United Nations, 2003) 24.
92 See, eg, ibid 17.
93 The securitisation process outlined by the Copenhagen School, discussed in the previous chapter, demonstrates this.
94 For discussion of 'sustainable security', see, eg, Sanjeev Khagram, William C Clark and Dana Firas Raad, 'From the Environment and Human Security to Sustainable Security and Development' (2003) 4 *Journal of Human Development* 289; Christina Voigt, 'Sustainable Security' (2009) 19(1) *Yearbook of International Environmental Law* 163. Thus far the concept has largely been limited to analysis from an environmental perspective, but can extend beyond, to social factors, just as sustainable development does.
95 United Nations Development Programme (UNDP), *Human Development Report 1994* (UNDP, 1994) 23.

Kaldor, Martin and Selchow describe human security as having the role of a 'bridging concept' between the long- and short-term needs.[96] On the one hand, human security is about responding to the immediate requirement for stabilisation and attention to pressing needs, while simultaneously, but over the long term, it seeks to address the structural conditions that allow such crises to occur.[97] 'From a human security perspective, the aim is not just political stability, it encompasses a notion of justice and sustainability.'[98]

III Transformative dimensions of human security (and the importance of this potential for international law)

The ultimate goal of human security discourse is a transformative project intended not only to deconstruct the traditional state-centric security paradigm, but to challenge some of the commonly held assumptions that are embedded in international relations scholarship (and which are commonly also held by international legal scholarship). As Newman observes, '[a]ttitudes and institutions that privilege "high politics" above disease, hunger or illiteracy' are embedded in international policy-making.[99] Human security is about re-evaluating the priorities of the international community and a redistribution of focus to issues, such as poverty, that have been previously neglected. Dunne and Wheeler argue that it is also about shifting 'our moral horizons' beyond constructions of citizenship into a more cosmopolitan outlook.[100] Thus, as Hammer points out, it is the transformative process itself that becomes more important than a concretised definition of human security.[101] The transformative process is one that is both cognitive and practical. It is necessary not only to promote change in the practices of the international community, but also to provoke a change in thinking.

Human security then is about addressing the imbalances and lacunae present in the current system. It seeks also to act, in the words of Asuncion St Clair, as an 'intellectual boundary object'.[102] A boundary object seeks to act as a bridge between different disciplines and between theorists and practitioners.[103] Human

96 Mary Kaldor, Mary Martin and Sabine Selchow, 'Human Security: A New Strategic Narrative for Europe' (2007) 83(2) *International Affairs* 273, 281.

97 Ibid.

98 Ibid 279.

99 Edward Newman, 'Human Security and Constructivism' (2001) 2 *International Studies Perspectives* 239, 240.

100 Tim Dunne and Nicholas J Wheeler, '"We the Peoples": Contending Discourses of Security in Human Rights Theory and Practice' in David Chandler and Nik Hynek (eds), *Critical Perspectives on Human Security: Rethinking Emancipation and Power in International Relations* (Routledge, 2011) 13, 13–14.

101 Leonard M Hammer, *A Foucauldian Approach to International Law* (Ashgate, 2007) 111.

102 Asuncion St Clair, 'The Role of Ideas in the United Nations Development Programme', in M Boas and D McNeill (eds) *Global Institutions and Development: Framing the World?* (Routledge, 2004) 178.

103 Ibid. See also, Asuncion St Clair, 'Ideas in Action: Human Development and Capability as Boundary Objects' (Working Paper, University of Bergen, 2004); Des

security can thus be used to engage in a multidisciplinary exercise, searching for common values and principles, and offering an organisational framework for shared commitment and multilateral responses for those issues that present the most pressing concerns for the international community. International law, like international relations, is seeking to bridge the gaps that have emerged between different normative systems.[104] The dominant contemporary models of thought in both international relations and international law are also seeking to overcome their entrenched state-centric structures, so as to acknowledge concerns and interests that extend beyond the Westphalian perspective of the world.[105] Human security offers itself as one tool that can be used in this broader transformative enterprise. Of course, as Hammer rightly stresses, this is not to say that human security can be used as a panacea for all the world's ills.[106]

The normative force of human security is one of the few elements of the discourse that is not criticised,[107] other than by those who believe that security should be an objective, apolitical concept.[108] Saul, who is highly critical of human security, concedes that '[t]he phrase neatly encapsulates a sense of compassion ("human") and realpolitik ("security"), which serves the useful polemical purpose of being difficult to oppose.'[109] He considers this a problem for its potential to be co-opted as will be discussed in Chapter Five, but it also demonstrates the positive potential of human security as both a discourse and rallying cry.

Suhrke places human security in the context of a broader movement in late 20th-century humanitarian ideas, serving as the principal normative reference for international action and international obligations.[110] While state security need not become redundant with the emergence of human security, it does carry with it a series of implications for the state and the notion of national security. It cannot be denied that despite the evolving nature of the international community, the state remains the dominant actor on the global stage. As such it remains a vital resource for the realisation of security, human or otherwise.[111] But as Gasper and others highlight, state security becomes both precarious and empty if not based

Gasper, 'Securing Humanity: Situating "Human Security" as Concept and Discourse' (2005) 6(2) *Journal of Human Development* 221, 235.

104 See Leonard M Hammer, *A Foucauldian Approach to International Law* (Ashgate, 2007) 98.

105 See, eg, Nancy Fraser, *Scales of Justice: Reimagining Political Space in a Globalizing World* (Polity Press, 2008).

106 Ibid.

107 See, eg, Roland Paris, 'Human Security: Paradigm Shift or Hot Air?' (2001) 26(2) *International Security* 87.

108 See, eg, David A Baldwin, 'The Concept of Security' (1997) 23 *Review of International Studies* 5.

109 Ben Saul, 'The Dangers of the United Nations' "New Security Agenda": "Human Security" in the Asia-Pacific Region' (2006) 1(1) *Asian Journal of Comparative Law* 1, 10.

110 Astri Suhrke, 'Human Security and the Interests of States' (1999) 30(3) *Security Dialogue* 265.

111 See, eg, Keith Krause, 'Towards a Practical Human Security Agenda' (Policy Paper No 26, Geneva Centre for the Democratic Control of Armed Forces (DCAF), 2007).

upon and consistent with the security of individuals.[112] Individuals then become the irreducible focus of all forms of security, not just human security.[113] In turn, human security can be a legitimating force for the state.

This does demonstrate however that human security discourse straddles a difficult line of trying to simultaneously produce what Newman refers to as 'problem solving' and 'critical' dimensions.[114] This, however, is problematic. The critical role of human security discourse is to challenge existing structures and normative assumptions, such as the role of the state, sovereignty and prevailing power structures.[115] The problem-solving dimension on the other hand requires an acceptance of the current international order as the platform for delivering required solutions.[116] These two functions cannot peacefully coexist, therein creating a paradox as human security discourse strives to serve two masters. Both functions however have their own value, especially in the context of international law. The critical lens of human security is essential to expose trends in international law that, by prioritising the interests of states and preserving state sovereignty, pose a threat to security of individuals and communities, especially the most disenfranchised, such as refugees, internally displaced and stateless persons.[117] And there is no question that states are part of the problem when it comes to human insecurity. Unfortunately, the international community can be collectively resistant to change, 'while clinging to outmoded mental models and dysfunctional solutions'.[118] The concerns of human security do not lie in justifying the discourse so much as determining how it might best be operationalised.[119]

Perhaps the most damning critique of human security comes from Chandler.[120] Chandler argues not that human security is marginalised in international discourse, nor that it has failed to translate into practice, as some have claimed. He in fact places human security as the dominant framework currently in international

112 Des Gasper, 'Securing Humanity: Situating "Human Security" as Concept and Discourse' (2005) 6(2) *Journal of Human Development* 221, 224.

113 Giorgio Shani, 'Securitising "Bare Life": Critical Perspectives on Human Security Discourse' in David Chandler and Nik Hynek (eds), *Critical Perspectives on Human Security: Rethinking Emancipation and Power in International Relations* (Routledge, 2011) 56.

114 Edward Newman, 'The United Nations and Human Security: Between Solidarism and Pluralism' in Mary Martin and Taylor Owen (eds), *Routledge Handbook of Human Security* (Routledge, 2014) 225, 231.

115 Ibid.

116 Ibid.

117 Such groups form the focus of Alice Edwards and Carla Ferstman (eds), *Human Security and Non-Citizens: Law, Policy and International Affairs* (Cambridge University Press, 2010).

118 Jorge Nef, 'Human Security, Mutual Vulnerability and Sustainable Development: A Critical View' (2006) 7 *Whitehead Journal of Diplomacy and International Relations* 55, 68.

119 See, eg, Dan Henk, 'Human Security: Relevance and Implications' (2005) Summer 2005 *Parameters* 91, 100.

120 David Chandler, 'Human Security II: Waiting for the Tail to Wag the Dog: Rejoinder to Ambrosetti, Owen and Wibben' (2008) 39(4) *Security Dialogue* 463.

relations.[121] What he argues, however, is that human security has been mainstreamed into international relations without producing any fundamental changes to the system, and in fact reinforcing existing power structures.[122] Thus human security has become the new orthodoxy, and its opportunity to change the world of international relations has passed. This point is also made by Christie, who argues that as human security has gained orthodoxy, it has lost all of its critical transformative potential.[123] There may be unfortunate truth in these assertions.

To produce results and to remain true to the original intent of the UNDP, the reality is that human security must be willing to find solutions within the current power structures of the globe.[124] The question then becomes whether human security loses its transformative potential if it embraces its problem-solving dimension. While the two dimensions of human security may seem diametrically opposed, arguably compromises can be made, and perhaps in the area of compromise is the true transformative potential of human security. One response might be that the changes which human security pursues as a pragmatic problem-solving approach are changes that are gradual and achieved over time. The role of human security then is to gradually promote normative shifts; to emphasise the ethical dimensions of security; to construct notions of sovereignty as responsibility; to question priorities and campaign for change; and to provide an overarching framework for *ongoing engagement* between different disciplines and policy circles.

Another response is to raise the question: if human security is growing stale, how might it be reinvigorated? International law has thus far been largely insulated from the human security discourse. Perhaps drawing international law into the human security discussion, and finding a place for human security in international law, might help human security find renewed purpose. In turn, human security discourse may allow us to 'interrogate, evaluate and criticise the practices that make people insecure in the first place.'[125] Indeed, it could be argued that such a transformation speaks to the heart of what some argue is the modern purpose of international law. Jouannet, for example, argues that international law has become more than a means of social regulation, and is 'becoming used to transform international society in order to make up for economic, social or equitable

121 Ibid 465.

122 David Chandler, 'Human Security: The Dog that Didn't Bark' (2008) 39(4) *Security Dialogue* 427.

123 Ryerson Christie, 'Critical Voices and Human Security: To Endure, to Engage or to Critique?' (2010) 41 *Security Dialogue* 169.

124 Though it should be noted that the UNDP itself recognised the critical role of human security, and the need for significant change: 'Much of this global security framework now needs change. In its place – or at least by its side – must be raised a new, more encompassing structure to ensure the security of all people the world over': United Nations Development Programme (UNDP), *Human Development Report 1994* (UNDP, 1994) 135.

125 Alex J Bellamy and Matt McDonald, '"The Utility of Human Security": Which Humans? What Security? A Reply to Thomas & Tow' (2002) 33(3) *Security Dialogue* 373, 376.

imbalances'.[126] Moreover, the human element of international law is increasingly emphasised. This is well encapsulated in a decision of the International Criminal Tribunal for Former Yugoslavia:

> A state-sovereignty-orientated approach has been gradually supplanted by a human-being-oriented approach. Gradually the maxim of Roman law *hominum causa omne jus constitutum est* (all law is created for the benefit of human beings) has gained a firm foothold in the international community as well.[127]

This discussion of the transformative potential of human security is predicated on a broad approach to human security, drawing on the original conceptualisation as framed by the UNDP.[128] The emphasis of the *Human Development Report* introducing the concept of human security was on the role of underdevelopment and poverty as root causes of human insecurity (and as insecurity in themselves).[129] The human security approach thus joins, in one integrated perspective, efforts to solve the problems generated by violent conflict and by economic and social deprivation.[130] As shall be seen in later chapters, however, international law more readily adapts to a narrower approach to human security.

IV Conclusion

In challenging the state-centric system of security on which international relations and international law continue to rest, human security is a deeply transformative idea. And it is a transformative idea that has captured the attention of international institutions, policy-makers and academics alike. Human security has in recent years begun to enter the common discourse of international relations in particular. Yet to many others it is widely viewed as 'vague, a ragtag of concepts' which, by adopting the security label, 'drink[s] from a poisoned chalice …'.[131] It has also splintered down the middle in a debate over what should constitute threats to human security. This debate has at times hindered the ability of the discourse to move forward, and will be explored in the following chapter.

But the questions that must be answered by human security (as with all forms of security discourse) are, or at least should be, much broader than merely a definition of threats. The security *problematique*, as modelled by Baldwin, is a multi-faceted

126 Emmanuelle Jouannet, 'What Is the Use of International Law? International Law as a 21st Century Guardian of Welfare' (2006–2007) 28 *Michigan Journal of International Law* 815, 821.

127 *Prosecutor v Tadíc (Interlocutory Appeal)* (International Criminal Tribunal for Former Yugoslavia, Appeals Chamber, Case No 94-1, 2 October 1995) [97].

128 The debate between broad and narrow approaches to human security will be addressed in Chapter Four.

129 United Nations Development Programme (UNDP), *Human Development Report 1994* (UNDP, 1994) 129.

130 Ibid.

131 Des Gasper, 'Securing Humanity: Situating "Human Security" as Concept and Discourse' (2005) 6(2) *Journal of Human Development* 221, 234.

and constructive way to engage with a concept of such importance. And when this *problematique* is applied to human security, the discourse can demonstrate that it does have the theoretical foundations, or at least the makings of them, that are critical for its continuing legitimacy – the discourse does not, in fact, have feet of clay. However, the gaps are clear to see: the discussion has focused for so long on the issue of threats that the other fundamentals that should make up the framework for human security have remained relatively unexplored.

The application of the *problematique* also demonstrates the delicate tightrope which human security must walk. It must steer between ambiguity on the one hand, which can lead to unrestrained discretion, and circumscription on the other, which can lead to the loss of normative clarity and context-specific responsiveness. In applying the *problematique*, we find few concrete certain or delineated answers. This allows the discourse to remain flexible and fluid. But this flexibility comes at the cost of clarity, frustrating those who require quantitative approaches to issues. It also exposes the discourse to misuse, allowing it to be twisted towards less than honourable ends. What we need to do now is reflect on the *problematique* of human security some more. What is needed is not necessarily narrow answers to these questions – that would prove counter-productive to the transformative project of human security. Instead it is time to start building a base of core principles for human security. These principles, which should have ties to notions of social justice, good governance, human rights and the rule of law could help provide the boundaries of human security without losing its normative relevance or fluidity.

3 The resistance of international legal scholarship to human security discourse

An examination

No great improvements in the lot of mankind [sic] are possible until a great change takes place in the fundamental constitution of their modes of thought. – John Stuart Mill

I Introduction

Despite the ongoing growth of the discourse, and its increasing influence on the operations of international organisations, in particular the United Nations, international legal scholarship continues to neglect the idea of human security. This is an intriguing oversight as proponents of human security attribute a range of international legal developments to the discourse.[1] The *Ottawa Convention*,[2] the *Optional Protocol in relation to Child Soldiers to the Convention on the Rights of the Child*,[3] the *Rome Statute* establishing the International Criminal Court,[4] and the *Arms Trade Treaty*[5] are all hailed as successes of human security discourse. This influence of the discourse on treaty development is the subject of Chapters Six and Seven. It is thus clear that notwithstanding the limited discussion and analysis that human security has received among the legal community, human security is of significant importance to international law.

It can be difficult to pin down reasons for the absence of something. Nonetheless, based on the limited literature that has engaged with the topic, and assuming some further reasons based on the nature and structure of international law, it is possible to postulate a set of rationales that explain the current dearth of attention given to human security:

1 See, eg, Gerd Oberleitner, 'Human Security: A Challenge to International Law?' (2005) 11 *Global Governance* 185.
2 *Convention on the Prohibition of the Use, Stockpiling, Production and Transfer of Anti-Personnel Mines and on their Destruction*, opened for signature 18 September 1997, 2056 UNTS 241 (entered into force 1 March 1999) ('*Ottawa Convention*').
3 *Optional Protocol to the Convention on the Rights of the Child on the Involvement of Children in Armed Conflicts*, opened for signature 25 March 2000, 39 ILM 1285 (entered into force 2 December 2002) ('*Optional Protocol*').
4 *Rome Statute of the International Criminal Court*, opened for signature 17 July 1998, 2187 UNTS 90 (entered into force 1 July 2002) ('*Rome Statute*').
5 *Arms Trade Treaty*, opened for signature 3 June 2013, 52 ILM 988 (entered into force 24 December 2014) ('*ATT*').

a The disciplinary divide between international law and international relations
b Security as a political, not legal, subject
c The fragmentation of international law
d Privileging of human rights – the perceived threat of human security
e Overstretch of the powers of the Security Council
f Theoretical discordance
g Lack of conceptual clarity – the potential for misuse

Only the first three of these rationales actually explain the absence of discussion; the latter concerns should be encouraging a healthy debate within international legal scholarship as to the place of human security. And as shall be discussed, while criticism of human security is to be expected from some inside the discipline, it is important that the discourse ceases to be simply ignored. This chapter speculates about and critically examines the potential reasons explaining why international legal scholarship has remained largely resistant and silent towards the increasingly dominant human security discourse.[6]

II Resistance of international legal scholarship

A The discipline divide

The first, and perhaps most fundamental, explanation for the lack of attention to the human security discourse lies in the divide between the disciplines of international law and international relations (IR). Human security is the child of international relations, and the chasm between the two disciplines may have made it more difficult for human security to gain a foothold on the legal side of international affairs. A simple lack of awareness of (or disinterest in) ideas emergent in IR could in part explain the dearth of attention by legal academics. However, as human security increasingly becomes a buzzword on the international stage, and is engaged by international organisations on an increasingly regular basis, lack of awareness becomes less able to explain the absence of discussion. Yet as political scientists and international legal scholars continue to 'talk past each other', as Keohane puts it,[7] drawing a discourse from one discipline into the other presents a continuing challenge.

6 It has arguably become the predominant model of human security within international organisations, as discussed in Chapters One and Two. Its dominance is also increasingly acknowledged within academic circles, though generally in a critical light; see, eg, Mandy Turner, Neil Cooper and Michael Pugh, 'Institutionalised and Co-opted: Why Human Security Has Lost Its Way' in David Chandler and Nik Hynek (eds), *Critical Perspectives on Human Security: Rethinking Emancipation and Power in International Relations* (Routledge, 2011) 83, 83–4. See also David Chandler, 'Human Security: The Dog that Didn't Bark' (2008) 39(4) *Security Dialogue* 427.

7 Robert O Keohane, 'International Relations and International Law: Interests, Reputations, Institutions' (1999) 93 *American Society International Legal Procedure* 375, 375.

The disciplinary divide can, however, be seen as a relatively weak reason for failing to engage with human security discourse. International legal scholarship has long acknowledged the role of politics and its effect on international law.[8] The disciplinary divide between international law and international relations has usually been a result of IR's resistance and criticism of international law, rather than the obverse.[9] And that resistance has mostly come in the form of realism, and the inability to reconcile the realist idea that power drives outcomes on the international stage with any meaningful function for international law.[10] As Krasner points out, for realism, 'international law is an oxymoron'.[11] So while realism held dominance in international relations theory, a gaping chasm formed between the two disciplines. But if it is the realist model that principally forms the rift between international law and international relations – the realist concern that engagement with international law results in descent into naïve utopian ideals[12] – then the gap is rendered meaningless for the purposes of human security. As has been demonstrated in Chapter One, human security is an explicit rejection of a realist construction of the global order, and is itself a target of realist criticism for its idealistic concerns.[13] Thus norm diffusion across the disciplinary borders seems at least feasible in the case of human security discourse. This stated, however, it is worth acknowledging the interesting quirk of existing interdisciplinarity noted by Dunhoff and Pollack. They highlight that all of the early major attempts by legal scholarship to engage with IR theory focused on realist approaches, and failed to really engage with other strands.[14] Although the literature has since become more diverse,[15] there is still a strong trend of orientation toward rationalist approaches.

8 See, eg, the seminal works of Louis Henkin, including *How Nations Behave: Law and Foreign Policy* (Council on Foreign Relations, 1979) and Kenneth Abbott, beginning with 'Modern International Relations Theory: A Prospectus for International Lawyers' (1989) 14 *Yale Journal of International Law* 335 (1989).

9 Though, as noted below, some scholars have sought to emphasise the autonomy of international law from political forces see, eg, Jeffrey L Dunhoff and Mark A Pollack, 'International Law and International Relations: Introducing an Interdisciplinary Dialogue' (Legal Studies Research Paper No 2012–18, Temple University Beasley School of Law, 2012) 1.

10 See, eg, Stephen D Krasner, 'International Law and International Relations: Together, Apart, Together?' (2000) 1 *Chicago Journal of International Law* 93, 94.

11 Ibid 98.

12 See, eg, Beth Simmons, 'International Law and International Relations: Scholarship at the Intersection of Principles and Politics' (2001) 95 *American Society International Legal Procedure* 271.

13 See, eg, S Neil MacFarlane and Yuen Foong Khong, *Human Security and the UN: A Critical History* (Indiana University Press, 2006). For further discussion, see Matt McDonald, 'Human Security and the Construction of Security' (2002) 16 *Global Society* 277.

14 Jeffrey L Dunhoff and Mark A Pollack, 'International Law and International Relations: Introducing an Interdisciplinary Dialogue' (Legal Studies Research Paper No 2012–18, Temple University Beasley School of Law, 2012) 9.

15 For example see analyses engaging with the Copenhagen School and Constructivists in Shirley V Scott, 'The Securitization of Climate Change in World Politics: How Close Have We Come and Would Full Securitization Enhance the Efficacy of Global Climate

This perhaps explains in part why legal scholarship has been so slow to acknowledge human security discourse.

It is vitally important for there to be a cross-fertilisation of ideas across the disciplines,[16] and human security offers one such framework, which can be truly effective only if an interdisciplinary approach to addressing its content can be formed. Beth Simmons' account of why there needs to be a greater cross-fertilisation of ideas across disciplines holds especially true for human security.[17] She writes: '[e]ach discipline holds part of a complex puzzle, and with a little patience and investment, I think more and more pieces will start to come together.'[18] This means, however, that human security discourse must find ways to overcome the challenges of interdisciplinary interaction. To quote Simmons again:

> after all, interdisciplinary cooperation is always difficult. There are usually a host of onlookers, like sceptics at an unlikely marriage, who at the first sign of trouble, argue that it will never last. The thrill of discovery of mutual interests and attractions gives way to the problem of real adjustment, mutual accommodation and criticisms from both disciplines about mistakes made along the way.[19]

Some international legal scholarship does challenge the idea of interdisciplinary approaches, which are seen to carry risks. One such risk, raised by Koskenniemi, is that law loses its unique functions. In adopting the language of interdisciplinarity, 'law is finally drained out of international law, conceived as a professional technique for the management of values, purposes, ideals' and becomes an instrumentalist project of politics.[20] Law is stripped of its 'sacredness', its profound symbolic meaning. This argument is not without merit, but runs the risk of treating law as an end unto itself.[21] It also promotes the idea that the law alone is enough – an argument that is not only naïve, but dangerous. Law also loses its sacred quality if

Change Policy?' (2012) 21(3) *Review of European Community & International Environmental Law* 220; David J Bederman, 'Constructivism, positivism, and empiricism in international law' (2000) 89 *Georgia Law Journal* 469; Jutta Brunnée and Stephen J Toope, 'International Law and Constructivism: Elements of an Interactional Theory of International Law' (2000) 39 *Columbia Journal of Transnational Law* 19.

16 Beth Simmons, 'International Law and International Relations: Scholarship at the Intersection of Principles and Politics' (2001) 95 *American Society International Legal Procedure* 271.

17 Ibid.

18 Ibid 275.

19 Ibid.

20 Martti Koskenniemi, 'International Law: between Fragmentation and Constitutionalism' (unpublished paper, ANU, Canberra, 27 November 2006) [22], [35].

21 On this point, see, eg, Christian Reus-Smit, *The Politics of International Law* (Cambridge University Press, 2004) 57; Francis Anthony Boyle, *Foundations of World Order: The Legalist Approach to International Relations* (Duke University Press, 1999) 12: '[i]nternational law was never perceived to be a transcendent end unto itself, but only a means to achieve the ultimate goal of peace in the human condition.'

it fails to keep up with shifting norms and needs in international society, and is rendered increasingly redundant as politics and other fields step in to fill the gap where international law has failed to engage with the ideas and principles of the international community. In an international legal framework that is increasingly more complex and places increasing weight on soft law, and with the increase in international (state and non-state) actors, law must begin to embrace the idea of normative pluralism, despite the challenges it presents. As human security increasingly enters 'our common international discourse'[22] it becomes all the more important that legal scholarship seeks to understand and evaluate its various dimensions, and the opportunities and challenges it presents to the future development and analysis of international law.

In a similar vein to Koskenniemi, Klabbers characterises interdisciplinarity as inevitable subjugation of law to politics.

> [I]nterdisciplinary scholarship is always, and inevitably, about subjection. Interdisciplinary scholarship is, more often than not, about imposing the vocabulary, methods, theories and idiosyncrasies of discipline A on the work of discipline B. Interdisciplinary scholarship, in a word, is about power, and when it comes to links between international legal scholarship and international relations scholarship, the power balance tilts strongly in favor of the latter.[23]

While this study is indeed borrowing from the theories of international relations, it does not intend to simply impose them on international law scholarship. Instead it seeks to determine points of commonality (hence the exploration of where human security sits in relation to the principal schools of international legal theory later in this chapter), and the extent to which human security aligns with existent trends in international law. Interdisciplinarity in this context aims to evaluate the extent to which human security discourse can assist in the furtherance of the aims and functions of international law.

While the difficulties of undertaking an interdisciplinary discussion of human security that engages both international relations and international legal scholarship are real and present, the task is surely not insurmountable. And while the challenges of interdisciplinarity are demanding, the need for this engagement is even more tangible and demands that we find a way past the current hurdles. The challenges that human security seeks to address are complex and multifaceted, and it is only through multilateral, multidisciplinary interventions that human security can flourish.

22 Keith Krause, 'Is Human Security More Than Just a Good Idea?' in M Brzoska and PJ Croll (eds), *Promoting Security: But How and for Whom?* (Bonn International Center for Conversion, 2004) 43.

23 Jan Klabbers, 'The Bridge Crack'd: A Critical Look at Interdisciplinary Relations' (2009) 23 *International Relations* 119, 120.

B Security as politics

A closely related concern is that human security discourse is not relevant to international law, because security is a political rather than legal construct. Securitisation literature contributes to this perspective by going a step further, putting security not only beyond the scope of legal process, but also beyond the ordinary functioning of politics.[24] This assumption seems to tie security closely to the idea of the state of exception – the area where law does not belong; where its norms may be suspended to produce the necessary results (in situations of emergency and crisis).[25] Noll, for example, describes security as 'closely related to the concepts of "emergency", "the exceptional" and the legitimacy of force'.[26]

In Noll's view, the individual becomes voiceless in the security discourse. As he observes:

> [a] further characteristic of the security concept is its trump function: invoking security concerns seemingly reduces the legal constraints put on actors and increases the leeway for discretion. Thus, 'securitising' the discourse on flight and protection means introducing a bias that ultimately works against the individual.[27]

Unfortunately, thus far there has seemed to be a neglect of the empowerment aspect of human security, raised in Chapter Two and discussed in more detail in the following chapter. But this is a failing of the application of the discourse, not the discourse itself.

There is certainly some merit in the idea that international law holds security apart from the regular function of the law. Key provisions derogating from international legal principles are often framed in terms of an exception for security purposes. Thus, for example, the General Agreement on Trade and Tariffs (GATT) contains Article XXI which provides an exception for GATT's provisions on the grounds of a state's 'essential security interests' (all framed, however, in traditional security concerns), or for the 'maintenance of international peace and security'.[28] Even more strikingly, human rights documents similarly accept

24 Barry Buzan, Ole Wæver and Jaap de Wilde, *Security: A New Framework for Analysis* (Lynne Rienner Publications, 1998) 23.

25 First developed by Carl Schmitt, but developed and analysed at length by Giorgio Agamben, *State of Exception* (University of Chicago Press, 2005). For excellent critical evaluation of this view, adopting constitutional models of accommodation, see Oren Gross and Fionnula Ní Aoláin, *Law in Times of Crisis: Emergency Powers in Theory and Practice* (Cambridge University Press, 2006).

26 Gregor Noll, 'Securitising Sovereignty? States, Refugees and the Regionalization of International Law' in Edward Newman and Joanne van Selm (eds), *Refugees and Forced Displacement: International Security, Human Vulnerability and the State* (United Nations University, 2003) 277, 280.

27 Ibid.

28 *General Agreement on Trade and Tariffs*, opened for signature 30 October 1947, 55 UNTS 194, (entered into force 29 July 1948) Article XXI ('GATT').

national security as a ground for derogation from some human rights principles.[29] It is worth noting that most of these principles explicitly limit the application of such an exception only if 'provided by law'. Thus, as Koskenniemi points out, '"law" and "discretion" do not exist in separate pigeon-holes in our minds'.[30] Even in relation to human security, the thematic debates held annually by the UN General Assembly reinforce the idea of security as a political construct, with many states demonstrating cautious or tacit acceptance of the concept on the proviso that it brings with it no new legal obligations.[31] Such a view has since found expression in the General Assembly Resolution 66/290 on human security, which states that '[h]uman security does not entail additional legal obligations on the part of States.'[32] This is not assisted by the lack of use of the term human security in any legally binding instruments, not even those that have been produced directly as a result of human security discourse.

Martti Koskenniemi notes that, in part, this assumption of security being reliant on ideas of discretion and being beyond the rule of law is because of an assumption that the idea that law can deter aggression and overcome state interests is so utopian that it seems 'anachronistic to suggest that law might have something to do with the high politics of international security.'[33] However, as the idea of security expands beyond aggression, as in the case of human security discourse, and moves beyond realist constructions of the world, this is no longer a sufficient explanation for the neglect of human security. Human security is, or perhaps should be, a rules-based concept. For example, the Helsinki Plus Report promoting the concept of human security in the EU–Russia relationship affirms that 'human security implies an extension of rule-governed security as opposed to war-based security'.[34] Many accounts of human security, including the Draft Declaration on the Right to Peace, associate human security explicitly with the rule of law, good governance and the observance of international law.[35] Because human security

29 See, eg, *International Covenant on Civil and Political Rights,* opened for signature 16 December 1966, 999 UNTS 171 (entered into force 3 January 1976) Articles 12, 13, 14, 19, 21, 22; *International Covenant on Economic, Social and Cultural Rights,* opened for signature 16 December 1966, 993 UNTS 3 (entered into force 3 November 1976) ('ICESCR') Article 8.

30 Martti Koskenniemi, 'The Place of Law in Collective Security' (1996) 17 *Michigan Journal of International Law* 455, 475.

31 The debates can be collectively located at UN Human Security Unit, Publications and Resources, <http://unocha.org/humansecurity/humansecurity/resources/publications-and-products/Human-Security-At-The-General-Assembly>.

32 *Follow-up to Paragraph 143 on Human Security of the 2005 World Summit Outcome,* 66/290, Sixty-sixth sess, Agenda Item 14 and 117, UN Doc A/RES/66/290 (25 October 2012) [3].

33 Martti Koskenniemi, 'The Place of Law in Collective Security' (1996) 17 *Michigan Journal of International Law* 455, 455.

34 EU–Russia Human Security Study Group, 'Helsinki Plus: Towards a Human Security Architecture for Europe' (First Report May 2010).

35 UN Human Rights Council, *Report of the Human Rights Council Advisory Committee on the Right of Peoples to Peace,* UN GAOR, Twentieth sess, Agenda Item 5, UN Doc A/HRC/20/31 (16 April 2012).

discourse lacks the voice of international legal scholarship, these dimensions have not been addressed in any significant depth. But reading between the lines, it is clear that the effective realisation of human security does not require a loosening of the constraints on actors, but exactly the opposite. Human security is a rights-based, and norms-based, concept.[36] Therefore Koskenniemi's account of law's contribution to security holds particular weight for human security:

> Law's contribution to security is not in the substantive responses it gives, but in the process of justification that it imports into institutional policy and in its assumption of responsibility for the policies chosen.[37]

Thus what international law can bring to human security is a legitimacy and sense of normative structure. Fears of instrumentalisation[38] can in part be addressed by drawing on international law principles and processes, and their subsequent incorporation into human security itself. 'Only in this way can "security" maintain its beneficial, altruistic orientation'.[39] Indeed, it is worth remembering that Jeremy Bentham, in *The Theory of Legislation*, argued that 'the principal object of law [is] the care of security.'[40] Furthermore, we can see already that security responses on the international stage are increasingly institutionalised – for example in the provision of humanitarian aid.[41] Such responses, while extraordinary in the sense that they are not the normal everyday functioning of law or politics, are nonetheless deeply rule-bound, following clear legal mandates and operating within guidelines and internal structures of rule and command.

Moreover, human security explicitly emphasises its preventative focus.[42] This means that it operates not out of an assumption of only being invoked at the inception of an emergency or crisis, but rather requires the establishment of long-term frameworks (as noted in Chapter Two) addressing the root causes of insecurity. Human security thus aligns well with existing moves in the direction of rule-based security – moves that already exist in international legal scholarship, such as in the work of Oren Gross and Fionnula Ní Aoláin.[43] In return, human security offers a framework and – potentially, when further developed – a set of principles to assist in the development and analysis of such rule-based responses.

36 UN Commission on Human Security, *Human Security Now* (United Nations, 2003) 107.
37 Martti Koskenniemi, 'The Place of Law in Collective Security' (1996) 17 *Michigan Journal of International Law* 455, 478.
38 Discussed below, Section G – 'Lack of conceptual clarity – potential for misuse'.
39 Martti Koskenniemi, 'The Place of Law in Collective Security' (1996) 17 *Michigan Journal of International Law* 455.
40 Jeremy Bentham, *The Theory of Legislation* (Elibron Classics, Reprint, 1896) I, 307.
41 For a discussion, see Scott Watson, 'The "Human" as Referent Object: Humanitarianism as Securitization?' (2011) 42 *Security Dialogue* 3, 12.
42 United Nations Development Programme (UNDP), *Human Development Report 1994* (UNDP, 1994) 21, 23.
43 See, eg, Fionnula Ní Aoláin and Oren Gross, 'A Skeptical View of Deference to the Executive in Times of Crisis' (2008) 41 *Israel Law Review* 545.

C The fragmentation of international law

Another, unexplored reason for the absence of human security in the minds of international legal scholars is the impact of the fragmentation and specialisation that now characterises international law.[44] The various branches of international law have developed largely in isolation from each other, and, as Doswald-Beck points out, 'there is the tendency to see branches of international law as discrete boxes and to think it possible to ignore or discard a box or two when it is perceived as inconvenient. This is the recipe for *in*security – indeed, for potential disaster.'[45] The fragmented nature of international law was commented upon by the International Law Commission (ILC) in a report published in 2006.[46] This report attributed the fragmentation largely to the paradox of globalisation: on the one hand there is increasing uniformisation of social life, while on the other hand, globalisation has also led to the emergence of 'functional differentiation', the increasing specialisation and automatisation of social actions and structures.[47] This institutional and structural separation has been accompanied by, and has undoubtedly influenced, a cognitive division between the fields of international law, with experts and academics specialising in fields and thus reinforcing the normative separation of the various regimes. Thus one of the greatest potential challenges to the recognition and comprehensive realisation of human security is this fragmentation in international law. Human security, with its broad overarching structure, intersects with all the various fields of international law without firmly belonging to any particular branch. International security law is traditionally concerned primarily with the use of force, and in the modern context, with the threats and consequences of terrorism.[48] Human security reaches far beyond this box, and requires integrated responses that recognise and are responsive to the complex interconnections between threats, and in particular, the nexus formed by security, development and human rights issues.[49]

44 See, eg, International Law Commission (ILC), *Fragmentation of International Law: Difficulties Arising from the Diversification and Expansion of International Law, Report of the Study Group of the International Law Commission* UN GAOR, Fifty-eighth sess, UN Doc A/CN.4/L.682 (18 July 2006); Bruno Simma and Dirk Pulkowski, 'Of Planets and the Universe: Self-contained Regimes in International Law' (2006) 17 *European Journal of International Law* 483; Andreas Fischer-Lescano and Gunther Teubner, 'Regime-Collisions: The Vain Search for Legal Unity in the Fragmentation of Global Law' (2004) 25 *Michigan Journal of International Law* 999.

45 Louise Doswald-Beck, 'Human Security: Can it be Attained?' (2003) 97 *American Society International Legal Procedure* 93, 93.

46 ILC, *Fragmentation of International Law: Difficulties Arising from the Diversification and Expansion of International Law, Report of the Study Group of the International Law Commission* UN GAOR, Fifty-eighth sess, UN Doc A/CN.4/L.682 (18 July 2006).

47 Ibid [7].

48 For example, a search of university teaching units and postgraduate degrees specialising in this area, demonstrates a dominance of issues relating to the use of force, terrorism and the laws of armed conflict, with relatively few exploring expanded understandings of security, and interconnected issues of peace and human security.

49 The integrative dimension of human security is discussed in more detail in the following chapter.

The institutional structures of international law have thus far proved largely ill-equipped for producing integrated responses.[50] These institutions have created a marked distinction between the fields of security and development. It has only been in the last two decades that it has been recognised that the disparate areas of international law do not in fact exist each in its own vacuum, and that greater coordination among these spheres has been pursued. Coordination, however, is not the same as integration. In examining the political dynamics of the security–development nexus within UN agencies, Sending points out that coordination 'is, in the final analysis a recommendation that two separate units should work together because their operations are interdependent.'[51] The more complex the issue, he points out, the more integration is necessary, as coordination says nothing about authority or responsibility. The same arguments can be made in relation to international law in this respect.

The specialisation of international law is unquestionably a vital aspect of the law, reflecting the pluralistic interests of a cosmopolitan global society.

> A law that would fail to articulate the experienced differences between fact-situations or between interests or values that appear relevant in particular problem-areas would seem altogether unacceptable, utopian and authoritarian simultaneously.[52]

As human security does not clearly fit into an area of specialisation, it is neglected in full. Paris once described human security as an issue that, in prioritising everything, prioritises nothing.[53] But perhaps, in relation to international law, the problem might more accurately be described thus: that in embracing all fields of international law, human security is embraced by no one.

The ILC Report, however, rejected the notion that specialised regimes constitute 'self-contained regimes'.[54] While acknowledging that different regimes may be said to express different social rationalities determined by their mandates and

50 See, eg, James Crawford and Penelope Nevill, 'Relations between International Courts and Tribunals: The "Regime Problem"' in Margaret A Young (ed) *Regime Interaction in International Law: Facing Fragmentation* (Cambridge University Press, 2012) 235; Frank Biermann et al, 'The Fragmentation of Global Governance Architectures: A Framework for Analysis' (2009) 9(4) *Global Environmental Politics* 14.

51 J Sending, 'The Political Dynamics of the Security-Development Nexus' (Working Paper for the Standing Group for International Relations of the European Consortium for Political Research, 9–11 September 2004) 14.

52 ILC, *Fragmentation of International Law: Difficulties Arising from the Diversification and Expansion of International Law, Report of the Study Group of the International Law Commission* UN GAOR, Fifty-eighth sess, UN Doc A/CN.4/L.682 (18 July 2006) [16].

53 Roland Paris, 'Human Security: Paradigm Shift or Hot Air?' (2001) 26(2) *International Security* 87, 91.

54 ILC, *Fragmentation of International Law: Difficulties Arising from the Diversification and Expansion of International Law, Report of the Study Group of the International Law Commission* UN GAOR, Fifty-eighth sess, UN Doc A/CN.4/L.682 (18 July 2006) [21].

the instruments that established them,[55] the categorisation of an issue as a 'trade law issue' or a 'human rights issue', and so on, is merely informal labelling, and no such classification scheme formally exists.[56] As Pierre-Marie Dupuy puts it, specialised institutions 'are essentially technical phenomena in the framework of the expansion of international law within an order that profoundly maintains its unity.'[57] In this view, not only does general international law continue to operate within various regimes, but so too does the law of other relevant specialised fields of international law. The relevance of this discussion to human security is that if specialisation is an artificial separation of the fields, and they can in fact inform one another, then human security should be able to find a place across the specialisations, rather than it being necessary to box it neatly into one. Moreover, its potential as an integrative concept (as will be addressed in the next chapter) means that human security could be of significant value for the future of international law as the latter seeks to overcome the limitations and fragmentation of international law that has occurred. Thus the real problem for the penetration of human security discourse is not the structure of international law itself, but the fragmentation of international legal scholarship. Nonetheless, the importance of addressing cross-cutting issues has in the past two decades been increasingly recognised, and human security can serve as one of the frameworks through which such cross-cutting discussion can be filtered.

D Privileging of human rights: presumption of threat

The one specialisation where one might expect human security to be discussed in the context of international law is international human rights law. However, with a few exceptions,[58] human rights scholarship is as silent on the topic as the rest of international law. What discussion does exist primarily treats human security as a threat to the 'precision and legality of the human rights framework', and as having little more than 'rhetorical appeal'.[59] Human security is seen as offering nothing beyond what human rights already provides, and human rights has the

55 Ibid [133].

56 Ibid [21]–[22].

57 Pierre-Marie Dupuy, 'International Law: Torn between Coexistence, Cooperation and Globalisation. General Conclusions' (1998) 9 *European Journal of International Law* 278, 284.

58 See, eg, Gerd Oberleitner, 'Porcupines in Love: The Intricate Convergence of Human Rights and Human Security' (2005) 6 *European Human Rights Law Review* 588; Rhoda E Howard-Hassmann, 'Human Security: Undermining Human Rights?' (February 2012) 34(1) *Human Rights Quarterly* 88; Wolfgang Benedek, 'Human Security and Human Rights Interaction' (2008) 59 *International Social Science Journal* 7; Dorothy Estrada-Tanck, *Human Security and Human Rights under International Law: The Protections Offered to Persons Confronting Structural Vulnerability* (Bloomsbury, 2016).

59 David Petrasek, 'Human Rights "Lite"? Thoughts on Human Security' (2004) 3 *Disarmament Forum* 59, 59.

advantage of time, recognition and established legal principles that human security lacks.[60]

As for the idea that human security is merely the relabelling of human rights, two responses to this can be made. The first, which will be outlined in more detail below, is that the interconnections between security, development and human rights justify a rethinking of these issues in terms of security.[61] Human security is not about putting the 'old wine' of human rights, or human development, in the 'new bottles' of human security.[62] They all three do share common core values, in that they are all concerned with the centrality of the individual, they all pursue equity and social justice, and all perceive human dignity as the core human value to be defended.[63] Human rights are also certainly central to the provision of human security and one of the best ways of ensuring it.[64] Any model of human security which directly challenges the validity or effect of human rights norms should be rejected. Human security can and has been framed as a rights-based concept, and human rights have even been described as the *sine qua non* of human security approaches.[65]

> It introduces a practical framework for identifying the specific rights that are at stake in a particular situation of insecurity and for considering the institutional and governance arrangements that are needed to exercise and sustain them.[66]

The rights-based dimensions of human security discourse are addressed in the next chapter. Here however it needs to be noted that if the concerns surrounding human security are the concerns that human security, as a nebulous political concept, will replace and/or undermine established human rights and the significant and well-developed normative legal force they provide, then this is an argument in favour of critically engaging with human security discourse to expose such dangers

60 See, eg, Ben Saul, 'The Dangers of the United Nations' "New Security Agenda": "Human Security" in the Asia-Pacific Region' (2006) 1(1) *Asian Journal of Comparative Law* 1. See also Rhoda E Howard-Hassmann, 'Human Security: undermining human rights?' (February 2012) 34(1) *Human Rights Quarterly* 88.
61 Shahrbanou Tadjbakhsh and Anuradha M Chenoy, *Human Security: Concepts and Implications* (Routledge, 2007) 68.
62 For use of this analogy, see, eg, Barbara von Tigerstrom, *Human Security and International Law: Prospects and Problems* (Hart Publishing, 2007).
63 Berma Klein Goldewijk, 'Why Human? The Interlinkages Between Security, Rights and Development' (2008) 1 *Security and Human Rights* 24.
64 See, eg, Human Security Study Group, 'A European Way of Security' (The Madrid Report of the Human Security Study Group comprising a Proposal and Background Report, 8 November 2007).
65 Eve Lester, 'Socio-economic Rights, Human Security and Survival Migrants: Whose Rights? Whose Security?' in Alice Edwards and Carla Ferstman (eds), *Human Security and Non-Citizens: Law, Policy and International Affairs* (Cambridge University Press, 2010) 317.
66 United Nations Trust Fund for Human Security, *Human Security in Theory and Practice* (United Nations, 2009) 9.

and offer analysis that will prevent such a result from materialising. The solution is not to bury our heads in the sand and hope that human security will just go away.

E Unfettered power for the Security Council?

The broadening of the definition of 'international peace and security' and the concomitant increase in the Security Council's purview presents another reason for resistance towards human security. It comes as no surprise that those with an interest in international law should be concerned about the increase in power of a largely political body with a selective membership and extensive mandate, even under a traditional conceptualisation of security. Ng, for example, argues that if the Security Council embraced human security, this would result in the application of its Chapter VII powers becoming practically limitless – conferred with 'a very expansive mandate to override the fundamental international law doctrine of state sovereignty.'[67] This links up with more general critiques of human security, and specifically the broad–narrow debate related to the definition of human security. A defence of the broad approach to human security will be mounted later in this chapter.

Despite what some have argued, however, a broadened interpretation of 'security' does not make the powers of the Security Council limitless. While the discretion of the Security Council is broad, it is not legally unfettered. The International Criminal Tribunal for Former Yugoslavia (ICTY)'s decision in *Tadić* is useful in this regard. The Appeals Chamber declared that a 'threat to the peace is more than a political concept. But the determination that there exists such a threat is not a totally unfettered discretion, as it has to remain, *at the very least*, within the Purposes and Principles of the Charter.'[68] The ICTY further went on to proclaim that 'neither the text nor the spirit of the Charter conceives of the Security Council as *legibus solutus* (unbound by law).'[69] This is a confirmation of Article 24(2) of the UN Charter which prescribes that the discharge of the Security Council's duties must be in line with the Charter itself. In light of the Purposes and Principles of the UN Charter, Article 1(3) then requires that Security Council action must be consistent with international human rights and humanitarian norms.[70] Concomitantly though, it should be noted, it also means that any efforts by the Security Council to protect human security must be restrained by the equal duty

67 Trina Ng, 'Safeguarding Peace and Security in our Warming World: A Role for the Security Council' (2010) 15(2) *Journal of Conflict and Security Law* 275, 280.

68 *Prosecutor v Tadić (Jurisdiction)* (Appeals Chamber) (1997) 105 ILR 453, 465 [27].

69 Ibid [28].

70 See, eg, Erika de Wet, *The Chapter VII Powers of the United Nations Security Council* (Hart Publishing, 2004); Greg Nolte, 'The Limits of the Security Council's Powers and Its Functions in the International Legal System: Some Reflections' in Michael Byers (ed), *The Role of Law in International Politics: Essays in International Relations and International Law* (Oxford University Press, 2000) 315; Nigel D White, 'The Security Council, the Security Imperative and International Law' in Matthew Happold (ed) *International Law in a Multipolar World* (Routledge, 2012) 4.

to be consistent with the principle of non-interference contained within Article 2(7) of the Charter.

As has been discussed above (and will be discussed in greater detail in Chapter Five), an appeal to human security *is* in line with the purposes and principles of the Charter, in some respects more so than traditional conceptualisations of security. Saul argues that the concept of human security should be avoided as it will dilute the purposes of the Security Council.[71] He argues that the Security Council 'was conceived as an institution of limited scope for addressing the most serious threats to world peace and security. In part, its competence was limited precisely so that it would remain focused on fixing acute dangers.'[72] Human security discourse does not disagree. What it does instead is expose and challenge the presumption that only armed conflict and direct violence constitute the most serious threats and dangers to the global community.

Many of the fears surrounding human security expanding the mandate of the Security Council conflate security with militarisation.[73] Human security does not implicitly allow an expansion of the Security Council's power in terms of military intervention. As discussed in Chapter One, human security is about finding alternatives to military might for the realisation of security.

> The concept of human security, if superficially understood, may expand the reach of traditional military-based strategies to areas originally considered outside its scope, including development, education, food security, etc. This unintended consequence can be avoided by emphasising human security as a process of inclusive dialogue that involves citizens and nonstate actors in identifying sources of insecurity and policies to address them …
>
> Human security should result in the democratisation of security policy-making, not the securitisation of development.[74]

The Security Council under Article 41 of the UN Charter has recourse to a wide range of non-military measures. It has increasingly employed these coercive and non-coercive measures, which have included economic sanctions, preventive diplomacy, multidimensional peacekeeping and peacebuilding operations, diplomatic engagement, security sector reform and the establishment of international tribunals.[75] Moreover, and of key relevance to human security discourse, some

71 Ben Saul, 'The Dangers of the United Nations' "New Security Agenda": "Human Security" in the Asia-Pacific Region' (2006) 1(1) *Asian Journal of Comparative Law* 1, 26.

72 Ibid.

73 See, eg, S Neil MacFarlane and Yuen Foong Khong, *Human Security and the UN: A Critical History* (Indiana University Press, 2006) 242.

74 Kristen Wall, Jenny Aulin and Gabriëlla Vogelaar (eds), *Empowerment and Protection: Stories of Human Security* (Global Partnership for the Prevention of Armed Conflict, 2014) 122.

75 For discussion, see, eg, Christoph Mikulaschek, 'The United Nations Security Council and the Responsibility to Protect: Policy, Process, and Practice' (Favorita Papers No 1/2010, 39th IPI Vienna Seminar, 15 January 2010).

Security Council Resolutions have increasingly taken on a 'quasi-legislative' function, or if they have not gone that far, they have at least taken on a role of norm entrepreneurship through thematic resolutions such as those discussed in Chapter Five.

Thus the benefit of human security being employed by the Security Council is not as a resort to interventionist military responses, but rather as a means of providing political gravitas and heightened attention, and the mainstreaming of human security into the activities of the Security Council, the UN more broadly and member states. Commentary within the UN has noted that the Security Council 'can do more to galvanise international humanitarian efforts and to lend political weight to them'.[76] Singapore has suggested in relation to climate change that the Security Council could potentially act as a vehicle to 'build greater awareness' and 'to help reinforce ongoing efforts to inject political momentum unto the UNFCCC negotiating process.'[77] Thus invoking human security within the Security Council is done with reference to the political, supportive and coordinating roles of the Council.[78] The Security Council is in a unique position to mobilise resources, raise awareness, emphasise global priorities and coordinate responses to human security issues.

The argument that predictability and certainty are needed in the interpretation of 'security', of Article 39, and of the jurisdiction of the Security Council generally, does hold merit.[79] It does not, however, preclude the application of human security. Indeed, if the Security Council expressly adopted human security, this would provide greater cohesion, order and consistency than the Security Council's current sporadic expansion of its mandate, as explored in Chapter Five.

This is not to say that the endemic concerns related to the operation of the Security Council are overcome or not relevant to human security. Of course, the Security Council's notorious selectiveness in its activities presents a serious challenge. The issues of its representativeness remain in play.[80] Also, when considering the expansion of the concept of security, it is axiomatic to assert that dedication to the

76 UNSC Verbatim Record, UN SCOR, UN Doc S/PV/5225 (12 July 2005) 33 (United Kingdom).

77 UNSC Verbatim Record, UN SCOR, UN Doc S/PV/6587 (Resumption 1) (20 July 2011) 16.

78 See, eg, Hitoshi Nasu, 'The Place of Human Security in Collective Security' (2012) 18 *Journal of Conflict and Security Law* 1, 34.

79 This argument is made, eg, by Ben Saul, 'The Dangers of the United Nations' "New Security Agenda": "Human Security" in the Asia-Pacific Region' (2006) 1(1) *Asian Journal of Comparative Law* 1, 17.

80 Critiques of the Security Council and discussions for reform continues to generate a huge amount of interest and literature. For a few select examples of the literature, see, eg, Ramesh Thakur, 'United Nations Security Council Reform' (2004) 13(3) *African Security Studies* 66; Klaus Schlichtmann, 'An Enduring Concept for Security Council Reform' (2011) 2 *Beijing Law Review* 97; Thomas G Weiss, 'The Illusion of UN Security Council Reform' (2003) 26(4) *Washington Quarterly* 147; Bardo Fassbender, *UN Security Council Reform and the Right of Veto: A Constitutional Perspective* (Martinus Nijhoff Publishers, 1998) vol 32; Dimitris Bourantonis, *The History and Politics of UN Security Council Reform* (Routledge London, 2005); Thomas G Weiss

old rhetoric of state sovereignty has kept the Security Council 'mired in inaction'.[81] These issues are beyond the scope of this discussion. What is relevant is that the role and activities of the Security Council should not act as an impediment to human security gaining a foothold in international legal discourse. Human security may be outside the original meaning of 'international peace and security' as conceived by the framers of the UN Charter, but it is not necessarily outside the ordinary meaning of that phrase, as this ordinary meaning is clearly evolving and broadening, as will be demonstrated in Chapter Five.

F Theoretical discordance and human security discourse

Another fundamental reason for neglecting the development of human security presents a challenge to some of the traditionally held notions embedded in the international legal system and within international legal theory. Human security discourse, with its emphasis on moving attention away from the state to the individual, does challenge the core elements of the Westphalian system, as originally conceived in 1648.[82] This system was intended to provide rules for peaceful interaction between states, and no more.[83] Ideas such as 'state sovereignty', 'territorial integrity' and 'non-interference in the domestic jurisdiction of states' are all ideas central to this system, and are encapsulated in the UN Charter. But the idea that human security fundamentally challenges the international legal system is an exaggeration. Many modern scholars depict international law as moving away from the traditional Westphalian structure according to which international law is purely concerned with governing the interaction of states.[84] International law has shifted away from solely coordinating the independent activities of states to a system of coordinated action in relation to a wide scope of considerations, with some arguing that '[a]t the outset of the 21st century, this system has become a guardian of welfare',[85] to the point that international law 'is widely considered the ultimate guarantor of collective well-being.'[86] It has done so by developing a Charter-oriented system, regulating the use of force, placing great emphasis on individual and group rights, developing international institutional structures, and

and Karen E Young, 'Compromise and Credibility: Security Council reform?' (2005) 36(2) *Security Dialogue* 131.

81 Dwight Newman, 'A Human Security Council? Applying a "Human Security" Agenda to Security Council Reform' (1999–2000) 31 *Ottawa Law Review* 213, 236.

82 *Treaty of Peace of Münster and Treaty of Peace of Osnabrück* (1648) 1 Parry 271; 1 Parry 119 (Peace of Westphalia).

83 As illustrated, eg, in the work of Grotius, *On the Rights of War and Peace* (Jean Barbeyrac trans, Nabu Press, 2010) [Trans of *De Jure Belli ac Pacis* (first published 1625)].

84 See, eg, Nancy Fraser, 'Who Counts? Dilemmas of Justice in a Post-Westphalian World' (2009) 41 *Antipode* 281.

85 Emmanuelle Jouannet, 'What Is the Use of International Law? International Law as a 21st Century Guardian of Welfare' (2006–2007) 28 *Michigan Journal of International Law* 815, 816.

86 Ibid 821.

the development and diffusion of international norms. Human security then contributes to this role of the international legal system by recognising that traditional, state-oriented security is a necessary but not a sufficient condition for securing human welfare.[87]

Certainly, it is difficult to reconcile human security with state-centric theories of international law such as positivism or legal realism. International legal positivism rejects the idea that international law has normative value. Positivists and realists alike argue that only actual state behaviour is relevant, and that the international prescription of behaviour on normative grounds is a utopian and unrealisable concept.[88] As these theories hold that the role of international law is governed by the self-interest of states, without taking into consideration the citizens (and non-citizens) within them, it is difficult for human security to gain any traction within these theories. However, many other equally influential schools of thought exist within international legal scholarship, and human security should not be rejected without due consideration of these viewpoints. Indeed, positivism is not the dominant school of thought in international law, but rather liberal international legal theory that is considered to hold sway in modern accounts of international law, at least in the Western world.[89]

(i) International legal positivism

As with all these classifications of schools of thought, the label positivism covers a significant array of arguments and approaches.[90] But at its core it is a commitment to the belief that the law is a unified system of rules emanating from state will, or at least from state consent.[91] Thus 'international law is "observable" from the practice and custom of states … it can be inferred rationally from their interactions'.[92] This is encapsulated in the well-known judgment of the Permanent Court of International Justice in *Lotus*:

> International law governs relations between independent States. The rules of law binding upon States therefore emanate from their own free will as

87 Dwight Newman, 'A Human Security Council? Applying a "Human Security" Agenda to Security Council Reform' (1999–2000) 31 *Ottawa Law Review* 213, 215.

88 See, eg, J Shand Watson, 'A Realistic Jurisprudence of International Law' (1980) 30 *Year Book of World Affairs* 265.

89 See, eg, Hilary Charlesworth and Christine Chinkin, *The Boundaries of International Law: A Feminist Analysis* (Manchester University Press, 2000) 28.

90 See, eg, Ulrich Fastenrath, 'Relative Normativity in International Law' (1993) 4 *European Journal of International Law* 305; Bruno Simma and Andreas Paulus' contribution to edited Symposium on Method in International Law, 'Appraising the Methods of International Law: A Prospectus for Readers' (1999) 93 *American Journal of International Law* 291.

91 See, eg, Francis Anthony Boyle, *Foundations of World Order: The Legalist Approach to International Relations* (Duke University Press, 1999) 11.

92 Frédéric Mégret, 'International Law as Law' in James Crawford and Martti Koskenniemi (eds), *The Cambridge Companion to International Law* (Cambridge, 2012) 64, 68.

> expressed in conventions or by usages generally accepted as expressing principles of law and established in order to regulate the relations between these co-existing independent communities or with a view to the achievement of common aims. Restrictions upon the independence of States cannot therefore be presumed.[93]

From a positivist's viewpoint, then, human security as a concept has no place in the international legal sphere until and unless it is expressly included in the formal sources of law.[94] Even then, it is only recognisable to the extent that states recognise the concept and expressly commit to relevant, objective, legal rules. However, given that this approach requires an abstraction of the law from non-legal factors such as political thought, moral and ethical concerns and social context, there seems little space within which human security discourse – which, as the previous chapter noted is highly contextualised – could comfortably sit in the positivist's view of international law. Moreover, applying human security discourse as a lens, we are reminded of the strong state-centricity inherent in the positivist tradition, which minimises concerns about the threats which states may pose to their own citizenry, or the structural violence that may be supported by existing national and international legal structures.

(ii) International legal liberal theory

Liberalism should be far more welcoming at least to a discussion of human security. However, as a system predicated on the consent of states, the possibility that human security might justify interventions in the affairs of states does present a possible area of objection. On the other hand, liberalism (as both a political and a legal theory) has long recognised

> that war can effectively be prevented only by tackling its root causes, that war is merely the external manifestation of the violence of the social institutions, that peace follows only from domestic enlightenment and justice.[95]

Modern legal liberal theorists argue that a state's legitimacy is dependent on the consent of the state's citizens.[96] This recognition that the function of states is to

93 *Lotus Case* (*France v Turkey*) (*Judgement*) [1927] PCIJ (ser A) No 10 (Judgment of 7 September 1927) 18.

94 See, eg, Bruno Simma and Andreas Paulus' contribution to edited Symposium on Method in International Law, 'Appraising the Methods of International Law: A Prospectus for Readers' (1999) 93 *American Journal of International Law* 291, 308.

95 See, eg, Immanuel Kant, *Perpetual Peace,* 1795 republished in *Kant's Political Writings* (HB Nisbet trans, Cambridge University Press, 1970). For discussion, see Fernando Tesón, 'The Kantian Theory of International Law' (1992) 92 *Columbia Law Review* 53.

96 See, eg, Thomas Franck's seminal work on this topic, *The Power of Legitimacy Among Nations* (Oxford University Press, 1990).

serve, protect and promote the interests of their constituents[97] should be able to accommodate a people-centred approach to security. Moreover, 'liberal institutionalism' is a branch of liberal theory that considers international organisations as vital to the maintenance of international peace and security, accommodating the centrality of UN mechanisms to most current approaches to human security.[98] Likewise, the idea in this strain of liberal thought, of finding the 'harmony of interests'[99] between states to pursue international cooperation, can be found expressed in terms of human security in the form of a concern for mutual vulnerability, discussed in the next chapter.

(iii) Human security and natural law

Human security also taps into the natural law roots of international law. Natural law views the international legal framework as based on universal values – from a historical standpoint, from divine law or 'right reason', but from a more modern standpoint, in the belief in a core of higher-order norms.[100] Indeed, from a natural law perspective there is a duty of states to provide assistance in situations of crisis. This natural law duty was captured in the writing of Emmerich de Vattel in 1758.[101] According to de Vattel,

> [t]o give assistance in such extreme necessity is so essentially conformable to humanity, that the duty is seldom neglected by any nation that has the slightest polish of civilisation ... if a Nation is suffering from famine, all those who have provisions to spare should assist it in its need ...[102]

Structural violence might not be included in the traditional framing of this duty, but it nonetheless complements the moral considerations and the principles of mutual vulnerability and responsibility within the discourse.[103] Likewise, human security sits well with more modern incarnations of natural law theory. The work of Fernando Tesón, for example, argues that international law's validity is dependent on making individuals, not States, the 'primary normative unit' of international law. This is an argument of 'normative individualism', which rests on the idea that

97 See, eg, Fernando Tesón, 'The Kantian Theory of International Law' (1992) 92 *Columbia Law Review* 53, 54.

98 David P Fidler, 'Caught between Traditions: The Security Council in Philosophical Conundrum' (1996) 17 *Michigan Journal of International Law* 411, 430.

99 See, eg, Hersch Lauterpacht, 'The Reality of the Law of Nations' in E Lauterpacht (ed) *International Law, being the Collected Papers of Hersch Lauterpacht* (Cambridge University Press, 2004) vol V, 26.

100 See, eg, JW Harris, *Legal Philosophies* (Butterworths, 2nd edn, 1997) 6.

101 Emmerich de Vattel, *The Law of Nations, or the Principles of Natural Law, Applied to the Conduct and to the Affairs of Nations and of Sovereigns* (Charles G Fenwick, trans 1916 edn) Book 11, Chapter 1.

102 Ibid [5].

103 On structural violence, see Johan Galtung, 'Violence, Peace and Peace Research' (1969) 6 *Journal of Peace Research* 170.

'the rights of states are derivative from the rights of individuals within their borders'.[104] Likewise, others have pointed to the thread of humanitarianism throughout the history of international law – international law as the 'gentle civiliser of nations',[105] demonstrated most clearly through the Martens Clause[106] – and in the perceived current processes of humanisation.[107] Human security thus aligns with the core values of such a theory, and could be a useful contribution in this school of thought.

(iv) Human security and idealism

Idealism as a theory of international law traces the development of international law from a system of coordination between states to one of cooperation, and moving towards communal action. This analysis highlights how this shift has led to a focus on the regulation of economic and social fields – that is, a focus on the needs and interests of people, and the effects of interdependence:

> … the emphasis of the law is increasingly shifting from the formal structure of the relationships between States and the delimitation of their jurisdiction to the development of substantive rules on matters of human concern vital to the growth of an international community.[108]

Thus human security's shift from statist constructions of the international order does not challenge the framework of idealist thinking. According to Koskenniemi, the test for international law by idealists is whether it corresponds to the interests and needs of international society.[109] It thus often expresses itself in general principles and rights, such as development and peace.[110] Human security would thus fit well in the toolbox of idealist norms and principles.

Mégret likewise points out that for idealists, sovereignty is not a value in and of itself, and that there must be a norm antecedent to it, justifying sovereignty and determining its proper uses.[111] 'This idea that there is something prior and,

104 Fernando Tesón, 'The Kantian Theory of International Law' (1992) 92 *Columbia Law Review* 53 54.

105 Martti Koskenniemi, *The Gentle Civiliser of Nations: The Rise and Fall of International Law 1870–1960* (Cambridge University Press, 2001).

106 *Hague Convention (IV) respecting the Laws and Customs of War on Land*, opened for signature 18 October 1907, 205 CTS (1907) 299, (entered into force 26 January 1910) preambular paragraph.

107 See, eg, Antônio Augusto Cançado Trindade, *International Law for Humankind: Towards a New Jus Gentium* (Martinus Nijhoff, 2010) vol 6; Theodor Meron, *The Humanization of International Law* (Martinus Nijhoff, 2006).

108 Jenks cited in Martti Koskenniemi, *From Apology to Utopia: The Structure of International Legal Argument* (Cambridge, 2nd edn, 2005) 211.

109 Ibid 212.

110 Ibid.

111 Frédéric Mégret, 'International Law as Law' in James Crawford and Martti Koskenniemi (eds), *The Cambridge Companion to International Law* (Cambridge, 2012) 64, 75–6.

unmistakably, higher – than the state is the defining mark of idealism',[112] and offers justification for example, of discussions of placing compliance with human rights as a precondition of legitimate statehood and sovereignty. This discussion shows a merge within idealism then of the precepts of liberalism and natural law. It also again shows that this school shares many of the same concerns as human security discourse.

(v) Human security and the New Haven School[113]

The New Haven School approach to international law is a particularly apt forum for the development of human security in international law. International law, according to the New Haven School, is a process of authoritative decision-making through which the international community clarifies and implements its common interests.[114] At the core of these common interests lies human dignity, which for this school should act as the driving force for all international legal activities.[115] For the founders of the New Haven School such as McDougal and Lasswell, international lawyers were implored to apply policy-driven skills to further the interests of human dignity.[116] Slaughter Burley points out that to best produce this global focus on 'human dignity', the next step, for the New Haven School, 'was to "invent and recommend" the principles and procedures necessary to a world public order consonant with the dignity and desires of all [humankind].'[117] Taking up this challenge, human security can be put forward as one such recommendation necessary for the pursuit of such a world order. As noted in the previous chapter, much of human security discourse places human dignity at the centre of the values which human security seeks to protect.

By moving away from formalistic approaches to concerns such as sources of law, the New Haven School also invites the elaboration of bottom-up approaches, and the empowerment of individuals in line with the values of human security. Moreover, the School also emphasises a self-consciousness about the position of the observer or analyst.[118] This, coupled with the inherently context-specific nature of

112 Ibid.

113 It should perhaps be noted that proponents of the school prefer the label 'Policy-Oriented Jurisprudence', but the more commonly used designation has been applied here for clarity's sake: Siegfried Wiessner and Andrew R Willard in Symposium on Method in International Law, 'Appraising the Methods of International Law: A Prospectus for Readers' (1999) 93 *American Journal of International Law* 291.

114 See, eg, Eisuke Suzuki, 'The New Haven School of International Law: An Invitation to a Policy-Oriented Jurisprudence' (1974) 1 *Yale Journal of International Law* 1, 36–7.

115 See, eg, Harold Lasswell, 'The Political Science of Science: An Inquiry into the Possible Reconciliation of Mastery and Freedom' (1956) 50 *American Political Science Review* 961.

116 H Lasswell and M McDonald, *Jurisprudence for a Free Society: Studies in Law, Science and Policy* (New Haven Press, 1992).

117 Anne-Marie Slaughter Burley, 'International Law and International Relations Theory: A Duel Agenda' (1993) 87 *American Journal of International Law* 205, 211.

118 Siegfried Wiessner and Andrew R Willard, 'Policy-Oriented Jurisprudence and Human Rights Abuses in Internal Conflict: Toward a World Public Order of Human Dignity' (1999) 93 *American Journal of International Law* 316, 323.

the social process theory is an important tool for the analysis of human security, which itself aims to be context-specific. Alongside this, the explicit law–policy nexus that is inherent in the New Haven School approach also makes it an ideal intellectual home for human security in international law scholarship. The policy path of 'clarification of values', 'identification of participants' and 'arenas of decision' to achieve 'social effects' could also be instrumental in rationalising the bottom-up approaches that are so essential to serving the multilateral and empowerment elements of human security. Moreover, as noted in the previous chapter, there are uncertainties about just what values or 'vital interests' human security serves to protect (though as noted, human dignity seems a common thread). The New Haven School contributes here by offering an inventory of the core human desires: power, enlightenment, wealth, well-being, skill, affection, respect and rectitude.[119]

(vi) New international legal process theory

New international legal process theory, as described by Koh, views

> the law's legitimacy as resting not just on process but also on its normative content. They view lawmaking as not merely the rubber-stamping of a pluralistic political process, but as a process of value-creation in which courts, agencies, and the people engage in a process of democratic dialogue.[120]

This approach emphasises the relationship between law and society. In so doing, it advocates that the development (and understanding) of the international legal system should be governed in terms of international society's values and in direct response to the contemporary challenges to that global society.[121] As human security becomes increasingly recognised by international and regional institutions, by political, media and academic minds, and enters the global lexicon, there is a powerful argument that international law and international legal scholarship must then engage with the discourse, to reflect these contemporary values. Moreover, the notion of democratic dialogue appeals to the empowerment and bottom-up dimensions of human security.

(vii) Critical theories of international law – 'newstream' theories and TWAIL

The so-called 'newstream' theories of international law themselves challenge its traditional foundations. The unifying argument of such theorists, that there is no objective truth in international legal rules and development, itself should invite at least the possibility of human security,[122] as a challenge to the status quo. Such

119 H Lasswell and M McDonald, *Jurisprudence for a Free Society: Studies in Law, Science and Policy* (New Haven Press, 1992).

120 Harold Hongju Koh, 'Transnational Legal Process' (1996) 75 *Nebraska Law Review* 181.

121 See, eg, Mary Ellen O'Connell, in Symposium on Method in International Law, 'Appraising the Methods of International Law: A Prospectus for Readers' (1999) 93 *American Journal of International Law* 291.

122 For discussion, see, eg, N Purvis 'Critical Legal Studies in Public International Law' (1991) 32 *Harvard International Law Journal* 81; Hilary Charlesworth and Christine

theories also seek to demonstrate the structural inequalities that reify and perpetuate social inequalities,[123] and are thus a useful lens through which to analyse human security and its attempt to reassess global priorities. Constructivist ideas of norm diffusion and the argument that international organisations can shape the interests of states and the content of norms,[124] are also of great potential interest to the analysis of human security. This is both because of the emergence of human security – initially within the UNDP and then continuing to be relevant in the context of the activities of the UN – and the normative power of the human security discourse.

Third World Approaches to International Law (TWAIL) scholarship counters the idea of the universality of international legal principles, arguing that the roots of most of these principles lie in Western values. 'Like a mastodon crushing the interests of the Third World countries', Mohammed Bedjaoui, a former President of the International Court of Justice writes, 'traditional international law is, as a whole, the embodiment of situations of predominance of the strong over the weak'.[125] That consideration resonates with the transformative potential of human security, which seeks to re-evaluate the priorities of the international community.[126] However, as will be discussed briefly in the next section, third world scholarship views human security with a healthy dose of scepticism. Moreover, TWAIL theory remains a largely state-oriented approach,[127] interested in the power balances between states, not the imbalances within states or the effect of imbalances on individuals' vulnerability to threats and insecurity. TWAIL scholarship also tends to show a steadfast commitment to the tenets of state sovereignty, which it sees as acting 'as a bulwark against perceived Western neo-colonialism'.[128]

(viii) Feminist theories of international law

Finally, a mutually beneficial relationship between human security and feminist theories is possible. On the one hand, feminist theory requires a conception of security that can take account of gendered experience.

> 'Engendering' security goes significantly beyond mainstreaming. It attempts to construct an alternative discourse, resocialising men and women into a qualitatively nuanced understanding of security … shifting priorities from

Chinkin, *The Boundaries of International Law: A Feminist Analysis* (Manchester University Press, 2000) 28, 34.

123 N Purvis 'Critical Legal Studies in Public International Law' (1991) 32 *Harvard International Law Journal* 81, 83.

124 See, eg, C Cora True-Frost, 'The Security Council and Norm Consumption' (2007–2008) 40 *NYU Journal of International Law & Politics* 115.

125 Cited in Hilary Charlesworth and Christine Chinkin, *The Boundaries of International Law: A Feminist Analysis* (Manchester University Press, 2000) 28, 36.

126 To be discussed in the following chapter.

127 Cited in Hilary Charlesworth and Christine Chinkin, *The Boundaries of International Law: A Feminist Analysis* (Manchester University Press, 2000) 28, 38.

128 Ibid.

threat perceptions and deterrence vocabularies to a language that cognises 'structural challenges' and 'enabling spaces'.[129]

Such an account of security is only possible through a people-centric approach to security, and cannot be achieved with a (supposedly) genderless account of national security. The feminist agenda can be advanced through a discourse such as human security, which seeks to challenge the traditional structures and concepts of the international order. In turn, legal feminist theory can offer a range of analytical tools for the development of human security – tools which can extend far beyond issues of gender. Charlesworth and Chinkin, in developing a framework for a feminist analysis of international law, noted that the tools they developed and employed had the potential for far broader scope.[130]

Feminist methods of analysis allow a useful examination of human security in a range of ways, including

- the identification of the silences and exclusions of international law that are integral to its structure;
- the analysis of the vocabulary of international law and the nature of basic concepts (including 'security');
- the analysis of seemingly 'neutral' principles;
- the recognition of the absence of the vulnerable from institutions and from the development of norms, procedures and policies;
- 'World Travelling', that is, the engagement with multiplicities of experiences, concerns and interests, and how this engagement affects how security needs are articulated and how this influences the capacity to address needs and mobilise resources; and
- the recognition of the risk of essentialism – reducing human experiences to a fixed set of characteristics.[131]

These tools of analysis are useful for exposing and examining structural injustices in all forms, not just gender. As such, these tools will be used extensively throughout this book. In turn, human security discourse can, if it is itself sufficiently engendered and critical, offer a constructive lens for the analysis of international law that promotes the interests of international legal feminist theory, deconstructing the role of the state, giving attention to issues of structural violence, and generating norms and policies on the basis of lived experience.

129 Meenakshi Gopinath and Sumona Das Gupta, cited in Amy Maguire, '"Security Starts with the Law": The Role of International Law in the Protection of Women's Security Post-Conflict' in Brett Bowden, Hilary Charlesworth and Jeremy Farrall (eds), *The Role of International Law in Rebuilding Societies After Conflict: Great Expectations* (Cambridge University Press 2009) 218, 223.

130 Hilary Charlesworth and Christine Chinkin, *The Boundaries of International Law: A Feminist Analysis* (Manchester University Press, 2000) 19.

131 Ibid. See also, Katharine Bartlett, 'Feminist Legal Methods' (1990) 103 *Harvard Law Review* 829.

G Lack of conceptual clarity – potential for misuse

The main criticism of human security is that its broad conceptualisation makes the concept vague, hollow and unworkable. Conceptual criticisms of human security have two broad fields of concern. First, there are concerns as to the 'grand theory' nature of human security.[132] This is a concern not specific to international legal scholarship, but represents one of the key concerns about human security as a discourse. The next section will mount a defence of the broad approach to human security, and wider concerns about its lack of conceptual clarity will be discussed there.

There are also concerns that, as a result of its combined depth and vagueness, it can be easily hijacked or manipulated in the self-interests of states or other actors.[133]

> Terms like 'humanitarianism' or 'democracy' have often been discredited as Orwellian types of Newspeak when wars are conducted in their name, precisely because they are empty linguistic vessels.[134]

Certainly there does exist a tangible risk of human security being misused in such a way. But this risk belongs to the concept of security more generally. The use of the security label is often condemned as misused when being employed in the national security context as well, for example, in the use of national security as a justification for curtailing individual liberties in the name of counter-terrorism. So while this is a relevant concern, it exposes a broader concern for the discussion of security more generally, and cannot be levelled at human security without these broader challenges being taken into consideration as well. However, as human security does broaden the scope of what may be placed under the umbrella of security, there are legitimate concerns about its misappropriation.

But this is precisely why international law's engagement with human security is so important. International law offers the legal framework – the 'operating system', to use Charlotte Ku's phrase – to give effect to norms and values.[135] In other words, this emphasises the importance of Hart's secondary rules, which give norms effect and legitimacy.[136] Even more importantly, '[e]ntering the legal culture compels a move away from one's idiosyncratic interests and preferences by

132 Shahrbanou Tadjbakhsh and Anuradha M Chenoy, *Human Security: Concepts and Implications* (Routledge, 2007) 60.

133 Sverre Lodgaard, 'Human Security: Concept and Operationalization', paper prepared for Expert Seminar on Human Rights and Peace, Geneva, 8–9 December 2000 (Harvard University's Program on Humanitarian Policy and Conflict Research), <http://www.hsph.harvard.edu/hpcr/events/hsworkshop/lodgaard.pdf> [26].

134 Mary Kaldor, Mary Martin and Sabine Selchow, 'Human Security: A New Strategic Narrative for Europe' (2007) 83(2) *International Affairs* 273, 274.

135 See also discussion by Beth Simmons, 'International Law and International Relations: Scholarship at the Intersection of Principles and Politics' (2001) 95 *American Society International Legal Procedure* 271, 278.

136 HLA Hart, *The Concept of Law* (Clarendon Press, 1994) 110.

insisting on their justification in terms of the historical practices and proclaimed standards of the community … it implies a recognition of the existence of a world beyond the speaker's immediate subjectivity.'[137] Jouannet describes international law as a means of combating arbitrariness and redressing the imbalances and injustices of international society.[138] Moreover, it is precisely where the critical voice of international legal scholarship is needed, to explore such misuse, and highlight the dangers that may lurk from uncritical approaches to human security discourse

Nonetheless, concerns about the current clarity of human security are of significance, and are perhaps the leading reason why the development of a human security–international law nexus has thus far been hindered. This is also demonstrated by an analysis of whether human security has the potential, as currently formed, to develop into international custom. These two topics are addressed in the following section and in the next chapter.

III Conclusion

The discussion in this chapter shows that resistance to human security discourse by international legal scholarship is multifaceted. But the points of resistance are not insurmountable. It is not to be expected that international legal scholarship will accept human security unadulterated and without question. It should, however, be a source of healthy debate within international legal analysis. Human security is not presumed to be a miracle cure-all for the panoply of current challenges the world faces. It does not provide us with a ready-made point-by-point for how to stop the HIV/AIDS pandemic, end global poverty, or resolve the effects of climate change. It does not provide an easy solution for internal unrest or international armed conflict, or produce from thin air the political will to address any of these problems. Nor is it a panacea to resolve the present and perceived weaknesses of the international legal system. It does not eliminate the need for states, guarantee global justice, or resolve the gaps and weaknesses in international human rights law. But it is an idea, and ideas can and do have power. It is an idea that seeks to reopen analysis of the world's priorities, to produce new integrated methodologies in analysing the most complex and pressing problems, and to give greater voice to individuals and communities in searching for solutions. This is the transformative potential discussed within the previous chapter. With these goals in mind, and in light of the fact that human security is playing an increasing role in international discourse, especially within the United Nations, it is high time for international law to join the party. Though taken out of context, a quote by Rizal Sukma is particularly apt to conclude:

137 Martti Koskenniemi, 'The Place of Law in Collective Security' (1996) 17 *Michigan Journal of International Law* 455, 478.

138 Emmanuelle Jouannet, 'What Is the Use of International Law? International Law as a 21st Century Guardian of Welfare' (2006–2007) 28 *Michigan Journal of International Law* 815, 836.

While it might be presumptuous to argue that the emphasis on human security will automatically ensure political and economic stability, one can make a reasonably strong claim that ignoring it will definitely serve as a recipe for disaster.[139]

139 Rizal Sukma, 'Indonesia' in Pranee Thiparat (ed) *The Quest for Human Security: The Next Phase of ASEAN?* (Institute of Security and International Studies, 2001) 62.

4 The intersection of human security discourse and international law

In search of principles

Without neglecting our existing system … we need to refocus on broad, simple and comprehensible principles of humanity. Broad principles and norms can sometimes be more effective than technical rules in ostracising and shaming violators
– Theodor Meron[1]

I Introduction

Human security has emerged in a period during which international law is re-evaluating approaches to the pursuit of global justice. As has been established in the preceding chapters, human security is an idea that not only challenges the role of states as the focal point for international society, but also the current priorities of the international community. Human security discourse seeks to redistribute international focus, so that it gives the same weight to issues such as poverty or climate change as has been traditionally given to national security concerns. Human security offers a potential conceptual framework for dealing with the broad encompassing crises of the modern world, the impact of which bleed across the varying specialisations of international law. It has the potential to provide a conceptual backdrop to deal with the lacunae of cross-specialisation and cross-discipline interaction, and provides a justification for the critical re-examination of how the international legal and policy structures determine priorities. In describing the impact of the international human rights programme on international law, Reisman described its impact as 'more than a piecemeal addition to the traditional corpus of international law. By shifting the fulcrum of the system from the protection of sovereigns to the protection of people, it works qualitative changes in virtually every component.'[2] Human security, if fully engaged by the international legal community, presents the potential for further momentum of this shifting fulcrum. The previous chapter examined why international legal scholarship has failed to truly engage with human security discourse. This chapter identifies the starting points for that conversation, by examining the shared principles between international law and human security.

1 Theodor Meron, *Bloody Constraint, War and Chivalry in Shakespeare* (Oxford University Press, 1998) 203–4.
2 W Michael Reisman, 'Sovereignty and Human Rights in Contemporary International Law' (1990) 84 *American Journal of International Law* 866, 872.

It discusses the ways in which these principles can operate both as a lens through which to evaluate existing international law, and as a framework for its future development. This will serve as an analytical framework for subsequent chapters, which will analyse the degree to which these principles manifest in international legal instruments and law-making processes. As will be seen, international law has been predominantly influenced by a narrow approach to human security. Therefore this chapter will conclude with an analysis of why a broad approach to human security is vital for the meaningful realisation of the principles of human security.

II Human security discourse: a principled approach

As has been previously noted throughout this study, bringing international law into the discussion of human security is vital for a number of reasons. As von Tigerstrom points out, 'the provision of security is one of the central purposes of legal systems'.[3] The referent of human security is humanity and/or the individual, and so justice is an important aspect to be considered and is a contributing factor to both security and development, along with accountability and the rule of law central to promoting good governance, peace and stability. As a number of discussions and definitions of human security point out, the rule of law, legal accountability, good governance and respect for international legal norms are essential to human security strategies.[4] The need for international law to embrace human security seems clear from Lloyd Axworthy's vision of human security:

> in essence, an effort to construct a global society where the safety of the individual is at the centre of the international priorities and a motivating force for international action; where international human rights standards and the rule of law are advanced and woven into a coherent web protecting the individual; where those who violate these standards are held fully accountable; and where our global, regional and bilateral institutions – present and future – are built and equipped to enhance and enforce these standards.[5]

Each element of this vision contains a clear role for international law. Another reason why it is essential that human security is embraced by international law is to give the concept greater legitimacy and authority,[6] and it is equally important that

3 Barbara von Tigerstrom, *Human Security and International Law: Prospects and Problems* (Hart Publishing, 2007) 3.
4 See, eg, UN Human Rights Council, *Report of the Human Rights Council Advisory Committee on the Right of Peoples to Peace*, UN GAOR, Twentieth sess, Agenda Item 5, UN Doc A/HRC/20/31 (16 April 2012) Article 2. See, also, Kofi Annan, 'Towards a Culture of Peace' (2000) <http://www.unesco.org/opi2/lettres/TextAnglais/AnnanE.html>.
5 Cited in Gerd Oberleitner, 'Human Security: A Challenge to International Law?' (2005) 11 *Global Governance* 185, 188.
6 Thomas M Franck, 'The Power of Legitimacy and the Legitimacy of Power: International Law in an Age of Power Disequilibrium' (2006) 100 *American Journal of International Law* 88; Anne-Marie Slaughter, 'Security, solidarity, and sovereignty:

international law not impede the pursuit of human security, or itself become an instrument for producing human insecurity. It is important, however, to assert that what is sought is not the deprivation of the political content of human security and a complete co-option of human security by legal architecture. Rather it is about human security discourse influencing the creation, interpretation and application of existing and future legal norms and approaches.

The establishment of clear principles of human security, with relevance and roots in existing international legal principles, offers the clearest opportunity for a mutually beneficial relationship between international law and human security. Principles offer a functionality to human security discourse, while allowing it to maintain its broad, transformative dimensions. In turn, principles offer the clarity and predictability which international law requires to fully engage with the discourse, if fully and clearly developed.

Rothschild identifies four purposes of principles of security.[7] Firstly, principles are intended to provide some form of guidance to the policies made by governments. One example of an existing principle of traditional security that operates in this way is the principle of non-intervention, which, while it does not find explicit written expression, is largely agreed to be comprised of the prohibition of the use of force within Article 2(4) of the UN Charter, the protection from interference encased in Article 2(7) of the Charter, and enshrined within customary international law, forming one of the bedrocks of the international legal order.[8]

The second purpose of principles of security, according to Rothschild, is to guide public opinion about policy.[9] This has been used to great effect by human security in the reframing of more traditional security issues, as will be seen in later chapters. The third purpose of security principles is to contest existing policies, and dispute their foundations.[10] This is arguably where human security discourse may be used to best effect. It acts as a lens through which to examine existing international law, creating a particular context and framework in which to rethink and analyse the underlying assumptions behind concepts of sovereignty, international legal subjects and indeed the role of international law.[11] Finally, the purpose of security principles is to influence the distribution of money and power.[12] This takes us back to core considerations about the power of the 'security' label.

The Grand Themes of UN Reform' (2005) 99 *American Journal of International Law* 619.

7 Emma Rothschild, 'What Is Security?' (1995) 124(3) *Daedalus* 53.

8 *Military and Paramilitary Activities in and against Nicaragua (Nicaragua v United States) (Merits)* [1986] ICJ Rep 14 [202]–[203].

9 Emma Rothschild, 'What Is Security?' (1995) 124(3) *Daedalus* 54.

10 Ibid.

11 See, eg, Math Noortmann, 'Human Securities, International Laws and Non-State Actors: Bringing Complexity Back In' in Cedric Ryngaert and Math Noortmann (eds), *Human Security and International Law: The Challenge of Non-State Actors* (Intersentia, 2014) 13, 27; Gerd Oberleitner, 'Human Security: A Challenge to International Law?' (2005) 11 *Global Governance* 185.

12 Emma Rothschild, 'What Is Security?' (1995) 124(3) *Daedalus* 54.

> The appeal of security-based arguments derives from the priority policy makers are perceived to give security threats … Recasting these problems as security threats provides the opportunity to change the nature of governance discourse about these problems and how to organise political responses to them.[13]

Thus, the application of human security stresses the urgency of issues, the need for an immediate response, and the need for increased attention, prevention, protection, response capabilities and – in the context of international law – regulatory frameworks.

Some limited attempts have been made by policymakers to provide human security with governing principles. The OSCE's Madrid Report offers six principles of human security:

a The primacy of human rights
b Legitimate political authority
c A bottom-up approach
d Effective multilateralism
e An integrated regional approach
f Clear and transparent strategic direction.[14]

Japan's International Cooperation Agency proposes seven principles for incorporating human security into its activities:

a Reaching those in need through a human-centred approach
b Empowering people as well as protecting them
c Focusing on the most vulnerable people whose survival, livelihood and dignity are at risk
d Comprehensively addressing both 'freedom from want' and 'freedom from fear'
e Responding to people's needs by assessing and addressing threats through flexible and inter-sectoral approaches
f Working with both governments and local communities to realize sustainable development
g Strengthening partnerships with various actors to achieve higher impact from assistance.[15]

The UN Trust Fund for Human Security declares the basic broad values of human security as its principles. That is, such action in the name of human security

13 David P Fidler, 'Governing Catastrophes: Security, Health and Humanitarian Assistance' (2007) 89(866) *International Review of the Red Cross* 247, 259.
14 Human Security Study Group, 'A European Way of Security' (The Madrid Report of the Human Security Study Group comprising a Proposal and Background Report 8 November 2007).
15 Institute for International Cooperation, 'Poverty Reduction and Human Security' (Report No 05-15, Japan International Cooperation Agency, March 2006) xvi.

is people-centred, multi-sectoral, comprehensive, context-specific and prevention-oriented.[16] Most of the principles thus cited for human security can be boiled down to the original four elements of human security as framed by the UNDP: people-centred, interconnected, universal and prevention-orientated. However, as can be seen, there is a lack of consistency in the focus of principles associated with human security, very little depth in the analysis or establishment of the principles, and no consideration at all has been given to the role of international law in the discussion. The following discussion focuses primarily on the latter, and examines the degree to which human security offers a normative framework for the interaction of existing legal norms and concepts, while retaining the structure of the UNDP's approach.

A People-centred approach

The most fundamental aspect of human security is of course the shift of the referent object of security from the nation-state to people. This also returns to the basic assumptions about the role of states: 'nations are not simply blocks of wood on a game-board. In reality, nations are collections of human beings and it's the security of those human beings that defines whether or not a nation is secure.'[17] As highlighted in the security *problematique* of human security outlined in Chapter Two, it is important not to equate human security with individual security, as the broader elements of human security discourse, and the lived experience of people in communities, is then lost. 'People-centred' is therefore the best way to frame this most fundamental principle of human security. This is a fundamental shift, but it is not without its precursors in the long history of international law.

(i) The existent people-centric trends in international law and principles of humanity

While it is accurate to state that, traditionally, international law has had the primary goal of regulating the relationships between states, this is not the whole story. From the inception of the United Nations a human-centred focus has been present, and become increasingly entrenched, in the international legal system, especially, though not exclusively, as a result of international human rights law.

The duty of states to protect their citizenry against abuse is one of the fundamental principles of the international human rights regime and has been firmly enshrined as such.[18] Beyond human rights, international humanitarian law is

16 United Nations Trust Fund for Human Security, *Human Security in Theory and Practice* (United Nations, 2009). See also UN Human Security Unit, *Strategic Plan 2014–2017* (United Nations, 2014).

17 Anthony Lake, *Address at High Level Human Security Symposium*, TICAD V: Tokyo International Conference on African Development High Level Human Security Symposium (2 June 2013) (Tokyo, Japan), <http://www.mofa.go.jp/policy/oda/sector/security/pdfs/sympo1306_unicef.pdf>.

18 Most notably in Article 2(1) of both the *International Covenant on Economic, Social and Cultural Rights*, opened for signature 16 December 1966, 993 UNTS 3 (entered

another reflection of international law that seeks to protect individuals. A number of norms emerging out of international humanitarian law, such as the humane treatment required by Common Article 3 of the *Geneva Conventions*, have attained the status of customary international law, and so form the bedrock of international norms and principles.[19] Indeed, it could be argued that from the modern perspective, international law is now dominated by people-centred concerns. Where once the principal concerns of international law had been statehood and territorial concerns, the modern proliferation of international law has been in areas of central concern to humankind (human rights, self-determination of people, environmental protection, development, and so on).[20]

One of the accepted general principles of international law (sometimes framed as a source of international law) is the concept of 'elementary considerations of humanity', first recognised by the International Court of Justice in the *Corfu Channel* case, which referred to obligations not based on treaty law but rather on

> certain general and well-recognised principles, namely elementary considerations of humanity, even more exacting in peace than in war.[21]

The roots of the concept are seen to lie in international humanitarian law, and specifically the Marten's Clause, formulated in 1899 and contained within the Hague Convention (II) with Respect to the Laws and Customs of War on Land:

> … the inhabitants and the belligerents remain under the protection and the rule of the principles of the law of nations, as they result from the usages established among civilized peoples, from the laws of humanity and the dictates of public conscience.[22]

The concept has since been recognised in a number of subsequent cases and advisory opinions, though the status of the principles have been variously described, from merely 'aspirational'[23] to 'intransgressible principles of international law'.[24] While the focus of such principles has been armed conflict, the principle

into force 3 November 1976) ('ICESCR') and the *International Covenant on Civil and Political Rights*, opened for signature 16 December 1966, 999 UNTS 171 (entered into force 3 January 1976) ('ICCPR').

19 See, eg, Jean-Marie Henckaerts and Louise Doswald-Beck, *Customary International Humanitarian Law: Volume I – Rules*, (ICRC and Cambridge, 2005).

20 On this point, see, eg, the work of Antônio Augusto Cançado Trindade, *International Law for Humankind: Towards a New Jus Gentium* (Martinus Nijhoff, 2010) vol 6, 4.

21 *Corfu Channel (United Kingdom v Albania) (Merits)* [1949] ICJ Rep 4.

22 *Hague Convention (IV) respecting the Laws and Customs of War on Land*, opened for signature 18 October 1907, 205 CTS 299, (entered into force 26 January 1910) preambular paragraph.

23 *South West Africa (Ethiopia v South Africa) (,Second Phase)* [1966] ICJ Rep 6, 34.

24 *Military and Paramilitary Activities in and against Nicaragua (Nicaragua v United States) (Merits)*, [1986] ICJ Rep 14, [79]. See also *Legal Consequences of the*

established in the *Corfu Channel case* – that these principles apply in peace as well as war – must be emphasised. Considerations of humanity have also been expressly recognised by other areas of international law, including the International Tribunal for the Law of the Sea, which in the *M/V Saiga Case (No 2)*, recognised that

> [c]onsiderations of humanity must apply in the law of the sea, as they do in other areas of international law. These principles have been followed over the years in law enforcement operations at sea.[25]

It should be noted, however, that the assessment of the normative force of such principles of humanity remains inconsistent. In the *South West Africa* cases, the majority decision in the ICJ asserted that

> [h]umanitarian considerations may constitute the ***inspirational basis*** for rules of law, just as, for instance, the preambular parts of the United Nations Charter constitute the moral and political basis for the specific legal provisions thereafter set out. Such considerations do not, however, in themselves amount to rules of law ... it is necessary not to confuse the moral idea with the legal rules intended to give it effect ...[26]

It is also true that the discussion of elementary considerations of humanity has not only centred around a predominantly narrow focus on armed conflict, but that '[h]umanity discourse' has often 'acted as a principled smokescreen for what was in effect a pragmatic and conservative conclusion', focused on more traditional principles such as military necessity, proportionality and the like.[27] Nonetheless, the pervasive trends in international case law and the common appeals to humanity-related concerns in the treaty law create a powerful basis for the conclusion that '[h]umanity is the lowest common denominator of most, if not all, international law.'[28]

Moreover recognition of 'principles of humanity' are littered throughout case law emanating from a range of courts and tribunals, and have enjoyed wiser usage, more in line with a protection of human security. In *Erdemovic*, the ICTY recognised

Construction of a Wall in the Occupied Palestinian Territory (Advisory Opinion) [2004] ICJ Rep 136, [157].

25 *M/V Saiga (No 2) (Saint Vincent and the Grenadines v Guinea)*, (1999) ITLS Case No 2, ICGJ 336, [155]–[156].

26 *South West Africa (Ethiopia v South Africa) (Second Phase)* [1966] ICJ Rep 6, [34]–[35].

27 See Matthew Zagor, 'Elementary Considerations of Humanity' in Karine Bannelier, Theodore Christakis and Sarah Heathcote (eds), *The ICJ and the Evolution of International Law: The Enduring Impact of the Corfu Channel Case* (Routledge, 2012) 264, 282. See also Theodor Meron, 'The Marten's Clause, Principles of Humanity and Dictates of Public Conscience' (2001) 94(1) *The American Journal of International Law* 78.

28 Robin Coupland, 'Humanity: What Is It and Does It Influence International Law?' (2001) 83(844) *International Review of the Red Cross* 969.

'minimum principles of humanity and dignity which constitute the inspiration for the international standards governing the protection of the rights of convicted persons',[29] while a French Court of Appeal noted that 'the principles of humanity and kindness [are] to be observed with regard to refugees.'[30] In a Separate Opinion in the Namibia case, Vice President Ammoun of the International Court of Justice (ICJ) identified what he considered

> the most essential principles of humanity, principles protected by the sanction of international law: equality, of which apartheid is the negation; freedom, which finds expressing in the rights of peoples to self-determination; and the dignity of the human person.[31]

People-centred concerns are also increasingly influencing the perception of the role of the international community in international peace and security. In an article written in 1999, Kofi Annan pointed out that '[w]hen we read the [UN] Charter today, we are more than ever conscious that its aim is to protect individual human beings, not to protect those who abuse them'.[32] The next chapter highlights, in particular, the changing perception of the Security Council and the increasing attention to the impact on individuals and communities in discussions of security. These comprise just a number of examples of how a 'humanisation of international law'[33] is evident in existing international law.

It is in light of this movement in international law that a shift away from the traditional paradigm of security to a focus on 'human security' can be considered. What it offers, however, is cohesion, and a clear normative framework through which to perceive the role of international law. It is essential to appreciate the purpose and depth of the concept of security as one of the central values of the system.[34] Human security's dual goals of protection and empowerment also indicate a future direction for the humanisation of international law – imbuing a sense of agency into the concept, engaging more and more with bottom-up approaches and with increased legal personality for individuals on the international stage. Thus human security demands from international law a system that is participatory, and not the exclusive domain of states.

29 *Prosecutor v Erdemovic (Sentencing Judgment)* (International Criminal Tribunal for former Yugoslavia (ICTY), Trial Chamber, Case No IT-96-22-T, 29 November 1996) [74].
30 *Compagnie des Phosphates et du Chemin de Fer de Gafsa v Weschler* (1967) 48 ILR 171 (France, Parisian Court of Appeal).
31 *Namibia (Legal Consequences of the Continued Presence of South Africa)(Advisory Opinion)* [1971] ICJ Rep 16, [8] (Separate Opinion of Vice President Ammoun).
32 Kofi Annan, 'Two Concepts of Sovereignty', *The Economist*, (London), 18 September 1999 <http://www.un.org/News/ossg/sg/stories/kaecon.html>.
33 Using the phrasing of Theodor Meron, *The Humanization of International Law* (Martinus Nijhoff, 2006).
34 Rosalyn Higgins, *Problems and Process: International Law and How We Use It* (Clarendon Press, 1994) 1–2.

(ii) Rights-based security

Just as human security has only received limited attention from human rights scholars (as discussed in the previous chapter), human rights has not received its due attention from human security scholarship. It is vitally important that this be rectified, and this is only possible if true engagement between international law and human security discourse is pursued.

Human rights offer a clear normative basis on which human security can build frameworks to deal with the world's most pressing crises. It also offers human security legitimacy, clarity and normative force, and the benefits of its decades of development. While there has only been limited discussion to date of how human rights and human security intersect, it was the intention of the United Nations that human security be realised through the application of international human rights law. This is demonstrated in the Commission on Human Security's Report: '[h]uman security helps identify the rights at stake in a particular situation. And human rights help answer the question: How should human security be promoted?'[35] While the advantages to a relationship between human security and human rights are quite clear, the benefits for human rights law are less so. Why engage with human security if it merely represents the same purposes, but without the clear frameworks or legal force? If we transform human rights back to a political enterprise, doesn't that undermine all that human rights law has achieved?[36]

However, there is little evidence that human security discourse is seeking to displace human rights law or take over its functions. Instead it is a normative framework which, if properly utilised, could be used to enhance and emphasise the role of human rights. Human security is at its core an assertion that security and human concerns are not in conflict with each other, and that indeed security can only be realised if there is a people-centred focus at its core. Moreover, in some ways human security is more flexible than human rights. International human rights law is deeply centred in the idea of states as the primary duty-bearers for the realisation, protection and promotion of human rights. Human security on the other hand does not require there to be a state violator – it addresses existential threats, such as climate change, pandemics and migration flows and focuses on broader ideas of communal responsibility (as discussed below).[37] It provides an innovative and comprehensive architecture for global legal and policy responses to situations, and emphasises (or at least has the potential to emphasise) that international law as a whole contributes to the realisation and promotion of the dignity of human beings, or to put it in the words of Estrada-Tanck, human security offers an

35 UN Commission on Human Security, *Human Security Now* (United Nations, 2003) 10.

36 See, eg, Ben Saul, 'The Dangers of the United Nations' "New Security Agenda": "Human Security" in the Asia-Pacific Region' (2006) 1(1) *Asian Journal of Comparative Law* 1.

37 See, eg, Rhoda Howard-Hassmann, 'Human Security: Undermining Human Rights?' (February 2012) 34(1) *Human Rights Quarterly* 88.

'enabling environment' for the realisation of human rights.[38] Human security should not, however, be seen as a substitute for human rights, and it is vitally important that the language of human security discourse does not supplant the vital role that human rights have to play.

(iii) Empowerment and participatory security

Human security has been described as

> a state that is achieved when and where individuals and communities have the options necessary to end, mitigate or adapt to threats to their human, environmental and social rights; have the capacity and freedom to exercise these options and actively participate in pursuing them.[39]

This approach to human security places empowerment squarely at the centre of the definition, and is closely tied to constructions of empowerment. Drydyk for example identifies empowerment as enhanced capacity for decision-making and the exercise of this capacity, and the opportunities to act upon this enhanced capacity.[40] From a legal standpoint, empowerment is most obviously associated with human rights, but it is also a relational concept reflective of vulnerability and/or marginalisation. This is because empowerment implies 'a lack of, or differential in, power or capacity'.[41] In the international law-making context, this in part relates to the limited capacity of non-state actors to be participants in the process, a subject of discussion in Chapter Six.

Human security is not merely the purview of states. Individuals and communities have equal responsibility in the promotion and protection of their own security and the security of others.

> Empowerment implies a 'bottom up' approach. It aims at developing the capabilities of individuals and communities to make informed choices and to act on their own behalf. Empowering people not only enables them to develop their full potential but it also allows them to find ways and to participate in solutions to ensure human security for themselves and others.[42]

38 Dorothy Estrada-Tanck, *Human Security and Human Rights under International Law. The Protections Offered to Persons Confronting Structural Vulnerability* (Bloomsbury, 2016).

39 Global Environmental Change and Human Security Project, 'Global Environmental Change and Human Security Science Plan' (IHDP Report International Human Dimensions Programme on Global Environmental Change, 1999) 6.

40 Drydyk cited in Susanne C Moser, 'Individual and Community Empowerment for Human Security' in Linda Sygna, Karen O'Brien and Johanna Wolf (eds), *A Changing Environment for Human Security: Transformative Approaches to Research, Policy and Action* (Routledge, 2013) 279, 285.

41 Ibid 280.

42 United Nations Trust Fund for Human Security, *Human Security in Theory and Practice* (United Nations, 2009) 8.

Human security demands that the processes for legal norm creation create opportunities for civil society and non-governmental organisation engagement. The system needs to be equally bottom-up and top-down to fulfil the vision of human security, and its protection and empowerment dimensions. Thus, to serve the people-centred component of human security, the core principles of rights-based security and participatory security should be emphasised.

B Interdependent

The UNDP, when outlining the interconnected nature of human security, emphasised that it comprised seven components: economic security; health security; personal security; community security; environmental security; political security; and food security.[43] What was important, however, was not the categories of security, which were created merely for conceptual convenience, but rather the understanding of the interconnected nature of the threats and the need for integrated, multi-sectoral solutions.[44] Bacon and Hobson correctly point out, however, that this critical point was unfortunately underdeveloped in both the UNDP account and the later report of the Commission on Human Security.[45] But this is a crucial point, as it has different dimensions.

The first is that human security, broadly speaking, is comprehensive or holistic security, taking into consideration the lived experience of people and an understanding that threats to security come in different forms. Secondly, it is an understanding that many of the complex issues that may create human insecurity contain threat multipliers, and thus a response focusing on only one dimension of human security will not adequately be able to respond to the issue. Thirdly, it recognises what Bacon and Hobson refer to as 'solution multipliers' – the understanding that it might be possible to redress multiple threats at the same time.[46] Its emphasis on the interconnected nature of threats requires the development of interconnected and complex networks engaging a diverse range of stakeholders from both the private and public sectors, and at the local, national, regional and international levels.

(i) Principle of integration

It would only be through systemic integration of international law – that is, recognising international law as comprising a coherent, cohesive normative

43 United Nations Development Programme (UNDP), *Human Development Report 1994* (UNDP, 1994) 87–8.

44 See, eg, United Nations Trust Fund for Human Security, *Human Security in Theory and Practice* (United Nations, 2009).

45 Paul Bacon and Christopher Hobson, 'Incorporating Natural Disasters into the Human Security Agenda' in Paul Bacon, Christopher Hobson and Robin Cameron (eds), *Human Security and Natural Disasters* (Routledge, 2014) 1, 6.

46 Ibid 7.

environment – that human security could possibly be pursued and supported within the framework of modern international law.[47] It is only under certain conditions – only if trade law is willing to recognise the human rights consequences of its policies, only if the Security Council is conscious of the effect of interventions in humanitarian and developmental terms, to take two examples – only then could strategies to realise human security be safeguarded. It requires intergovernmental agencies and the states they represent to be willing to proactively engage with other bodies of international law, and with norms from other fields, and to be conscious of the importance of prevention and empowerment as two of the cornerstones of human security. Human security could then bring with it a framework for determining the integration of such issues.

The institutional structures of international law have thus far proved largely ill-equipped to produce integrated responses. These institutions have created a marked distinction between the fields of security and development.[48] It has only been in the last two decades that the realisation that the disparate areas of international law do not each exist in a vacuum has gained traction, and that greater coordination among spheres has been pursued. Coordination, however, is not the same as integration. In examining the political dynamics of the security–development nexus within UN agencies, Sending points out that coordination is 'in the final analysis a recommendation that two separate units should work together because their operations are interdependent.'[49] The more complex the issue, he points out, the more integration is necessary, as coordination says nothing about authority or responsibility.[50] The same arguments can be made in relation to international law in this respect.

47 A detailed examination of systemic integration, however, is unfortunately beyond the scope of this book. There is an increasing body of work in this area. For a more detailed examination of the issues related to systemic integration (especially in areas most relevant to human security), see, eg, Violeta Moreno-Lax, 'Systematising Systemic Integration: "War Refugees", Regime Relations, and a Proposal for a Cumulative Approach to International Commitments' (2014) 12(5) *Journal of International Criminal Justice* 907; Bruno Simma and Dirk Pulkowski, 'Of Planets and the Universe: Self-contained Regimes in International Law' (2006) 17 *European Journal of International Law* 483; Jörg Kammerhofer, 'Systemic Integration, Legal Theory and the ILC' (2009) 19 *Finnish Yearbook of International Law* 157; Erika De Wet and Jure Vidmar, 'Conflicts Between International Paradigms: Hierarchy Versus Systemic Integration' (2013) 2(02) *Global Constitutionalism* 196; Anne van Aaken, 'Defragmentation of Public International Law Through Interpretation: A Methodological Proposal' (2009) 16 *Indiana Journal of Global Legal Studies* 483; Marko Milanovic, 'Norm Conflict in International Law: Whither Human Rights?' (2009) 20 *Duke Journal of Comparative and International Law* 69.

48 A point discussed in more detail in Chapter Three.

49 J Sending, 'The Political Dynamics of the Security-Development Nexus' (Working Paper for the Standing Group for International Relations of the European Consortium for Political Research, 9–11 September 2004) 14.

50 Ibid.

(ii) Existing integrative frameworks in international law

ARTICLE 31(3)(C)

In addressing measures of conflict resolution between conflicting legal norms, the ILC draws on a principle from the *Vienna Convention on the Law of Treaties* (VCLT), referring to Article 31(3)(c) of the Convention as the 'Principle of Systemic Integration'. Article 31(3)(c) comprises part of the general rules for interpretation of treaties, and states:

> 3. There shall be taken into account, together with the context:
> (c) any relevant rules of international law applicable in the relations between the parties...[51]

The International Law Commission (ILC) highlights the importance of this principle as one that goes beyond restating the applicability of general international law, and in that '[i]t points to the need to take into account the normative environment more widely.'[52] The ILC Report asserts that this does not extend the role of institutions beyond their jurisdiction, for although such institutions may only have jurisdiction with regard to a particular treaty of international law, the *application* of that treaty can only take place by situating that instrument in its normative environment.[53] A similar principle of note is made by Joost Pauwelyn in his work on the conflict of norms within the World Trade Organisation (WTO). Pauwelyn reveals that norms of international law interact in two ways – they conflict or they accumulate.[54] Thus if two norms do not conflict[55] they automatically accumulate.

51 For a detailed analysis of the meaning and substance of Article 31(3)(c), see, eg, Ulf Linderfalk, 'Who Are "The Parties"? Article 31, Paragraph 3(C) of the 1969 Vienna Convention and the "Principle of Systemic Integration" Revisited' (2008) 55(03) *Netherlands International Law Review* 343; Vassilis P Tzevelekos, 'The Use of Article 31(3)(c) of the VCLT in the Case Law of the ECtHR: An Effective Anti-fragmentation Tool or a Selective Loophole for the Reinforcement of Human Rights Teleology? Between Evolution and Systemic Integration. (Vienna Convention on the Law of Treaties, European Court of Human Rights)' (2010) 31(3) *Michigan Journal of International Law* 621; Campbell McLachlan, 'The Principle of Systemic Integration and Article 31(3)(c) of the Vienna Convention' (2005) 54(2) *International & Comparative Law Quarterly* 279; Panos Merkouris, 'Debating the Ouroboros of International Law: The Drafting History of Article 31 (3)(c)' (2007) 9(1) *International Community Law Review* 1.

52 International Law Commission (ILC), *Fragmentation of International Law: Difficulties Arising from the Diversification and Expansion of International Law, Report of the Study Group of the International Law Commission* UN GAOR, Fifty-eighth sess, UN Doc A/CN.4/L.682 (18 July 2006) [415].

53 Ibid [423].

54 Joost Pauwelyn, *Conflict of Norms in Public International Law: How WTO Law Relates to other Rules of International Law* (Cambridge University Press, 2003) 161–63.

55 Using Pauwelyn's broad definition of conflict to include 'inconsistent', 'incompatible' and 'contradictory'.

Of course, the principle of systemic integration as stated in the VCLT and as discussed by the ILC is used in the very limited context of treaty interpretation, and is subject to a number of limitations. The term refers explicitly to 'rules' and thus does not include considerations of principles, soft law, or broader considerations of international law. Moreover, the object and purpose of the provision is to assist in giving meaning to a particular treaty provision, rather than to assert the operation or relevance of relevant rules in any broader sense. Nonetheless, utilisation of this principle may be essential for the realisation of the integrative nature of human security. If international law remains a 'system' of law where the wider legal environment remains relevant, even in the operation of specialised institutions, then the principle of systemic integration makes sense as a broader tool – one to be utilised not only in dispute resolution but in the creation and application of norms within regimes, and reflected in their activities in their entirety. However, as Broude points out, another problem is that along with the fragmentation of international law itself has come institutional fragmentation, which results in forum shopping, as different institutions and different decision-making authorities will approach the issue with a particular focus.[56] That said, Broude also points out that where substantive norms are sufficiently integrated or harmonised, 'normative commonality overcomes institutional differences'.[57] Of particular relevance to human security, the International Court of Justice has shown its capacity for integrative reasoning in recent cases concerning the relationship between international human rights and international humanitarian law.[58] The benefit, then, of human security may be the creation of regimes that provide integration. This has to some extent been achieved with some of the recent 'human security treaties' discussed in Chapter Seven, which have brought together norms from different fields of international law.

SUSTAINABLE DEVELOPMENT AS A MODEL

One other clear opportunity for studying means of integrating human security approaches into international law is a study of sustainable development. Sustainable development is an established integrative concept,[59] and can serve as a

56 Tomer Broude, 'Principles of Normative Integration and the Allocation of International Authority: The WTO, the Vienna Convention on the Law of Treaties and the Rio Declaration' (2008–2009) 6 *Loyola University Chicago International Law Review* 173, 178.

57 Ibid 179.

58 *Legality of the Threat or Use of Nuclear Weapons* (Advisory Opinion) [1996] ICJ Rep 226, 240; *Legal Consequences of the Construction of a Wall in the Occupied Palestinian Territory (Advisory Opinion)* [2004] ICJ Rep 136, 178; *Armed Activities on the Territory of the Congo (Democratic Republic of the Congo v Uganda) (Judgment)* [2005] ICJ Rep 116, [216].

59 See, eg, Bob Giddings, Bill Hopwood and Geoff O'Brien, 'Environment, Economy and Society: Fitting Them Together into Sustainable Development' (2002) 10(4) *Sustainable Development* 187; Sébastien Jodoin, 'The Principle of Integration and Interrelationship in Relation to Human Rights and Social, Economic and

possible model from which human security could learn lessons and adopt an integrative approach. Integration is central to the issue of sustainable development, and has been described as one of the guiding central principles of the concept.[60] A key example of the principle of integration is seen to lie within Principle 4 of the Rio Declaration, which states that

> In order to achieve sustainable development, environmental protection shall constitute an integral part of the development process and cannot be considered in isolation from it.[61]

It has since been expanded to encompass the three pillars of sustainable development – that is, the social, economic and environmental aspects – and is enshrined in a range of international instruments related to sustainable development. It is perhaps best captured in paragraph 7.1 of the New Delhi Declaration, which states that

> [t]he principle of integration reflects the interdependence of social, economic, financial, environmental and human rights aspects of principle and rules of international law relating to sustainable development as well as of the needs of current and future generations.[62]

Broude argues that the 'soft' character of Principle 4 of the Rio Declaration offers it greater opportunities for adoption on the international stage, and by institutions such as the WTO, as it offers a 'path of least resistance', as opposed to imposing definitive obligations that may seem to undermine institutional authority, and therefore be avoided by such institutions.[63] Furthermore, the structure of the principle of integration for sustainable development is such that it does not refer to conflict of rules, but rather to policy considerations, operating at 'a meta-level, causing norms to take into account the objectives of other norms but not their substance'.[64] Human security would be well served developing such a

Environmental Objectives' (A Legal Working Paper in the Recent Developments in International Law Related to Sustainable Development Series CISDL, March 2005).

60 See, eg, Christine Voight, *Sustainable Development as a Principle of International Law: Resolving Conflicts between Climate Measures and WTO Law* (BRILL, 2009) chapter 2.

61 Commision on Sustainable Development, *Rio Declaration on Environment and Development*, UN ESCOR, Fifth sess, UN Doc E/CN.17/1997/8 (10 February 1997).

62 *ILA New Delhi Declaration of Principles of International Law Relating to Sustainable Development*, 70th Conference of the International Law Association, New Delhi, India (2–6 April 2002).

63 Tomer Broude, 'Principles of Normative Integration and the Allocation of International Authority: The WTO, the Vienna Convention on the Law of Treaties and the Rio Declaration' (2008–2009) 6 *Loyola University Chicago International Law Review* 173, 202.

64 Ibid.

principle – one which reflects the interconnected nature of threats and the need for an integrated response.

Thus far the Human Security Reports issued by the Secretary-General and the Human Security Resolution have all emphasised that human security 'recognizes the interlinkages between peace, development and human rights, and equally considers civil, political, economic and social rights'.[65] Thus in the same way that the environment and economic and social dimensions stand as the three pillars of sustainable development, human security may see these three pillars as the core of human security discourse, and emphasise human security integral relationship with sustainable development and human rights. This then aligns with other conceptions of human security that focus on freedom from want, freedom from fear and freedom from indignity.

This also shows the added value of human security to existing human rights law. The three-pillars approach emphasises that on the one hand human security is a rights-based approach and plays a supportive role and ensures the minimum necessary conditions for development, as previously discussed.[66] But framing it in this way also emphasises that there is not a trade-off between rights and security, and advances a security culture that supports rather than undermines human rights.[67] Moreover human security places the focus primarily on threats. It thus balances against the perspective of human rights that focuses on actors (and principally the relationship between individual and state) and the goals-based orientation of development.[68] Integrative approaches that collectively consider these different dimensions will assist in the realisation of human security.

C Universal approach

'Human security is a universal concern.'[69] Unpacked, this idea has a number of dimensions. First, it is a recognition that all individuals are threatened by forms of human insecurity, and hence that the protection of human security is in the

65 *Follow-up to Paragraph 143 on Human Security of the 2005 World Summit Outcome*, GA Res 66/290, Sixty-sixth sess, Agenda Item 14 and 117, UN Doc A/RES/66/290 (25 October 2012) [3]; United Nations General Assembly, *Report of the Secretary-General on Human Security*, UN GAOR, Sixty-fourth sess, Agenda Item 48 and 114, UN Doc A/64/701 (8 March 2010); General Assembly, *Report of the Secretary-General: Follow-up to General Assembly Resolution 66/290 on Human Security*, Sixty-eighth sess, Agenda Item 14 and 118, UN Doc A/68/685 (23 December 2013).

66 See, eg, *Human Security Resolution*, UN Doc A/RES/66/290 [4].

67 See, eg, Tim Dunne and Nicholas J Wheeler, '"We the Peoples": Contending Discourses of Security in Human Rights Theory and Practice' in David Chandler and Nik Hynek (eds), *Critical Perspectives on Human Security: Rethinking Emancipation and Power in International Relations* (Routledge, 2011) 13, 21; Stephen J Toope, 'Fallout from "9-11": Will a Security Culture Undermine Human Rights' (2002) 65 *Saskatchewan Law Review* 281.

68 See, eg, Gerd Oberleitner, 'Porcupines in Love: The Intricate Convergence of Human Rights and Human Security' (2005) 6 *European Human Rights Law Review* 588.

69 United Nations Development Programme (UNDP), *Human Development Report 1994* (UNDP, 1994) 22.

interests of all. Secondly, and relatedly, it draws in ideas of vulnerability, and a need to give particular concern to the most vulnerable. Connected to that idea are ideas of mutual vulnerability – that is, an understanding that threats must be responded to by global governance, because threats to human insecurity in one part of the globe have ramifications for the security of the rest of the world.[70] It thus gives rise to the underlying foundations of the Responsibility to Protect (discussed below) – the idea that

> [s]overeign states have the responsibility to protect their own citizens from avoidable catastrophe – from mass murder and rape, from starvation – but that when they are unwilling or unable to do so, that responsibility must be borne by the broader community of states.[71]

The universality component of human security addresses a number of relevant concerns for international law. On the one hand it emphasises the importance of protection for the most vulnerable. While human rights law ostensibly guarantees equal protection of the human dignity of each and every individual,[72] the reality is that insecurities reduce the ability of individuals to assert those rights. Human security then becomes a matter of ensuring the immediate protection of vulnerable individuals, so that the longer-term measures to improve conditions (eg, sustainable development, or more formal invocations of their human rights) can have an opportunity to work.[73] The most vulnerable are often, then, the least protected. The more vulnerable are affected by crises and threats to security far more than other individuals. This brings to mind Tawney's earlier mentioned depiction of poverty in rural China.[74]

Secondly, and perhaps even more importantly for the application of international law, human security's universal nature emphasises that security is a global concern. It thus invokes a sense of shared responsibility within the international community. Thus the Millennium Declaration states:

> [w]e recognise that, in addition to our shared responsibilities to our individual societies, we have a collective responsibility to uphold the principles of human dignity, equality, and equity at the global level. As leaders we have a duty

70 See, eg, Jorge Nef, *Human Security and Mutual Vulnerability* (IDRC, 1999); Jorge Nef, 'Human Security, Mutual Vulnerability and Sustainable Development: A Critical View' (2006) 7 *Whitehead Journal of Diplomacy and International Relations* 55.

71 International Commission on Intervention and State Sovereignty (ICISS), *The Responsibility to Protect* (International Development Research Centre, December 2001), viii.

72 *Universal Declaration of Human Rights*, GA Res 217A (III), UN GAOR, Third sess, 183rd plen mtg, UN Doc A/810 (10 December 1948) Preamble.

73 Ibid.

74 Cited in PH Liotta and James F Miskel, 'Towards an Ethical Framework for Security' in Hans Günter Brauch et al (eds), *Globalization and Environmental Challenges* (Springer Berlin Heidelberg, 2008) vol 3, 879. See also, Astri Suhrke, 'Human Security and the Interests of States' (1999) 30(3) *Security Dialogue* 265, 271.

> therefore to all the world's people, especially the most vulnerable ... Responsibility for managing worldwide economic and social development, as well as threats to international peace and security, must be shared among the nations of the world and should be exercised multilaterally.[75]

Moreover, it acknowledges the potential role for non-state actors as well as state actors to fulfil the role of securitising agent.

> Human security can therefore lead to the establishment of synergies and partnerships that capitalise on the comparative advantages of each implementing organization and help empower individuals and communities to act on their own behalf.[76]

The General Assembly Resolution acknowledged the need for interconnected and multilateral responses, expressly recognising the need to for greater collaboration and partnership between governments, international and regional organisations and civil society.[77]

A true sense of responsibility is best formed when a concept is accompanied by clear legal norms and principles, driving the decision-making of the international community. A genuine duty to human security therefore must find some expression in international law.

(i) The Responsibility to Protect

As has been discussed, the duty of states to protect their citizenry against abuse is one of the fundamental principles of the international legal regime and has been firmly enshrined as such. 'State sovereignty implies responsibility, and the primary responsibility for the protection of its people lies with the state itself.'[78] The Responsibility to Protect (R2P) doctrine is based on this principle, but it extends it further, recognising a role for the universal concern of the international community. It recognises that in situations of egregious human rights violations, the international community does share the responsibility to protect individuals from harm, in situations where the state is the perpetrator or has systematically failed to uphold its duty to protect. The R2P doctrine gained its first recognition in the Report of the International Commission on Intervention and State Sovereignty (ICISS) and has subsequently been recognised by both the UN General Assembly and the Security Council.[79]

75 *United Nations Millennium Declaration*, GA Res 55/2, Fifty-fifth sess, Agenda Item 60(b), UN Doc A/RES/55/2 (18 September 2000) I.6.

76 United Nations Trust Fund for Human Security, *Human Security in Theory and Practice* (United Nations, 2009).

77 *Human Security Resolution*, UN Doc A/RES/66/290.

78 Report of the International Commission on Intervention and State Sovereignty (ICISS) *The Responsibility to Protect* (December 2001) Synopsis, Basic Principles.

79 *World Summit Outcome Document*, GA Res 60/1, UN GAOR, Sixtieth sess, Agenda Item 46 and 120, UN Doc A/RES/60/1 (24 October 2005) [138]–[140]; Security

Human security has recently been uncoupled from the Responsibility to Protect (R2P) by the United Nations. The General Assembly Resolution on Human Security carefully states:

> (d) The notion of human security is distinct from the responsibility to protect and its implementation.[80]

This is expanded upon in the first Report on Human Security by the UN Secretary-General. There it is highlighted that '[t]he use of force is not envisaged in the application of the human security concept.'[81] Instead, the Report points out that the focus of human security is on preventive solutions, strengthening local capacity and resilience to threats.[82] It goes on to associate R2P with protection of populations, suggesting that the use of force is relevant to R2P, as distinct from human security. This demonstrates a 'pervasive connection' between R2P and military intervention.[83] This narrow view of the role of R2P not only deviates from the ICISS approach to the doctrine, which was itself a child of human security discourse, but also from the three-pillar approach that the UN itself adopted in the 2005 World Summit Outcome Document.[84] This three-pillar approach acknowledged, firstly, the idea of sovereignty as responsibility – that states had the primary duty to protect their own citizens – and secondly, that

> [o]ur goal is to help States succeed, not just to react once they have failed to meet their prevention and protection obligations. It would be neither sound morality, nor wise policy, to limit the world's options to watching the slaughter of innocents or to send in the marines.[85]

Thirdly, there was the pillar involving a responsibility to react, with Security Council authorisation, when states fail to protect their populations from genocide,

Council Resolution 1674 (2006), On the protection of civilians in armed conflict, UN SCOR, UN Doc S/RES/1674 (28 April 2006) and Security Council Resolution 1706 (2006) Concerning the situation in the Sudan, UN SCOR, UN Doc S/RES/1706 (31 August 2006); UN Security Council, Security Council Resolution 1973 (2011) [on the situation in the Libyan Arab Jamahiriya] UN SCOR, UN Doc S/RES/1973 (17 March 2011).

80 Ibid.

81 United Nations General Assembly, *Report of the Secretary-General on Human Security*, UN GAOR, Sixty-fourth sess, Agenda Item 48 and 114, UN Doc A/64/701 (8 March 2010) [23].

82 Ibid.

83 See, eg, Alex J Bellamy, 'The Responsibility to Protect and the Problem of Military Intervention' (2008) 84(4) *International Affairs* 615, 633.

84 *World Summit Outcome Document*, GA Res 60/1, UN GAOR, Sixtieth sess, Agenda Item 46 and 120, UN Doc A/RES/60/1 (24 October 2005) [38].

85 Press Release, Secretary-General, 'Secretary-General Defends, Clarifies "Responsibility to Protect" at Berlin Event on "Responsible Sovereignty: International Cooperation for a Changed World"', UN Doc, SG/SM/1 1701 (15 July 2008) <http://www.un.org/News/Press/docs/2008/sgsml 1701.doc.htm>.

war crimes, ethnic cleansing and crimes against humanity.[86] However, this was expected to be the narrow end of the R2P doctrine.[87] Thus it was designed, in both the Outcome document and the original ICISS construction, to be a doctrine of prevention, thus responding to the final element of human security discussed below.[88] The literature, however, universally agrees that while prevention is the most important dimension of R2P, it has been woefully underdeveloped and largely neglected.[89]

Moreover, the shift from the ICISS Report to the 2005 World Summit demonstrates the tendency – one to be highlighted throughout the following chapters – of a narrow approach to human security.[90] While the ICISS Report had explicitly listed natural disasters[91] as a threat that would allow the doctrine to be invoked, the UN document narrowed the scope explicitly to atrocity crimes. This narrow scope was justified by the Secretary-General in a 2009 Report:

> The responsibility to protect applies, until Member States decide otherwise, only to the four specified crimes and violations: genocide, war crimes, ethnic cleansing and crimes against humanity. To try to extend it to cover other calamities such as HIV/AIDS, climate change or the response to natural disasters would undermine the 2005 consensus and stretch the concept beyond recognition or operational utility.[92]

As such, efforts by France and by a range of commentators, academics and others failed successfully to invoke the doctrine in 2008 when Myanmar refused

86 *World Summit Outcome Document,* UN Doc A/RES/60/1, [39].

87 'Prevention is the single most important dimension of the responsibility to protect', International Commission on Intervention and State Sovereignty (ICISS), *The Responsibility to Protect* (International Development Research Centre, December 2001), Synopsis, Priorities.

88 See, eg, Sheri P Rosenberg, 'Responsibility to Protect: A Framework for Prevention' (2009) 1 *Global Responsibility to Protect* 442, 443; Louise Arbour, 'The Responsibility to Protect as a Duty of Care in International Law and Practice' (2008) 3 *Review of International Studies* 445; Foluke Ipinyomi, 'Is Côte d'Ivoire a Test Case for R2P? Democratization as Fulfilment of the International Community's Responsibility to Prevent' (2012) 56(2) *Journal of African Law* 151; Natalie Oman, 'The "Responsibility to Prevent": A Remit for Intervention?' (2009) 22(2) *Canadian Journal of Law and Jurisprudence* 355; Marie-Joelle Zahar, 'Intervention, Prevention and the "Responsibility to Protect"' (2005) 60 *International Journal* 723.

89 Ibid. See also Emma McClean, 'The Responsibility to Protect: The Role of International Human Rights Law' (2008) 13 *Journal of Conflict and Security Law* 123.

90 On the historical development (and shifts) of R2P, see, eg, Teresa Chataway, 'Towards Normative Consensus on Responsibility to Protect' (2007) 16 *Griffith Law Review* 193; Carsten Stahn, 'Responsibility to Protect: Political Rhetoric or Emerging Legal Norm?' (2007) 101 *American Journal of International Law* 99.

91 International Commission on Intervention and State Sovereignty (ICISS), *The Responsibility to Protect* (International Development Research Centre, December 2001) 33.

92 United Nations General Assembly, Implementing the Responsibility to Protect, Report of the Secretary General, UN GAOR, Sixty-third sess, Agenda Item 44 and 107, UN Doc A/63/677 (12 January 2009) [10(b)].

international aid efforts access to the country in the wake of Cyclone Nargis.[93] It was argued that such attempts to utilise R2P in this manner would destroy the legitimacy of the principle. However, this ignores the normative challenges made to such narrow constructions of human security, as discussed in the previous chapter.[94] As Axworthy and Rock asked at the time,

> Is there a moral difference between an innocent person being killed by a machete or AK 47, and starving to death or dying of a cholera epidemic that could have been avoided by a proper humanitarian response? If R2P does not apply to situations where a government is actively working to deprive large numbers of people of life saving assistance, then we must ask how far the international community has come in saying that it will never again sit idly by in the face of human catastrophe.[95]

The experiences of R2P are valuable lessons as human security begins to find a place in international legal discourse. Because the focus on R2P has coalesced around its relationship to intervention, human security discourse may have to divorce itself from the doctrine and, as far as possible, from issues relating to the use of force, if it wants to develop an expansive agenda. Indeed, invoking human security may be a way of revitalising the lost elements of R2P – a way of returning to expansive ideas of threat, the idea of shared responsibilities, and above all, the need to focus on prevention. R2P is also a cautionary tale for human security about the risks of co-option and abuse of the concept.

(ii) Common concern for humankind

For Tigerstrom, the universality of human security is the core entry point for international law's relationship with human security.[96] The starting point for this relationship then is the principles of cooperation to be found within (among

93 See, eg, Rebecca Barber, 'The Responsibility to Protect the Survivors of Natural Disaster: Cyclone Nargis, A Case Study' (2009) 14 *Journal of Conflict and Security Law* 3.

94 For further discussion of the application of R2P to Nargis (and similar scenarios), see, eg, John Langmore and Ashley McLachlan-Bent, 'A Crime against Humanity? Implications and Prospects of the Responsibility to Protect in the Wake of Cyclone Nargis' (2011) 3 *Global Responsibility to Protect* 37; Alpaslan Özerdem, 'The "Responsibility to Protect" in Natural Disasters: Another Excuse for Interventionism? Nargis Cyclone, Myanmar' (2010) 10(5) *Conflict, Security & Development* 693; Jürgen Haacke, 'Myanmar, the Responsibility to Protect and the Need for Practical Assistance' (2009) 1 *Global Responsibility to Protect* 156; Jarrod Wong, 'Reconstructing the Responsibility to Protect in the Wake of Cyclones and Separatism' (2009) 84 *Tulane Law Review* 219.

95 Lloyd Axworthy and Allan Rock, 'R2P: A New and Unfinished Agenda' (2009) 1 *Global Responsibility to Protect* 54, 55. See also, Julie MacArthur, 'A Responsibility to Rethink? Challenging Paradigms in Human Security' (2007–2008) 63 *International Journal* 422.

96 Barbara von Tigerstrom, *Human Security and International Law: Prospects and Problems* (Hart Publishing, 2007) 72–88.

other sources) the UN Charter and the 1970 Declaration on Friendly Relations.[97] After all,

> States have the duty to co-operate with one another, irrespective of the differences in their political, economic and social systems, in the various spheres of international relations, in order to maintain international peace and security and to promote international economic stability and progress, the general welfare of nations and international cooperation free from discrimination based on such differences.[98]

The relationship between human security and the UN Charter will be examined in more detail in Chapter Five. More specifically, Tigerstrom attaches human security to the principle of 'common concern for humankind', a principle contained within international environmental law.[99] She argues that the value of this approach is the two core implications for the status of 'common concern': first, that the issue is deemed as a transnational issue, and therefore outside of the exclusive sphere of domestic sovereignty of any one state; and secondly that is imposes a common responsibility for assistance and protection.[100] It is necessary to look to environmental law for such a principle, as this sense of extraterritorial obligation is rarely found elsewhere in international law, as Tigerstrom herself acknowledges.[101]

While the approach to human security as a common concern for humankind could potentially be of great value to approaching the relationship between human security and international law, it cannot do so without acknowledging the two intersecting principles of human security that Tigerstrom neglects, that is the integrative dimensions discussed above, and the next topic of attention, the principle of prevention.

D Preventative dimension

'Human security is easier to ensure through early prevention than later intervention. It is less costly to meet these threats upstream than downstream.'[102] Thus at the core of the comprehensive vision of human security is the identification and redress of the root causes of human insecurity. This is yet another justification for the broad approach to human security; even if forms of structural violence are not

97 *Charter of the United Nations*, arts 1(3) and 56; *Declaration on Principles of International Law Concerning Friendly Relations and Cooperation Among States in Accordance with the Charter of the United Nations*, GA Res 2625 (XXV) UN GAOR, Twenty-fifth sess, Agenda item 85, UN Doc A/RES/25/2625 (24 October 1970).

98 *Declaration on Principles of International Law Concerning Friendly Relations*, UN Doc A/RES/25/2625.

99 Barbara von Tigerstrom, *Human Security and International Law: Prospects and Problems* (Hart Publishing, 2007) 80–2.

100 Ibid 82.

101 Ibid 83–4.

102 United Nations Development Programme (UNDP), *Human Development Report 1994* (UNDP, 1994) 23.

regarded as themselves human security threats, social inequality, poverty, environmental degradation, pandemics and the like are all triggers of social unrest, and can lead to the more traditional security concerns.

(i) Addressing international law's characterisation as a discipline of crisis

The preventative dimension of human security is something that offers enormous transformative potential to international law, which has traditionally been largely reactive in nature. In describing the nature of international law as a discipline, Gerry Simpson observes that '[b]y the time we have put some distance between ourselves and a particular human tragedy, we have moved on to the next "international incident". This is a discipline that leaves you jet lagged, breathless and numb'.[103] A result of this is that a 'crisis orientation of our discipline promotes a narrow agenda for international law.'[104] Such an orientation offers little attention to the bigger picture, or the politics and realities of everyday life. Problems of structural violence, long-term trends and the details of complex contexts are often overlooked as a result.[105]

> A concern with crises skews the discipline of international law. Through regarding 'crises' as its bread and butter and the engine of progressive development of international law, international law becomes simply a source of justification for the status quo … One way forward is to refocus international law on issues of structural justice that underpin everyday life.[106]

Human security seeks to explore causal links – the bigger picture – and build a normative framework for situations of crisis that challenges the traditional notion of crisis, while retaining the sense of urgency that justifies a call to action. Moreover, human security is about how the international community responds to threats. From a human security perspective, the aim is not just political stability; it encompasses a notion of justice and sustainability.[107]

(ii) First, do no harm

While cataloguing the largest challenges to the implementation of a human security approach, Tadjbakhsh concludes that '[i]n the final analysis, human security is about not doing harm.' This should be the cornerstone of the human security–international law nexus.[108]

103 Gerry Simpson, cited in Hilary Charlesworth, 'International Law: A Discipline of Crisis' (2002) 65(3) *Modern Law Review* 377, 384.
104 Ibid 386.
105 Ibid 389.
106 Ibid 390.
107 Mary Kaldor, Mary Martin and Sabine Selchow, 'Human Security: A New Strategic Narrative for Europe' (2007) 83(2) *International Affairs* 273, 279.
108 Shahrbanou Tadjbakhsh, 'Human Security: The Seven Challenges of Operationalizing the Concept' (Speech delivered at the Human Security: 60 Minutes to Convince, Paris, France, 13 September 2005).

> It should therefore be used as a measuring rod against which aid and interventions are assessed for their impacts on the lives of people. Human security provides the framework to assess both the positive and the negative impacts of relief or developmental interventions and their secondary effect and externalities.[109]

This is an important message of significant value for international law. Interventions in the affairs of other states can in certain circumstances be justified – such as when the R2P is invoked, as discussed above.[110] But the impact of such intervention must be carefully considered. The international community has already learned that sanctions can have unintended detrimental side-effects on the people they seek to protect.[111] This is the minimum threshold for human security. Real engagement needs to go further. Introducing structural change, but while 'not doing harm', would be a useful first step by means of which international law could engage more constructively with human security discourse.

III The broad conceptualisation of human security

The emphasis of the *Human Development Report* introducing the concept of human security was on the role of underdevelopment and poverty as root causes of human insecurity.[112] This is, however, just one of an increasing cacophony of definitions that have emerged in relation to human security, in both academic circles and policy-making circles at the international and domestic levels. The UNDP in its seminal discussion of human security did not in fact work to define human security, as Frerks points out.[113] Instead, the focus of that report was to circumscribe rather than define the notion.[114] While the definitions are diverse, the proponents of human security have been polarised into two general groups: those supporting a broad theory of human security as framed originally by the UNDP (or more recently by the Commission on Human Security), and those advocating a narrow approach, retaining the people-centred focus of human security, but confining itself to direct threats of personal violence and

109 Ibid.

110 International Commission on Intervention and State Sovereignty (ICISS), *The Responsibility to Protect* (International Development Research Centre, December 2001).

111 See, eg, United Nations Inter-Agency Standing Committee, *Sanctions Assessment Handbook: Assessing the Humanitarian Implications of Sanctions,* (OCHA, October 2004); *Making Targeted Sanctions More Effective: Guidelines for the Implementation of UN Policy Options,* Final Report of the Stockholm Process on the Implementation of Targeted Sanctions, (Department of Peace and Conflict Research, Uppsala University, February 2003).

112 United Nations Development Programme (UNDP), *Human Development Report 1994* (UNDP, 1994).

113 Georg Frerks, 'Human Security as a Discourse and Counter-Discourse' (2008) 19(1) *Security & Human Rights* 8, 12.

114 Ibid.

conflict.[115] The final section of this chapter engages with this debate, because uncertainty about the content and role of human security discourse may contribute to the lack of engagement by legal minds, and it is important to be clear about how the principles discussed above should be mobilised for the benefit of promoting human security.

A The broad conceptualisation of human security

While the United Nations Development Programme (UNDP) discussion of human security, first introduced in 1994,[116] remains the starting point for most analysis of human security, a major rift has developed among proponents of human security regarding the appropriate and most effective definition of the concept. In its original conceptualisation, the UNDP definition of human security was formulated to correspond to the rights of individuals in the forms of 'freedom from fear' and 'freedom from want'.[117] From a legal perspective there are a range of reasons why the narrow approach to human security might be preferred, which are explored below.[118] However, as the discussion in this section will show, the advantages of adopting a narrow perspective of human security are outweighed by normative, ethical, and pragmatic considerations.

Moreover, many of the definitional challenges for human security are really those that are paralleled in the broader discourse of security generally, something that is rarely appreciated. Thus many of the criticisms of human security as ill-defined, or alternatively, having too many competing definitions, are merely mirrors of the bigger challenges of defining security as discussed in Chapter Two. Nonetheless, as will be seen, there are some valid criticisms that emerge in relation to human security. However, as will also be explored, these do not work to undermine human security as a valid discourse, but merely demonstrate future directions within which the discourse must begin to move. The critiques of human security will be explored, with the general criticism combined with critiques of the broad approach, as it is the broad approach that is most specifically targeted in criticism of the discourse. These critiques are clearly closely related to the potential concerns of international legal scholarship in relation to the discourse. Again however, it must emphasised that legal scholars need to put voice to these concerns rather than ignore the discourse entirely.

115 On the classification of the divide, see, eg, Taylor Owen, 'Human Security – Conflict, Critique and Consensus: Colloquium Remarks and a Proposal for a Threshold-Based Definition' (2004) 35(3) *Security Dialogue* 373; David Roberts, 'Empowering the Human Security Debate: Making It Coherent and Meaningful' (2005) XXII(4) *International Journal on World Peace* 3; David Roberts, 'Human Security or Human Insecurity? Moving the Debate Forward' [249] (2006) 37 *Security Dialogue* 249.

116 United Nations Development Programme (UNDP), *Human Development Report 1994* (UNDP, 1994) 46–8.

117 Ibid 47–8.

118 See III.C Narrow approach to human security, below.

The broad conceptual approach to human security belongs not only to the UNDP, and the UN agencies which have since reflected this approach, but is also captured by the definitions of human security by the Japanese government,[119] and a wide host of academics. The broad approach seeks to treat human insecurity as a holistic problem, facing a wide range of potential threats. As Ewan puts it, human security seeks to break down the distinction between 'high' and 'low' politics, a distinction that has traditionally privileged the direct violence of armed conflict over broader forms of violence, including structural violence.[120] As Booth asks,

> Why should certain issues – human rights, economic justice, and so on – be kept off the security agenda? They are, after all, crucial security questions for somebody, if not for those benefiting from statist power structures.[121]

As discussed in the previous chapter, this then encompasses concerns of structural violence, as conceived by Galtung.[122] The justification for a broad approach to human security is well captured by the former Director-General of the Foreign Ministry of Japan, Yukio Takaso:

> Human security is a much broader concept. We believe that freedom from want is no less critical than freedom from fear. So long as its objectives are to ensure the survival and dignity of individuals as human beings, it is necessary to go beyond thinking of human security solely in terms of protecting human life in conflict situations.[123]

James and other authors explain the rationale of a broad approach to human security. Recognising a broad range of potential threats allows an acknowledgement of how insecurities are dynamic and interactive.[124] It also highlights the fact that the aspects of security are complex and multidimensional. The broad, holistic approach to human security thus creates the possibility for integrated

119 Although it should be noted that the Japanese approach focuses almost exclusively on the 'freedom from want' dimensions of human security, rather than the more properly stated broad approach of incorporating 'freedom from want', 'freedom from fear' and 'freedom from indignity'.

120 Pauline Ewan, 'Deepening the Human Security Debate: Beyond the Politics of Conceptual Clarification' (2007) 27(3) *Politics* 182, 182.

121 Ken Booth, 'Security and Self: Reflections of a Fallen Realist' in Keith Krause and Michael Williams (eds), *Critical Security Studies: Concepts and Cases* (UCL Press, 1997) 83, 111.

122 Johan Galtung, 'Violence, Peace and Peace Research' (1969) 6 *Journal of Peace Research* 170, 171.

123 Yukio Takaso, Director-General, Foreign Ministry of Japan, Statement at the International Conference on Human Security in a Globalised World (8 May 2000), cited in Sung Won Kim, 'Human Security with an Asian Face?' (2010) 17 *Indiana Journal of Global Legal Studies* 83, 92.

124 Stephen James, 'Human Security: Key Drivers, Antecedents and Conceptualisation' (Working Paper No 1, Institute for Human Security, La Trobe University, 2010) 5–6.

policy action, and for systematic comparisons of prioritisations across policy spheres and policy levels.[125] As noted in Chapter Two, human security is also more attuned to the costs incurred at the policy level, and Oquist argues that it permits greater sensitivity in the trade-offs between policy priorities.[126] It also provides a framework in which the comparative advantage of various players can be assessed and capitalised on, as noted by Alkire.[127]

Kerr argues that broadly defined human security can be justified on normative, utilitarian and consequentialist grounds.[128] Recognising poverty and social inequalities in developing countries requires the urgent attention that the security label can provide. Furthermore, using the security label is a recognition that poverty and inequality are among the root causes of conflict and the more traditionally labelled security concerns. An empirical assessment also supports the broader approach to human security – as highlighted by Thomas, it is estimated that the total number of people killed by World War One and World War Two was around 30 million. The estimated number of people who currently die of hunger-related causes each year is approximately 15 million. Thus just two years of hunger reach the equivalent casualty rate of eleven years of world war.[129]

B Critiques of the broad conceptualisation of human security

Proponents of the narrow approach to human security argue that it is necessary to limit the definition for pragmatic reasons.[130] They view the broad definition as too unworkable, vague and unquantifiable in relating threats and vulnerabilities to security-based criteria. The narrow view, with its attention to physical violence, is considered by these theorists to be more practical. The arguments of both critics of human security generally and the proponents of the narrow view will be categorised into four general topics for discussion: (i) conceptual clarity; (ii) analytical rigour; (iii) policy utility/implementation challenges; and (iv) the capture and instrumentalisation of human security.

(i) Conceptual clarity

The primary critique raised of human security is that the broad conceptualisation makes the concept vague, hollow and unworkable. Conceptual criticisms relate to

125 Paul Oquist, 'Basic Elements of a Policy Framework for Human Security' in Moufida Goucha and John Crowley (eds), *Rethinking Human Security* (Wiley-Blackwell, 2008) 101, 112.
126 Ibid.
127 Sabine Alkire, 'A Conceptual Framework for Human Security' (Working Paper No 2, Centre for Research on Inequality, Human Security and Ethnicity [CRISE] 2003) 3.
128 Pauline Kerr, 'The Evolving Dialectic between State-Centric and Human-Centric Security' (Working Paper No 2003/2, Australian National University, 2003) 10.
129 Caroline Thomas, 'Global Governance, Development and Human Security: Exploring the Links' (2001) 22(2) *Third World Quarterly* 150, 163–4.
130 The starting point for critique of human security remains Roland Paris, 'Human Security: Paradigm Shift or Hot Air?' (2001) 26(2) *International Security* 87.

two broad fields of concern. On the one hand, there are concerns as to the 'grand theory' nature of human security.[131] The concern is that if insecurity embraces all forms of harm, the term will cease to have any descriptive power. Human security is then reduced to a shopping list of 'bad things that happen', according to Krause.[132] Others argue similarly that in trying to explain everything, human security ultimately explains nothing.[133] A related concern is the open-ended definitions of human security that are contextually based.[134] Academics such as Roland Paris condemn such open-endedness as 'emptily conclud[ing] … that the content of human security really is in the eye of the beholder'.[135] This broadness has particular implications for international law. To function, law should not be vague, inconstant or impossible to be fulfilled.[136]

Proponents of the broad approach to human security respond to these critiques in a variety of ways and are equally scathing of narrow approaches to human security. Thakur acknowledges that the broad approach 'sacrifices precision for inclusiveness'.[137] But this lack of precision is necessary, as the expansion of security to focusing on the individual inherently requires attention to be given to a wider range of threats.[138] This argument is perhaps put best by Newman:

> The reality is that, by far, the biggest killers in the world are extreme poverty, preventable disease and the consequences of pollution. According to this approach, any conception of security which neglects this reality is conceptually, empirically and ethically inadequate.[139]

In other words, the narrow approach to human security renders the entire concept of security meaningless if it does not aim to protect human life and dignity (which are endangered by a range of threats, not merely direct violence). King and Murray likewise acknowledge the imprecision of the broad approach, but advocate human security as an 'organising' concept or principle, which is forward-looking in

131 Shahrbanou Tadjbakhsh and Anuradha M Chenoy, *Human Security: Concepts and Implications* (Routledge, 2007) 60.
132 Keith Krause, 'The Key to a Powerful Agenda, If Properly Defined' (2004) 35 *Security Dialogue* 367, 367.
133 Andrew Mack, 'A Signifier of Shared Values' (2004) 35 *Security Dialogue* 365, 366. See also, Barry Buzan, 'Human Security in International Perspective' (Paper presented at the 14th Asia-Pacific Roundtable, Kuala Lumpur, Malaysia, 3–7 June 2000); Roland Paris, 'Human Security: Paradigm Shift or Hot Air?' (2001) 26(2) *International Security* 87.
134 For example, the definition adopted by the UN Commission on Human Security, *Human Security Now* (United Nations, 2003).
135 Roland Paris, 'Still an Inscrutable Concept' (2004) 35(3) *Security Dialogue* 370, 371.
136 See, eg, Lon L Fuller, *The Morality of Law* (Yale University Press, revised edition, 1969).
137 Ramesh Thakur, 'A Political Worldview' (2004) 35 *Security Dialogue* 347, 347.
138 Ibid.
139 Edward Newman, 'Critical Human Security Studies' (2010) 36 *Review of International Studies* 77, 80.

nature.[140] A better way to approach this may be the acknowledgment of human security as a discourse, one that seeks to explore the interconnections between the threats to people, interconnections that can only be understood by taking a broad approach to the threats that people face.

Many other proponents of the broad approach argue that the very appeal of human security lies in its vagueness. Scholars such as Grayson and Acharya argue that the broad-based concept opens the way to progressive and dynamic responses to security problems.[141] Similarly, Winslow and Hylland Eriksen bring an anthropological perspective to the issue, arguing for the importance of a concept that can develop over time and space, and that can draw on cross-cultural perspectives. They point out that concepts that are intuitively understood but difficult to pin down scientifically are not uncommon to the social sciences, and therefore a lack of clarity on the definition of human security does not invalidate the concept.[142] Thus they question equating conceptual clarity with conceptual utility. From the political and legal perspective, many other concepts could be mentioned to demonstrate this point – ranging from the 'state', 'democracy', 'development' and, of course, 'law', all of which present conceptual challenges and yet whose value *as concepts* is undisputed. A related point is made by Hubert, who describes human security as a concept that works in practice but not in theory, and argues that even if the definition is not clear, this does not, and has not prevented the concept from producing results.[143]

Peter Uvin argues that the concept of human security resembles a 'process definition', and therefore that the importance of the concept is its flexibility about specific aims in light of context and temporality, focusing instead on the sort of policy and mindset changes that are necessary, rather than a concretised definition of security.[144] Many others also make the point that human security must be viewed as relative, so as to be meaningful to different communities and within different contexts. Alkire, for example, argues that the generality of the concept is a virtue, allowing for local interpretation and application, and accommodating the different policies and resources of the implementing body.[145] Another argument, made by Grayson, is that the act of defining is in itself an act of hegemonic discourse, and human security's lack of structured definition is not a weakness but a refusal 'to succumb to the political trappings of the discipline's definitional

140 Gary King and Christopher Murray, 'Rethinking Human Security' (2001) 116(4) *Political Science Quarterly* 585, 606.

141 Kyle Grayson, 'A Challenge to the Power over Knowledge of Traditional Security Studies' (2004) 35 *Security Dialogue* 357. See also Amitav Acharya, 'A Holistic Paradigm' (2004) 35 *Security Dialogue* 355, 355.

142 Drawing on 'culture' as an example, Donna Winslow and Thomas Hylland Eriksen, 'A Broad Concept that Encourages Interdisciplinary Thinking' (2004) 35 *Security Dialogue* 361, 362.

143 Don Hubert, 'An Idea that Works in Practice' (2004) 35 *Security Dialogue* 351, 351.

144 Peter Uvin, 'A Field of Overlaps and Interactions' (2004) 35 *Security Dialogue* 352, 352.

145 Sabine Alkire, 'A Conceptual Framework for Human Security' (Working Paper No 2, Centre for Research on Inequality, Human Security and Ethnicity (CRISE) 2003) 10.

project'.[146] This argument also ties into concerns about analytical rigour, as Hubert's position is that human security's unstructured nature ensures it is free of analytical prejudices.[147]

Thus, from a legal perspective, certainty is not needed in the form of the concept itself. After all, concepts such as justice and sustainable development are equally broad, without losing their relevance to legal culture. What makes those concepts work, however, and what human security arguably lacks are clear principles to guide the development, interpretation, and application of law and policy. Of course, the human element of discretion in applying the concept of human security remains. This is an inherently political element that remains open to abuse or misinterpretation. But this is true of any concept, norm or principle. Furthermore, as Lon Fuller points out,

> if the human element is a possible source of failure, it is also an indispensable ingredient in any just and humane legal system.... The complex undertaking we call 'law' requires at every turn the exercise of judgment, and that judgment must be exercised by human beings *for human beings*.[148]

With the development of clear principles, rooted in international legal norms, human security can act as a framework against which rules, standards and behaviour can be evaluated, against a backdrop of a developing common vocabulary and a set of shared values. While abuse is possible, it is engagement with international law and more precisely international legal norms and processes that will reduce this possibility.

(ii) Analytical rigour

Another common criticism made of the broad approach to human security, one closely related to concerns about conceptual clarity, is that the vagaries of the concept make it unworkable from the analytical perspective of the academic community. One argument made in this regard relates to the inability of the broad approach to generate a clear research agenda.[149] Newman describes human security as a concept that is 'normatively attractive but analytically weak.'[150] Newman's point is that human security has lacked a critical academic focus, being primarily policy-oriented.[151] Others argue that being so broad and requiring interdisciplinary study makes it unattractive from the analytical perspective as it

146 Kyle Grayson, 'A Challenge to the Power over Knowledge of Traditional Security Studies' (2004) 35 *Security Dialogue* 357, 357.

147 Don Hubert, 'An Idea that Works in Practice' (2004) 35 *Security Dialogue* 351, 351.

148 Lon L Fuller, *Anatomy of the Law* (Penguin, 1969) 59, emphasis added.

149 Roland Paris, 'Rational and Irrational Approaches to Human Security: A Reply to Ralph Pettman' (2005) 18(3) *Cambridge Review of International Affairs* 479, 481.

150 Edward Newman, 'A Normatively Attractive but Analytically Weak Concept' (2004) 35 *Security Dialogue* 358.

151 Ibid.

cannot produce clear results. A related concern is that the vague definition undermines appreciation of causal relationships. For example, Paris argues that 'it is impractical to talk about factors "causing" an increase of decline in human security, given that these factors are themselves part of the definition of human security'.[152] It is commonly argued that variables need independent examination to be understood, and that the broad conceptualisation of human security undermines this by conflating and confusing the issues.[153] Mack, for example, recognises that issues of war, poverty and bad governance are interconnected, but argues that they must be treated separately for the purposes of analysis.[154]

Many of the counter-arguments made by broad-approach proponents regarding the lack of conceptual clarity are also relevant to arguments of analytical weakness. Edward Newman, while critical of the vagaries of the definition of human security, acknowledges that the concept has stimulated new lines of inquiry in security discourse, ranging from the relationship between the individual and the state and the nature of state sovereignty to fundamental questions about the division of power in society, the role of human agency and the continued relevance of existing social and political structures.[155] Stimulating debate and rethinking traditionally accepted paradigms gives human security an inherent analytical value that should not be underestimated.

Many scholars stress that the analytical value lies in the very thing to which critics object, namely, that human security not only encourages, but requires interdisciplinary thinking.[156] They point out that as the threats facing the world are increasingly pluralistic and interconnected, research and policy should respond in kind.[157] Peter Uvin emphasises that lack of interdisciplinary study and intersectoral policy work is leading not only to redundancies in studies and programming, but actually proving counter-productive to finding practical solutions to global problems.[158] Owen highlights the analytical freedom that human security offers: any variable can be studied as an independent or dependent variable, since

152 Roland Paris, 'Human Security: Paradigm Shift or Hot Air?' (2001) 26(2) *International Security* 87, 93.
153 See, eg, Andrew Mack, 'A Signifier of Shared Values' (2004) 35 *Security Dialogue* 365; S Neil MacFarlane and Yuen Foong Khong, *Human Security and the UN: A Critical History* (Indiana University Press, 2006) 240–2; Keith Krause, 'Towards a Practical Human Security Agenda' (Policy Paper No 26, Geneva Centre for the Democratic Control of Armed Forces (DCAF), 2007) 5.
154 Andrew Mack, 'A Signifier of Shared Values' (2004) 35 *Security Dialogue* 365, 367.
155 Edward Newman, 'A Normatively Attractive but Analytically Weak Concept' (2004) 35 *Security Dialogue* 358, 359.
156 See, eg, Donna Winslow and Thomas Hylland Eriksen, 'A Broad Concept that Encourages Interdisciplinary Thinking' (2004) 35 *Security Dialogue* 361.
157 Caroline Thomas, 'A Bridge Between the Interconnected Challenges Confronting the World' (2004) 35 *Security Dialogue* 353; Shahrbanou Tadjbakhsh and Anuradha M Chenoy, *Human Security: Concepts and Implications* (Routledge, 2007); Fen Olser Hampson, 'A Concept in Need of a Global Policy Response' (2004) 35 *Security Dialogue* 349.
158 Peter Uvin, 'A Field of Overlaps and Interactions' (2004) 35 *Security Dialogue* 352, 353.

the interconnected nature of threats makes them both cause and consequence of insecurity.[159] The broader concern about human security conflating variables by including them all within the definition can also be overcome, at least in part, by appreciating human security as a discourse rather than as a concept. Thus, as a discourse, it is the focus on understanding the relationships between the variables that is more important for human security to be meaningful from an analytical standpoint. While Paris does not take his discussion in this direction, he does at least acknowledge human security's potential value as a *category of research.*[160] However, in casting human security as a taxonomical label of research, he argues that this label would then presuppose no normative agenda.[161] Given that much of the value of human security lies in its normative force, treating human security as a discourse, rather than a category of research, is to be preferred.

Newman's general argument about the underdevelopment of human security as an analytical discourse does nevertheless have merit. Much like the realists who preceded them, very few of those undertaking human security scholarship have engaged seriously with the question of what security actually means. Furthermore, though increasing in numbers, very few have analysed human security within the broader context of security studies. Newman argues that the reason for this neglect of analytical rigour is to keep human security accessible to the policy community. Over-attention to the theory might come at the cost of alienating the policy makers who are seeking real-world 'problem-solving' in the form of human security.[162] Human security as a result has become the poor cousin to critical security studies in academic circles, or critical security studies-*lite*, as Newman puts it. While there is merit in this criticism, it does not render human security meaningless. Instead it highlights the necessary future direction of human security, that is, engaging more with the body of security studies more generally, so as to ensure that the discourse has both theoretical and practical merit.

Again, from a legal perspective, the development of discrete principles attached to the discourse would help alleviate at least some concerns of analysis, by providing a clearer framework for analysis and application. Sustainable development shares many of the same basic issues as human security both in terms of the nebulous nature of the concept and in challenges for effective analysis. But sustainable development has developed a rich body of legal literature as a result of the substantive evolution of a clear set of principles through which to realise the concept.[163]

159 Taylor Owen, 'Human Security – Conflict, Critique and Consensus: Colloquium Remarks and a Proposal for a Threshold-Based Definition' (2004) 35(3) *Security Dialogue* 373, 380.

160 Roland Paris, 'Human Security: Paradigm Shift or Hot Air?' (2001) 26(2) *International Security* 87, 96–7.

161 Ibid, 97.

162 Edward Newman, 'Critical Human Security Studies' (2010) 36 *Review of International Studies* 77, 89–90.

163 Principles such as inter- and intra-generational equity, common but differentiated responsibilities, the precautionary principle, polluter pays principle, etc.

(iii) Policy utility and implementation challenges

The third major critique of the broad approach relates to its policy utility. With respect to this issue, it is argued that while there may be normative value to a broad approach, it is simply infeasible and incapable of producing quantitative results.[164] Further arguments are made that the economic and social concerns of the broad view of human security are already addressed by human development strategies, and that human security offers nothing new to the existing processes.[165] MacFarlane argues that broad human security entails the relabelling of human development as security to secure a larger share of public resources, and that even if there is normative value in that argument, it has not produced results.[166]

The final criticism of broad conceptualisations of human security is rooted in the nature of security studies. Securitisation is about priorities, and by prioritising everything, human security makes it impossible for anything to be actually prioritised.[167] Thus human security renders the entire enterprise of security and security studies meaningless, nullifying the potential effects of a security approach. Furthermore, the securitisation of what have been traditionally known as 'soft' issues draws resources and urgency away from traditional security issues and makes the broad approach impractical.[168]

A number of academics point to the overstatement of the value and usefulness of quantitative results.[169] These authors point out that security might be better assessed by perception of gravity rather than objective indicators,[170] and that such measures must be contextually specific.[171] Grayson in particular is critical of approaches that seek to reduce human security to a science. He asks: what of those (in)securities that cannot be readily quantified?[172] Moreover, the 'impulse to quantify' changes our perception of what is being analysed, '[b]ody counts,

164 See, eg, Roland Paris 'Human Security: Paradigm Shift or Hot Air?' 26(2) *International Security* 87.

165 Yuen Foong Khong, 'Human Security: A Shotgun Approach to Alleviating Human Misery?' (2001) 7 *Global Governance* 231.

166 S Neil MacFarlane, 'A Useful Concept that Risks Losing Its Political Salience' (2004) 35 *Security Dialogue* 368, 369.

167 Keith Krause, 'Towards a Practical Human Security Agenda' (Policy Paper No 26, Geneva Centre for the Democratic Control of Armed Forces (DCAF), 2007) 5.

168 Roland Paris, 'Rational and Irrational Approaches to Human Security: A Reply to Ralph Pettman' (2005) 18(3) *Cambridge Review of International Affairs* 479; Keith Krause, 'Towards a Practical Human Security Agenda' (Policy Paper No 26, Geneva Centre for the Democratic Control of Armed Forces (DCAF), 2007); S Neil MacFarlane and Yuen Foong Khong, *Human Security and the UN: A Critical History* (Indiana University Press, 2006) 237–40.

169 See also Owen's point discussed above on the analytical value of human security in examining variables.

170 Jennifer Leaning, 'Psychosocial Well-Being over Time' (2004) 35 *Security Dialogue* 354, 354.

171 Kanti Bajpai, 'An Expression of Threats Versus Capabilities Across Time and Space' (2004) 35 *Security Dialogue* 360, 361.

172 Kyle Grayson, 'Human Security as Power/Knowledge: The Biopolitics of a Definitional Debate' (2008) 21(3) *Cambridge Review of International Affairs* 383, 392.

generalised poverty models and epidemiological data may reveal the biological limits and distributions that define our species, but they remain silent on what makes us human(e).'[173]

Regarding concerns about prioritisation, it is possible to return to Uvin's process-based definition. Using a process-model of human security, priorities are made flexible and capable of being adapted to the particular needs of societies and communities. For Uvin, human security makes the establishment of hierarchies of priorities a discursive process among a range of actors based on the individual context of the situation. Grayson similarly argues that there is a fundamental misunderstanding in the arguments over the importance of concrete definitions in the policy-making process. He convincingly argues that '[d]efinitional malleability has great political utility' because it makes the narrowing or broadening of agendas easier to justify than would be possible with concretised definitions.[174]

As for the idea that human security is merely the relabelling of human development (or human rights) two responses may be made. The first, which will be outlined in more detail below, is that the interconnections between security, development and human rights justify a rethinking of these issues in terms of security.[175] Secondly, there is a large body of authoritative literature on the ways in which human security and human development interrelate but differ, and the Commission on Human Security's report in particular is informative in this regard. Human security is no more about putting the 'old wine' of human development in the 'new bottle' of human security than it is in relation to human rights, as mentioned above.

The distinction between human security and human development is perhaps best encapsulated by Amartya Sen. He describes human development as an expansionist concept, 'growth with equity', concerned with expanding human potential. Human security, by contrast, is concerned with 'downturns with security'. It is about creating insulation from crises and pervasive threats, and it focuses on those left behind by growth.[176] It provides safety nets, on the one hand, for when the crises occur, and it reduces the impact of those threats, by protecting human rights, establishing good governance and so forth. Human security is, in short, about creating a platform of minimum protection from which development can then be pursued. Kaldor similarly classes human security at the 'sharp end' or 'crisis end' of human rights and human development.[177] Gasper argues

173 Ibid 396.
174 Ibid 395.
175 Shahrbanou Tadjbakhsh and Anuradha M Chenoy, *Human Security: Concepts and Implications* (Routledge, 2007) 68.
176 UN Commission on Human Security, *Human Security Now* (United Nations, 2003) 8–9.
177 See, eg, Human Security Study Group, 'A European Way of Security' (The Madrid Report of the Human Security Study Group comprising a Proposal and Background Report 8 November 2007) 8. See also Mary Kaldor, Mary Martin and Sabine Selchow, 'Human Security: A New Strategic Narrative for Europe' (2007) 83(2) *International Affairs* 273, 278.

that human security attempts to combine 'human development's discourse's broad focus and stress on reasoned freedoms, basic human needs discourse's stress on prioritisation, and human rights' discourse's unwillingness to sacrifice anyone'.[178]

(iv) The capture and co-option of human security

Criticisms of human security are not only conceptual but also rooted in political concerns. The South has received the concept of human security with much scepticism. Of particular concern to members of the G77 is the fear that human security is a political tool to justify interventions and violations of their state sovereignty.[179] Moreover, they share specific concerns that human security could be used to impose further conditionality on aid that they receive.[180]

> For many G77 countries, human security is yet another ethnocentric paradigm that emphasises subjective aspects and values while reinforcing the economic might of the North, another attempt by the West to impose its liberal values and political institutions on non-Western societies.[181]

These concerns have manifested in a North–South divide in discussions of human security in the General Assembly of the UN.[182]

This is disappointing to advocates of human security, who view human security as the triumph of the South's interests because human security puts developmental-related concerns on an equal footing with the traditional (Northern) interests of state security.[183] Human security is an acceptance of the idea that human survival is multi-faceted and needs protection from a range of threats. This is reflected in the early documents pre-dating human security, such as the Brandt Report, issued by the International Commission on International Development Issues in 1980:

> Our Report is based on what appears to be the simplest common interest: that mankind [sic] wants to survive, and one might even add has the moral obligation to survive. This raises not only traditional questions of peace and war,

178 Des Gasper, 'Securing Humanity: Situating "Human Security" as Concept and Discourse' (2005) 6(2) *Journal of Human Development* 221, 233.

179 Shahrbanou Tadjbakhsh and Anuradha M Chenoy, *Human Security: Concepts and Implications* (Routledge, 2007) 35.

180 Ibid.

181 Ibid 36.

182 Such as in the informal thematic debates. Transcripts and recordings of the debates are located at UN Human Security Unit, Publications and Resources, <http://unocha.org/humansecurity/humansecurity/resources/publications-and-products/Human-Security-At-The-General-Assembly>.

183 See, eg, Shahrbanou Tadjbakhsh and Anuradha M Chenoy, *Human Security: Concepts and Implications* (Routledge, 2007) 35.

> but also how to overcome world hunger, mass misery, and alarming disparities between the living conditions of the rich and poor.[184]

Proponents of the human security paradigm call on the South to take up the mantle of human security advocacy as a means of challenging current priorities and of vindicating the economic and social rights of their people.[185] Mahbub ul-Haq, the architect of the original conception of human security presented by the UNDP, wanted to emphasise the potential of human security for the South.[186] He defined human security as a means for instituting a 'new partnership between the North and the South based on justice not on charity; on an equitable sharing of global market opportunities, not on aid; on two-way compacts, not one-way transfers; on mutual cooperation, not on unilateral conditionality or confrontation'.[187]

Beyond the South-centric concerns, there are broader concerns that as a result of its combined depth and vagueness, human security can be easily hijacked or manipulated to serve the self-interest of states or other actors,[188] a concern raised above. It is the use of the human security label by states that makes critical security studies inherently suspicious of the discourse, regardless of how those states employ the term. As Newman points out, the critical theorists fundamentally question existing structures and institutions of power, and the willingness of the proponents of human security to engage with those existing structures in the pursuit of results alienates the critical scholarship.[189]

> According to this critical line of reasoning, human security can never overcome its central paradox: it apparently calls for a critique of the structures and norms that produce human insecurity, yet the ontological starting point of most human security scholarship and its policy orientation reinforce these structures and norms.[190]

There is a measure of truth in this paradox. But human security's policy-oriented focus highlights the importance of strategies that can produce results. As such the philosophy of human security must, unless and until more fundamental structural

184 Independent Commission on International Development Issues, *North–South: A Program for Survival* (MIT Press, 1980) 13. Discussed in more detail in Chapter Five.

185 Shahrbanou Tadjbakhsh and Anuradha M Chenoy, *Human Security: Concepts and Implications* (Routledge, 2007) 38.

186 Ul Haq, 'Human Rights, Security and Governance', (1998) 3(2) *Peace and Policy Journal of the Toda Institute for Global Peace and Policy Research: Dialogue of Civilizations for World Citizenship*, 3(2), cited in ibid, 37.

187 Ibid.

188 Sverre Lodgaard, 'Human Security: Concept and Operationalization' (Paper prepared for Expert Seminar on Human Rights and Peace, Geneva, 8–9 December 2000) [26] <http://www.hsph.harvard.edu/hpcr/events/hsworkshop/lodgaard.pdf>.

189 Edward Newman, 'Critical Human Security Studies' (2010) 36 *Review of International Studies* 77, 88.

190 Ibid.

changes are made possible, remain one of changing the system from within. Moreover, as Newman points out, critical security studies' unwillingness even to engage with human security 'seems guilty of the sort of exclusionary analytical practices they claim exists in orthodox security studies.'[191] Critical security studies' own unwillingness to become involved in the same policy-relevant problem solving of human security shows a potential failing in, or at least limit of, the school itself, rather than a failing of the human security discourse. It highlights the importance of critical assessment of approaches taken in the name of human security, but does not convince as an argument to sacrifice human security on the ground that it is a servant of self-interest.

C Narrow approach to human security

In response to the limitations they perceive in the broad approach, proponents of the narrow view of human security see its practical utility if it is confined to forms of direct violence.[192] This approach is commonly referred to as the 'Canadian Approach' to human security, as it was first adopted as the approach of the Canadian government in pursuing human security. For Canada, human security comprised 'freedom from pervasive threats to people's rights, safety or lives', with pervasive threats construed narrowly.[193] Human security under a narrower view is concerned with 'violent' threats to human security, that is, direct forms of violence. The value of human security according to this approach lies in the recognition of the changing character of conflict and the willingness to treat internal forms of conflict and violence under the security mantle.

Given the choice of being broad and ideal, or narrow and operable, by focusing on violence – only a small component of human vulnerability – the Canadian government has clearly sided with pragmatism.[194]

One argument that has been put forward in justifying the narrow approach is that deliberate organised physical harm should be the sole focus of human security because it relates to notions of responsibility and human agency.[195] Bajpai, for example, suggests a 'focus on threats that can be traced back to identifiable human agents … not to structural … causes.'[196]

191 Ibid 91.
192 Andrew Mack, 'A Signifier of Shared Values' (2004) 35 *Security Dialogue* 365.
193 Cited in Roland Paris, 'Human Security: Paradigm Shift or Hot Air?' (2001) 26(2) *International Security* 87, 91.
194 P H Liotta and Taylor Owen, 'Why Human Security' (2006) 7 *Whitehead Journal of Diplomacy and International Relations* 37, 42.
195 See, eg, Morgan's concern that '[b]roadening security studies to cover other "harms" – economic environmental and so forth – is unfortunate for it lumps together deliberate, organised physical harm (or threats thereof) with other threats and pains': cited in Steve Smith, 'The Concept of Security in a Globalizing World' in Robert G Patman (ed) *Globalization and Conflict: National Security in a 'New' Strategic Era* (Routledge, 2006) 33, 45.
196 Cited in David Roberts, 'Empowering the Human Security Debate: Making It Coherent and Meaningful' (2005) XXII(4) *International Journal on World Peace* 3, 6.

From a legal perspective, much could be gained by preferring the narrow approach over the broad approach. The narrow approach offers far greater clarity and runs less of a risk than the broad approach of being perceived as 'vague, inconstant or impossible to be fulfilled'. It offers clear directional paths for legal discussion of human security, such as further developing the legal frameworks of peacebuilding, the protection of civilians in armed conflict, and the Responsibility to Protect. The narrow approach can also more easily find a place in the specialisations of international law, by primarily locating itself in international humanitarian law. There are, however, as will be shown, a number of fundamental problems with the narrow approach.

(i) Critique of the narrow approach to human security

The narrow approach rests on two problematic assumptions. The first assumption is that structural violence and the deprivation of economic, social and cultural rights are of less urgency or importance than the more direct and obvious forms of physical violence and the violation of civil and political rights. Whether at the core of the notion of security is survival,[197] or survival-plus (that is, the opportunity to make choices),[198] it stands to reason that structural violence and the devastating effects of poverty are no less a concern than direct forms of violence. As Mack notes, disease kills tens of millions of people a year while wars currently kill tens of thousands.[199] The proponents of the narrow approach make conceptual and analytical arguments in favour of their approach, but generally fail to provide a normative justification for why direct violence deserves priority. From a human rights perspective, these arguments return to a long-running debate relating to the relative importance of the civil and political rights on the one hand, and economic, social and cultural rights on the other. While this debate is far from resolved, it is increasingly reiterated that rights are indivisible and of equal importance.[200] Moreover, while emphasising a people-centred approach, the narrow vision largely reinforces the status quo of what are deemed acceptable security problems, ignoring what people actually perceive to be the most dangerous threats to their daily lives.[201]

197 The position, taken for example, by the Copenhagen School, a securities studies school of thought focused on notions of securitisation, propounded by Barry Buzan, Ole Wæver and Jaap de Wilde, *Security: A New Framework for Analysis* (Lynne Rienner Publications, 1998).

198 For a discussion see Chapter One.

199 Andrew Mack, 'A Signifier of Shared Values' (2004) 35 *Security Dialogue* 365, 367.

200 See, eg, *Vienna Declaration and Programme of Action: Report of the World Conference on Human Rights*, UN GAOR, UN Doc A/CONF.157/23 (25 June 1993). See also, Louise Doswald-Beck, 'Human Security: Can It Be Attained?' (2003) 97 *American Society International Legal Procedure* 93, 94.

201 Shahrbanou Tadjbakhsh, 'In Defense of the Broad View of Human Security' in Mary Martin and Taylor Owen (eds), *Routledge Handbook of Human Security* (Routledge, 2014) 43, 46.

The one normative argument that has been put forward in favour of the narrow approach is the argument that links direct violence with notions of responsibility and human agency. James points out that such a position underestimates the complex networks of human activity and responsibility that influence other kinds of crises.[202] He uses natural disasters as an example and points out that human agency has a significant role to play in the magnitude of such disasters. Deforestation can lead to desertification, uneven development and poor urban planning can increase vulnerabilities, and the poorest members of communities are the most exposed to environmental calamities. James uses Hurricane Katrina as a vivid demonstration of how unsustainable development, racism, poverty and governmental failings culminated in a 'natural' disaster far worse than just the storm system itself.[203] Roberts is also critical of the normative argument for the narrow approach, arguing that it ignores the role that human agency plays in the very creation of unequal structures, and in populating and reinforcing the structures with action and beliefs.[204]

The second assumption behind the narrow approach of human security is the idea that security from direct violence and armed conflict can be achieved without giving attention to economic and social concerns. This idea ignores the nexus of security and development, and between direct physical violence and other forms of harm, and the realities that demonstrate that to produce sustainable security, economic and social concerns cannot be ignored. It is important, however, to stress the complicated nature of the security–development nexus. Some academics point out that clear causal connections between underdevelopment and security have not been empirically proven.[205] There are, however, clear *indirect* causal links highlighted in a range of studies. In particular, *relative deprivation,* that is, structural inequalities in distribution of resources, has been demonstrated as a predictor for internal conflict and violence.[206] Likewise, underdevelopment is usually accompanied by, and contributes to, weak institutions, poor governance and lack of accountability, all of which are recognised triggers for conflict.[207] Rather than undermine the security–development nexus as a component of human security, the lack of clear causal links merely demonstrates the importance of taking into account the interconnections between threats, and looking at the whole picture of contributing factors to human insecurity. Moreover, even when

202 Stephen James, 'Human Security: Key Drivers, Antecedents and Conceptualisation' (Working Paper No 1, Institute for Human Security, La Trobe University, 2010), 13.

203 Ibid.

204 David Roberts, 'Empowering the Human Security Debate: Making It Coherent and Meaningful' (2005) XXII(4) *International Journal on World Peace* 3, 6.

205 See, eg, Charles Saliba-Couture, 'The Security–Development Nexus: From Obviousness to Ambiguity' (Paper presented at the International Studies Association Annual Conference Global Governance: Political Authority in Transition, Montreal, Canada, 16 March 2011) <http://www.allacademic.com/meta/p502091_index.html>.

206 For a survey of the relevant literature and data see World Bank Conflict Crime and Violence Team, *Making Societies More Resilient to Violence: A Conceptual Framework for the Conflict, Crime And Violence Agenda* (World Bank, 2008) 2, fn 6.

207 Ibid 2.

structural inequalities are not the direct causes of crises, they are nonetheless contributing factors to a community's or individual's *vulnerability* to that crisis. The inequality will serve to limit the capacity of the person or society to respond and cope with the crisis, and the inequality itself will be further exacerbated by the crisis as well.[208]

Thus while the threats of structural violence are important in their own right, and while their resolution is vital for the protection of the well-being of individuals affected by such behaviour, the threats of physical and structural violence are closely interrelated and should be treated as such. Acknowledging the nexus is vital if effective policy making is to occur. It is important, however, not to put too much emphasis on these arguments at the cost of the earlier argument that non-traditional threats to security are of equal importance. There is the risk of making economic and social concerns an instrumentality of conflict and losing sight of the intrinsic value of human dignity in the form of economic and social rights, and the fact that concerns such as the effects of the HIV/AIDS pandemic or poverty are themselves forms of insecurity, and not merely contributing factors to insecurity, in a more traditional sense.

D The benefits of the debate

While some argue that the rupture of human security into two competing schools of thought paralyses or negates the value of human security,[209] others see the debate as a fruitful exercise in exploring and challenging our conception of security. Ewan, for example, argues that

> calls to delimit human security on analytical and policy grounds often rest on positivist assumptions that obscure the ethico-political implications of conceptual choices about security. Decisions about what counts as 'security' raise profoundly political concerns that cannot be resolved through greater methodological rigour or conceptual clarification.[210]

The debate on the scope of human security has also produced beneficial results for the concept. The broad perspective has been forced to become far more critical and precise in its arguments for how to achieve security without losing the benefits of its breadth, or in making normative judgments on what is appropriately viewed as a threat. What has been produced as a result is a threshold approach to human security, in terms of which threats are not limited by reference to their type but rather by reference to their impact. This approach was briefly introduced in

208 See, eg, Mary Kaldor, Mary Martin and Sabine Selchow, 'Human Security: A New Strategic Narrative for Europe' (2007) 83(2) *International Affairs* 273, 281.

209 See, eg, Georg Frerks, 'Human Security as a Discourse and Counter-Discourse' (2008) 19(1) *Security & Human Rights* 8, 12.

210 Pauline Ewan, 'Deepening the Human Security Debate: Beyond the Politics of Conceptual Clarification' (2007) 27(3) *Politics* 182, 183.

Chapter One. Taylor Owen has been a significant contributor to this approach and describes its value thus:

> A threshold-based conceptualization, one that limits threats by their severity rather than their cause, allows all possible harms to be considered, but selectively limits those that at any time are prioritized with the security level.[211]

Other academics have also taken up the threshold approach and offer possible tests for determining when a threat becomes a human security issue. Renner argues that the test is 'whether the well-being and integrity of society are so compromised that they lead to possibly prolonged periods of instability and mass suffering.'[212] Thakur and Newman, on the other hand, argue that issues become security concerns when they 'undermine and diminish the survival chances' of a large number of people, or agreeing with Renner, when the stability and integrity of the society is threatened.[213] That approach is heavily limited, however, to a rather narrow vision of security. A focus on survival chances ignores threats to the quality, and not just quantity, of life as security issues. Ullman's treatment of threats as limits to policy choices seems more useful for human security, and Alkire's model while arguably too broad can also be a useful gauge of where the threshold of human security lies, as was discussed in Chapter One.

The challenges of such an approach are clear. While the approach has enormous potential, since it allows the concept to remain flexible without losing all meaning, and reconciles the two sides to the debate to some extent, where the threshold should be drawn is no easy matter and unlikely to be resolved with any form of widespread consensus. Nevertheless, the approach correctly makes the point that the issues of human security should be less about the prioritisation of competing goals for policy makers, and more about the identification of minimum levels of welfare, human dignity and considerations of humanity. For human security discourse to meaningfully contribute to international law, it is argued here that the broad approach must be adopted.

IV Conclusion

This chapter has explored the transformative potential of human security discourse. As mentioned in Chapter One, human security discourse emerged as it

211 Taylor Owen, 'Human Security – Conflict, Critique and Consensus: Colloquium Remarks and a Proposal for a Threshold-Based Definition' (2004) 35(3) *Security Dialogue* 373, 384. See also Taylor Owen, 'Human Security Thresholds' in Mary Martin and Taylor Owen (eds), *Routledge Handbook of Human Security* (Routledge, 2014) 58.

212 Michael Renner, 'Security Redefined' in Michael Renner (ed), *The State of the World 2005: Redefining Global Security* (Worldwatch Institute, 2005) 3, 5.

213 Ramesh Thakur and Edward Newman, 'Introduction: Non-Traditional Security in Asia' in Ramesh Thakur and Edward Newman (eds), *Broadening Asia's Security Discourse and Agenda: Political, Social and Environmental Perspectives* (United Nations University Press 2004) 1, 3.

became increasingly clear that traditional conceptualisations of security, sovereignty and state, and non-state actors no longer represented the way the world actually operates today. Human security discourse became a way to challenge the priorities and structuring of the international political canvas, and while not producing a revolution in the reordering of the international system, it has nonetheless provided a useful lens through which to critically assess the international political order and a framework for policy development. These same functions of human security discourse, as critical lens and normative framework, can provide the same benefits to the international legal system. Indeed, as has been seen, much of the change that human security wishes to produce is already occurring within international law, albeit in a fractured, ad hoc and sometimes inconsistent way. Human security discourse offers an overarching way to observe the interaction of these trends in international law and a normative and principled approach for suggesting future direction. However, it also has become clear that the conceptual division between broad and narrow approaches to human security highlighted in the previous chapter is playing out in the development of international law. To the extent that international law is moving towards compliance with and promotion of human security, it has done so predominantly only in relation to the narrow approach, keeping a focus firmly on traditional security threats such as armed conflict. This is perhaps demonstrated in the way in which the Responsibility to Protect, a child of human security discourse, has been operationalised. The narrow approach to human security is important. It shifts the focus of analysis from state interests to the human impact of direct violence. But it also greatly hinders the transformative capacity of human security discourse to expand what is meant by security, and to enlarge the role of the international community in response to the increasingly prevalent non-traditional threats. The next chapter examines the degree to which the interpretation of 'international peace and security' has developed, and whether human security, broadly understood, is accommodated within the perspective of international security architecture.

5 Human security discourse

An 'authoritative interpretation' of the UN Charter?

When we read the [UN] Charter today, we are more than ever conscious that its aim is to protect individual human beings, not to protect those who abuse them
– Kofi Annan[1]

I Introduction

In their seminal work on the sources of human rights in international law, Simma and Alston move beyond the traditional focus on Article 38 of the *Statute of the International Court of Justice*, and suggest an alternative approach for identifying human rights obligations.[2] They suggest that one way to form an understanding of human rights obligations independent of specific treaty obligations is to treat the *Universal Declaration of Human Rights* as an authoritative interpretation of Articles 55 and 56 of the UN Charter.[3] Moreover, they attach the definition of human rights to 'the virtually unanimous practice of the relevant organs of the United Nations'.[4] This is an interesting approach through which to view the related issues of human security, especially at a time when 'human security' is increasingly being mainstreamed into the policies and practices of the UN and its organs.

The International Court of Justice (ICJ) has acknowledged that interpretation of the Charter generally involves the traditional rules and principles of treaty interpretation:

1 Kofi Annan, 'Two Concepts of Sovereignty', *The Economist*, (London), 18 September 1999 <http://www.un.org/News/ossg/sg/stories/kaecon.html>.
2 Bruno Simma and Philip Alston, 'The Sources of Human Rights Law: Custom, Jus Cogens and General Principles' (1988–1989) 12 *Australian Yearbook of International Law* 82.
3 Ibid 100–2. They note that this approach has been undertaken by a number of respected authorities, including Louis B Sohn, 'The New International Law: Protection of the Rights of Individuals Rather Than States' (1982) 32 *American University Law Review* 1, 17; and Thomas Buergenthal, 'International Human Rights Law and Institutions: Accomplishments and Prospects' (1988) 63 *Washington Law Review* 1.
4 In support of this they point to a similar approach adopted by the Inter-American Court of Human Rights: *Interpretation of the American Declaration of the Rights and Duties of Man Within the Framework of Article 64 of the American Convention on Human Rights (Advisory Opinion)* (1990) 29 ILM 379, 389.

> On the previous occasions when the Court has had to interpret the Charter of the United Nations, it has followed the principles and rules applicable in general to the interpretation of treaties, since it has recognised that the Charter is a multilateral treaty, albeit a treaty having certain special characteristics.[5]

Article 5 of the *Vienna Convention on the Law of Treaties* explicitly states that the Convention is applicable 'to any treaty which is the constituent instrument of an international organization'.[6] An authoritative interpretation must therefore meet the conditions of treaty interpretation outlined in the Article 31 of the *Vienna Convention on the Law of Treaties*, which states

> 1. A treaty shall be interpreted in good faith in accordance with the ordinary meaning to be given to the terms of the treaty in their context and in the light of its object and purpose.[7]

It is of no small importance to assess the appropriate interpretation of the UN Charter, and to classify human security as an authoritative interpretation. After all, '[t]he power to interpret is the power to create law'.[8] With 'security' as a contested concept, as explored in Chapter Two, an 'ordinary meaning' of 'international peace and security' is not readily apparent. Furthermore, Brölmann argues that the 'object and purpose' is given special weight in interpretation of constitutive instruments.[9] In determining that interpretation, 'subsequent practice in the application of the treaty which establishes the agreement of the parties regarding its interpretation'[10] is to be taken into account. Indeed, this is also given special weight, according to Justice Lauterpacht:

5 *Certain Expenses of the United Nations (Article 17, paragraph 2, of the Charter)* (Advisory Opinion) [1962] ICJ Rep 151, 157.

6 *Vienna Convention on the Law of Treaties*, opened for signature 23 May 1969, 1155 UNTS 331 (entered into force 27 January 1980) art 5. Note, however, that the preceding Article 4 holds that the treaty's provisions are only applicable to treaties concluded after the *Vienna Convention* entered into force. This may not, however, be a serious bar to the application of the Convention to the UN Charter, given that it largely accepted to represent the codification of existing customary international law; see, eg, Blaine Sloan, 'The United Nations Charter as a Constitution' (1989) 1 *Pace International Law Review* 61, 116. On interpretation of the UN Charter generally, see also Oscar Schachter, 'United Nations Law' (1994) 88 *American Journal of International Law* 1; Constance Jean Schwindt, 'Interpreting the United Nations Charter: From Treaty to World Constitution' (2000) 6 *UC Davis Journal of International Law and Policy* 193; Carin Kahgan, 'Table of Content. Jus Cogens and the Inherent Right to Self Defence' (1997) 3 *ILSA Journal of International and Comparative Law* 767.

7 *Vienna Convention on the Law of Treaties*, art 31.

8 Oscar Schachter, 'United Nations Law' (1994) 88 *American Journal of International Law* 1, 6.

9 Catherine Brölmann, 'Specialized Rules of Treaty Interpretation: International Organizations' in Duncan B Hollis (ed) *The Oxford Guide to Treaties* (Oxford University Press, 2012) 507, 512.

10 *Vienna Convention on the Law of Treaties*, art 31(3)(b).

> A proper interpretation of a constitutional instrument must take into account not only the formal letter of the original instrument, but also its operation *in actual practice* and in light of revealed tendencies in the life of the Organization.[11]

This is a key point, given that it places more weight on the practices of the United Nations than on Member States, making the practice of UN where human security is increasingly being mainstreamed as central to the processes of interpretation.

This chapter examines whether human security could appropriately be considered an authoritative interpretation of 'international peace and security' within the UN Charter. It begins by examining the UN Charter through the lens of human security discourse, and through an analysis of how 'security' is used in the Charter. It then broadens this discussion to how security has been approached in other significant documents from the UN, and the degree to which human security principles can be identified within those documents. Finally, it examines the broadening interpretation of international peace and security, particularly under Article 39 of the UN Charter. As the Security Council holds the primary responsibility for the maintenance of international peace and security, its interpretation of 'security' is of central concern to how international peace and security should be understood by international law. The chapter thus finishes with an analysis of Security Council Resolutions, examining the degree to which the Council has formally expanded its understanding of its mandate and what constitutes a 'threat to peace'.

II Human security and the UN Charter

Human security not only complements but potentially unifies the overarching principles and goals established in the UN Charter. The Preamble to the UN Charter establishes the goals of the UN to promote and protect international peace and security; to promote economic and social progress and improve standards of living; and to promote justice, respect human dignity and reaffirm universal human rights.[12] Human security considers these goals to be interconnected and mutually reinforcing, and seeks to protect the core of these principles – to establish a safe and stable environment in which these goals can be fully realised.

> The UN Charter as the principal document in international law offers space for both the security and the human aspects of the concept – concern for security as a concept based on the sovereign state and concern for the fate of the individual human being.[13]

11 *Voting Procedures on Questions Relating to Reports and Petitions Concerning the Territory of South-West Africa* [1955] ICJ Rep 67, 106 (June 7) (Judge Lauterpacht) 106.

12 *Charter of the United Nations*, Preamble, art 1.

13 Gerd Oberleitner, 'Human Security: A Challenge to International Law?' (2005) 11 *Global Governance* 185, 191. See also Miltiadis Sarigiannidis, 'Legal Discourses on Peacemaking/Peacekeeping/Peacebuilding: International Law as a New Topos for Human Security' (2007) 62 *International Journal* 519, 524. Human security

Great emphasis is also placed on the opening wording of the UN Charter, 'We the peoples', which is a stark departure from the formalistic, state-centred opening of the League of Nations Covenant, 'The High Contracting Parties'. Thus:

> The opening words of the Charter, 'we the peoples' root 'the sovereign authority of the Member States, and thus the legitimacy of the Organisation which they were to compose, in the will of their peoples.[14]

In the General Assembly thematic debates on human security it was acknowledged that 'human security was characterised as a framework to further the principles of the UN Charter.'[15] A similar point was made by the UN High Level Panel on Threats, Challenges and Change, namely, that human security represented a point of convergence for the central aims and purposes of the United Nations.[16] Thus human security, like Article 1 of the UN Charter, pairs the objectives to 'maintain international peace and security' and to 'achieve international cooperation in solving international problems of an economic, social, cultural, or humanitarian character'. Likewise, Article 55, regarding the establishment of ECOSOC, states:

> With a view to the creation of conditions of stability and well-being *which are necessary for peaceful and friendly relations among nations* ... the United Nations shall promote:
>
> a Higher standards of living, full employment, and conditions of economic and social progress and development;
> b Solutions of international economic, social, health and related problems...; and
> c Universal respect for, and observance of, human rights and fundamental freedoms for all without distinction as to race, sex, language, or religion.[17]

On the other hand, however, such a reading of the UN Charter can only go so far. It is important to note that the structure of the organs of the UN created a very clear separation between issues of security, to be addressed by the Security Council, and the institutions charged with promoting and protecting the social

'encapsulates the UN Charter's Preamble and furnishes the notion of security in the realm of human rights international instruments'.

14 Boutros Boutros-Ghali, *An Agenda for Democratization* (United Nations 1996) 12. See also Tim Dunne and Nicholas J Wheeler, '"We the Peoples": Contending Discourses of Security in Human Rights Theory and Practice' in David Chandler and Nik Hynek (eds), *Critical Perspectives on Human Security: Rethinking Emancipation and Power in International Relations* (Routledge, 2011) 13.

15 The debates can be collectively located at UN Human Security Unit, Publications and Resources, <http://unocha.org/humansecurity/humansecurity/resources/publications-and-products/Human-Security-At-The-General-Assembly>.

16 UN High Level Panel on Threats, Challenges and Change, *A More Secure World* (UN, 2004) 11.

17 *Charter of the United Nations*, art 55, emphasis added.

progress and welfare of individuals, for example, ECOSOC.[18] Indeed it may be worth returning to the principles of interpretation at this stage and noting that the ICJ has held that

> The imperatives associated with the effective performance of its functions, as well as its own practice, are all elements which may deserve special attention when the time comes to interpret these constitutive treaties.[19]

However, the UN Secretary-General's Report on Human Security asserts that equal weight is given to each concern and, more importantly, that '[t]he indivisibility of security, development and human rights is also well articulated in the Charter'.[20]

A Security and the UN Charter

The maintenance of international peace and security is considered the essential 'Purpose' of the United Nations, as established in both the Preamble and Article 1.[21] The term 'international peace and security', which had its origins in the Covenant of the League of Nations, is littered throughout the Charter,[22] but the term 'international security' is used in isolation. This is an interesting fact, as the term peace and occasionally 'universal peace' are used separately within the Charter.[23]

The idea of security conceived in the United Nations Charter was indisputably state-centric. The principles of territorial integrity, political independence, sovereign equality, and non-interference in the internal affairs of sovereign states are the foundations of the international order developed under the UN, and are laid out in Article 2 of the Charter.[24] The collective security idea embedded in the UN

18 A discussion on this point is made by Charlotte Ku, 'Collective Security and the Personalization of Peace' in Steve Charnovitz, Debra P Steger and Peter Van Den Bossche (eds), *Law in the Service of Human Dignity* (Cambridge University Press, 2005) 336, 343.

19 *Legality of the Use by a State of Nuclear Weapons in Armed Conflict (Request by WHO)* (Advisory Opinion) [1996] ICJ Rep 66, 74–5.

20 United Nations General Assembly, *Report of the Secretary-General on Human Security*, UN GAOR, Sixty-fourth sess, Agenda Item 48 and 114, UN Doc A/64/701 (8 March 2010) [21], [22].

21 *Charter of the United Nations*, Preamble, art 1(1). See also Rüdiger Wolfrum, 'Article 1' in Bruno Simma (ed), *The United Nations Charter: A Commentary* (Oxford University Press, 2nd edn, 2002) vol I [3]; Jean-Philippe Thérien, 'Human Security: The Making of a UN Ideology' (2012) 26(2) *Global Society* 191, 191.

22 *Charter of the United Nations,* Preamble; arts 1(1); 2(3) and 2(6); 11 (1) and (2); 12 (2); 18(2); 23(1); 24(1); 26; 33(1); 34; 37(2); 39; 42; 43(1); 47; 48(1); 51; 52(1); 73; 76; 84; 99; 106.

23 For discussion see, eg, Rüdiger Wolfrum, 'Article 1' in Bruno Simma (ed), *The United Nations Charter: A Commentary* (Oxford University Press, 2nd edn, 2002) vol I, 83.

24 For a discussion see Gerd Oberleitner, 'Human Security: A Challenge to International Law?' (2005) 11 *Global Governance* 185, 192. Alice Edwards and Carla Ferstman, 'Humanising Non-Citizens: The Convergence of Human Rights and Human Security' in

Charter is itself a state-centred vision of the world order, and one that privileges ensuring the national security of member states.[25]

> The preoccupation of the United Nations founders was with State security. When they spoke of creating a new system of collective security, they meant it in the traditional military sense: a system in which States join together and pledge that aggression against one is aggression against all, and commit themselves in that event to react collectively. *But* they also understood well, long before the idea of human security gained currency, the indivisibility of security, economic development and human freedom.[26]

Edwards and Ferstman point out that realist doctrines, while playing up the role of sovereignty, non-interference and national security as the cornerstones of the UN Charter, play down the other central tenets of the UN Charter: human rights, social justice, non-discrimination and international cooperation.[27] It is also widely accepted that the principles of the UN Charter must be interpreted in their contemporary context and current human realities, and not solely by reference to the intent of the drafters. To do otherwise would be to 'ossify international law ... and diminish its contemporary relevance ... we cannot ... regard the Charter as immutable'.[28]

Wolfrum asserts that in distinguishing 'peace' and 'security' in the UN Charter, security is 'generally understood as encompassing the activity which is necessary for maintaining the conditions of peace.'[29] Thus even if 'peace' were to be narrowly defined as not extending beyond the absence of organised force (that is, not extending beyond the role of Article 2(4) – 'negative peace'), security under this definition would still contain elements of the notion of 'positive peace'.[30] Or put in a different context, it would contain elements of the idea of human security.

A broad reading of 'international peace and security' is also supported by the Proclamation of the International Year of Peace. The Proclamation stated that the

Alice Edwards and Carla Ferstman (eds), *Human Security and Non-Citizens: Law, Policy and International Affairs* (Cambridge University Press, 2010) 3–47, 9.

25 Charlotte Ku, 'Collective Security and the Personalization of Peace' in Steve Charnovitz, Debra P Steger and Peter Van Den Bossche (eds), *Law in the Service of Human Dignity* (Cambridge University Press, 2005) 336, 344.

26 UN High Level Panel on Threats, Challenges and Change, *A More Secure World* (UN, 2004) synopsis, 1.

27 Alice Edwards and Carla Ferstman, 'Humanising Non-Citizens: The Convergence of Human Rights and Human Security' in Alice Edwards and Carla Ferstman (eds), *Human Security and Non-Citizens: Law, Policy and International Affairs* (Cambridge University Press, 2010) 3, 9.

28 Javier Pérez de Cuellar, *Report of the Secretary-General on the Work of the Organisation*, UN GAOR, Forty-sixth sess, UN Doc GA/46/404 (23 September 1991) reprinted in [1991] 45 *UN Yearbook* 7, 13–14.

29 Rüdiger Wolfrum, 'Article 1' in Bruno Simma (ed), *The United Nations Charter: A Commentary* (Oxford University Press, 2nd edn, 2002) vol I, [4].

30 Ibid.

promotion of international peace and security requires continuing and positive action by states and peoples towards a collection of goals including, but not limited to: the prevention of war; the removal of various threats to peace; non-use of force; resolution of conflict; respect for economic development of states; the promotion and exercise of human rights and freedom; the enhancement of quality of life; the satisfaction of human needs; and the protection of the environment.[31]

The definition of the 'maintenance of international peace and security' and how it relates to human security is also important, as this interpretation forms the scope of the powers of the Security Council.[32] The Security Council's influence and broad discretion in determining its own authority make it important to examine the decision-making of the Council, especially in regard to Resolutions, to determine the scope of the international peace and security in the modern context. This will be explored below.

It has been argued that recognising human security stretches the limits of the interpretation of 'international peace and security' beyond their ordinary meaning,[33] thus contravening the rules of interpretation as set out in the *Vienna Convention of the Law of Treaties.*[34] But in many ways, the ordinary meaning of the term 'security' is precisely what human security is about. When the United Nations Development Programme (UNDP) advocated the approach in 1994, it used anecdotal evidence of what people in different parts of the world considered security to be, to demonstrate that the ordinary meaning was much broader than traditionally conceived.[35] The meanings of terms can and do change over time, and the discussion of the relationship between human security and the UN Charter above demonstrates that human security is not the conceptual overstretch that some believe. This is especially true when it is remembered, as discussed earlier, that both the objects and purposes and subsequent practice of the organisation (and not the treaty parties) bear special weight when interpreting the Charter.[36] It is thus relevant to discover whether discourse in both the United Nations generally, and the Security Council specifically, has expanded sufficiently to demonstrate a conceptual shift in the meaning of 'international peace and security', and whether human security could in fact be considered the authoritative interpretation of 'international peace and security' in the modern context.

31 Proclamation of the International Year of Peace, cited in Wolfrum, 'Article 1' in Bruno Simma (ed), *The United Nations Charter: A Commentary* (Oxford University Press, 2nd edn, 2002) vol I, [5].

32 *Charter of the United Nations*, art 24.

33 See, eg, Ben Saul, 'The Dangers of the United Nations' "New Security Agenda": "Human Security" in the Asia-Pacific Region' (2006) 1(1) *Asian Journal of Comparative Law* 1, 20.

34 *Vienna Convention on the Law of Treaties*, art 31.

35 United Nations Development Programme (UNDP), *Human Development Report 1994* (UNDP, 1994).

36 Catherine Brölmann, 'Specialized Rules of Treaty Interpretation: International Organizations' in Duncan B Hollis (ed) *The Oxford Guide to Treaties* (2012) 507, 511–12.

III Interpretation of 'security' in other significant documents

While human security increasingly gains a place in the operations of a range of UN bodies, much of the discussion of security in the dominant documents of the UN shuns the use of the term 'human security'. Nonetheless, the influence of human security on these documents may be detected, though each fails in different ways to fully adopt the idea of human security. Indeed, many of the core elements of human security actually predate the concept of human security (as formed by the UNDP) itself, and are evidenced in the series of independent commissions undertaken in the 1980s in consideration of development, security and the environment. What this demonstrates is that use of the term security by states and international institutions is changing and broadening. This is of key relevance when discussing a viable interpretation of 'international peace and security' as used in the UN Charter and other key international legal documents.

A Brandt Commission

Early recognition of the need for a broader, people-centred approach to security can be traced back to at least as early as the Brandt Commission in 1980.[37] This Commission was founded with the purpose of analysing development-related issues and the North–South divide. Summarising the findings of the Reports, Quilligan asserts that the Brandt Reports had found that

> ... security must be reconceived with people foremost in mind. The purely defensive concept of security should be enlarged to include hunger, disease, poverty, environmental stress, repression, and terrorism, all of which endanger human security as much as any military provocation.[38]

The Reports of the Brandt Commission repeatedly emphasise that security cannot be understood as a military problem alone:

> True security cannot be achieved by mounting buildup of weapons (defence in a narrow sense) but only by providing basic conditions for solving non-military problems which threaten them. Our survival depends not only on military balance, but on global cooperation to ensure a sustainable environment.[39]

The Commission sought to illustrate that '[m]uch of the insecurity in the world is connected with the divisions between the rich and poor countries.'[40] The other

37 Independent Commission on International Development Issues (ICIDI), *North–South: A Program for Survival* (MIT Press, 1980).

38 J B Quilligan, 'The Brandt Equation: 21st Century Blueprint for the New Global Economy', *Brandt 21 Forum*, (2002) <http://www.brandt21forum.info/BrandtEquation-19Sept04.pdf>.

39 Independent Commission on International Development Issues (ICIDI), *North–South: A Program for Survival* (MIT Press, 1980) 119.

40 Ibid 124, 125.

element of human security which is emphasised in the work of the Commission is that security and world order must be predicated on 'people and respect for their essential rights.'[41] Ultimately, however, the focus of the report was on development, not security, so while moving international discussion in the direction of people-centric security, it did not develop a comprehensive understanding of the idea of human security as raised in the Report.

B Palme Commission

The Palme Commission, established in 1982, followed the Brandt Commission, with a mandate related to disarmament and security issues. Like the Brandt Commission, the Palme Commission emphasised that 'military strength alone cannot provide real security.'[42] Likewise, the Palme Report emphasised the nexus between security and development, arguing that the development of the global South was 'the only basis for lasting security.'[43] The idea of 'common security' in the Palme Report was influenced by a people-centric vision, and obliquely recognised the importance of rights discourse for the realisation of security, '[c]ommon security requires that people live in dignity and peace'.[44]

However, unlike the Brandt Commission, the Palme Commission did not employ the term 'human security' but favoured the term 'common security'.[45] While emphasising the importance of addressing the security needs of individuals, it did so in the service of the common security of states, not the other way around, in the language of the report. The human security issues highlighted were also marginalised in the report, which was heavily weighted towards the disarmament rather than the broader security component of its mandate, in this way being very much a product of its times. And while the Brandt and Brundtland Commissions forged a place for their Reports in the development of international law and policy, the Palme Report 'passed remarkably unnoticed',[46] with little discernible impact on the global approach to security.

C The Brundtland Commission

The Brundtland Commission carved out a name for itself, and is best known for having placed sustainable development firmly on the global agenda. Like the two preceding Commissions, the Brundtland Commission sought to participate in 're-centering international affairs on individuals rather than states',[47] with

41 Ibid 268.
42 Independent Commission on Disarmament and Security Issues, *Common Security: A Blueprint for Survival* (Simon and Schuster, 1982) 4, 71.
43 Ibid 173.
44 Ibid 172.
45 See, eg, ibid.
46 Johan Galtung, 'The Palme Commission Report on Disarmament and Security a Critical Comment' (1983) 14(2) *Security Dialogue* 147, 147.
47 Philippe Thérien, 'Human Security: The Making of a UN Ideology' (2012) 26(2) *Global Society* 191, 197–8.

the Report emphasising that it was '[f]irst and foremost...concerned with people'.[48] Considerations of security, while certainly not a major component, were also present in the report. The Commission was, unsurprisingly, particularly concerned with the environmental dimensions of security:

> The whole notion of security as traditionally understood must be expanded to include the growing impacts of environmental stress ... There are no military solutions to 'environmental insecurity'.[49]

The report emphasised that unsustainable development constitutes a source of insecurity, which in turn feeds into more traditional conflict-centric dimensions of security. This acknowledgment thus reaffirms both the broad-ranging character of the concept of security and the interconnected nature of sources of insecurity, in line with human security discourse.

D Millennium Declaration

The Millennium Declaration, adopted at the Millennium Summit of the General Assembly in 2000, is most significant for its establishment of the Millennium Development Goals.[50] It is the first of the discussed documents to emerge after the UNDP Report establishing human security. While this document isolated security and framed it in the (predominantly) traditional terms of conflict and violence, there are two interconnected elements of the document which stand out from a human security perspective. One of the values espoused in the document is the notion of shared responsibility. This is expressly framed thus:

> Responsibility for managing worldwide economic and social development, as well as threats to international peace and security, must be shared among the nations of the world, and should be exercised multilaterally. As the most universal and most representative organization in the world, the United Nations must play the central role.[51]

However, the connection to human security is perhaps better encapsulated earlier in the document:

> We recognise that, in addition to our shared responsibilities to our individual societies, we have a collective responsibility to uphold the principles of human

48 World Commission on Environment and Development, *Our Common Future* (Oxford University Press, 1987) 23.

49 Ibid 19.

50 United Nations General Assembly, *United Nations Millennium Declaration*, UN GA Res 55/2, Fifty-fifth sess, Agenda Item 60(b), UN Doc A/RES/55/2 (18 September 2000).

51 Ibid [6].

> dignity, equality, and equity at the global level. As leaders we have a duty therefore to all the world's people, especially the most vulnerable ...[52]

This draws together a series of ideas closely connected to human security – in particular, shared responsibility and the universality of human security, and human dignity with an emphasis on the protection of the vulnerable. The protection of the vulnerable is an important element of the Millennium Declaration, and the section dedicated to it demonstrates, at least to an extent, a human security mentality:

> We will spare no effort to ensure that children and all civilian populations that suffer disproportionately the consequences of natural disasters, genocide, armed conflicts and other humanitarian emergencies are given every assistance and protection so that they can resume normal life as soon as possible.[53]

On the other hand, the term 'human security' is not employed once in the document, and the interconnections between the various elements of the Declaration – most specifically between development, security and human rights issues – are not only left unexplored by the Declaration but fail to be referenced at all.

E A more secure world

In 2003 the UN Secretary General commissioned a High Level Panel to explore the future of the role of the UN in international peace and security, in light of a more interconnected world, and a new range of threats.[54] This report is one of the single most authoritative contributions to the discussion by the UN of an expanded definition of security. It also expressly uses the term 'human security' in the document, particularly emphasising the concept in the synopses for each chapter.[55] Most significantly, the conclusions of the panel are boiled down to one core idea: that the 'dignity, justice, worth and safety' of the citizens of every state 'should be at the heart of any collective system for the 21st century.'[56] While not directly engaging significantly and expressly with human security discourse in the Report, the Panel did nonetheless highlight many of the core elements of human security.

52 Ibid [2].
53 Ibid [26].
54 UN High Level Panel on Threats, Challenges and Change, *A More Secure World* (UN, 2004).
55 *Contra* discussion of Taylor Owen, 'In All but Name: The Uncertain Future of Human Security in the UN' in Moufida Goucha and John Crowley (eds), *Rethinking Human Security* (Wiley-Blackwell 2008) 113, 119. Owen claims that no mention of human security is made in the Report. The term is in fact employed seven times in the main body of the Report, and is emphasised in particular in the synopses, employed in the first paragraph of the primary Synopsis.
56 UN High Level Panel on Threats, Challenges and Change, *A More Secure World* (UN, 2004) [30].

More than anything else, the Report demonstrated an awareness of the *integrated* nature of security and the interconnections between the various threats to it:

> Poverty, infectious disease, environmental degradation and war feed into one another in a deadly cycle.
>
> Poverty is strongly associated with the outbreaks of civil war. Such diseases as malaria and HIV/AIDS continue to cause large numbers of deaths and reinforce poverty. Disease and poverty, in turn, are connected to environmental degradation; climate change exacerbates the occurrence of such infectious disease … Environmental stress, caused by large populations and shortages of land and other natural resources can contribute to civil violence.[57]

While the interconnected nature of threats is vital for the advancement of human security, it should be noted that the Panel's perspective is heavily one-sided. It is interested in how poverty, disease and environmental crises contribute to direct forms of violence.[58] Despite arguing that it is a vicious circle, no real consideration is given in the Report to how, in turn, armed conflict and violence contribute to poverty, disease and environmental stress. This arguably demonstrates a lingering perception that security is related to armed conflict, and raises the question of whether the Panel genuinely saw poverty (and so on) as insecurity in itself, or only as a consequential threat, given that these phenomena can lead to direct violence. The Panel may have fallen into a perceptual trap it had itself highlighted:

> Difference of power, wealth and geography do determine what we perceive as the gravest threats to our survival and well-being. Differences of focus lead us to dismiss what others perceive as the gravest of all threats to their survival. Inequitable responses to threats further fuel division.[59]

The *preventative* focus of human security, however, does find a place in the report:

> The primary challenge for the United Nations and its members is to ensure that of all the threats in the categories listed, those that are distant do not become imminent, and those that are imminent do not actually become destructive.[60]

The Report acknowledges the challenges of prevention – most notably, a lack of sustained political will to address it. Significantly, the first suggested reform to address these challenges is better international regulatory frameworks and norms.[61] It is for precisely this reason that international legal engagement with human security is so important.

57 Ibid [22].
58 Ibid.
59 Ibid Synopsis [12].
60 Ibid Synopsis [2]–[3].
61 Ibid [89]–[97].

The Report acknowledges the universality of human security by acknowledging mutual vulnerability. That is, that 'a threat to one is a threat to all',[62] as discussed in Chapter Four. This, then, goes back to the idea of shared responsibility that is raised in the Millennium Declaration. As the Panel pointed out, the 'mutual vulnerability of weak and strong has never been clearer'.[63] This then also aligns closely with the idea of sovereignty as responsibility. This argument is expressly made in the Report:

> In signing the Charter of the United Nations, States not only benefit from the privileges of sovereignty but also accept the responsibilities.[64]

The Panel also demonstrated an understanding of the importance of human rights to security. The Report as a whole is littered with references to the importance of human rights to the realisation of its objectives. It was as a direct result of this Report that the problematic Human Rights Commission was replaced with the Human Rights Council.[65] There is, however, a lack of a sophisticated analysis in the report of the relationship between security and human rights, and it does not at any point expressly frame security as a rights-based concept.

While the Report as a whole significantly advances an international agenda for a broader and more comprehensive approach to security, it should be acknowledged that, despite the many relevant observations made by the Panel in the Report, the latter at no stage engages in a systematic or comprehensive analysis of human security. And while it acknowledges the importance of human rights, the Report fails to take the extra step taken in *Human Security Now*,[66] released the year before, of acknowledging human agency in security and the importance of promoting the empowerment of individuals and groups.

F In Larger Freedom

A Secretary-General Report, *In Larger Freedom*, followed up on the findings of the High-Level Panel.[67] As indicative of the work of Kofi Annan in general during his tenure as Secretary-General of the UN, the Report advances a strongly people-centric worldview. However, unlike *A More Secure World*, this Report largely avoids the explicit use of the phrase 'human security'. There is a single use of the phrase in reference to the Millennium Declaration (a document which itself had not used the term), asserting that the Declaration emphasised the importance of rule of law for advancing human security.[68]

62 Ibid [17].
63 Ibid.
64 Ibid [29].
65 Ibid 88–90.
66 UN Commission on Human Security, *Human Security Now* (United Nations, 2003).
67 Kofi Annan, *In Larger Freedom: Towards Development, Security and Human Rights for All*, UN GAOR, Fifty-ninth sess, Agenda Item 45 and 55, UN Doc A/59/2005/Add.3 (26 May 2005).
68 Ibid [133].

Despite the conspicuous absence of the term 'human security', the basic elements of human security are evident in the Report. The substance of human security is largely distilled into a single paragraph, which reads:

> On this interconnectedness of threats we must found a new security consensus, the first article of which must be that all are entitled to freedom from fear, and that whatever threatens one threatens all. Once we understand this, we have no choice but to tackle the whole range of threats. We must respond to HIV/AIDS as robustly as we do to terrorism and to poverty as effectively as we do to proliferation. We must strive just as hard to eliminate the threat of small arms and light weapons as we do to eliminate the threat of weapons of mass destruction. Moreover, we must address all these threats preventively, acting at a sufficiently early stage with the full range of available instruments.[69]

This paragraph alone demonstrates most of the elements of human security: the scope and interconnected nature of threats, the universality and mutual vulnerability, and the preventative focus are all in evidence, and people-centred concerns are implicit in the discussion. Perhaps most importantly, the paragraph emphasises the importance of giving equal attention and gravity to the non-traditional threats as to armed conflict and terrorism.

The interlinkages of security, development and human rights are strongly emphasised in the Report:

> Accordingly, we will not enjoy development without security, we will not enjoy security without development, and we will not enjoy either without respect for human rights. Unless all these causes are advanced, none will succeed.[70]

However, by and large, the analysis of the Report structurally separates its discussion of freedom from fear and freedom from want. And despite acknowledging a broad understanding of potential threats to security, in a similar vein to *A More Secure World* the Report treats these threats as potential hazards to more traditional security concerns, rather than as security issues in themselves.[71]

G World Summit Outcome Document

In Larger Freedom was produced for consideration ahead of the largest meeting of heads of state ever conducted within the General Assembly in 2005. The World Summit Outcome Document produced at this meeting is significant as it contains

69 Ibid [81].

70 Ibid [17], see also [128]: 'No security agenda and no drive for development will be successful unless they are based on the sure foundation of respect for human dignity.'

71 A similar point is made by Ben Saul, 'The Dangers of the United Nations' "New Security Agenda": "Human Security" in the Asia-Pacific Region' (2006) 1(1) *Asian Journal of Comparative Law* 1, 5.

the first formal acknowledgment of human security by the General Assembly.[72] The General Assembly in this document asserted:

> We stress the right of people to live in freedom and dignity, free from poverty and despair. We recognise that all individuals, in particular vulnerable people, are entitled to freedom from fear and freedom from want, with an equal opportunity to enjoy all their rights and fully develop their human potential. To this end, we commit ourselves to discussing and defining the notion of human security in the General Assembly.[73]

This, however, is the only explicit reference to human security in the document, demonstrating that the absence of a clear, universal definition of the concept has impeded its development at the intergovernmental level. The commitment to discuss human security expressed in the Outcome Document has resulted in an annual thematic debate of human security within the General Assembly, with several reports produced by the Secretary-General in anticipation of these discussions.

H The 2012 Human Security Resolution, and the reports on human security by the Secretary-General

In 2010, a shift began in the way the General Assembly approached the issue of human security. It began with a resolution in 2010 raising the issue of human security.[74] This resolution is extremely brief (comprising only four paragraphs), but announces the commencement of the first formal debate on human security (the informal thematic debates had begun two years prior, in 2008) and committed the Assembly to 'continue its consideration of human security'.[75] This formal debate was set to accompany the first issued report of the Secretary General on human security. In it, the Secretary General committed to producing progress reports on human security every two years. Most of the core messages contained in that 2010 Report eventually made their way into what to date remains the most significant recognition of human security, the 2012 General Assembly Resolution expressly recognising and committing to the concept of human security.[76]

The Resolution does not provide a definition of human security. This had been one of the chief areas of concern raised again and again at the informal (and

72 *World Summit Outcome Document,* GA Res 60/1, UN GAOR, Sixtieth sess, Agenda Item 46 and 120, UN Doc A/RES/60/1 (24 October 2005).

73 Ibid [143].

74 United Nations General Assembly, *Follow-up to Paragraph 143 on Human Security of the 2005 World Summit Outcome*, 64/291, UN GAOR, Sixty-fourth sess, Agenda Item 48 and 114, UN Doc A/RES/64/291 (27 July 2010).

75 Ibid [4].

76 General Assembly, *Follow-up to Paragraph 143 on Human Security of the 2005 World Summit Outcome*, 66/290, Sixty-sixth sess, Agenda Item 14 and 117, UN Doc A/RES/66/290 (25 October 2012) ('Human Security Resolution').

formal) debates. It had also been raised in the 2010 Report, in which the Secretary-General briefly surveyed some of the more authoritative definitions produced by regional bodies and intergovernmental institutions.[77] Instead the Resolution describes human security as

> An approach to assist Member States in identifying and addressing widespread and cross-cutting challenges to the survival, livelihood and dignity of their people.[78]

The following elements were identified as central to 'a common understanding of the notion of human security':

- the right of people to live in freedom and dignity;
- people-centred, comprehensive, context-specific and prevention-oriented responses;
- recognition of the interlinkages between peace, development and human rights;
- human security is distinct from responsibility to protect; it does not entail the threat or use of force or coercive measures; it does not replace state security;
- is based on national ownership; it seeks national solutions, which are compatible with local realities;
- governments retain primary responsibility for ensuring the survival, livelihood and dignity of their citizens; international community complements these efforts, while greater cooperation and partnership is required among Governments, international and regional organisations and civil society;
- human security does not entail additional legal obligations to states.[79]

While the document was inherently people-centred, as a resolution issued by the General Assembly, it should be unsurprising that it reflected the problem-solving, and not critical, dimensions of the human security discourse. That is, it emphasised the role of human security within the current power structures of the international order, emphasising, as the list above provides, that human security does not replace state security, and observing that human security must be implemented with full respect of the sovereignty of states and the principle of non-interference.[80] This had likewise been stressed in the 2010 Report, with the Secretary-General asserting that '[t]he advancement of human security requires strong and stable institutions', the most relevant of which is national governments.[81]

77 United Nations General Assembly, *Report of the Secretary-General on Human Security*, UN GAOR, Sixty-fourth sess, Agenda Item 48 and 114, UN Doc A/64/701 (8 March 2010).
78 *Human Security Resolution*, UN Doc A/RES/66/290, [3].
79 Ibid.
80 Ibid [3].
81 *2010 Human Security Report*, UN Doc A/64/701, [20].

Other people-centred components endorsed by the Resolution are an emphasis on the vulnerable,[82] and a recognition of the rights-based nature of the concept. First it is recognised that all people are entitled to the opportunity to enjoy all their rights, and that human security equally considers civil, political, economic, social and cultural rights. The Resolution then ties the rights-based component to the interconnectedness of human security.

> Human security recognises the interlinkages between peace, development and human rights …
>
> Recognises that … development, peace and security and human rights are the pillars of the United Nations and are interlinked and mutually reinforcing.[83]

This draws from the 2010 Report which explored the nexus between security and development and concluded that 'no country can enjoy development without security, security without development and neither without respect for human rights.'[84] The Resolution also acknowledged the need for interconnected and multilateral responses, expressly recognising the need for greater collaboration and partnership between governments, international and regional organisations and civil society.[85] It also recognises that human security has the two components of protection and empowerment.[86]

The divorce of human security from the responsibility to protect has been previously noted, but the Resolution also explicitly states that human security 'does not entail the threat or the use of force or coercive measures.'[87] Interestingly however, the report does not refute the relevance of other, non-coercive measures. Finally, the 2010 Report concluded with the recommendation to mainstream human security into United Nations activities.[88]

The most recent Report of the Secretary General largely echoes the 2012 Resolution and the findings of the 2010 Report.[89] One interesting area of novelty is raised, however. The 2012 Report raises the importance of human security to the post-2015 development agenda. Citing civil society advocates of this inclusion, it observes that

> the human security approach, by underscoring the importance of inclusive, targeted and comprehensive solutions to widespread and cross-cutting

82 *Human Security Resolution*, UN Doc A/RES/66/290, [3].
83 Ibid [4].
84 *2010 Human Security Report*, UN Doc A/64/701, [10].
85 *Human Security Resolution*, UN Doc A/RES/66/290, [3].
86 Ibid.
87 Ibid.
88 *2010 Human Security Report*, UN Doc A/64/701, [72].
89 General Assembly, *Report of the Secretary General: Follow-up to General Assembly Resolution 66/290 on Human Security*, Sixty-eighth sess, Agenda Item 14 and 118, UN Doc A/68/685 (23 December 2013).

> challenges, provides the appropriate methodology for the analysis and development of policies and programmes in the formulation of the post-2015 sustainable development goals ...[90]

One of the final recommendations of the Report then asks the General Assembly '[t]o consider human security as an overarching framework in the post-2015 development agenda'.[91]

I Post-2015 Development Agenda Report

A High Level Panel was appointed to consider the consequences of the end of the Millennium Development Goals (MDGs) and the post-2015 development agenda.[92] The Report of the High Level Panel in its recommendations only contains one reference to human security:

> At the same time there is unprecedented prosperity and dynamism in many countries ... This means it is now possible to **leave no one behind** – to give every child a fair chance in life, and to achieve a pattern of development where dignity and human rights become a reality for all, where an agenda can be built around human security.[93]

It thus ties human security primarily to its first 'transformative shift', to leave no one behind. This recommendation centres around issues of social justice, and in particular on the needs of the vulnerable. By raising the issue in the context of social justice and the 'unprecedented prosperity' noted above, it is also raising the issue of human security as one of universal concern and mutual responsibility, two interconnected principles identified in Chapter Four. This is expressly noted in the summary of the Report: '[t]his is a universal agenda, for which everyone must accept their proper share of responsibility.'[94] To this end, the universal concern and empowerment components of human security are also evident in the Report's call for global partnerships, expressly noting the range of stakeholders who can contribute the future Agenda. What is lacking however, is a clear understanding of how such partnerships should be undertaken, and how genuinely participatory the processes will be.

Human security is otherwise little evidenced in the Post-Development Report. In particular, the emphasis on the interconnected nature of threats is entirely lacking from the report. This is unfortunate, as one of the criticisms levelled at the MDGs had been that it cast the goals into demarcated, isolated categories that

90 Ibid [40].
91 Ibid [67].
92 The Report of the High-Level Panel of Eminent Persons on the Post-2015 Development Agenda, *A New Global Partnership: Eradicate Poverty and Transform Economies through Sustainable Development,* (United Nations, 2013).
93 Ibid 4.
94 Ibid Executive Summary.

needed to be addressed in a more systematic fashion.[95] Moreover, the importance of human rights is an issue raised repeatedly in the Report. However, as civil society commentators have already noted, the human rights discussed in the Report are almost exclusively civil and political rights, despite the core relevance of economic, social and cultural rights to the concerns of the Agenda.[96]

J The limits of the influence of human security discourse

What is clear is that while human security discourse is increasingly being employed, there is still considerable lack of consistency in its application and its focus. All four of the core principles of human security – its people-centredness; interconnectedness; universality and prevention-orientation – are all important for the realisation of human security and the creation of effective responses. Thus far however, the only consistently recognised component is that human security relates to people.

It must also be noted that while documents such as the Post-2015 Development Agenda Report contain evidence of the influence of human security discourse, and while the United Nations Human Security Unit continues to operate and disseminate materials in collaboration with other UN organs and specialised agencies, there have been no new Secretary-General Reports on the issue since 2014, and the annual General Assembly human security debate has ceased. In its place is an increased emphasis on the 2030 development agenda, and concerns of human security largely subsumed within that model. In a global environment of increased nationalism, this loss of explicit engagement is simultaneously troubling, and not surprising. While it is likely that the discourse will have an enduring impact on the framing of pressing transnational issues, the less human security is explicitly engaged with, the less we are likely to see a comprehensive approach that engages with the full potential of the discourse.

IV 'Threat to the Peace' and the role of the Security Council

Under Article 24 of the UN Charter, the Security Council is vested with the 'primary responsibility for the maintenance of international peace and security'. The Security Council has been vested with considerable political and legal clout to discharge this responsibility, and under the auspices of Chapter VII of the UN

95 See, eg, Gabriele Koehler et al, 'Human Security and the Next Generation of Comprehensive Human Development Goals' (Research Paper Institute of Development Studies, April 2012) 18.

96 See, eg, Global Call to Action against Poverty, 'Leave No One Behind! Initial GCAP Response to the UN Post-2015 High Level Panel Report' (June 2013) <www.un-ngls.org/IMG/doc/CivilSocietyResponsestoHLPReport.doc>. For the importance of human rights in the post-development agenda, see, eg, Gabriele Koehler et al, 'Human Security and the Next Generation of Comprehensive Human Development Goals' (Research Paper Institute of Development Studies, April 2012); Ved P Nanda, 'Human Rights Must be at the Core of Post-2015 International Development Agenda' (April 2014) 75 *Montana Law Review* 1.

Charter has the unique authority to make decisions that are binding on all Member States. The Security Council, in exercising the power asserted by Article 24, has the authority to define its own jurisdiction. This is particularly relevant in the search for an authoritative interpretation, as the Permanent Court of International Justice stated that 'it is an established principle that the right of giving an authoritative interpretation of a legal rule belongs solely to the person or body who has the power to modify or suppress it.'[97]

The Security Council has the authority to act under Chapter VII, specifically Articles 41 and 42, of the UN Charter, if the Council determines that there exists a 'threat to the peace, breach of the peace, or act of aggression' under Article 39. The Security Council thus has the most authoritative voice, from a legal perspective, regarding what security in fact consists in at the international level.[98] After all, 'il n'y a pas de "menaces contre la paix" en soi dont l'existence empirique n'aurait qu'à être constatée par le Conseil …'[99] Indeed, the justiciability of the Security Council's decisions under Article 39 is questionable, with many arguing that the decision of what constitutes a threat to international peace and security is a purely political question, and that courts and tribunals must not substitute their own views for the views of the Council.[100]

While a human security vision cannot be presently said to inform the decision-making of the Security Council, what is discernible is a gradually broadening of the idea of security under the Council, and a move, albeit uneven in application, towards a more people-centric view of the threats that give rise to international attention.

The issue of 'threat to the peace' poses the most relevant avenue for human security concerns for a number of reasons. It is acknowledged as the broadest and most nebulous concept in Article 39, 'the true grey area in the practice of the Security Council'.[101] Both breach of the peace and act of aggression are reactive concepts, capable of being invoked only once violence occurs.[102] Threat to the peace on the other hand is a *prospective* concept, and thus vital for the

97 *Question of Jaworzina*, (Advisory Opinion) [1923] PCIJ (series B), No 8, 37.

98 While the role of the Security Council in relation to international peace and security is broad, this study is primarily interested in interpretation of 'security' and as such, will limit its examination of the role of the Security Council to its interpretation and application of Article 39 of the Charter of the United Nations.

99 Jean Combacau, 'Le Chapitre VII de la Charte des Nations Unies: resurrection ou metamorphoses?' in RB Archour and S Laghmi (eds), *Les Nouveaux Aspects du Droit International* (Pedone, 1994) 139, 145.

100 See, eg, Hans Kelsen, *The Law of the United Nations* (Stevens 1950) 727; Louis Henkin, 'Conceptualizing Violence – Present and Future Developments in International Law' (1997) 60 *Alberta Law Review* 571, 577. Others, however see at least justiciability of the issue as possible, see, eg, Erika de Wet, The *Chapter VII Powers of the United Nations Security Council* (Hart Oxford, 2004) 133,

101 Helmut Freudenschauβ, 'Article 39 of the UN Charter Revisited: Threats to the Peace and the Recent Practice of the UN Security Council' (1993) 46 *Austrian Journal of Public and International Law* 1, 3.

102 See, eg, Jan Klabbers, 'Intervention, Armed Intervention, Armed Attack, Threat to Peace, Act of Aggression, and Threat or Use of Force: What's the Difference?' in Marc

preventative focus of human security. As Frowein notes, '[t]he concept of threat to the peace is of central significance for the system of the UN Charter, according to which the SC should also be active particularly in a preventive manner.'[103]

Some authorities argue that while the concept of 'international peace and security' can be defined widely in Article 1(2) of the Charter, this broad definition should not be applied to Chapter VII. Instead 'peace' as used in Chapter VII cannot be extended beyond the 'absence of organised use of force between states.'[104] Certainly when agreed upon, the Charter's considerations in relation to peace and security 'had a predominantly military connotation'.[105] However, it can be argued that the term has since evolved, and become a far broader and more people-centred concept. According to Sir Arthur Watts, '[t]his evolution was in a sense inevitable because the term was open to normatively justifiable interpretation or reinterpretation.'[106] State and institutional practice in relation to the concept is a relevant consideration in interpreting the Charter.[107]

It is also important to note that the Security Council does not often invoke Article 39 when discussing less traditional threats. As Wellens points out, '[t]he strict formalistic determination that a threat exists seems to have been overtaken in recent years by other formulations such as the council expressing (grave) concern that particular situations (may) constitute a threat.'[108] He highlights the fact that while the Security Council has increasingly expanded its attention, this has not necessarily resulted in a concomitant expansion of its mandate under Article 39. Rather, it has introduced an informal attention to threats, making pronouncements which stop short of formal determinations under Article 39, which Wellens argues has resulted in an increasing growing autonomy of the notion, not dependent on instrumentalisation under Article 39, as well as a blurring of the line between Chapters VI and VII.[109] Thus many of the concerns of human security that have been recognised by the Security Council are expressed in terms such as 'disturbs' the peace, not threat or breach of the peace – deliberately falling short of invoking Article 39.[110]

Weller (ed) *The Oxford Handbook of the Use of Force in International Law* (Oxford University Press, 2015) 1729.

103 Jochen Abr. Frowein, 'Article 39. Chapter VII. Action with Respect to Threats to the Peace, Breaches of Peace and Acts of Aggression' in Bruno Simma et al (ed), *The United Nations Charter: A Commentary* (2nd edn, 2002) vol I, 612.

104 Ibid 611.

105 Sir Arthur Watts during the discussion at the 1992 Kiel Symposium, cited in Karel Wellens, 'The UN Security Council and New Threats to the Peace: Back to the Future' (2003) 8 *Journal of Conflict and Security Law* 15, 28.

106 Ibid.

107 Thus, eg, *Vienna Convention on the Law of Treaties,* opened for signature 23 May 1969, 1155 UNTS 331 (entered into force 27 January 1980), art 31 (3)(b).

108 Karel Wellens, 'The UN Security Council and New Threats to the Peace: Back to the Future' (2003) 8 *Journal of Conflict and Security Law* 15, 18.

109 Ibid 53, 68.

110 A point also noted by Jochen Abr. Frowein, 'Article 39. Chapter VII. Action with Respect to Threats to the Peace, Breaches of Peace and Acts of Aggression' in Bruno

A Interpretation of 'security' – Security Council resolutions

In its early decades it is clear from the practices of the Security Council (impeded as they were by the Cold War) that threats to international peace and security were situations of inter-state armed conflict.[111] Where internal conflict was considered, this was almost exclusively in the context of potential externalities. The Security Council condemnation of the Apartheid regime in South Africa is often cited as one of the first examples of recognition that human rights violations can constitute threats to international peace and security. However, the resolutions made by the Security Council were largely focused on the potential impact of Apartheid on South Africa's neighbours:

> ... *Recognising* that the military build-up by South Africa and its persistent acts of aggression against the neighbouring States seriously disturb the security of those states ...[112]
>
> *Convinced* that the violence and repression by the South African racist regime have greatly aggravated the situation in Southern Africa and will certainly lead to violent conflict and racial conflagration with serious international repercussions ...[113]

An early exception seems to be that of the Security Council's approach to Southern Rhodesia. It is never made clear in the Security Council resolutions regarding Southern Rhodesia what precisely made the situation a threat to international peace and security. The focus of the resolutions, however, seems to emphasise the illegal nature of the regime, arguably indicating that (serious) breaches of international law might be a contributing factor to this classification.[114] Likewise, returning to the example of Apartheid, while not connecting it clearly with the maintenance of peace and security, several resolutions on the situation asserted the practices to be contrary to the purposes and principles of the United Nations Charter and the obligations of Member States.[115] This is an interesting perspective on international peace and security, especially working from the premise that human security is a rule-based approach to security, as previously discussed.

Simma et al (ed), *The United Nations Charter: A Commentary* (2nd edn, 2002) vol I, 609.

111 Discussion of this point may also be found in Michael Bothe, 'Security in International Law Since 1990' in Hans Günter Brauch et al (eds), *Globalization and Environmental Challenges* (Springer Berlin Heidelberg, 2008) vol 3, 475.

112 Security Council Resolution 418 (1977), UN SCOR, UN Doc S/RES/418 (4 November 1977).

113 Security Council Resolution 417 (1077) UN SCOR, UN Doc S/RES/417 (31 October 1977).

114 Security Council Resolution 221 (1966) UN SCOR, UN Doc S/Res/221 (9 April 1966).

115 Security Council Resolution 182 (1963) UN SCOR, UN Doc S/Res/182 (4 December 1963); see also Security Council Resolution 181 UN SCOR, UN Doc S/Res/181 (7 August 1963).

The beginnings of conflict in the Democratic Republic of Congo also seem to show an early somewhat broadened understanding of peace and security. As Bothe points out, it seems to be simultaneously the internal and international elements of the conflict that led to recognition of this situation as a threat to international peace and security.[116] While it is the international implications that seem to be the focus of the resolutions, in particular the withdrawal of Belgian personnel, Resolutions 161 and 169 seem equally concerned with the internal violence itself:

> Deeply concerned at the grave repercussions of these crimes and the danger of widespread civil war and bloodshed in the Congo and the threat to international peace and security[117]

Nonetheless, other than a few rare exceptions such as those highlighted above, the view of 'security' in the early decades of the Security Council, at least up to the end of the Cold War, was clearly a narrow vision. 'International peace and security' was concerned with military violence of state upon state. Internal conflicts and violence normally only constituted a threat to international peace and security if the repercussions of that violence spilling across territorial borders seemed imminent. This concept of security as the absence of inter-state conflict was largely in keeping with the realist model of security which was dominant at the time. However, just as the end of the Cold War encouraged academic discussion of the broadening and deepening of security, so too does the Security Council's interpretation of its mandate and the maintenance of international peace and security begin to become a broader, more inclusive, concept.[118] The change is particularly significant as it came at a time when the Security Council was no longer impacted by the Cold War blocs that had stymied its role for so long.

Emerging from the Cold War, a meeting of Heads of State and Government was conducted for the first time by the Security Council on 31 January 1992. This meeting (which, it should be noted, occurred *before* the emergence of human

116 Michael Bothe, 'Security in International Law Since 1990' in Hans Günter Brauch et al (eds), *Globalization and Environmental Challenges* (Springer Berlin Heidelberg, 2008) vol 3, 475, 582.

117 Security Council Resolution 161 (1961) UN SCOR, UN Doc S/Res/161 (21 February 1961) and reiterated in Security Council Resolution 169 (1961) UN SCOR, UN Doc S/Res/169 (24 November 1961).

118 For discussion of the expansion, see, eg, Jane E Stromseth, David Wippman, and Rosa Brooks, *Can Might Make Rights? Building the Rule of Law after Military Interventions* (Cambridge University Press, 2006); Michael J Matheson, *Council Unbound: The Growth of UN Decision Making on Conflict and Post-conflict Issues after the Cold War* (United States Institute of Peace Press, 2006) 41–64; PJ Kooijmans 'The Enlargement of the Concept Threat to the Peace' RJ Dupuy (ed) *The Development of the Role of the Security Council* (Nijhoff, 1993) 111–21; JM Sorel 'L'élargissement de la notion de menace contre la paix' in Société Française pour le Droit International *Le Chapitre VII de la Charte des Nations Unies* (Pedone, 1996) 3–57; Lois E Fielding, 'Taking a Closer Look at Threats to Peace: The Power of the Security Council to Address Humanitarian Crises' (1995) 73 *University of Detroit Mercy Law Review* 551.

security) acknowledged that international peace and security was not simply a military matter or the absence of armed conflict:

> The absence of war and military conflicts among States does not in itself ensure international peace and security. The non-military sources of instability in the economic, social, humanitarian and ecological fields have become threats to peace and security. The United Nations membership as a whole, working through the appropriate bodies, needs to give the highest priority to the solution of these matters.[119]

Freudenschauβ, who participated in this meeting, recalls his surprise 'at how easy it was to arrive at this text'.[120] This comprehensive view has been consistently reaffirmed by the Council in non-binding statements. In 2001 the Council asserted that 'the quest for peace requires a comprehensive, concerted and determined approach that addresses the root causes of conflicts, including their economic and social dimensions'.[121] This reinforced previous statements as to the importance of the eradication of poverty, the promotion of democracy, sustainable human development and respect for human rights.[122] In turn, the Security Council has acknowledged the interconnections travel in both directions, as ensuring 'peace, security and stability' is a necessary prerequisite for economic development.[123] The significant relationship between peace and development has also been recognised in Security Council Resolutions, most explicitly in Resolution 1159, regarding the situation in the Central African Republic in 1998:

> Recognizing the link between peace and development and that a sustained commitment by the international community to assist and support the economic, social, and institutional development of the Central African Republic is indispensable for long-term peace and stability in the country, and in that regard welcoming the cooperation between the Government of the Central African Republic and the international financial institutions in developing an economic reform programme.[124]

119 UN Security Council, Statement by the President of the Security Council, UN SCOR, UN Doc S/23500 (31 January 1992).

120 Helmut Freudenschauβ, 'Article 39 of the UN Charter Revisited: Threats to the Peace and the Recent Practice of the UN Security Council' (1993) 46 *Austrian Journal of Public and International Law* 1, 28.

121 UN Security Council President, Peace-building: towards a comprehensive approach, UN SCOR, UN Doc S/PRST/2001/5 (20 February 2001).

122 UN Security Council, Statement of the President, UN SCOR, UN Doc S/PRST/1998/29 (24 September 1998).

123 UN Security Council, Statement of the President, UN SCOR, UN Doc S/PRST/2002/31 (31 October 2002).

124 Security Council Resolution 1158 (1998) UN SCOR, UN Doc S/RES/1158 (27 March 1998).

Generally, the broadened perspective of the Security Council can be lumped under several categories.

(i) Refugee flows

Non-military threats to international peace and security were first recognised by the Security Council in the form of flows of refugees escaping internal conflict. Thus in 1991, in response to the ongoing repression of the Kurdish population of Northern Iraq, the Security Council issued Resolution 688 (1991) which stated:

> *Gravely concerned* by the repression of the Iraqi civilian population in many parts of Iraq, including most recently in Kurdish-populated areas, which led to a massive flow of refugees towards and across international frontiers and to cross-border incursions which threaten international peace and security in the region,
> *Deeply disturbed* by the magnitude of the human suffering involved ...[125]

However, that same resolution was also at pains to emphasise the precepts of sovereignty and territorial integrity as governing considerations. Refugees nonetheless thus constituted one of the first non-military considerations of threats to international peace and security. Likewise, in 1993, addressing the situation in Haiti after the coup deposing President Aristide, the Security Council's concern for international peace and security, at least initially, focussed on the potential for refugee flows:

> *Concerned* that the persistence of this situation contributes to a climate of fear of persecution and economic dislocation which could increase the number of Haitians seeking refuge in neighbouring Member States...[126]

Here can also be noted the recognition, albeit indirect, of the impact of 'economic dislocation' as a threat to international peace and security. Later resolutions in relation to Haiti demonstrated a broader range of concerns and a general interest in the restoration of democracy in the country.[127] Recognition of refugee flows does show a broader understanding of security threats, but still remains focused only on how internal problems can impact on other states to be a concern for the international community. It does, however, also indicate a developing understanding of the interconnected nature of threats. The so-called once-in-a-generation refugee crisis generated by the situation in Syria has demonstrated once again a

125 Security Council Resolution 688 (1991) UN SCOR, UN Doc S/Res/688 (5 April 1991).
126 Security Council Resolution 841 (1993) UN SCOR, UN Doc S/Res/841 (16 June 1993).
127 See, eg, Security Council Resolution 917 (1994), UN SCOR, UN Doc S/RES/917 (6 May 1994); Security Council Resolution 940 (1994) UN SCOR, UN Doc S/RES/940 (31 July 1994).

failure of the Security Council to recognise that the refugee crisis is in itself a threat to international peace and security, but has seen the Security Council invoke the language of mutual responsibility, calling on the use of burden-sharing principles to address the crisis:

> *Expressing grave concern* at the more than 4.8 million refugees, including more than 3.4 million women and children, who have fled Syria as a result of ongoing violence, and recognizing that the continued deterioration of the humanitarian situation in Syria is further contributing to the movement of refugees and poses risks to regional stability,
>
> ...
>
> *Noting with concern* that the international response to the Syrian and regional crisis continues to fall short of meeting the needs as assessed by host governments and the United Nations, therefore *urging* once again all Member States, based on burden-sharing principles, to support the United Nations and the countries of the region, including by adopting medium and long-term responses to alleviate the impact on communities, providing increased, flexible and predictable funding as well as increasing resettlement efforts.[128]

The need for successive resolutions repeatedly pointing out that the international community has not pulled its collective weight in addressing the crisis, however, demonstrates the continued normative weakness of ideas of transnational responsibility, despite their vital importance to truly addressing issues of international peace and security.

(ii) Humanitarian and human rights violations

Humanitarian and human rights violations were increasingly acknowledged by the Security Council over the 1990s and into the 21st century. Most were, however, still tied directly to events of armed conflict. The Rwandan genocide was treated by the Security Council as a fairly traditional armed conflict, calling for cease-fires and resolutions between the Parties.[129]

While often the external consequences of threats were still at work in justifying the classification of these violations as threats to international peace and security, the emphasis on the human suffering in such circumstances shows that an increasingly people-centred perspective on security was beginning to emerge:

128 Security Council Resolution 2332 (2016), UN SCOR, UN Doc S/RES/2332 (21 December 2016), echoing the language of Security Council Resolution 2258 (2015) UN SCOR, UN Doc S/RES/2258 (22 December 2015) and SC Res 2014.

129 See, eg, Security Council Resolutions 912 (1994) UN SCOR, UN Doc S/RES/912 (21 April 1994); Security Council Resolution 925 (1994) UN SCOR, UN Doc S/RES/925 (8 June 1994).

> *Appalled* at the ensuing large-scale violence in Rwanda, which has resulted in the death of thousands of innocent civilians, including women and children, the displacement of a significant number of the Rwandese population ...[130]
>
> *Deeply disturbed* by the magnitude of the human suffering involved [In the repression of the Kurdish population of Iraq] ...[131]
>
> *Determining* that the magnitude of the human tragedy caused by the conflict in Somalia ... constitutes a threat to international peace and security ...[132]

Systematic, flagrant and widespread human rights violations were identified as a potential threat to international peace and security in the general, declaratory Resolution 1314 (2000).[133] Application of the Responsibility to Protect doctrine in instances such as the situations in the Sudan[134] and Côte d'Ivoire,[135] and the overthrow of Gaddafi in Libya,[136] and Resolutions on the Protection of Civilians in Armed Conflict demonstrate a further step in recognising human rights violations as a threat to international peace and security. Taking the issue even further, the UN Secretary-General has urged the permanent members of the Security Council to refrain from using the threat of the veto in situations which manifestly invoke the R2P doctrine, and to reach a mutual understanding to that effect.[137] Clearly, however, this understanding is far from being achieved, as demonstrated by the employment of the veto in the situation in Syria in 2012 (and subsequent vetos on this situation), though since 2012, proposed resolutions have not explicitly invoked the Syrian government's failure to protect its citizens. Furthermore, as Wellens points out, human rights violations have never 'provided the exclusive underpinning of a pronouncement or determination of a threat

130 Security Council Resolution 912 (1994) UN SCOR, UN Doc S/RES/912 (21 April 1994).

131 Security Council Resolution 688 (1991) UN SCOR, UN Doc S/RES/688 (5 April 1991).

132 Security Council Resolution 794 (1992) UN SCOR, UN Doc S/RES/794 (3 December 1992).

133 Security Council Resolution 1314 (2000) UN SCOR, UN Doc S/RES/1314 (11 August 2000). For discussion see Karel Wellens, 'The UN Security Council and New Threats to the Peace: Back to the Future' (2003) 8 *Journal of Conflict and Security Law* 15, 43.

134 Security Council Resolution 1706 (2006) UN SCOR, UN Doc S/RES/1706 (31 August 2006) citing paragraphs 138–9 on R2P in the 2005 World Summit Outcome Document and Security Council Resolution 1674 (2006) on the Protection of Civilians in Armed Conflict UN SCOR, UN Doc S/RES/1674 (28 April 2006). However the subsequent Resolution 1769 (2007) UN SCOR, UN Doc S/RES/1769 (31 July 2007) enlisting a more extensive peacekeeping operation failed to refer to R2P.

135 Security Council Resolution 1975 (2011), UN SCOR, UN Doc S/RES/1975 (30 March 2011).

136 Security Council Resolutions 1970 (2011), UN SCOR, UN Doc S/RES/1970 (26 February 2011) and 1973 (2011) UN SCOR, UN Doc S/RES/1973 (17 March 2011).

137 United Nations General Assembly, Implementing the Responsibility to Protect, Report of the Secretary General, UN GAOR, Sixty-third sess, Agenda Item 44 and 107, UN Doc A/63/677 (12 January 2009) [61].

[to the peace]'.[138] In fact, in relation to political unrest in Myanmar, and a proposed Security Council resolution calling for the release of political prisoners and the cessation of human rights violations, including military attacks on ethnic minorities, both China and Russia employed their vetoes (the first double veto since the end of the Cold War), with China asserting that the situation fell within the domestic jurisdiction of Myanmar, while Russia discouraged the Security Council from considering 'issues outside its purview'.[139] Moreover, the urgency of situations has often been ignored as a result of the 'glacial speed'[140] with which the Security Council has responded to serious human rights violations, such as the more than two year gap between the onset of the Darfur crisis and the Security Council Resolution recognising the 'ongoing humanitarian crisis and widespread human rights violations'.[141]

Perhaps the most significant breakthrough in the acknowledgment of the relationship between human rights and international peace and security is Resolution 2331 (2016) dedicated to the issue of human trafficking. This Resolution:

> *Condemns* in the strongest terms all instances of trafficking in persons in areas affected by armed conflicts, and stresses that trafficking in persons undermines the rule of law and contributes to other forms of transnational organized crime, which can exacerbate conflict and foster insecurity and instability and undermine development.[142]

This landmark resolution is the first time that human trafficking has received such attention by the Security Council. The language (and very existence) of this Resolution is significant for a number of reasons, from the perspective of human security discourse. First, the language is deeply people-centric. Rather than focusing on the impact of human trafficking on states and on international peace and security in its broadest construction, the language of the resolution is strongly driven with concerns for the victims of human trafficking:

> *Expressing solidarity* with victims of trafficking in persons, including victims of trafficking in persons in armed conflict and post-conflict situations and in humanitarian crisis derived from them; *noting in this regard* the importance of assistance and services for the physical, psychological and social recovery,

138 Karel Wellens, 'The UN Security Council and New Threats to the Peace: Back to the Future' (2003) 8 *Journal of Conflict and Security Law* 15, 44.
139 The Draft Resolution and a discussion of the debate can be found in UN Security Council Press Release, Security Council Fails to Adopt Draft Resolution on Myanmar, Owing to Negative Votes by China, Russian Federation, UN SCOR, 5619th mtg, UN Doc SC/8939 (12 January 2007).
140 UN High Level Panel on Threats, Challenges and Change, *A More Secure World* (UN, 2004) 42.
141 Security Council Resolution 1556 (2004) UN SCOR, UN Doc S/Res/1556 (30 July 2004).
142 Security Council Resolution 2331 (2016) UN SCOR, UN Doc S/Res/2331 (20 December 2016).

> rehabilitation and reintegration; *recognizing* the extreme trauma experienced by the victims of trafficking in persons in the context of armed conflict and sexual violence in conflict, and that humanitarian organizations should consider this vulnerability in humanitarian planning,

The language of vulnerability employed by the Security Council is addressed further below. The Resolution also calls upon Member States to implement robust mechanisms in support of the protection, identification and redress of victims of trafficking. The multilateral dimensions of human security discourse are acknowledged in terms of encouraging states to develop partnerships with the private sector and to engage relevant groups, particularly local women's organisations to assist with effecting justice for the victims, and also through the need for information sharing, capacity building and technical assistance to effectively address the issue. By acknowledging the need to address issues such as supply chains, corruption and terrorism, and ensuring the criminalisation of such behaviour as a method of deterrence, there is also evidence of a preventative dimension, though the focus is primarily on redressing the situation of people already affected by trafficking. But the resolution does restrict itself to addressing trafficking that is occurring in conflict and post-conflict situations. This arbitrary line dividing those affected by conflict situations and those trafficked in peacetime shows both the limits and the continuing influence of more traditional notions of security.

(iii) Humanitarian assistance

Another aspect of the developing notion of security was that the Security Council increasingly addressed obstruction of humanitarian assistance as a contributor to, if not in itself, a 'threat to peace'. Thus the 'human tragedy' of Somalia, which constituted a threat to international peace and security, was acknowledged as

> further exacerbated by the obstacles being created to the distribution of humanitarian assistance.[143]

Likewise the impact of such obstruction is noted in Resolutions regarding the situation in Bosnia-Herzegovina in the wake of events in Sarajevo:

> *Dismayed* by the continuation of conditions that impede the delivery of humanitarian supplies to destinations within Bosnia and Herzegovina and the consequent suffering of the people of that country …[144]

The same resolution emphasised obstruction of humanitarian assistance as a serious impediment to peace and security, recognising that

143 Ibid.

144 Security Council Resolution 770 (1992) UN SCOR, UN Doc S/RES/770 (13 August 1992); reiterated in Security Council Resolution 787 (1992) UN SCOR, UN Doc S/RES/787 (16 November 1992).

> … the provision of humanitarian assistance in Bosnia and Herzegovina is an important element in the Council's effort to restore international peace and security in the area.

Most recently the Council has required all parties to the conflict in Syria (addressing the relevance of non-state actors in the provision and hindrance of human security):

> shall enable the immediate and unhindered delivery of humanitarian assistance directly to people throughout Syria …[145]

Recognition of the importance of humanitarian assistance seems an important step in the direction of human security, as it is an acknowledgment of the broader implications of conflict, and the interconnected nature of conditions necessary for human survival and dignity. The language also demonstrates far greater consideration by the Security Council of the human element of international peace and security. However, this recognition needs to be tempered with an acknowledgement that thus far the Security Council has recognised the impediment of humanitarian assistance only when directly related to a situation of armed conflict. No statements regarding the prevention of human suffering through the provision of international assistance were made by the Security Council following the military junta of Myanmar's obstruction to aid following Cyclone Nargis in 2008, Nor in relation to the obstruction and hijacking of aid by Al-Shabaab insurgents in Somalia during the 2011 Horn of Africa famine. As to the latter, however, the Security Council did expressly note that the asset-freeze related sanctions established in Resolution 1844 would not apply to funds 'necessary to ensure the timely delivery of urgently needed humanitarian assistance in Somalia'.[146] This arguably demonstrates a balancing of different security considerations, with human security being prioritised over other more traditional security priorities.

(iv) Vulnerability and security

Vulnerability (another key concern of human security) is also increasingly a consideration of the Security Council in discussion of international peace and security. The vulnerability of specific groups first began to be recognised in relation to particular conflicts. Thus in relation to East Timor and the Sudan, as two examples:

> *Appalled* by the worsening humanitarian situation in East Timor, particularly as it affects women, children and other vulnerable groups;[147]

145 Security Council Resolution 2165 (2014) UN SCOR, UN Doc S/Res/2165 (14 July 2014). See also a number of subsequent Resolutions, including Security Council Resolution 2332 (2016) UN SCOR, UN Doc S/Res/2332 (21 December 2016).

146 Security Council Resolution 1916 (2010) UN SCOR, UN Doc S/RES/1916 (19 March 2010).

147 Security Council Resolution 1264 (1999) UN SCOR, UN Doc S/RES/1264 (15 September 1999).

> ... expressing its utmost concern at the consequences of the conflict in Darfur on the civilian population, including women, children, internally displaced persons, and refugees...[148]

The role of Security Council resolutions has expanded beyond addressing specific conflicts, and vulnerability has been one area of such consideration. These general declaratory resolutions have moved the Security Council in a new direction. They demonstrate a recognition that particular threats and concerns are common to many of the situations that come before the Council, and thus show a willingness on the part of the Council to become more proactive and prospective in its activities, which aligns with the preventative focus of human security. Indeed, these non-coercive resolutions on thematic issues of peace and security have been described by some as 'human security resolutions'.[149] True-Frost, for example, argues that the description is appropriate since these resolutions focus on the needs and rights of individuals and blur the conventional boundaries between the doctrines of human rights, development and *jus in bello.*[150]

The Security Council has issued a series of specific Resolutions about addressing the particular vulnerabilities experienced by civilians,[151] and specifically women[152] and children[153] in situations of armed conflict and their susceptibility to serious human rights violations. The resolutions on Women and Armed Conflict are particularly important as a range of them emphasise the importance of not merely

148 Security Council Resolution 1556 (2004) UN SCOR, UN Doc S/RES/1556 (30 July 2004).

149 See, C Cora True-Frost, 'The Security Council and Norm Consumption' (2007–2008) 40 *NYU Journal of International Law & Politics* 115, 118.

150 Ibid, 118 fn 7.

151 Security Council Resolutions 1265 (1999) UN SCOR, UN Doc S/RES/1265 (17 September 1999); 1296 (2000) UN SCOR UN Doc S/RES/1296 (19 April 2000); 1502 (2003) UN SCOR UN Doc S/RES/1502 (26 August 2003); 1674 (2006) UN SCOR, UN Doc S/RES/1674 (28 April 2006); 1894 (2009) UN SCOR UN Doc S/RES/1894 (11 November 2009).

152 Security Council Resolutions 1325 (2000) UN SCOR, UN Doc S/RES/1325 (31 October 2000); 1820 (2008) UN SCOR, UN Doc S/RES/1820 (19 June 2008); 1888 (2009) UN SCOR, UN Doc S/RES/1888 (30 Sept 2009); 1889 (2009) UN SCOR, UN Doc S/RES/1889 (5 October 2009); 1894 (2009) UN SCOR, UN Doc S/RES/1894 (11 November 2009); 2122 (2013) UN SCOR, UN Doc S/RES/2122 (18 October 2013).

153 Security Council Resolutions 1261 (1999) UN SCOR, UN Doc S/RES/1261 (25 August 1999); 1314 (2000) UN SCOR, UN Doc S/RES/1314 (11 August 2000); 1379 (2001) UN SCOR, UN Doc S/RES/1379 (20 November 2001); 1460 (2003) UN SCOR, UN Doc S/RES/1460 (30 January 2003); 1539 (2004) UN SCOR, UN Doc S/RES/1539 (22 April 2004); 1612 (2005) UN SCOR, UN Doc S/RES/1612 (26 July 2005); 1882 (2009) UN SCOR, UN Doc S/RES/1882 (4 August 2009); 1998 (2011) UN SCOR, UN Doc S/RES/1998 (12 July 2011); 2068 (2012) UN SCOR, UN Doc S/RES/2068 (19 September 2012); and 2143 (2014) UN SCOR, UN Doc S/RES/2143 (7 March 2014).

treating women as victims,[154] but also granting them agency via strategies for empowering them and involving them in the peacebuilding process:

> *Noting* that women in situations of armed conflict and post-conflict situations continue to be often considered as victims and not as actors in addressing and resolving situations of armed conflict and *stressing* the need to focus not only on protection of women but also on their empowerment in peacebuilding ...[155]

Again this draws on ideas that are encapsulated by human security discourse and not largely found in other conceptualisations of security. Also found within these resolutions are multi-dimensional considerations of security, focused on peace-building, but nonetheless recognising the importance of, *inter alia*, health and economic considerations for a comprehensive and sustainable realisation of security.

Terrorism and concerns related to weapons of mass destruction are, of course, also relevant in considering other possible 'threats to peace'.[156] Growing attention to illegal flows of arms and light weapons and the exploitation of natural resources to finance conflict are also part of this deepened understanding. But the most remarkable and relevant 'new' threat to peace and security came in the recognition of HIV/AIDS as a potential threat by the Security Council.[157] The first acknowledgment of the spread of HIV as a threat to international peace and security came in Resolution 1308 in 2000. Since then extensive attention has been given to the issue. Again, however, the Security Council, while recognising the breadth of threats by considering this issue, has limited its primary attention to conflict and post-conflict situations. Indeed, in terms of response, Resolution 1308 largely narrowed the focus to the potential effect of the pandemic on peacekeepers. It has, however, also acknowledged the broader importance of prevention, which does necessitate incorporating a vision beyond conflict.

154 There is extensive literature on the role of Security Council Resolution 1325 and the rise of transnational women's security on the global stage, which is beyond the scope of this book. It does however demonstrate the significance of civil society and frameworks of positive peace promoting a more human security approach of the Security Council.

155 Security Council Resolution 1889 (2009) UN SCOR, UN Doc S/RES/1889 (5 October 2009).

156 On terrorism, see, eg, Security Council Resolutions 1373 (2001) UN SCOR, UN Doc S/RES/1373 (28 September 2001); 1450 (2002) UN SCOR, UN Doc S/RES/1450 (13 December 2002); 1624 (2005) UN SCOR, UN Doc S/RES/1624 (14 September 2005); 2082 (2012) UN SCOR, UN Doc S/RES/2082 (17 December 2012). On Weapons of Mass Destruction, see, eg, Security Council Resolutions 1172 (1998) UN SCOR, UN Doc S/RES/1172 (6 June 1998); 1696 (2006) UN SCOR, UN Doc S/RES/1696 (31 July 2006); 1803 (2008) UN SCOR, UN Doc S/RES/1803 (3 March 2008); 1929 (2010) UN SCOR, UN Doc S/RES/1929 (9 June 2010); and 2049 (2012) UN SCOR, UN Doc S/RES/2049 (7 June 2012).

157 See Security Council Resolution 1308 (2000) UN SCOR, UN Doc S/RES/1308 (17 July 2000).

While not embracing the language of human security, nor yet moving towards an idea of international insecurity that exists independent of conflict, the most recent and significant Resolution in relation to the threat of HIV/AIDS is demonstrative of a number of the ideals driving elements of human security. The *people-centred* dimension of human security is inherent in the concern about HIV, but is particularly evident in the way that the Resolution does not discuss how HIV might destabilise nation-states, but focuses on the very human impact of the disease. The *multilateral* nature of human security is acknowledged in the endorsement and promotion of public private partnerships, the role of international institutions, joint operations (most notably UNAIDS) and civil society as being central to addressing the problems related to the pandemic. The resolution repeatedly stresses the need for a comprehensive, coordinated and global response. The *preventative* aspect is stressed by the Resolution, in particular through the prevention of conflict-driven sexual violence. The *interconnected* quality of human security is also evident in the resolution:

> *Further recognizing* that conditions of violence and instability in conflict and post-conflict situations can exacerbate the HIV epidemic, *inter alia*, through large movements of people, widespread uncertainty over conditions, conflict-related sexual violence, and reduced access to medical care …

Vulnerability is given special attention in the resolution,

> *Recognizing* that women and girls are particularly affected by HIV,
> *Notes* that the disproportionate burden of HIV and AIDS on women is one of the persistent obstacles and challenges to gender equality and empowerment of women …

This approach is part of a general trend that Wellens traces within the Security Council of a growing awareness and importance attached to 'a movement towards a global, integrated approach to peace, not only to the interlinkage of causes and consequences of threats to the peace, but also to the interlinkages between various threats and conflicts.'[158] He argues that the combination of these general declaratory statements alongside the situation-specific resolutions and determinations has produced a degree of order and consistency in the Security Council's practice.[159] However, the fact remains that the Security Council's approach to its mandate is not guided by any clear methodology, nor any specific conceptual framework. Explicit adoption of human security discourse within the Security Council would promote far greater consistency and predictability to its operation, which would in turn lend greater legitimacy to its operation.

158 Karel Wellens, 'The UN Security Council and New Threats to the Peace: Back to the Future' (2003) 8 *Journal of Conflict and Security Law* 15, 33.
159 Ibid 47.

B The limitations of the Security Council's approach – pre-2014

Some discussions by members of the Security Council during debates have expressly recognised 'international peace and security' as extending to human security. Argentina asserted that 'threats to international peace and security are not exclusively related to the threat or use of force ... they instead encompass a broader criterion that has been called human security.'[160] Rwanda has noted '[i]t is indeed true that through a broad Security Council agenda, including human security, the Council's legitimacy and credibility hinges on its ability to act as a guarantor of civilian protection.'[161] The African Union commented that 'the Security Council should take an interest in issues of human security, including social and economic development. There is a great need to stress the linkage between peace and security, and economic development.'[162] Azerbaijan perhaps has gone the furthest, expressing the opinion that '[p]roviding human security is one of the main responsibilities of the Security Council.'[163] However, while recourse to discussions of human security is an increasing facet of Security Council debates,[164] 'human security' has yet to feature in a single UN Security Council Resolution, or any other form of formal statement from the Council. Moreover, while there has been a widening of the problems that the Security Council acknowledges as threats to international peace and security, prior to 2014, the additional matters have only been recognised in so far as they directly relate to the threat of armed conflict. As one member noted, '[c]onflict is the business of the Council'.[165] This has been observed in the above discussion, particularly in the cases of humanitarian assistance and the proliferation of HIV/AIDS. It demonstrates that there has been wider consensus on adopting a narrow view of human security, but that much uncertainty still exists over the broader interpretation of human security.

It seems, however, that the reticence is not always a matter of whether or not the issues are security concerns, but can rather be attributed to merely functional questions as to what the Security Council can in fact do. Thus when food security was discussed within the Security Council it was widely recognised as an issue with an 'incontrovertible link' to peace and security.[166] The UK likewise acknowledged that '[t]he underlying causes of hunger are very complex, but there is no doubt

160 UNSC Verbatim Record, UN SCOR, UN Doc S/PV/4087 (Resumption 1) (10 January 2000) 2.
161 UNSC Verbatim Record, UN SCOR, UN Doc S/PV/7019 (19 September 2013).
162 UNSC Verbatim Record, UN SCOR, UN Doc S/PV/7015 (Resumption 1) (6 August 2013).
163 UNSC Verbatim Record, UN SCOR, UN Doc S/PV/3980 (Resumption 1) (22 February 1999) 2.
164 For discussion see, eg, Hitoshi Nasu, 'The Place of Human Security in Collective Security' (2012) *Journal of Conflict and Security Law* 1.
165 UNSC Verbatim Record, UN SCOR, UN Doc S/PV/5766 (23 October 2007) 17 (United Kingdom).
166 UNSC Verbatim Record, UN SCOR, UN Doc S/PV/5220 (30 June 2005) (Philippines).

that there are links both to governance and to peace and security – and these are the principal concern of the Security Council.'[167] While discussion rapidly turned to the link between conflict and food security, the discussion indicates that this was more a matter of confusion of what the Security Council's role should be. Algeria, for example, noted that the General Assembly and the Economic and Social Council were better equipped to determine and respond to the structural causes of food insecurity.[168]

Similar issues occurred when the issue of climate change was raised for discussion in the Security Council. The first time it was raised, in 2007 by the United Kingdom, the topic of discussion was expressly the potential of climate change to act as a driver of armed conflict.[169] While Small Island Pacific States emphasised the direct and urgent nature of the security threat, they focused on the threat to their national security, and did not raise the issue of human security.[170] Furthermore, they ultimately aligned themselves with proponents of the link between climate change and conflict.[171] Human security was only sparingly raised during the discussion.[172] However, the louder voices in this debate (most notably the Group of 77, endorsed by China and Russia) viewed the issue as beyond the scope of the Security Council, and criticised the 'ever-increasing encroachment by the Security Council on the roles and responsibilities of other principal organs of the United Nations.'[173] The issue returned to the Security Council in 2011, in an open debate on the emerging challenges to international peace and security. During this debate greater recourse to human security was had, and the broader range of implications of climate change beyond conflict were acknowledged, such as concerns about environmental and food security, economic instability and health implications.[174] Again, however, the Group of 77, China and Russia all emphasised that this was not a security issue but an issue of development. Interestingly, Bolivia's concern was not about the definition of security or the mandate of the Security Council, but a political concern. The Security Council was an inappropriate forum for dealing with climate change since 'the representatives of

167 Ibid 9 (United Kingdom).
168 Ibid 14 (Algeria).
169 'Letter dated 5 April 2007 from the Permanent Representative of the United Kingdom of Great Britain and Northern Ireland to the United Nations addressed to the President of the Security Council' UN Doc S/2007/186 (5 April 2007).
170 UNSC Verbatim Record, UN SCOR, UN Doc S/PV/5663 (17 April 2007) 28–9 (Papua New Guinea); UNSC Verbatim Record, UN SCOR, UN Doc S/PV/5663 (Resumption 1) (17 April 2007) 8–9 (Tuvalu); 25 (Micronesia).
171 See, eg, Hitoshi Nasu, 'The Place of Human Security in Collective Security' (2012) *Journal of Conflict and Security Law* 1, 25.
172 UNSC Verbatim Record, UN SCOR, UN Doc S/PV/5663 (17 April 2007), 29 (Japan); UNSC Verbatim Record, UN SCOR UN Doc S/PV/5663 (Resumption 1) (17 April 2007) 29 (Bolivia); 32 (Costa Rica, as a collective statement on behalf of the Human Security Network).
173 UNSC Verbatim Record, UN SCOR, UN Doc S/PV/5663 (17 April 2007) 24 (Pakistan).
174 See, eg, UNSC Verbatim Record, UN SCOR, UN Doc S/PV/6587 (20 July 2011) 28 (El Salvador); 6 (United States); 29 (EU); 8 (Brazil).

the largest emitters of greenhouse gases are precisely those States with permanent seats in the Council and the right to veto.'[175] Ultimately neither discussion amounted in any Security Council Resolutions, as was also the case with food security and most recently water security. Thus, up until 2014, unless a human security issue could be firmly placed in the context of armed conflict, there was a distinct reluctance to recognise it as falling within the purview of the Security Council.

C The Ebola crisis, human security and Resolution 2177 (2014) – watershed moment, or flash in the pan?

On 18 September 2014, the Security Council held an emergency meeting on a public health crisis for the first time in its history.[176] While, as discussed above, the Council had previously met to discuss the AIDS pandemic, it had never before treated a health crisis as a sufficiently imminent threat to call an emergency session of the Council, though pandemics broadly had been discussed at the aforementioned open debate on emerging challenges in November 2011. Indeed, at that time Portugal had, with significant prescience given the current epidemic, noted '[i]ntegrating the fight against pandemics into the peacebuilding strategies of post-conflict countries ... is an essential measure to avoid jeopardizing the gains made in the consolidation of peace'.[177] If due attention had been paid to this concern, the preventative dimension of human security would have been fulfilled, and the current situation mitigated.

The Ebola outbreak had been briefly discussed earlier in the year, during the meeting on the UN Office for West Africa.[178] At the time, however, it remained firmly categorised as purely a health issue and not a security threat. The Security Council issued a press statement expressing concern about the situation and highlighting the need for prompt international assistance, but was otherwise satisfied that no further response to the situation was required by the Council. This sentiment began to change as the outbreak began to develop at an exponential rate: the World Health Organisation declared the situation a public health emergency on 8 August and the Security Council briefing on Liberia demonstrated the social upheaval and broader implications of the crisis. The emergency meeting was called for by the US, and resulted in the adoption of Resolution 2177.[179] The Resolution had a record 130 co-sponsors, the highest sponsorship of any Resolution issued in

175 Ibid 26 (Bolivia).

176 UNSC Verbatim Record, UN SCOR, UN Doc S/PV/7268 (18 September 2014) 7 (President's Statement).

177 UNSC Verbatim Record, UN SCOR, UN Doc S/PV/6668 (23 November 2011) (Portugal). This was highlighted by the Security Council Report, <http://www.securitycouncilreport.org/>.

178 UNSC Verbatim Record, UN SCOR, UN Doc S/PV/7213 (8 July 2014).

179 Security Council Resolution 2177 (2014) UN SCOR, UN Doc S/Res/2177 (18 September 2014).

the history of the Council,[180] demonstrating the universal concern about and support for addressing this human security crisis.

Resolution 2177 determines that 'the unprecedented extent of the Ebola outbreak in Africa constitutes a threat to international peace and security.' This assertion is undiluted, with no qualifying reference back to its relationship to armed conflict. It thus represents the first recognition by the Council, not only of the threat posed by an epidemic to international peace and security, but of any threat to human security not linked to direct violence. The Resolution calls on action from all capable and relevant actors – from member states, regional organisations, the UN and the private sector, recognising the need for a coordinated and integrated response, and the significant contribution non-state actors can make to dealing with such a human security crisis. One of the principal aims of the meeting and the Resolution itself was to draw attention to the crisis and lend the Security Council's considerable weight to emphasising the urgency and high priority of the issue.

Unlike previous open debate on human security issues, the debate on the outbreak was not dominated by discussions of whether or not the crisis constituted a threat to international peace and security, or whether the crisis was within the mandate of the Council. However, also unlike previous debates, 'human security' was not a phrase used once during extensive debates – not by Member States (not even members of the Human Security Network or Japan, who most regularly bring discussion of human security into the Council), nor by the UN representatives who spoke, despite the increasing mainstreaming of human security within the organisation. Nonetheless, the imprints of human security discourse are found across the debate. Yet, as will be seen, the lack of direct recourse to human security has also had an impact on the scope and nature of the discussion.

The concerns around the issue are indisputably *people-centric.*

> If we do not respond with urgency and from the heart, with health policies on treatment, prevention and education, the living conditions of peoples around the world may be dramatically affected, as the lives of thousands of people in the countries of West Africa are being affected.[181]

Representatives of WHO and *Médecins Sans Frontières* related hands-on experiences of the suffering.

> None of us experienced in containing outbreaks has ever seen in our lifetimes an emergency on this scale, with such a degree of suffering and such a magnitude of cascading consequences.[182]

180 UNSC Verbatim Record, UN SCOR, UN Doc S/PV/7268 (18 September 2014) 8 (President's Statement).
181 UNSC Verbatim Record, UN SCOR, UN Doc S/PV/7268 (18 September 2014) (Argentina).
182 UNSC Verbatim Record, UN SCOR, UN Doc S/PV/7268 (18 September 2014) 5 (Ms Chan speaking on behalf of WHO).

Yet despite the inherent human-security-centricity of the situation, the Resolution at no point refers to human suffering, unlike previous Resolutions discussed above. The language of the Resolution is instead broadly stated in terms of the wide sweeping effects on states and the region, expressing grave concern about the 'impact on West Africa', instead of any explicit recognition of the direct impact felt by the populations within the region, or beyond. The only exception to this state-centric language is in the recognition of the particular *vulnerability* of women to the impact of the outbreak:

> ... that responses to the Ebola outbreak should address the specific needs of women and *stresses* the importance of their full and effective engagement in the development of such responses ...[183]

This direct reference to the unique vulnerability of women is in keeping with the commitments of the Security Council in Resolution 1325, and the express concerns raised by a number of representatives in the debate. Australia, for example, noted that '[w]omen are disproportionately affected, as always, accounting for as much as 70 per cent of Ebola cases. Female nurses represent the majority of medical personnel killed.'[184] Similar statements were made by other speakers, sometimes recognising other classes of vulnerable persons, most notably children, but with a firm focus on women. Positively though, and again in accordance with Resolution 1325, it was not simply the vulnerability of women that was acknowledged, but also issues of *agency and empowerment*, by stressing engagement with the response effort, and not reducing women to an instrumentalist or essentialist 'victim'.[185] Missing from the Resolution itself however is a recognition of other forms of vulnerability to related human insecurity, most notably the impact of stigmatisation experienced by the infected and their families.[186]

Nor are human rights (and most obviously the right to health) mentioned in the Resolution, or indeed in the records of the Meetings themselves. This is problematic, not only because of the failure to take a rights-based approach to security, but also for missing the opportunity to strengthen its approach in relation to the universality of the issue.

The *universality* of the issue is recognised in the Resolution's call for an international coordinated response, and in the recognition that this is a crisis that 'may

183 UNSC Verbatim Record, UN SCOR, UN Doc S/PV/7268 (18 September 2014) [2]. See also Preamble, '*Expressing concern* about the particular impact of the Ebola outbreak on women.'

184 UNSC Verbatim Record, UN SCOR, UN Doc S/PV/7268 (18 September 2014) 16 (Australia).

185 See, eg, Aili Mari Tripp, 'Toward a Gender Perspective on Human Security' in Aili Mari Tripp, Myra Marx Ferree and Christina Ewig (eds), *Gender, Violence and Human Security: Critical Feminist Perspectives* (New York University Press, 2013) 11, 27.

186 See, eg, UNSC Verbatim Record, UN SCOR, UN Doc S/PV/7268 (18 September 2014) 22 (Chile).

exceed the capacity of the governments concerned to respond'.[187] Concerns of mutual vulnerability and responsibility found greater expression in the debate.

> The suffering and spillover effects in the region and beyond demand the attention of the entire world. Ebola matters to us all.[188]

Universality and responsibility also found expression in repeated calls in the Resolution and the debate for states to resist the urge to isolate themselves, which was deemed both unhelpful and counterproductive as it undermined efforts to respond to the outbreak.[189]

> Today, instead of isolating the affected countries, we call for flooding them with the resources that are desperately needed to turn the tide in this fight.[190]

However, the Resolution fails to acknowledge any explicit international legal obligations for international cooperation and assistance. The Committee on Economic, Social and Cultural Rights, in its General Comment 14 (and reiterating the obligation outlined in General Comment 3), stressed that 'states parties should recognise the essential role of international cooperation and comply with their commitment to take joint and separate action to achieve the full realization of the right to health', in keeping not only with their human rights obligations but also under the commitment contained in Article 55 of the United Nations Charter.

The *interconnected* nature of threats and the complex comprehensive insecurities posed by the outbreak were universally attested across the debate. Almost every speaker began with a commentary on how the epidemic was not merely a health crisis, but 'a social crisis, a humanitarian crisis, an economic crisis and a threat to national security well beyond the outbreak zones.'[191] The varying impacts of the disease were spoken of with varying degrees of specificity among the speakers. The Resolution itself, however, is more constrained. In relation to international peace and security, there was a focus on the more traditional forms of security threat:

> *Recognizing* that the peacebuilding and development gains of the most affected countries concerned could be reversed in light of the Ebola outbreak and *underlining* that the outbreak is undermining the stability of the most affected

187 Security Council Resolution 2177 (2014) UN SCOR, UN Doc S/Res/2177 (18 September 2014) Preamble.
188 UNSC Verbatim Record, UN SCOR, UN Doc S/PV/7268 (18 September 2014) 2 (Secretary General).
189 Security Council Resolution 2177 (2014) UN SCOR, UN Doc S/Res/2177 (18 September 2014) [4].
190 UNSC Verbatim Record, UN SCOR, UN Doc S/PV/7268 (18 September 2014) 8 (President).
191 See, eg, UNSC Verbatim Record, UN SCOR, UN Doc S/PV/7268 (18 September 2014) 5 (WHO).

> countries concerned and, unless contained, may lead to further instances of civil unrest, social tensions and a deterioration of the political and security climate ...[192]

There is also a reference to the impact on food security posed by existing travel and trade restrictions, but otherwise the varying dimensions of human security are not addressed. Furthermore, and more troubling, the broader dimensions of the crisis seem to be deemed the responsibility of the affected states, and the affected states alone:

> *Encourages* the governments of Liberia, Sierra Leone and Guinea to continue efforts to resolve and mitigate the wider political, security, socioeconomic and humanitarian dimensions of the Ebola outbreak ...[193]

Further detracting from a genuine human security effort, no reference to human rights is made in the resolution. Nor were human rights referred to at all during the debate. While this neglect is not surprising, it does undermine the potential for a comprehensive account of human security.

Resolution 2177 is nevertheless of significance for human security discourse. It shows a genuine shift in perspective as to what constitutes a threat to international peace and security, and is as such an important step in the recognition of human security as the appropriate account of security on the world stage. However, whether it demonstrates a sustainable shift – one that points to the future direction of the Security Council – is questionable. After all, the Ebola outbreak has been described as an unprecedented, unique crisis – 'likely the greatest peacetime challenge that the United Nations and its agencies has ever faced'.[194] It may well be that it will take another such unparalleled crisis before the Security Council advances the scope of international peace and security again. Furthermore, the need to wait until a crisis reaches such a point undermines the potential of human security discourse to promote the prevention of insecurity. Yet it is unlikely that another non-traditional threat will be accorded the attention demonstrated in Resolution 2177 until a comparable crisis level is reached, and even then, the lack of clarity on the interpretation of 'security' means the international community can have no certainty in terms of response.

There may, however, be an enduring influence of human security discourse on the Council's consideration of international peace and security. This is demonstrated in a recent Presidential Statement on the issue of 'Inclusive Development'.[195] While this statement once again eschews usage of the term 'human security', the fingerprints of the discourse are undeniable in its content. The statement 'underlines that security and development are closely interlinked and

192 UNSC Verbatim Record, UN SCOR, UN Doc S/PV/7268 (18 September 2014).
193 Security Council Resolution 2177 (2014) UN SCOR, UN Doc S/Res/2177 (18 September 2014) [2].
194 UNSC Verbatim Record, UN SCOR, UN Doc S/PV/7268 (18 September 2014) 5 (WHO).
195 UN Security Council, Statement by the President of the Security Council on Inclusive Development, UN SCOR, UN Doc S/PRST/2015/3 (19 January 2015).

mutually reinforcing and key to attaining sustainable peace. The Council recognizes that their relationship is complex, multifaceted and case-specific.'[196] This is language almost directly paralleling the Reports of the Secretary-General on Human Security, as discussed above. As in the Draft Declaration on the Right to Peace's article on human security, security is deemed to require coherence between security, human rights, development and rule of law activities.[197] Throughout the statement the need for an integrative, comprehensive approach is taken, and the protection of civilians and vulnerable individuals highlighted. This statement, the general trend of a broadening scope of threats to the peace, and Resolution 2177 collectively indicate a growing understanding of security that is steadily shifting beyond a focus on states as the referent objects of security, the core unit entitled to international protection.

V Conclusion

It may currently be too presumptuous to describe human security, which still remains a relatively new conceptualisation of 'security', as the authoritative interpretation of international peace and security within the UN Charter. It is, however, an increasingly dominant discourse, and the UN itself has acknowledged the interlinkages between human welfare and international peace and security. There is no denying that the understanding of what security constitutes has broadened since the Charter was originally drafted, and that much of this broadening supports consideration of human security. But the vision of human security as it has expanded so far has largely been a narrow approach to human security, with a continued emphasis on the consequences of direct violence. It remains to be seen if recent developments, as a result of the Ebola crisis, signal a change in perspective that will lead to a warmer embrace of comprehensive human security. Even if they do, the relationship between human security discourse and international security architecture has a long way to go. Human security could provide a useful normative framework for the future work of the Security Council, allowing it to produce both a clear working methodology and a discourse of security when fulfilling its role on the international stage. Human security discourse may be one means of bringing international law, and in particular, human rights considerations, firmly into the Security Council's deliberation processes, thus enabling the power of the 'better argument' to add greater legitimacy and bring certainty to its decision-making and the broadening scope of its work.[198] It would also allow greater opportunity to determine the Security Council's role in the prevention of and not merely mitigation of and reaction to threats.

196 Ibid.

197 UN Human Rights Council, *Report of the Human Rights Council Advisory Committee on the Right of Peoples to Peace*, UN GAOR, Twentieth sess, Agenda Item 5, UN Doc A/HRC/20/31 (16 April 2012) art 2.

198 Ian Johnstone, 'Security Council Deliberations: The Power of the Better Argument' (2003) 14 *European Journal of International Law* 437. See also Ian Johnstone, 'Legislation and Adjudication in the UN Security Council: Bringing Down the Deliberative Deficit' (2008) 102 *American Journal of International Law* 275.

6 International law-making and a human security template

I Introduction

The previous chapter looked at the way in which human security discourse, and in particular the principles articulated in Chapter Four, has had an influence on the interpretation of international peace and security. This chapter examines the ways in which human security discourse has influenced the development of international legal instruments. A number of international treaties have been given the label 'human security treaties'. These treaties are examined in detail in the next chapter. This chapter begins with an examination of the processes of their creation, which in reality has been the primary determinant thus far for the label 'human security treaty'. Primarily this has been applied specifically to the Ottawa Process, which led to the creation of a comprehensive ban on the use of anti-personnel mines (APMs), as well as the series of treaties which followed in its wake and built on the momentum achieved by the Ottawa Process. This chapter examines the elements that made up this process, as a blueprint for future development of international human security treaty law.

It is increasingly recognised in both international law and international relations that effective responses require the efforts of not just the UN (and other international organisations) and states, but of a range of actors, including NGOs, affected populations and the business community. Traditionally, international law works because it is made up of norms made for states, by states, and 'compliance with the rules of international law might be thought of as the price of membership' in the international community.[1] However, as discussed elsewhere, human security, as a universal concern, requires action from all relevant actors, most particularly those directly affected. As Boutros-Ghali noted, prior to the development of the UNDP discourse, '[i]f UN efforts are to succeed, the roles of the various players need to be carefully coordinated in an integrated approach to human security.'[2]

This chapter will examine the scope of human security discourse as an 'organisational platform' for norm entrepreneurship within international law.[3] According

1 Carlos M Vásquez, 'Direct v Indirect Obligations of Corporations under International Law' (2005) 43 *Columbia Journal of Transnational Law* 927, 955.
2 Boutros Boutros-Ghali, *An Agenda for Peace* (UN, 1992) [82].
3 See Martha Finnemore and Kathryn Sikkink, 'International Norm Dynamics and Political Change' (1998) 52 *International Organization* 887, 898.

to Wexler, the development, transmission and promotion of norms requires a force 'dedicated to changing the meaning ascribed to certain material practices within the relevant community.'[4] The development of norms involves a reasoning process, and norm entrepreneurs who share not only a common agenda, but a shared set of principles and notions of validity.[5] This is also achieved by framing issues through the development or use of a shared language that 'names, interprets and even dramatises' the issue.[6] This chapter will examine the degree to which human security discourse provides such a shared language. Norm entrepeneurs then pursue social change through '(a) signaling their own commitment to change, (b) creating coalitions, (c) making defiance of norms seem or be more costly, and (d) making compliance with new norms seem or be more beneficial.'[7] While norm entrepreneurs can be comprised of a widespread selection of actors, both state and non-state, this chapter will primarily focus on the role of coalitions of actors, and particularly the role of NGOs within those coalitions.

This chapter examines two ways in which international norm production has moved beyond the traditional constraints of state-centric law development. The first is the crucial role of coalition building for the development of the human security treaties discussed in the following chapter. Secondly, the chapter moves beyond the scope of traditional international law development into the field of soft law and quasi-legislative measures, examining the degree to which human security has been facilitated through the development of multi-stakeholder initiatives.

II The template of human security treaty making

A The emergence of the 'human security formula': the Ottawa Process

The Ottawa Process came about as a result of the failure of the negotiations at the First Review Conference of the 1980 *Convention on Prohibitions or Restrictions on the Use of Certain Conventional Weapons* (CCW).[8] During the review

4 Lesley Wexler, 'The International Deployment of Shame, Second-Best Responses and Norm Entrepreneurship: The Campaign to Ban Landmines and the Landmine Ban Treaty' (2003) 20(3) *Arizona Journal of International and Comparative Law* 561, 562.

5 PM Haas, 'Introduction: Epistemic Communities and International Policy Coordination' (1992) 46 *International Organization* 1, 3. See also the discussion of shared understandings in Jutta Brunnée and Stephen J. Toope, *Legitimacy and Legality in International Law: An Interactional Account* (Cambridge University Press, 2010) chapter 2.

6 Martha Finnemore and Kathryn Sikkink, 'International Norm Dynamics and Political Change' (1998) 52 *International Organization* 887, 897.

7 Cass R Sunstein, 'Social Norms and Social Roles' (1996) 96 *Columbia Law Review* 903, 929.

8 *Convention on Prohibitions or Restrictions on the Use of Certain Conventional Weapons Which May Be Deemed to be Excessively Injurious or to Have Indiscriminate Effects*, opened for signature 10 October 1980, 1342 UNTS 137 (entered into force 2 December 1983) ('CCW').

conference in 1996 not only were minimal gains made, the use of landmines remaining legal under international law, but the definition of an anti-personnel mine in fact became less rigorous.[9] More than 40 states had called for the prohibition on the use of these weapons during this conference, and Canada, in negotiation with both like-minded states and NGOs, decided to use this interest and build momentum by announcing a meeting to be conducted later in the year on the issue of producing a global ban on anti-personnel mines. Thus began the Ottawa Process. At this time human security was at the forefront of Canada's policy development, spearheaded by the Foreign Minister at the time, Lloyd Axworthy.[10] Thus the Ottawa Process and the subsequent Convention are correctly touted as one of the largest successes to date of the human security discourse.[11] The Oslo Process that culminated in the *Convention on Cluster Munitions* was almost a perfect duplication of the Ottawa Process conducted a decade later. Variations begin to appear in the other negotiations, however. For example, while the Oslo and Ottawa Processes were conducted independently of the traditional UN forums, the negotiations for the International Criminal Court, the *Optional Protocol on Child Soldiers* and the *Arms Trade Treaty* were all successfully conducted within the UN framework. However, they all share unifying factors, most notably the clear messaging and the shifting human-centred focus in the negotiations, and the presence of coalition building, with states acting in concert with NGOs and each other. The negotiating processes and policy considerations behind their creation have been the central considerations in the use of the label 'human security treaty'. This section will examine the core components that made up these negotiating conditions.

B Rules of procedure and negotiating conditions

(i) Consensus rule v majority voting

One of the most striking features of the Rules of Procedure for the Ottawa Process was a return of decision-making by two-thirds majority voting. It is worth

9 For discussion on the background of the Ottawa Process, and the previous attempts to initiate a ban on APMs, see, eg, Stuart Maslen and P Herby, 'An International Ban on Anti-personnel Mines: History and Negotiation of the "Ottawa Treaty"', in Louis Maresca and Stuart Maslen (eds), *The Banning of Anti-Personnel Landmines: The Legal Contribution of the International Committee of the Red Cross 1955–1999* (Cambridge University Press, 2000) 606; Jody Williams and Stephen Goose, 'The International Campaign to Ban Landmines' in Maxwell A Cameron, Robert J Lawson and Brian W Tomlin (eds), *To Walk Without Fear: The Global Movement to Ban Landmines* (Oxford University Press, 1998) 20

10 See, eg, Lloyd Axworthy, 'Notes for an Address by the Honourable Lloyd Axworthy, Minister of Foreign Affairs, Canada' (Speech delivered at the Woodrow Wilson International Center for Scholars, Washington, DC, United States of America, 16 June 2000) <http://www.peace.ca/axworthyaddresstwoodrow.htm>.

11 See, eg, Gerd Oberleitner, 'Human Security: Idea, Policy and Law' in Mary Martin and Taylor Owen (eds), *Routledge Handbook of Human Security* (Routledge, 2014) 319.

remembering that there are no restrictions imposed on the creation of rules of procedure. Participating states are free to lay down the conditions deemed appropriate for the Conference proceedings, the decision-making processes and the threshold for adoption of the prospective convention. In the past the practice of two-thirds majority voting reigned supreme.[12] Since the 1970s and the negotiations of the Third Conference of the Law of the Sea, the consensus approach has become the favoured approach for conventions formulated in UN forums.[13] It has been noted that conventions adopted via consensus have a better chance of being signed and ratified, and thus also of entering into force more rapidly.[14] Another rationale for the consensus rule becoming popular at this time was that it prevented negotiations from leaving out ideological, regional or political blocs during the Cold War.[15] The consensus rule dominated international decision-making despite there being some disagreement over the definition of 'consensus', a point that was raised by Mexico at the *ATT* Conference.[16]

The general view is that '"consensus" means the absence of any formal objection', such as is stated in Article 161 (8) (e) *UN Convention on the Law of the Sea*,[17] and similarly in Article IX(1) of the *WTO Agreement*.[18] 'Consensus' is framed slightly differently in Rule 69 of the Final Recommendation of the Helsinki Consultations of the Conference on Security and Cooperation in Europe (OSCE).

12 Particularly noted in the case of humanitarian treaty creation: see, eg, Stuart Maslen and P Herby, 'An International Ban on Anti-personnel Mines: History and Negotiation of the "Ottawa Treaty"', in Louis Maresca and Stuart Maslen (eds), *The Banning of Anti-Personnel Landmines: The Legal Contribution of the International Committee of the Red Cross 1955–1999* (Cambridge University Press, 2000) 606, 620. See also CW Jenks, 'Unanimity, the Veto, Weighted Voting, Special and Simple Majorities and Consensus as Modes of Decisions in International Organizations' in Arnold Duncan McNair Baron McNair (ed), *Cambridge Essays in International Law: Essays in Honour of Lord McNair* (Stevens Publishing Company, 1965) 48.

13 On discussion of the introduction of the consensus process in UNCLOS proceedings, see Daniel Vignes, 'Will the Third Conference on the Law of the Sea Work According to the Consensus Rule?' (1975) 69 *American Journal of International Law* 119. See also L B Sohn, 'United Nations Decision-making, Confrontation of Consensus?' (1974) 15 *Harvard International Law Journal* 438; and Barry Burzan, 'Negotiating by Consensus: Developments in Technique at the United Nations Conference on the Law of the Sea' (1981) 75 *American Journal of International Law* 324.

14 See, eg, Oliver Dörr and Kirsten Schmalenbach, *The Vienna Convention of the Law of Treaties: A Commentary* (Springer Science & Business Media, 2011) 143.

15 Ken Rutherford, 'The Hague and Ottawa Conventions: A Model for Future Weapons Ban Regimes' (1999) Spring–Summer *The Nonproliferation Review* 36, 40.

16 This call echoed the commentary of Amerisinghe, during the Third Law of the Sea Conference, who doubted that one could 'possibly write into the rules of procedure a rule to the effect that there should be a consensus, because a consensus is beyond definition; it is impossible of definition.' Cited by Louis Sohn, 'Voting Procedures in United Nations Conferences for the Codification of International Law' (1975) 69 *American Journal of International Law* 310, 333.

17 *UN Convention on the Law of the Sea*, opened for signature 10 December 1982, 1833 UNTS 3 (entered into force 16 November 1994).

18 *Marrakesh Agreement Establishing the World Trade Organization*, opened for signature 15 April 1994, 1867 UNTS 3 (entered into force 1 January 1995).

There consensus is defined as 'the absence of any objection expressed by a representative and submitted by him as constituting an obstacle to the taking of the decision'. However, such definitions make it difficult to distinguish between consensus and unanimity, which provides a veto power.[19] However, where they can be distinguished is that consensus can be gained through abstention and silences, and only an express contrary view prevents consensus.[20] Consensus is ultimately determined by the President or Chair of the Conference, making the role of the person presiding over the conference particularly central, and further confounding attempts at definition. For example, during the Cancun Climate Change Conference in 2010, the President of the Conference (Mexico's Foreign Minister) overruled Bolivia's express objection to the texts of the final decisions and declared consensus 'to thunderous applause.'[21] On the other hand, at the *ATT* Conference, the President upheld the last-minute objections of Iran, Syria and North Korea, concluding that no consensus had been reached. In the case of the *ATT*, the overwhelming 154 states in support of the treaty text brought the matter to the General Assembly which, being based on majority voting principles, was thus able to adopt the treaty.[22]

The return to majority voting was deemed a particularly important inclusion in the Ottawa Process, given that the consensus rule applied in the CCW negotiations was a significant contributing factor to the failure of CCW Review Conferences in regard to APMs.[23] The same thing occurred again in the third CCW Review Conference in relation to the call to outlaw cluster munitions, and once again states opted to circumvent the CCW Review process entirely, culminating in the Oslo Process and the subsequent creation of the *CCM*:

> When adopting Rule 34 of its Rules of Procedure (stating that decision making in the Conference is governed by Art 8 CCW Convention), the third CCW Review (2006) affirmed that 'in the deliberations and negotiations relating to the Convention and its annexed Protocols, High Contracting Parties have proceeded on the basis of consensus and no decisions have been taken by vote.'[24] In view of the fact that the conference did not reach a consensus on outlawing cluster munitions, the Norwegian government announced on 17

19 Rüdiger Wolfrum and Jakob Pichon, 'Consensus' in Rüdiger Wolfrum (ed) *Max Planck Encyclopedia of Public International Law* (online ed).

20 See, eg, Daniel Vignes, 'Will the Third Conference on the Law of the Sea Work according to Consensus Rule?' (1975) 69*American Journal of International Law* 119, 120.

21 L Rajamani, 'The Cancun Climate Agreements: Reading the Text, Subtext and Tea Leaves', (2011) 60 *International & Comparative Law Quarterly* 499, 515.

22 See, United Nations Office for Disarmament Affairs, *ATT Voting Chart*, <http://www.un.org/disarmament/update/20130402/ATTVotingChart.pdf>.

23 See, eg, Stuart Maslen and P Herby, 'An International Ban on Anti-personnel Mines: History and Negotiation of the "Ottawa Treaty"', in Louis Maresca and Stuart Maslen (eds), *The Banning of Anti-Personnel Landmines: The Legal Contribution of the International Committee of the Red Cross 1955–1999* (Cambridge University Press, 2000) 606.

24 *Final Document of the Third Review Conference of the Conventional Weapons Convention*, UN Doc CCW/CONF.III/I (15 December 2006) 1 (Part 1) [19].

> November 2006, the final day of the CCW Conference, that it would convene an intergovernmental conference to negotiate a convention outside the CCW context. The negotiations of the Convention on Cluster Munitions have been finalized in May 2008. And the Convention was opened for signature in December 2008 in Oslo.[25]

The consensus rule has been particularly popular in the area of disarmament, where it has been considered that universal support is necessary for effective regime development.[26] The consensus approach, at least theoretically, would seem to foster the universality and notions of shared responsibility which are also a part of human security discourse. On the other hand, the proceedings of the CCW and the Conference on Disarmament (CD) are criticised for lowest common denominator approaches and long, drawn-out negotiations – in the case of the CD often lasting decades.[27] Neither of these conditions is fruitful for the development of strong, responsive human-security-oriented norms. The other problem with the consensus approach is that it allows Conference proceedings to be utterly dominated by major powers. By not applying the rule during the Ottawa Process, the US was prevented from derailing the negotiations with its list of packaged demands, which included exceptions for landmine use in Korea, a withdrawal clause in case of national emergencies, deferral of the entry into force of the treaty, and narrowing of the definition of APMs.[28] These requests would have significantly impacted on the human security value of the treaty and the goals it sought to achieve.

It should be noted that during the Ottawa Process discussions, votes were never actually taken, despite the majority voting rule. It has been argued that the value of the rule in this instance was as a deterrent to those who aspired to water down the commitments of the Convention and the comprehensive ban it sought.[29] Moreover, it can also be seen that majority voting need not compromise the pursuit of universal coverage of conventions. The *Ottawa Convention* currently has 162 state parties, and the frequently commented upon de facto compliance on the part of non-member states makes a powerful argument that the Convention has assisted in the creation of an emergent customary norm.[30] The preference for

25 Diplomatic Conference for the Adoption of a Convention on Cluster Munitions, UN Doc CCM/77 (30 May 2008) <http://www.clustermunitionsdublin.ie/pdf/ENGLISHfinaltext.pdf>.

26 See, eg, Oliver Dörr and Kirsten Schmalenbach, *The Vienna Convention of the Law of Treaties: A Commentary* (Springer Science & Business Media, 2011), 143, commentary on Article 9: Adoption of the Text [21].

27 Ken Rutherford, 'The Hague and Ottawa Conventions: A Model for Future Weapons Ban Regimes' (1999) Spring–Summer *The Nonproliferation Review* 36, 39.

28 See, eg, Kenneth Anderson, 'The Ottawa Convention Banning Landmines, the Role of International Non-Governmental Organizations and the Idea of International Civil Society' (2000) 11(1) *European Journal of International Law* 91.

29 Ken Rutherford, 'The Hague and Ottawa Conventions: A Model for Future Weapons Ban Regimes' (1999) Spring–Summer *The Nonproliferation Review* 36, 40.

30 Stuart Maslen and P Herby, 'An International Ban on Anti-personnel Mines: History and Negotiation of the "Ottawa Treaty"', in Louis Maresca and Stuart Maslen (eds),

two-thirds majority voting is replicated in the rules of procedure for the other human security treaties,[31] with the exception of the *Arms Trade Treaty*, which saw what was ultimately an unwelcome return of the consensus approach. As noted above, the consensus approach meant that the final conference on the treaty failed to adopt the text, and recourse to the General Assembly was necessary for the treaty's success.[32] However, this also demonstrates that another core element of success for human security issues is an appreciation by member states of the urgency and importance of the issue at hand. Despite the lack of consensus for the *Arms Trade Treaty*, the solution was not the traditional approach of consensus – to return to the drawing board in search of that lowest common denominator for compromise. Instead, states decided that it was time to produce results in the area of arms control and pushed forward without diluting the core message determined at the conference.

(ii) Fast track strategy

Another feature of the Ottawa Process, and those processes modelled on its procedures, was the fast track strategy of negotiation. The pioneers of the process had been disillusioned by the drawn-out negotiations of the CCW, and were aware both of the urgency of the issue and the need to capitalise on the policy window they had – the public attention surrounding the issue and the political will of states – before that window closed.[33] A strict deadline was set – negotiations would cease, and the Convention ready for adoption by December 1997. Thus the Ottawa Process refers to the 14-month period from the call for a new process during the CCW negotiations in October 1996 to its conclusion in December 1997. Indeed, only a few weeks after Canada had called for the Process, Austria circulated the first draft of a treaty to ban the use of anti-personnel mines.[34] The deadline effectively heightened pressures (internal and external) to

The Banning of Anti-Personnel Landmines: The Legal Contribution of the International Committee of the Red Cross 1955–1999 (Cambridge University Press, 2000) 606; Richard Price, 'Emerging Customary Norms and Anti-Personnel Landmines' (2004) 96 *Cambridge Studies in International Relations* 106; Susan Benesch, Cristina Rodriguez and Robert Sloane, 'International Customary Law and Antipersonnel Landmines: Emergence of a New Customary Norm' in Landmine Monitor (ed), *Landmine Monitor Report 1999: Toward a Mine-Free World* (Human Rights Watch, 1999) 1020. Note, however, that while the ICRC recognised a series of restrictions in the use of landmines, in their landmark study on international customary humanitarian law, this did not extend to the comprehensive ban on their use.

31 See, eg, United Nations Diplomatic Conference of Plenipotentiaries on the Establishment of an International Criminal Court, *Official Record Vol II*, Rome, Italy, 15–17 June 1998, UN Doc A/CONR183/13(Vol.II) (15–17 June 1998).

32 *The Arms Trade Treaty*, General Assembly Resolution 67/234, GAOR, Sixty-seventh sess, Agenda Item 94, UN Doc A/Res/67/234 B (11 June 2013).

33 See, eg, Brian W Tomlin, 'On a Fast Track to a Ban: The Canadian Policy Process' in Maxwell A Cameron, Robert J Lawson and Brian W Tomlin (eds), *To Walk Without Fear: The Global Movement to Ban Landmines* (Oxford University Press, 1998).

34 Stuart Maslen and P Herby, 'An International Ban on Anti-personnel Mines: History and Negotiation of the "Ottawa Treaty"', in Louis Maresca and Stuart Maslen (eds),

produce results, provided significant momentum to the campaign, and helped ensure that the process was not bogged down in procedural issues or backroom deals. In doing so, it helped highlight the core elements of the 'security' label – urgency, priority, and an uncompromising need for effective and comprehensive solutions.

(iii) Forum choice

The choice to conduct the Ottawa Process outside the sanctified halls of the United Nations is often credited as one of the reasons for its success.[35] However, while there are advantages to independent processes, it is clear that this need not be a crucial feature of human security campaigns. While the Oslo Process followed in the footsteps of Ottawa, the Rome Statute establishing the ICC and the *Arms Trade Treaty* were negotiated under the auspices of the United Nations, and the *Optional Protocol on Child Soldiers* within the UN Commission on Human Rights. Nonetheless, there are advantages to be had by conducting human security negotiations via independent processes. The most obvious advantage is the flexibility available to tailor procedures in light of the issues at stake and the outcomes sought.[36] Moreover, removing human security issues from the specialised bodies of the UN, such as the Office for Disarmament Affairs, Human Rights Bodies and so on, will better enable the more comprehensive vision of human security and its integrative dimensions. It would make it easier to arrive at a broader perspective on issues and make it easier to draw on relevant expertise and perspectives across relevant fields of interest, rather than adopting the more traditional and narrower processes of the selected UN forum. Moreover, it prevents issues emerging in regard to member states – an issue faced by the original landmine negotiations at the CCW. At the time there were only 41 state parties, and these states represented only a small number of the global landmine producers, users, and states affected by landmine use.[37] Moreover, the issue of forum was not simply one of where to negotiate, but also an issue of the relevant legal instruments, and their

The Banning of Anti-Personnel Landmines: The Legal Contribution of the International Committee of the Red Cross 1955–1999 (Cambridge University Press, 2000).

35 Miguel de Larrinaga and Claire Turenne Sjolander, '(Re)Presenting Landmines from Protector to Enemy: The Discursive Framing of a New Multilateralism' in Maxwell A Cameron, Robert J Lawson and Brian W Tomlin (eds), *To Walk Without Fear: The Global Movement to Ban Landmines* (Oxford University Press, 1998) 392; Lesley Wexler, 'The International Deployment of Shame, Second-Best Responses and Norm Entrepreneurship: The Campaign to Ban Landmines and the Landmine Ban Treaty' (2003) 20(3) *Arizona Journal of International and Comparative Law* 561.

36 See, eg, Don Hubert, 'The Landmine Ban: A Case Study in Humanitarian Advocacy' (Occasional Paper No 42, Institute for International Studies, Brown University, 2000).

37 See, eg, Lesley Wexler, 'The International Deployment of Shame, Second-Best Responses and Norm Entrepreneurship: The Campaign to Ban Landmines and the Landmine Ban Treaty' (2003) 20(3) *Arizona Journal of International and Comparative Law* 561, 582.

respective relationship to human security. The provisions of the CCW relevant to landmine use are contained in Protocol II,[38] but this Protocol applies only to international, not internal, armed conflicts. As such it retains a highly state-centric focus, does not reflect the current landscape of global conflict and as such is a poor instrument for promoting considerations of human security and producing effective results. One of the most important issues at stake with regard to forum choice for human security, however, is the issue of who has access and the ability to participate. NGO access and involvement in the processes and rules of procedure that allow for this access have proven to be among the most significant elements in successful human security law-making. NGO involvement with human security and international legal development is examined below.

(iv) Simple messages

As discussed earlier in this book, human security is a complex entity which can lack conceptual clarity.[39] This, however, can be counterbalanced through simple messaging to address specific human security issues. Below it will be shown that the core purpose of each treaty is identified as addressing human suffering and this shows one dimension of human security discourse assisting in the framing of issues. But what has also proven to be important is having a simple uncompromising core at the heart of the negotiation process.[40] For the *Ottawa Convention* this was the need for a comprehensive ban on APMs. Likewise, the *CCM* required a similar ban on cluster munitions. For the *Optional Protocol*, the core message was the 'Straight 18' – the prohibition of the involvement of children under the age of 18 in armed conflict. The establishment of a strong independent court to provide justice to victims was the objective of the ICC campaign. The complexities of the arms trade, however, presented challenges, and explains, in part, the lengthy processes and previously stalled attempts to gain ground. Nonetheless, the central message of the need for a regulated arms trade was sufficient to see the eventual success of the *Arms Trade Treaty*. It is clear that strong human security campaigning requires clear simple rallying points. Such arguments allow for solidarity, and make it clear where the limits for compromise lay, and the human security focus provides significant weight, emphasising both the human dimension and the need for an urgent and decisive response.

38 *Protocol on Prohibitions or Restrictions on the Use of Mines, Booby-Traps and Other Devices as amended on 3 May 1996* opened for signature 5 March 1996, 2048 UNTS 133 (entered into force 12 March 1998) ('*Amended Protocol II*').

39 See, in particular, relevant discussion in Chapter Three.

40 For discussion, see, eg, Don Hubert, 'The Landmine Ban: A Case Study in Humanitarian Advocacy' (Occasional Paper No 42, Institute for International Studies, Brown University, 2000); Miguel de Larrinaga and Claire Turenne Sjolander, '(Re)Presenting Landmines from Protector to Enemy: The Discursive Framing of a New Multilateralism' in Maxwell A Cameron, Robert J Lawson and Brian W Tomlin (eds), *To Walk Without Fear: The Global Movement to Ban Landmines* (Oxford University Press, 1998) 392.

III Coalition building for international treaty development

A 'Coalition of the angels' – coalition building for human security

Perhaps the most crucial element for effective human security norm and regime development is effective coalition building.[41] This coalition building comes at different levels – between states; between states and international organisations; between states and non-state actors (NSAs), most notably non-governmental organisations (NGOs); and among NGOs. Each of the human security treaties discussed in Chapter Seven owes much of its development, adoption and subsequent successes to the involvement of cohesive coalitions committed to a strong human security message. Coalitions committed to such messages have sometimes been derided by states clinging to realist perceptions of international security: the inception of the Ottawa Process was openly criticised by powerful states, who argued that this 'coalition of the angels' would have little effect on global security (indeed that a ban on landmines was in fact a threat to security, as traditionally conceived), and were particularly critical of the close ties being forged between Canada and the other state authors of the Ottawa Process and the NGO community.[42] The Ottawa Process forged ahead despite this criticism, and has since produced the paradigm for effective human-security-oriented negotiation.

B Leadership of coalitions

The first important element of coalition building is, of course, strong leadership.[43] In the case of the Ottawa Process, the 'Core Group' quickly emerged from those that had been particularly vocal in their concerns over the limits of the CCW process. They agreed to meet with the leading NGO representatives to form the initial Ottawa Conference on Landmines in October 1996. This brought together the core group of Canada, Norway, Belgium, Austria, Switzerland, Ireland, Mexico, South Africa, the Philippines, Germany and the Netherlands.[44] The work of the core group has been commended as producing a remarkably cohesive sense of purpose and drive, developing an intensive working strategy towards the clear

41 See, eg, Lloyd Axworthy, 'Human Security and Global Governance: Putting People First' (2001) 7 *Global Governance* 19; Burkard Eberlein and Abraham L Newman, 'Escaping the International Governance Dilemma? Incorporated Transgovernmental Networks in the European Union' (2008) 21(1) *Governance* 25.

42 On use of 'coalition of angels' see Phillip S Winslow, 'Canadians taking lead in mine fight: United States "miffed" as nation to north forms coalition against weapon', *Baltimore Sun* (Baltimore, Maryland), 10 August 1997 <http://articles.baltimoresun.com/1997-08-10/news/1997222014_1_anti-personnel-mines-ban-on-anti-personnel-campaign-to-ban>.

43 See, eg, Fen Osler Hampson and Holly Reid, 'Coalition Diversity and Normative Legitimacy in Human Security Negotiations' (2003) 8(1) *International Negotiation* 7.

44 The basic composition of much of this list may seem familiar (Canada, Norway, Austria, Switzerland, Ireland, South Africa, the Netherlands); two years later many of these states came together to form a more permanent coalition – the Human Security Network, discussed in Chapter One.

goal of a comprehensive ban.[45] Part of the success of the coalition is attributed to the idealism for which they had been criticised – the absence of direct self-interest on the part of the process leadership allowed for a focus on norm entrepreneurialism.[46] For the development of the ICC, the 'like-minded group', as they came to be called, was a group of 60 states, again led by Canada, whose goal was the development of a strong court. It again worked closely with NGOs as discussed below. Hubert argues that the lack of such a like-minded group at the table for the *Optional Protocol on Child Soldiers* is one of the principal reasons explaining why compromises weakened the final text, as well as the failure of the NGO campaign for a 'Straight 18' as the age restriction for the recruitment of soldiers.[47] The *ATT* was likewise challenged, as small arms are a matter that falls squarely within the state-interest of all states, making it more difficult to form a disinterested coalition.[48]

C Threshold approach – detractors not invited

Another dimension of coalition building in the Ottawa Process returns to the independent process, outside of the forum of the United Nations. Only states that were willing to commit to the goal of 'the earliest possible conclusion of a legal binding agreement to ban antipersonnel mines' were permitted as participants at the conferences.[49] Thus the initial conference in Ottawa, held on 3–5 October 1996, saw 50 states attending as participants, and another 24 attending as observers. In a reversal of traditional conference proceedings, while states sat as observers, an NGO coalition, the International Campaign to Ban Landmines (ICBL) and the International Committee of the Red Cross (ICRC), were invited to the conference as full participants. At the follow-up conference, held in Brussels in June 1997, 156 states attended, with 97 signing the Brussels Declaration committing to a comprehensive ban. Only states that were willing to sign this political declaration were permitted to be official participants at the Oslo Conference, held in September 1997, where the draft of the treaty was to be finalised.

45 See, eg, Robert J Lawson, Mark Gwozdecky, Jill Sinclair and Ralph Lysyshyn, 'The Ottawa Process and the International Movement to Ban Anti-Personnel Mines' in Maxwell A Cameron, Robert J Lawson and Brian W Tomlin (eds) *To Walk Without Fear: The Global Movement to Ban Landmines* (Oxford University Press, 1998) 160, 166f.

46 See, eg, Ken Rutherford, 'The Hague and Ottawa Conventions: A Model for Future Weapons Ban Regimes' (1999) Spring–Summer *The Nonproliferation Review* 36, 38.

47 Don Hubert, 'The Landmine Ban: A Case Study in Humanitarian Advocacy' (Occasional Paper No 42, Institute for International Studies, Brown University, 2000) 40.

48 See, eg, Barbara von Tigerstrom, *Human Security and International Law: Prospects and Problems* (Hart Publishing, 2007), 146–56.

49 For discussion of the background to the Ottawa Process, see, eg, Stuart Maslen and P Herby, 'An International Ban on Anti-personnel Mines: History and Negotiation of the "Ottawa Treaty"', in Louis Maresca and Stuart Maslen (eds), *The Banning of Anti-Personnel Landmines: The Legal Contribution of the International Committee of the Red Cross 1955–1999* (Cambridge University Press, 2000) 606.

Wexler notes that part of the strength of such an approach is not only in providing the ingredients for developing strong (human-security-oriented) norms, but also in shaming those states that elected not to participate.[50] The return to UN forums, however, for the later treaties (with the exception of the *CCM*), meant that such a threshold approach could not be taken.

D Multi-stakeholder coalitions

While the nature of the state–state coalitions discussed above were innovative developments of the Ottawa Process, and characteristic of the human security model that has continued, what made the Ottawa Process particularly unique was the level of partnership between state and non-state actors.[51] This level of partnership was described by Axworthy as the 'new multilateralism'.[52] This drew on the idea of capitalising on the comparative advantages for human security of the diverse actors: 'only states could sign a binding convention; the [ICBL] had the tools to mobilise public opinion; the [ICRC] had the detailed knowledge and practical experience gained from undertaking mine action in the most affected countries'.[53] NGOs had 'unparalleled' access during the Ottawa Process,[54] and have had formal observer or participant status (without the right to vote) in the subsequent rules of procedures for the human security treaty conferences. Indeed, as noted earlier, the ICBL and ICRC were given participant status at conferences where states unwilling to commit to a comprehensive ban were only permitted observer status. In particular, there was a high degree of cooperation between the Canadian government and the ICBL throughout the Process, with strategising and regular meetings ensuring an alignment of the shared values and objectives that characterised the campaign.[55]

E Regional preparatory meetings

An important dimension of effective coalition building that must be mentioned is having processes of regional meetings and consultations in preparation for negotiation conferences. These events could include states, NGOs, civil society actors and individuals, or any combination thereof. While regional meetings and/or

50 Lesley Wexler, 'The International Deployment of Shame, Second-Best Responses and Norm Entrepreneurship: The Campaign to Ban Landmines and the Landmine Ban Treaty' (2003) 20(3) *Arizona Journal of International and Comparative Law* 561, 582.

51 Which should be noted included not only NGOs, but international organisations, individual victims and other civil society actors.

52 Lloyd Axworthy, 'Towards a New Multilateralism' in Maxwell A Cameron, Robert J Lawson and Brian W Tomlin (eds), *To Walk Without Fear: The Global Movement to Ban Landmines* (Oxford University Press, 1998) 448.

53 Ibid 453.

54 See, eg, Nicola Short, 'The Role of NGOs in the Ottawa Process to Ban Landmines' (1999) 4(3) *International Negotiation* 483.

55 Ibid.

conferences were conducted with all of the treaty conferences, they were perhaps used to best effect in relation to the Oslo Process to establish the *CCM* (which had been closely modelled on the Ottawa Process). What makes the Oslo Process unique is that it did not merely pursue meetings based on regional lines, but also dealt with matters of particular interest and for those most affected. Thus in October 2007 the Belgrade Conference for States Affected by Cluster Munitions was held by Serbia, itself a former user, stockpiler and producer of cluster munitions. The purpose of this conference was to ensure that communities and states most affected by cluster munitions could identify their expectations and concerns, and ensure that these concerns were central in the development of the treaty:

> Affected countries represent the reason why there is a process. These are the states that matter most in this context. This conference is the first conference ever dedicated specifically to the problems of affected countries. It is an opportunity to learn about the concerns and considerations of affected countries and to demonstrate commitment to address them.[56]

While this conference was significant, and the goal of addressing the most affected important, it does however need to be observed that this is a return to state-centric language. Rather than the most affected populations, the attention is on states that matter most, not the people within those states. Participants at this conference included a high concentration from Africa, including Chad, the Democratic Republic of Congo (DRC), Ethiopia, Guinea-Bissau, Sierra Leone, Sudan and Uganda.[57] African states can be seen to have had a significant influence in reframing perspectives on international peace and security in human terms. This was a point emphasised at the All-Africa Regional Conference on Cluster Munitions in Livingstone. This conference was opened with a clear commitment to human security expressed by the Zambian Foreign Minister, Mr Kabinga J Pande:

> we do not have the technical and financial capacity to deal with cluster munitions when they are left in our backyards long after war. Rather than direct our resources to the acquisition of these weapons, we should be spending those resources on making our peoples' lives better ...[58]

The Norwegian representative also noted that participation by African states was essential for the successful outcome, a reality which also proved to be true for the

56 Ambassador Steffen Kongstad, 'Opening Statement by Norway at the Belgrade Conference of States Affected by Cluster Munitions, the Way Ahead: Achieving an Effective International Response to the Problem of Cluster Munitions', 3–4 October 2007, <http://www.w3c.org/TR/1999/REC-html401-19991224/>.

57 Gugu Dabe, 'Negotiating the Convention on Cluster Munitions: The Role of African States' (ISS Paper 187 June 2009).

58 Minister Kabinga J Pande, Opening statement delivered by Zambia at the Livingstone Conference on Cluster Munitions, 31 March–1 April 2008.

Arms Trade Treaty.[59] Regional meetings were particularly important for engaging with non-state actors – those without the resources or capacity to attend the global conferences. They are thus an essential means of drawing participation directly from the individuals and communities whose human security is being threatened.

Regional conferences were also used to great effect for the *Optional Protocol*, largely organised by the NGO Coalition.[60] Like-minded governments were called on to host these conferences and to ensure that state representatives from the regions attended. The first conference was hosted in Mozambique in April 1999 for the African region, attended by states in the region as well as like-minded states from outside the region, including Brazil, Canada, Denmark, Finland, Germany, Norway, Switzerland and Uruguay. Participants were invited at the end of the Conference to sign unto the Maputo Declaration, unequivocally condemning the use of child soldiers and calling for legal standards and measures at every level to prohibit any military service by children under the age of 18.[61] During the Conference a number of African states also committed to ratifying the *African Charter on the Rights and Welfare of the Child*,[62] the only regional instrument that set 18 as the minimum age for recruitment and participation of children in armed conflict. Likewise the regional conference for Latin America and the Caribbean held in Uruguay resulted in the Montevideo Declaration.[63] However, the third conference in Europe was not able to maintain momentum for the so-called 'Straight-18' position.[64] This provides one example of how human security discourse still finds it difficult to penetrate some states' state security positions. Nonetheless, the regional conference still had an effect, and after the Conference, the European

59 After all it was Kenya that led the push for the issue of the *ATT* to be brought before the General Assembly, after the consensus vote had failed during its last conference, and African states who were vocal in its development and eventual adoption: United Nations, 'Deputy Secretary-General, Hailing Historic Adoption of Arms Trade Treaty During High-level Event, Urges Its Early Ratification, Entry into Force' (2013) <http://www.un.org/press/en/2013/dsgsm704.doc.htm>. See also, Guy Lamb, 'African States and the ATT Negotiations' (Arms Control Today 2012) <http://www.armscontrol.org/act/2012_09/African-States-And-the-ATT-Negotiations>.

60 See, eg, Rachel Stohl, 'Armed and Dangerous: Stopping the Use of Child Soldiers' in Ken Rutherford, Stefan Brem, and Richard Anthony Matthew, *Reframing the Agenda: The Impact of NGO and Middle Power Cooperation in International Security Policy* (Greenwood, 2003) 60, 66–67; 76–77.

61 Maputo Declaration on the Use of Child Soldiers, 22 April 1999, <http://www.hrw.org/campaigns/crp/maputo-declaration.htm>.

62 *African Charter on the Rights and Welfare of the Child*, opened for signature 11 July 1990, OAU Doc CAB/LEG/24.9/49 (1990) (entered into force 29 November 1999).

63 Montevideo Declaration on the Use of Child Soldiers, Montevideo, Uruguay, 8 July 1999 <http://www.unesco.org/cpp/uk/declarations/montevideo.htm>.

64 See, eg, Don Hubert, 'The Landmine Ban: A Case Study in Humanitarian Advocacy' (Occasional Paper No 42, Institute for International Studies, Brown University, 2000) 45–6. Coalition to Stop the Use of Child Soldiers, 'Europe Accused of Double Standards on Child Soldiers' (20 October 1999) *Press Release*.

Parliament called on EU member states to support the adoption of an optional protocol to prohibit the recruitment and use of children under 18 in armed conflicts.

F NGO coalitions

As with states, NGOs likewise learned that an effective way to consolidate their power and influence was to form coalitions.[65] Coalitions of the nature and scope that have been generated for human security issues have been unparalleled.[66] The comprehensive nature of human security allows for organisations with vastly disparate foci to find common ground and universal objectives. This section briefly analyses the nature and role of the NGO coalitions built for the human security treaties. It then concludes with some commentary on the drawbacks of relying on the coalition approach.

The International Campaign to Ban Landmines (ICBL) was formally launched in 1992, and began with a coalition of six member organisations: Handicap International; Human Rights Watch; Medico International; Mines Advisory Group; Physicians for Human Rights; and the Vietnam Veterans of America Foundation.[67] These six would become the steering committee of a coalition with more than 1,200 member organisations. It should be noted that in 2011 the ICBL merged with the Cluster Munition Coalition, its counterpart in the Oslo Process. It brought together groups who aligned themselves with the ban on landmines from different perspectives – as a human rights issue, an environmental threat, an arms control issue, a health issue, etc. This synthesis of such disparate groups, mandates and mission statements was only made possible by drawing on human security discourse to identify a common objective, namely, a comprehensive ban on landmines, and a shared vision – that this was an issue about humanity, not arms control.[68]

Broadly speaking, the ICBL framed the core objectives of the Ottawa Process, formulated strategy for the negotiations, targeted important states at both regional conferences and at the international conferences, provided assistance to states with less resources, provided commentary on the draft provisions of the treaty, and gave invited speeches.[69] The role of the ICBL in formal negotiations took two

65 On the role and development of NGO coalitions generally, see, eg, Cyril Ritchie, 'Coordinate? Cooperate? Harmonise? NGO Policy and Operational Coalitions' (1995) 16(3) *Third World Quarterly* 513; Helen Yanacopulos, 'The Strategies That Bind: NGO Coalitions and Their Influence' (2005) 5(1) *Global Networks* 93; Helen Yanacopulos, 'Patterns of Governance: The Rise of Transnational Coalitions of NGOs' (2005) 19(3) *Global Society* 247.

66 See, eg, Fen Osler Hampson and Holly Reid, 'Coalition Diversity and Normative Legitimacy in Human Security Negotiations' (2003) 8(1) *International Negotiation* 7.

67 Jody Williams and Stephen Goose, 'The International Campaign to Ban Landmines' in Maxwell A Cameron, Robert J Lawson and Brian W Tomlin (eds), *To Walk Without Fear: The Global Movement to Ban Landmines* (Oxford University Press, 1998) 20

68 For more information on the ICBL, see ibid 20.

69 See, eg, Nicola Short, 'The Role of NGOs in the Ottawa Process to Ban Landmines' (1999) 4(3) *International Negotiation* 483.

broad forms: in 'closed' negotiations on the text, two representatives participated on behalf of the ICBL as a whole, while at the other negotiations NGOs participated more broadly in a wide range of capacities. This participation included briefing sessions and the contribution of technical expertise, and representatives were generally provided a high degree of access to governmental delegates.[70] Particular achievements that the ICBL are credited with in the final text are the general language of the treaty and the maintained focus on human security concerns, and the inclusion of Article 6 providing for Victim Assistance, which was something for which the Coalition had lobbied hard.

In relation to the ICC and the *Rome Statute*, the NGOs coordinated their diverse objectives through the NGO Coalition for the International Criminal Court (CICC). The CICC comprises more than 2500 organisations spread across 150 countries around the world.[71] At the time of negotiating the *Rome Statute*, the CICC represented more than 800 groups, with 236 actually represented at the negotiations themselves and accredited to participate.[72] Indeed, as Boyle and Chinkin point out, this number exceeded the number of participating states (160).[73] The CICC divided itself into three types of groups during the conference: regional caucuses, who met with state representatives; issue-oriented groups dealing in speciality areas such as gender justice, victims, children and peace; and teams with legal expertise working along the same divisions as the conference – establishment; general principles; definitions; and so on. As with the ICBL, the organisations that form the CICC are extremely diverse.

The NGO role in relation to the *Rome Statute* conference included the production of informational materials; lobbying for support for the idea of an international criminal court; organisation of regional meetings with both NGO and governmental representatives; development of the position papers; and the forging of ties with governments.[74] During the Rome Conference, one role of the CICC was to increase the transparency of the negotiations by providing daily reporting of the states' positions and the progress of the negotiations. Some states also recruited NGO members as a part of their own delegations, giving these members greater access, but also requiring alignment with state interests. Furthermore, some NGOs, such as No Peace Without Justice, provided technical assistance to state delegations.[75]

70 Ibid 486.

71 The Coalition of the International Criminal Court, <http://www.iccnow.org/?mod=coalition>.

72 United Nations Diplomatic Conference of Plenipotentiaries on the Establishment of an International Criminal Court, *Non-governmental organizations accredited to participate in the Conference: note by the Secretary-General*, Official Records of the United Nations Diplomatic Conference of Plenipotentiaries on the Establishment of an International Criminal Court (Reports and other documents), Vol III, UN Doc A/CONF/183/INF/3 (5 June 1998). See also, Marlies Glasius, *The International Criminal Court: A Global Civil Society Achievement* (Routledge, 2006) 27.

73 Alan Boyle and Christine Chinkin, *The Making of International Law* (Oxford University Press, 2007) 73.

74 Ibid 148.

75 Ibid 73.

In relation to the ICC, the CICC has maintained a significant role, and committed itself to three core ongoing principles: a) promoting universal ratification of the *Rome Statute* and strengthening international cooperation with the Court; b) ensuring the court is fair, effective and independent; and c) advancing strong national laws that deliver justice to victims of international crimes.[76] NGOs are strongly represented at the meeting of the Assembly of States Parties (ASP), and provide insights into the policy decisions of the ASP. They provide background research for the investigations, and are sometimes better able to cultivate relationships with victims and communities than the ICC could achieve on its own.[77] They provide information about crimes, locate victims and witnesses, and promote and assist with victim participation in the court. Analysing the varying roles of NGOs in the ongoing work of the ICC, Schiff concludes: 'NGOs are at once assets for the organization and sources of criticism, exhortation and pressure upon it. Perhaps more than for any other international organization, the ICC depends upon NGOs for its operation.'[78] Human security requires such participation, and this is reflected across all of the relevant treaties and their realisation.

In 1998, the NGO Coalition to Stop the Use of Child Soldiers was launched, with its campaign to end the recruitment and use of children in armed conflict.[79] The Steering Committee for this campaign was again comprised of six member groups: Amnesty International, Human Rights Watch, International Federation Terre des Hommes, the International Save the Children Alliance, the Jesuit Refugee Service and the Quaker UN Office in Geneva. Like the other coalitions, this coalition also benefited from diverse membership, ranging from the large credible human rights and humanitarian organisations, such as Human Rights Watch and Amnesty International, to local groups that worked on the ground dealing with the reintegration and rehabilitation of former child soldiers. The coalition adopted a four-pronged strategy, closely reflected in all of the human security coalitions, of regional mobilisation, work of national coalitions to ensure local ownership, supporting partnerships with like-minded state partners, and influencing public opinion and raising awareness of the issues.[80]

For the development of the *ATT*, the launch of the Control Arms Campaign in 2003 was essential. Control Arms spanned more than 100 countries and engaged in a decade-long campaign, remaining a driving force through to the adoption of

76 The Coalition of the International Criminal Court, <http://www.iccnow.org/?mod=coalition>.

77 Marlies Glasius, '"We Ourselves, We Are Part of the Functioning": The ICC, Victims, and Civil Society in the Central African Republic' (2009) 108(430) *African Affairs* 49.

78 Benjamin N Schiff, *Building the International Criminal Court* (Cambridge University Press, 2008), 144.

79 Now known as Child Soldiers International, <http://www.child-soldiers.org/our_history.php>.

80 See, eg, Don Hubert, 'The Landmine Ban: A Case Study in Humanitarian Advocacy' (Occasional Paper No 42, Institute for International Studies, Brown University, 2000), chapter 4. See also Coalition to Stop the Use of Child Soldiers, *Global Report 2008* (CICC, 2008); Michael Wessels, *Child Soldiers: From Violence to Protection* (Harvard University Press, 2007).

the treaty in 2013. The coalition and its members were essential in highlighting the weaknesses of the draft that had been produced in 2012. It was NGOs who vocally campaigned on issues such as the omission of ammunition from this text and the need to address the risk of diversion and to exclude national security exemptions, and successfully pressured states into taking up these issues in the final 2013 conference.[81] Their role has been accurately described as indispensable to the creation of the treaty.[82]

NGO coalitions are a vital component of human security. The bringing together of diverse perspectives and the integration of these perspectives into a targeted message is a cornerstone of the human security formula, necessary to respond to the principle of integration for human security. Forming a coalition gives NGOs greater legitimacy and credibility, and a louder voice through which to campaign.[83] It allows smaller, particularly grassroot campaigners, to participate, and to draw on the influence of more established NGOs such as Amnesty International or the ICRC. However, one of the core roles of an NGO presence at international conferences is arguably to present critical voices.[84] By centralising the leadership of coalitions, and provisions that allow only token representatives of NGOs to attend or participate in key negotiating sessions, critical perspectives and genuine dialogue may be lost.[85] This yet again demonstrates the difficult balance that human security maintains between critical approaches and problem-solving capacities. On the one hand more diversity in the participation would allow the role of NGOs to be more critical, and to push for more fundamental change. On the other hand however, too many voices, and the message may be diluted or lost, NGOs lose legitimacy and results may not be achieved.

G NGOs and standard setting: reframing towards human security

As highlighted in the previous chapter, one of the key ingredients in the success of the discussed treaties was the use of human security discourse to reframe the issue

81 '[A] treaty which includes weapons and guns but does not include bullets and ammunitions would simply be perverse': Presentations by the Representatives of the Control Arms Coalition, Arms Trade Treaty Diplomatic Conference, 11 July 2012, New York.

82 Zeray Yihdego, 'The Arms Trade Treaty and Human Security: What Role for NSAs?' in Cedric Ryngaert and Math Noortmann (ed), *Human Security and International Law: The Challenge of Non-State Actors* (Routledge, 2014) 135.

83 See, eg, Lesley Wexler, 'The International Deployment of Shame, Second-Best Responses and Norm Entrepreneurship: The Campaign to Ban Landmines and the Landmine Ban Treaty' (2003) 20(3) *Arizona Journal of International and Comparative Law* 561.

84 Jean d'Aspremont, 'International Law-Making by Non-State Actors: Changing the Model or Putting the Phenomenon into Perspective' in Math Noortman and Cedric Ryngaert (eds) *Non-State Actor Dynamics in International Law: From Law Takers to Law Makers* (Ashgate 2010) 171, 185.

85 Short raises a similar point in relation to the ICBL, see Nicola Short, 'The Role of NGOs in the Ottawa Process to Ban Landmines' (1999) 4(3) *International Negotiation* 483, 495.

in human, not state-centric terms. NGOs have proven essential to accommodating this shift. In the case of the creation of the ICC, the NGO campaigners 'emphasized a new justice victim orientation'.[86] It was largely the advocacy of a coalition of women's groups that ensured, *inter alia,* the comprehensive acknowledgment of sexual violence,[87] that judges with legal experience dealing with violence against women sat on the bench,[88] and that the Registry's Victims and Witnesses Unit included staff experienced in trauma related to crimes of sexual violence.[89]

In the case of the *ATT*, the ICRC early on in small arms discussions recognised the broadening notions of responsibility addressed by human security discourse:

> While the primary responsibility for compliance with IHL falls upon users of weapons, states and enterprises engaged in production and supply of weapons bear a degree of political, moral and, in some cases, legal responsibility to the international community for the use made of their weapons and ammunition.[90]

Control Arms went further, and after the failure in 2012 to reach agreement on the text, explicitly drew on human security:

> Ultimately, the ATT will be judged according to its success in preventing arms transfers that risk contributing to or facilitating human suffering. An ATT that does not serve to enhance human security will represent a hollow victory for all those who have advocated for a robust treaty.[91]

But it was the *Ottawa Convention* that kicked off the use of human security discourse to reframe the issue in human, not state-centric terms, as discussed in the previous chapter. And here too, it was the NGOs involved in the campaign, the International Campaign to Ban Landmines (ICBL) and the ICRC, who are predominantly credited with this shift. One of the core initial functions for NGOs was to generate and maintain public interest and outrage over the use of landmines and the need for a ban, with the knowledge of how such public interest would positively drive state action on the issue.[92] Thus the way that the ICBL

86 Benjamin N Schiff, *Building the International Criminal Court* (Cambridge University Press, 2008), 148.

87 *Rome Statute*, art 7.1(g), 'Rape, sexual slavery, enforced prostitution, forced pregnancy, enforced sterilisation or any other form of sexual violence of comparable gravity'. See also the gender violence provisions in art 8.2(b)(xxii) and 8.2(e)(vi).

88 Ibid art 36.8.b.

89 Ibid art 43.6.

90 ICRC, *Arms Availability and the Situation of Civilians in Armed Conflict* (Geneva, June 1999) 25 [2].

91 Control Arms, *Finishing the Job: Delivering a Bullet-Proof ATT* (CA, 2012) <http://speakout.controlarms.org/wordpress/wp-content/uploads/2012/01/FinishingtheJob-1-format.pdf>.

92 Thus the ICBL, HRW and Physicians for Human Rights, and the ICRC all produced reports on the impact of landmines and case-studies of affected regions: see, eg, Physicians for Human Rights, *Hidden Enemies: Landmines in Northern Somalia* (PHR,

approached the issue 'elevated [it] beyond a particular state's national interest',[93] and this was achieved through framing the issue in human security terms – placing emphasis on the impact on civilians, the potential threat to children,[94] and the preservation of the environment and human health.[95] Narratives of victims became the story of landmines, rather than issues of state and sovereignty.[96] It was this reframing of the issue that made it a particularly effective campaign for raising awareness of the issue, and established the potential role of international law in redressing the problem.[97] The ICBL disseminated information to the public and governments alike, publicising the harm caused by landmines and their indiscriminate nature.[98]

What was also demonstrated by effective human security campaigning is the role of NGOs in not only framing issues in human security terms, but also in refuting the arguments generated from traditional security constructions. NGOs are better equipped than states to generate such arguments, as they are detached from national security concerns, and thus viewed as a more legitimate source for such commentary.[99] This was most effectively demonstrated by the ICRC in the Ottawa Process. Traditional security concerns were being raised by states reluctant to agree to a ban. Defence analysts asserted that the continued employment of APMs was necessary, in particular, in areas such as the demilitarised zone in Korea, to 'secure military installations, to divert enemy forces, to deny areas of strategic interest to the enemy.'[100] Particularly crucial to combatting such views was the publication of

1992); Human Rights Watch, *Hidden Death: Land Mines and Civilian Casualties in Iraqi Kurdistan* (HRW, 1992).

93 Lesley Wexler, 'The International Deployment of Shame, Second-Best Responses and Norm Entrepreneurship: The Campaign to Ban Landmines and the Landmine Ban Treaty' (2003) 20(3) *Arizona Journal of International and Comparative Law* 561, 562.

94 For example raised awareness of so-called 'butterfly mines', Soviet ПФМ-1 APMs which because of their toylike appearance and bright colours attracted children to pick them up; see, eg, ICRC, *Anti-Personnel Mines – Friend or Foe? A Study of the Military Use and Effectiveness of Anti-personnel Mines* (ICRC, 1997).

95 Lesley Wexler, 'The International Deployment of Shame, Second-Best Responses and Norm Entrepreneurship: The Campaign to Ban Landmines and the Landmine Ban Treaty' (2003) 20(3) *Arizona Journal of International and Comparative Law* 561, 562.

96 See, eg, Miguel de Larrinaga and Claire Turenne Sjolander, '(Re)Presenting Landmines from Protector to Enemy: The Discursive Framing of a New Multilateralism' in Maxwell A Cameron, Robert J Lawson and Brian W Tomlin (eds), *To Walk Without Fear: The Global Movement to Ban Landmines* (Oxford University Press, 1998) 392.

97 See, eg, Andrew Latham, 'The Politics of Stigmatization: Global Cultural Changes and the Transnational Campaign to Ban Antipersonnel Landmines', Address Before the International Studies Association, *Columbia International Affairs Online* <www.ciaonet.org/isa/laa01/>.

98 Shawn Roberts and Jody Williams, *After The Guns Fall Silent: The Enduring Legacy of Landmines* (ICBL, 1995).

99 See, eg, Nicola Short, 'The Role of NGOs in the Ottawa Process to Ban Landmines' (1999) 4(3) *International Negotiation* 483, 492.

100 Rae McGrath, 'The Reality of the Present Use of Mines by Military Forces' in ICRC (ed), *ICRC Report of the Symposium on Anti-Personnel Landmines* (ICRC, 1993) 7.

the ICRC's comprehensive study *Friend or Foe?*[101] This study comprehensively dismantled arguments about the military value of using APMs. It drew on extensive research and was co-authored by a Group of Military Experts who concluded:

> The limited military utility of AP mines is far outweighed by the appalling humanitarian consequences of their use in actual conflicts. On this basis their prohibition and elimination should be pursued as a matter of utmost urgency by governments and the entire international community.[102]

As Hubert concludes, '[i]f governmental coalitions are the key to the successful conclusion of humanitarian campaigns, NGO coalitions are the key to their emergence and development. NGOs are most effective at identifying the overarching objectives and are securing governmental support.'[103] These demonstrates the fundamental role of NGOs to the processes of standard setting for human security. The Ottawa Process has been focused on, but similar roles for NGOs can be found for each of the treaties discussed in Chapter Seven.

H NGO involvement – addressing the democratic deficit and offering empowerment?

Lloyd Axworthy described the involvement of NGOs in the Ottawa Process as a form of democratising the processes of international law-making:

> One can no longer relegate NGOs to simple advisory or advocacy roles in this process. They are now part of the way decisions have to be made. They have been the voice saying that government belongs to the people, and must respond to the people's hopes, demands and ideals.[104]

This ties in to broader arguments about addressing the democratic deficit of international decision-making, such as the criticisms made during the 1999 Ministerial Conference of the World Trade Organisation to the effect that 'international systems lack transparency, accountability and citizen inclusiveness', and that international institutions were 'remote, bureaucratic, elite driven and unresponsive to popular will'.[105] Ryngaert, for example, makes the point that procedural rules of

101 ICRC, *Anti-Personnel Mines – Friend or Foe? A Study of the Military Use and Effectiveness of Anti-personnel Mines* (ICRC, 1997). ICRC, above n 44.
102 Ibid XI Conclusions [8].
103 Don Hubert, 'The Landmine Ban: A Case Study in Humanitarian Advocacy' (Occasional Paper No 42, Institute for International Studies, Brown University, 2000), 62.
104 Lloyd Axworthy, 'Notes for an Address by the Honourable Lloyd Axworthy, Minister of Foreign Affairs, to the Oslo NGO Forum on Banning Anti-Personnel Landmines', DFAIT (Canada) Statement, Oslo, Norway, 10 September 1997.
105 Steven Wheatley, 'Democratic Governance Beyond the State: The Legitimacy of Non-state Actors as Standard-setters' in Anne Peters et al (eds), *Non-State Actors as Standard Setters* (Cambridge, 2009) 214, 215.

inclusive or participatory governance are essential if substantive rules are to be considered legitimate, and that this fact, when combined with NGOs' ability to produce results, 'militate[s] strongly in favour of enhanced participatory rights of non-state actors' in international governance.[106] It also aligns closely to the goal of empowerment and principles of participatory security.

NGO participation is thought to provide legitimacy via a range of means. As noted above, NGOs lend their expertise, vocalise interests, provide information and criticism, and often act as the voice of opposition, thereby improving the quality of debates and people's understanding of complex issues, such as those posed by human security threats.[107] The independence of NGOs lends credibility to such functions. Coalition building is seen as a measure that strengthens this legitimacy further, by increasing the diversity and effectiveness of NGOs.[108]

However, caution must be exercised in assuming that NGO involvement necessarily contributes to the promotion of human security, or that NGO involvement itself fulfils the empowerment element of human security. Anderson, for example, notes that NGOs should not be construed as standing in for the 'people'. He writes:

> International NGOs collectively are not conduits from the 'people' or the 'masses' or the 'world citizenry' from the bottom up. They are rather a vehicle for international elites to talk to other international elites about the things – frequently of undeniably critical importance – that international elites care about. The conversation is not vertical, it is horizontal. It has a worthwhile, essential function in making the world, sometimes at least, a better place, but it does not reduce the democratic deficit.[109]

In the case of the Ottawa Process, for example, it should be noted that a survey of the Ottawa Treaty Signing NGO Forum found that only 20 per cent of the NGOs were not from Europe or North America.[110] While this was partly mitigated through the regional conferences, it is difficult to determine what effect this may

106 Cedric Ryngaert, 'Imposing International Duties of Non-State Actors and the Legitimacy of International Law' in Math Noortmann and Cedric Ryngaert (eds) *Non-State Actor Dynamics in International Law: From Law Takers to Law Makers* (Ashgate, 2010) 69, 81.

107 See, eg, Anne Peters, Till Förster and Lucy Koechlin, 'Towards Non-State Actors as Effective, Legitimate and Accountable Standard Setters' in Anne Peters et al (eds), *Non-State Actors as Standard Setters* (Cambridge, 2009) 492, 516–17.

108 Ibid 521.

109 Kenneth Anderson, 'The Ottawa Convention Banning Landmines, the Role of International Non-Governmental Organizations and the Idea of International Civil Society' (2000) 11(1) *European Journal of International Law* 91, 118. See also Anne Peters, Till Förster and Lucy Koechlin, 'Towards Non-State Actors as Effective, Legitimate and Accountable Standard Setters' in Anne Peters et al (eds), *Non-State Actors as Standard Setters* (Cambridge, 2009) 492, 519–20.

110 Nicola Short, 'The Role of NGOs in the Ottawa Process to Ban Landmines' (1999) 4(3) *International Negotiation* 483, 495.

have had on adequate representation of the diverse interests. Ultimately, the diversity of NGOs in structure, goals, and governance makes it very difficult to draw any sort of universal conclusions about their contributions or their ability to contribute. As Bennoune points out,

> In the last 20 years or so, NGOs have been variously heralded as *the* solution for all manner of international law difficulties, and lambasted as undemocratic manifestations of global inequality, political puppets and dangerously unaccountable at that. Of course, like most academic assertions each of these things has been true in particular instances, and each completely false at many other times.[111]

More fundamentally, however, no matter how much access is granted to NGOs, the processes of international law-making are still absolutely state-centric. NGOs participate only with the permission of states, and are not guaranteed the right to participate.[112] Moreover, as NGO participation is sometimes reduced to lobbying outside of the formal structures of negotiations, fundamental concerns can be raised about the transparency, predictability and legitimacy of the participation.[113] This is not the fault of NGOs, but of the lack of any formalisation of their role, despite decades of involvement in the processes of treaty creation.[114]

The human security treaties may not have even been considered without the efforts of NGOs, and this should not be forgotten, but the development of those treaties would also not have been possible without states that were willing to commit to human security discourse. However, to truly capture the transformative potential of human security discourse, it should be used as a tool to drive international law-making more fully in the direction of participatory and transparent decision-making processes. The next section examines whether initiatives further removed from formal international law-making structures better serve the interests of human security.

IV Multi-stakeholder initiatives and human security

A large part of the emphasis human security discourse places on multilateralism rests on the acknowledgement that many challenges to human security are 'neither

111 Karima Bennoune, 'Productive Tensions: Women's Rights NGOs, the "Mainstream" Human Rights Movement, and International Lawmaking' in Cecilia M Bailliet (ed), *Non-State Actors, Soft Law and Protective Regimes: From the Margins* (Cambridge University Press, 2012) 125, 128.

112 On this point, see, eg, Menno T. Kamminga, 'The Evolving Status of NGOs under International Law: A Threat to the Inter-State System?' in Philip Alston (ed), *Non-State Actors and Human Rights* (Oxford University Press, 2005) 93, 110.

113 Cedric Ryngaert, 'Imposing International Duties of Non-State Actors and the Legitimacy of International Law' in Math Noortmann and Cedric Ryngaert (eds) *Non-State Actor Dynamics in International Law: From Law Takers to Law Makers* (Ashgate, 2010) 69, 74–5.

114 See, eg, Boyle and Christine Chinkin, *The Making of International Law* (Oxford University Press, 2007), chapter 2.4.

owned nor solved by individual stakeholders'.[115] Collaborative approaches are necessary, pooling the combined knowledge, resources and social capital of governments, corporations, civil society organisations, researchers and local communities to produce effective results.

The most effective strategy for addressing transnational or global problems involves mixed networks of public, private and civic actors created under the rubric of public–private partnerships (PPPs), global alliances, global campaigns or collaborative networks. Although not a panacea, such arrangements can stretch scarce government resources and ensure that they leverage other contributions of money, expertise and other in-kind resources.[116]

In recent decades there has been a movement towards multi-stakeholder initiatives, viewed by some as the 'future of international cooperation'.[117] Multi-stakeholder initiatives (MSIs) have emerged, particularly in response to the corporate social responsibility agenda, and they are a key component of the United Nations Guiding Principles on Business and Human Rights.[118] Most typically, multi-stakeholder initiatives have pursued dialogue between states, business and NGOs. The importance of engaging with NGOs in the pursuit of human security has been explored above. The engagement of business is particularly important when the norms and mechanisms are directed towards regulating business practices and national or international markets, which can be both threats and solutions to issues of human insecurity.[119] MSIs, it has been argued, are in a better position than traditional governance frameworks to pool local knowledge and experience from diverse actors.[120] Just as local communities are needed to produce effective, contextualised approaches, corporations have a more intimate understanding not only of their own working structures but also of the complexities of the international market and their particular industry – they know what will work and what will not. That said, it is also important to heed Surya Deva's warning that too great an emphasis on dialogue and the cooperation of business can create the impression that human rights are negotiable.[121] The same could be said of human security.

115 Rob van Tulder, foreword to Mariëtte van Huijstee, 'Multi-stakeholder Initiatives: A guide for civil society organisations' (Report SOMO, March 2012) 8.
116 Anne-Marie Slaughter, 'A Grand Strategy of Network Centrality' in Richard Fontain and Kristin Lord (eds), *America's Path: Grand Strategy for the Next Administration* (Center for American Security, May 2012) 43, 54.
117 See, eg, Jens Martens, 'Multistakeholder Partnerships – Future Models of Multilateralism' (Occasional Paper No 29, Dialogue on Globalization, January 2007).
118 UN Guiding Principles on Business and Human Rights, <http://www.ohchr.org/Documents/Publications/GuidingPrinciplesBusinessHR_EN.pdf>.
119 Claude Bruderlein, 'The Role of Non State Actors in Building Human Security' (Working Paper Centre for Humanitarian Dialogue, May 2000).
120 See, eg, Scott Jerbi, 'Assessing the Roles of Multi-stakeholder Initiatives in Advancing the Business and Human Rights Agenda' (2012) 94(887) *International Review of the Red Cross* 1027, 1032.
121 Surya Deva, 'Human Rights Violations by Multinational Corporations and International Law: Where from Here?' (2003–2004) 19 *Connecticut Journal of International Law* 1, 20.

Yihdego for example raises the counter-productive role played by the arms industry during the negotiation of the *ATT*.[122] The same tensions can play out in less formalised settings, such as MSIs.

A The nature of multi-stakeholder initiatives

It is widely accepted that the emergence of multi-stakeholder approaches to addressing international challenges began in the 1990s in the area of environmental governance, following the Rio Conference on Environment and Development in 1992.[123] Partnerships between public, private and community-based organisations lie at the centre of Agenda 21.[124] According to MSI Integrity, an initiative assessing the impact and value of MSIs, an MSI is defined as the following:

> Multi-Stakeholder Initiatives (MSIs) bring together various stakeholders – such as corporations, civil society, government, and local communities – to collaborate in addressing a specific issue. In the context of business and human rights, this is frequently done by developing standards for specific industries, regions or issues relevant to human rights. Some MSIs focus on a narrow issue, such as child labor in cocoa, while others attempt to look at the general human rights, environmental and social issues relevant to a particular industry. While many focus on setting standards for industry and monitoring, others have chosen to focus on promoting policy engagement or learning amongst stakeholders to improve business systems. Many include certification schemes and some also include grievance mechanisms to handle complaints.[125]

The definition provided is vague, since the only true unifying factor of MSIs is their multi-stakeholder involvement.[126] The actors and instruments vary from MSI to MSI, and by contrast with the more traditional public–private partnerships (PPPs) paradigm, there is no guarantee of the role of governments as a key participant, nor is there in all cases formalised structures and partnerships. The lack of a specified structure is one of the perceived advantages of such approaches,

122 Zarey Yihdego, 'The Arms Trade Treaty and Human Security: What Role for NSAs?' in Cedric Ryngaert and Math Noortmann (ed), Human Security and International Law: The Challenge of Non-State Actors (Routledge, 2014) 135, 159.

123 See, eg, Scott Jerbi, 'Assessing the Roles of Multi-stakeholder Initiatives in Advancing the Business and Human Rights Agenda' (2012) 94(887) *International Review of the Red Cross* 1027, 1029; Jens Martens, 'Multistakeholder Partnerships – Future Models of Multilateralism' (Occasional Paper No 29, Dialogue on Globalization, January 2007) 7.

124 *Agenda 21: Programme of Action for Sustainable Development*, UN GAOR, Forty-sixth sess, Agenda Item 21, UN Doc A/Conf.151/26 (14 June 1992).

125 MSI Integrity, What Are MSIs?, <http://www.msi-integrity.org/?page_id=557>.

126 See also, Jens Martens, 'Multistakeholder Partnerships – Future Models of Multilateralism' (Occasional Paper No 29, Dialogue on Globalization, January 2007).

which 'are seen as pragmatic, solution-oriented, flexible, efficient and un-bureaucratic'.[127] These attributes, along of course with their inherently collaborative structure, make MSIs appear to be the ideal candidate for the development of human security strategies.

MSIs greatly blurred the lines between voluntary and mandatory obligations. While these initiatives do not have the direct force of law, between market inducements, social pressure and possible national implementation of the principles of such initiatives, they can be equally effective: 'what matters is not whether the approach is voluntary or mandatory, but whether it can effect positive change.'[128] It has also been noted that while most MSIs begin as voluntary initiatives, there is a trend towards formalisation, and that such initiatives can also play a key role in norm development and diffusion.[129] For this reason it is worth examining their value in the relationship between human security discourse and the development of international law norms.

While there are a range of existent multi-stakeholder initiatives, this chapter focuses its analysis on one example of particular relevance to human security concerns: the Kimberley Process Certification Scheme. While there are many other schemes that are relevant to human security, including the Voluntary Principles on Security and Human Rights, the Extractive Industries Transparency Initiative, and the Global Fund to Fight AIDS, Tuberculosis and Malaria, the Kimberley Process provides an excellent model as it contains a mix of non-binding and binding elements, has been endorsed via the United Nations General Assembly and the Security Council, raises a number of issues that highlight the benefits and challenges of addressing threats to human security and has been described as a key example of informal international law-making.[130]

B The Kimberley Process

(i) Background: the issue of conflict diamonds

The UN defines conflict diamonds as 'diamonds that originate from areas controlled by forces or factions opposed to legitimate and internationally recognised governments, and are used to fund military opposition to those governments, or in contravention of the decisions of the Security Council.'[131]

127 Ibid 5.

128 Office of the Global Compact, *Enabling Economies of Peace: Public Policy for Conflict-Sensitive Business*, (UN, 2005) 28.

129 See, eg, Scott Jerbi, 'Assessing the Roles of Multi-stakeholder Initiatives in Advancing the Business and Human Rights Agenda' (2012) 94(887) *International Review of the Red Cross* 1027, 1032.

130 Victoria Vidal, 'Informal International Lawmaking: The Kimberley Process' Mechanism of Accountability' in Ayelet Berman et al (ed), *Informal International Law-making: Case Studies* (Torkel Opsahl Academic EPublisher, 2012) 505.

131 UN Department of Public Information, 'Sanctions and War: General Assembly adopts resolution on conflict diamonds' (2002) <http://www.un.org/peace/africa/Diamond.html>.

The trade in conflict diamonds began in the early 1990s, first employed by Jonas Savimbi's National Union for the Total Independence of Angola (UNITA) in Angola, and copied in Sierra Leone by the Revolutionary United Front (RUF). Rebel armies in the Democratic Republic of Congo also began to use diamonds to fuel the conflict and since then the practice has touched Guinea, Liberia and Côte d'Ivoire as well.[132]

There can be little doubt that the use of conflict diamonds constitutes a human security crisis. The atrocities of the armed groups that have used conflict diamonds have become well known. In describing the physical and psychological terrorisation of the civilian population in Sierra Leone, the Prosecutor for the Special Court of Sierra Leone began:

> This is a tale of horror, beyond the gothic into the realm of Dante's Inferno.[133]

Chopping off limbs, burning both adults and children alive, recruiting child soldiers, using young girls as sex slaves, massive internal displacement and much more were all in significant part financed via the sale of diamonds and in turn these terror tactics were used to gain greater access to more diamonds.[134] At the height of the conflict diamond trade it is estimated that they may have constituted as much as 15 per cent of the global trade in rough diamonds.[135] As an example of the sort of revenue diamonds provided these groups, it is estimated that UNITA obtained at least between US$ 3.7 and 4 billion between 1992 and 1998.[136] According to Holly Burkhalter, conflict diamonds may generate as much as US$ 7 billion per year in revenue. She states that '[i]n some African countries $1 million could buy 100 000 second hand Kalashnikov rifles.'[137] Diamonds in these parts of Africa are collected from alluvial streams and are easy to smuggle across borders. There is no reliable way to determine their origins and even the legitimate diamond trade operated on a largely cash basis.[138]

132 Partnership Africa Canada, 'Killing Kimberley? Conflict Diamonds and Paper Tigers' (Occasional Paper No 15, PAC, November 2006) 2.

133 *Prosecutor v Issa Sesay, Morris Kallon and Augustine Gbao, (Proceedings)* (Special Court for Sierra Leone, Case No SCSL-2004-15-PT, 5 July 2004) 1, Opening Statement, David M Crane.

134 See, eg, Daniel L Feldman, 'Conflict Diamonds, International Trade Regulation and the Nature of Law' (2003) 24 *University of Pennsylvania Journal of International Economic Law* 835, 840–1.

135 Partnership Africa Canada, 'Killing Kimberley? Conflict Diamonds and Paper Tigers' (Occasional Paper No 15, PAC, November 2006) 2.

136 Margo Kaplan, 'Carats and Sticks: Pursuing War and Peace through the Diamond Trade' (2003) 35 *International Law and Politics* 559, 574.

137 Holly Burkhalter, 'Between the Lines: A Diamond Agreement in the Rough' (2003) 135 *Foreign Policy* 72, 72.

138 Partnership Africa Canada, 'Killing Kimberley? Conflict Diamonds and Paper Tigers' (Occasional Paper No 15, PAC, November 2006), 2.

(ii) The Kimberley Process

The Kimberley Process emerged to address these problems. After two years of negotiations a final agreement was reached on 5 November 2002, when the representatives of a range of States, the diamond industry and a number of NGOs convened in Interlaken, Switzerland, to announce an agreement on the Kimberley Process Certification Scheme (KPCS). The Kimberley Process Certification Scheme became effective from 1 January 2003. It currently has 54 participants, representing 81 countries.[139] The governmental membership of the Kimberley Process is estimated to account for 99.8 per cent of the world's legal trade and production in rough diamonds.[140] The Kimberley Process has received endorsement both from the UN General Assembly and the Security Council.[141] The Kimberley Process Chair country's Permanent Representative to the UN reports to the UN General Assembly on an annual basis.[142]

The Kimberley Process Certification Scheme requires all shipments of rough diamonds that are exported from a Member State to be transported in a tamper-resistant container and accompanied by a certificate validated by the exporting government.[143] The shipment can only be sent to other members of the Kimberley Process, and no uncertified shipments are to be allowed into the jurisdiction of participants. After export the diamonds are subject to a voluntary system of warranty, acknowledging that they were obtained from legitimate sources. Though the regulations of the scheme apply only between Kimberley Process participants, all the major producers and importers of diamonds are involved, and as such the Process attained de facto universal coverage,[144] and has encouraged almost all of the relevant countries involved in the diamond trade to come on board.

Originally the Kimberley Process negotiations only included government representatives.[145] Eventually, however, the process became a joint effort

139 As the European Union represents a single participant. See <http://www.kimberleyprocess.com/background/index_en.html>.

140 Daniel L Feldman, 'Conflict Diamonds, International Trade Regulation and the Nature of Law' (2003) 24 *University of Pennsylvania Journal of International Economic Law* 835, 864.

141 *The Role of Diamonds in Fuelling Conflict*, GA Res 55/56, UN GAOR, Agenda Item 175, UN Doc A/RES/55/56 (29 January 2001) – endorsing and legitimising the negotiation process; *The Role of Diamonds in Fueling Conflict*, GA Res 56/263, UN GAOR, Agenda Item 37, UN Doc A/RES/56/263 (13 March 2002). Also endorsed by Security Council Resolution 1459 (2003) UN SCOR, UN Doc S/RES/1459 (28 January 2003).

142 Ann C Wallis, 'Data Mining: Lessons from the Kimberley Process for the United Nations' Development of Human Rights Norms for Transnational Corporations' (2005) 4 *Northwestern Journal of International Human Rights* 388, 397.

143 See Kimberley Process website, <http://www.kimberleyprocess.com>.

144 Victoria Vidal, 'Informal International Lawmaking: The Kimberley Process' Mechanism of Accountability' in Ayelet Berman et al (ed), *Informal International Lawmaking: Case Studies* (Torkel Opsahl Academic EPublisher, 2012) 505, 512.

145 Daniel L Feldman, 'Conflict Diamonds, International Trade Regulation and the Nature of Law' (2003) 24 *University of Pennsylvania Journal of International Economic Law* 835, 850.

between states, NGOs and the diamond industry. Thus the process does not only involve the various stakeholders but was also developed in partnership with all parties.

The direct buy-in and responsibility for development of the process certainly has contributed to the rapid universal acceptance of the Kimberley Process standards and their legitimacy. Further, the process itself, having been developed by those to whom it applies, is presumably practical and workable.[146]

The Kimberley Process participant group is uniquely structured. The World Diamond Council, participant NGO Partnership Africa Canada (PAC),[147] and representatives from participant states all serve equally on the various working groups and committees that operate under the Kimberley Process Chair.[148]

In relation to the relationship between the Kimberley Process and international trade law, Member States chose to pre-empt any concerns about the validity of the scheme under WTO provisions, and sought a waiver allowing participants to discriminate in their imports and exports of rough diamonds, '*recognising* the extraordinary humanitarian nature of this issue … and the systematic and gross human rights violations that have been perpetrated' as a result of conflict diamonds.[149] Concerns have been raised over the existence of the waiver, as some fear it implies that without it the Kimberley Process is contrary to WTO rules.[150] It is also criticised for taking the easy way out, and not providing any long-term solutions to the relationship between international trade rules and international human rights law. This shows an example where the integrative nature of human security discourse was not able to overcome the fragmented nature of international law.

As Ann Wallis observes, '[p]erhaps the most striking quality of the Kimberley Process is that it exists at all.'[151] Moreover, the Process has had an appreciable effect on the conflict diamond trade. The Kimberley Process is acknowledged as

146 Ann C Wallis, 'Data Mining: Lessons from the Kimberley Process for the United Nations' Development of Human Rights Norms for Transnational Corporations' (2005) 4 *Northwestern Journal of International Human Rights* 388, 389–90.

147 As will be discussed below, prior to 2011, there were two participant NGOs prior to the withdrawal of Global Witness; see below.

148 Ann C Wallis, 'Data Mining: Lessons from the Kimberley Process for the United Nations' Development of Human Rights Norms for Transnational Corporations' (2005) 4 *Northwestern Journal of International Human Rights* 388, 397.

149 Waiver Concerning the Kimberley Process Certification Scheme for Rough Diamonds, Decision of 15 May 2003, WTO Doc WT/L/518 (27 May 2003); It has since been renewed and now extends to 2018: *Decision of 27 December 2012, Request for Extension*, WTO Doc WT/L/518 (27 November 2012).

150 See Krista Nadakavukaren Schefer, 'Chilling the Protection of Human Rights: What the Kimberley Process Waiver Can Tell Us about the WTO's Effect on International Law' (Working Paper No 2007/03, NCCR Trade Regulation: Swiss National Centre of Competence in Research, January 2007).

151 Ann C Wallis, 'Data Mining: Lessons from the Kimberley Process for the United Nations' Development of Human Rights Norms for Transnational Corporations' (2005) 4 *Northwestern Journal of International Human Rights* 388, 398.

having reduced the global trade in conflict diamonds to less than 1 per cent of the global market in rough diamonds.[152]

It is also important to recognise the reasons why the industry was eager to develop and cooperate in the process to begin with. As an expensive luxury item, consumer demand is flexible and crucial to the price of diamonds.[153] Conflict diamonds constituted a small portion of the total market, but if consumers reacted to concerns about conflict diamonds, the whole industry would be affected. According to Holly Burkhalter:

> It was the atrocities in Sierra Leone that moved the non-governmental community to say out loud what the industry knows well: diamonds have no intrinsic value and they are not rare. If the public learns to associate them with hacked off limbs and the rape of children, the notion of the diamond as a symbol of love could evaporate forever.[154]

Previously in this chapter the power of NGO campaigning on treaty development was shown. Here it is demonstrated that there is equal effectiveness of NGO campaigning and public awareness raising both on informal lawmaking processes, and on other non-state actors, in this case on the diamond industry. And the approach of focusing on the human elements of the issue were once again the key to the success of the campaign.

Of the concerns that surround the Kimberley Process, none is more threatening than the potential for waning or splintering interest. The Kimberley Process, and especially the diamond industry's continuing participation, are entirely dependent on maintaining commitment to and public interest in the project. With the perception that the worst of the diamond-fuelled conflicts are over, there is an increasing sense that the Kimberley Process has fulfilled its purpose.[155] But, as Kaplan points out, '[t]he conflict diamonds issue is not only about ending civil wars but also about ensuring they do not arise'.[156] This shows another of the key challenges of pursuing human security norms. It is easy to capture attention when a situation has reached a crisis level. But for human security to fulfil its

152 Special Representative of the Secretary-General (SRSG) on the issue of human rights and transnational corporations and other business enterprises, UN GAOR, Human Rights Council Comm, Fourth sess, Agenda Item 2, UN Doc A/HRC/4/035 (9 February 2007) [59]. Kimberley Process, *Background* <http://www.kimberleyprocess.com/background/index_en.html>.

153 Leiv Lunde and Mark Taylor, 'Commerce or Crime? Regulating Economies of Conflict' (Report No 424, FAFO Institute, 2003) 17.

154 Cited in Jamila D Holmes, 'The Kimberley Process: Evidence of Change in International Law' (2006–2007) 3 *International Law and Management Review* 213, 218.

155 See, eg, Ann C Wallis, 'Data Mining: Lessons from the Kimberley Process for the United Nations' Development of Human Rights Norms for Transnational Corporations' (2005) 4 *Northwestern Journal of International Human Rights* 388, 401.

156 Margo Kaplan, 'Carats and Sticks: Pursuing War and Peace through the Diamond Trade' (2003) 35 *International Law and Politics* 559, 572–3.

preventative function, it must be able to harness the power of the security label without such crisis dimensions.

(iii) The Kimberley Process, 'conflict diamonds' and human security

In recent years the Kimberley Process has come under heavy pressure, and there are renewed questions about its ongoing relevance, surrounding particularly the narrow definition of diamonds covered by the KPCS. As noted above, the UN defines 'conflict diamonds' as those 'diamonds that originate from areas controlled by forces or factions opposed to legitimate and internationally recognised governments, and are used to fund military opposition to those governments, or in contravention of the decisions of the Security Council.' The KPCS definition is even narrower: 'Conflict diamonds, also known as "blood" diamonds, are rough diamonds used by rebel movements or their allies to finance armed conflicts aimed at undermining legitimate governments.'[157] While both definitions retain the narrow perspective of internal armed conflicts, which in itself is problematic (as will seen below), the KPCS definition fails to account for the possibility of the governments of states themselves abusing their power in relation to the diamond trade, and only refers to the Security Council insofar as it relates to this narrow definition. The Core Document's Preamble expresses concern for the 'peace, safety and security of people in affected countries and … systematic and gross human rights violations' but only insofar as these occur within conflicts. Despite this language, the narrow definition demonstrates that the primary concern of the KPCS is in fact with the preservation of national sovereignty, and that it targets only threats against the state. The KP Civil Society Coalition has nevertheless seized on the language of the Preamble to assert that:

> Civil society believes that human rights have always been at the core of the Kimberley Process mandate and that this commitment should be clarified through the introduction of explicit human rights language in Kimberley Process documents.[158]

In stark contrast, however, the KP Chair, Bernard Esau, explicitly asserted in 2009 that '[t]he Kimberley Process is not a human rights organisation.'[159]

To the extent that the KPCS is a response to human insecurity, it can be seen that a narrow perspective on human security has prevailed within the operation of the Kimberley Process. The Process is capable of responding to the direct relationship between diamonds and conflict, but not to systemic abuse, or the structural violence of depriving a country of the benefits of its resources. The effects of the narrow

157 KPCS Core Document, <http://www.kimberleyprocess.com/en/kpcs-core-document>.

158 KP Civil Society Coalition, *A Guide to the Kimberley Process* (PAC, September 2013).

159 'Blood diamonds watchdog washes its hands', *Independent Online*, 29 August 2009 <http://www.iol.co.za/news/africa/blood-diamonds-watchdog-washes-its-hands-1.456713>

definition were most starkly revealed when the Kimberley Process authorised exports from two companies operating in the Marange diamond fields in Zimbabwe, and called for the end of US sanctions on diamonds sourced from the region.

(A) HUMAN SECURITY, DIAMONDS AND THE RESOURCE CURSE: ZIMBABWE'S MARANGE DIAMONDS

> The story of Zimbabwe's contested diamond fields is about many things: smuggling and frontier hucksterism; a scramble fuelled by raw economic desperation and unfathomable greed; and, of course, heart-wrenching cases of government-sponsored repression and human rights violations ... It is also about political intrigue, ambition and a complete disregard for decency or the rule of law.[160]

In March 2006, a diamond rush began in the rich alluvial deposits in the Marange region of Zimbabwe. The Marange diamond fields stretch across approximately 66,000 hectares, and while there have been conflicting estimates as to the worth of the deposits, some have estimated it to be one of the world's richest reserves of diamonds.[161] One estimate stated that Zimbabwe's Marange diamond fields were expected to produce 16.9 million carats in 2013, which would make the project the largest in the world in terms of carats produced annually.[162] From October 2006 the diamond fields have been under government control, with state-controlled mining company ZMDC taking over operations, and Marange is a heavily militarised region, like much of Chaidzwa, the district in which it lies.[163]

Since the assumption of government control, reports of violence and human rights abuse allegedly perpetrated by state security agents have emerged. A range of reports and testimonials from workers in the diamond fields and local communities have reported deaths, forced evictions, assaults, rape, arbitrary detention and forced labour (including child labour) occurring in the region.[164] This violence reached a peak in 2008 when the military seized complete control of the diamond

160 Partnership Africa Canada (PAC), 'Diamonds and Clubs: The Militarized Control of Diamonds and Power in Zimbabwe' (Report PAC, June 2010).

161 See, eg, Global Witness, 'Return of the Blood Diamond: The Deadly Race to Control Zimbabwe's New Found Diamond Wealth' ibid. (14 June 2010). See also ibid.

162 Kitco Report, cited in 'Zimbabwe to Lead Diamond Producers: Report', *NewsDay* (Zimbabwe) 2 September 2013 <https://www.newsday.co.zw/2013/09/02/zimbabwe-lead-diamond-producers-report/>; *Business Times Africa magazine* (Edition 1, 2012) puts the potential output of the Marange diamonds deposits at 60 million carats a year – worth about $3 billion, or more than 15% of the global diamond supply. Canadian jeweller Brilliant Earth suggests that the total value of Marange gems may be as high as $800 billion, making them the richest fields ever found.

163 See, eg, Partnership Africa Canada (PAC), 'Diamonds and Clubs: The Militarized Control of Diamonds and Power in Zimbabwe' (Report PAC, June 2010), 4.

164 Ibid. See also, Human Rights Watch, *Deliberate Chaos: Ongoing Human Rights Abuses in the Marange Diamond Fields of Zimbabwe* (HRW, 2010), Human Rights Watch, *Diamonds in the Rough: Human Rights Abuses in the Marange Diamond Fields of Zimbabwe* (HRW, 2009).

fields, in an effort to stamp out all illegal mining in the area under *Operation Hakudzokwi* ('area of no return'), and killed over 200 people according to NGO estimates. The soldiers at this time took over mining syndicates that had previously been run by the police.

In 2009, a Kimberley Process Review Mission was sent to Zimbabwe to investigate the violence and to assess compliance with the Kimberley Process. The Mission was, as is customary for KP reviews, made up of representatives from Member States, participating NGOs and industry experts. The review found evidence of human rights abuses, of security-agent-run syndicates and smuggling of diamonds to non-KP participants, specifically Mozambique.[165] The Review Mission concluded that it had 'identified several areas in which Zimbabwe is non-compliant with the minimum requirements of the KPCS' and made the recommendation that Zimbabwe should have its membership suspended for at least six months.[166]

As noted earlier, the KPCS operates on a consensus-based system of decision-making, which means that a single dissenting voice can impede the scheme's ability to produce results, and undermine the legitimacy of the Kimberley Process as a whole. In 2009 the KP members decided not to suspend Zimbabwe, but instead to enact a Joint Work Plan to bring the country into compliance. The Joint Work Plan did not specifically address the violence noted by the review mission, and failed to mention human rights at all. Instead it focused on stopping the smuggling and on the demilitarisation of the diamond fields. Efforts were made by the companies that had been given licences to mine in the area to meet the conditions of the Joint Work Plan, and by September 2010, the Kimberley Process authorised two companies, Mbada and Canadille, to resume exports of diamonds from the region, despite ongoing reports of human rights abuses occurring, and declared the diamonds to be 'conflict-free'.[167] Further allowances were made by the Administrative Decision on Zimbabwe [Marange] of 1 November 2011, adopted by the Kinshasa plenary meeting, allowing rough diamond exports from the Marange area.[168] In 2013, the Kimberley Process Plenary Meeting was opened with calls by the Chair for the US to follow the path of the European Union and other states in lifting sanctions imposed on diamonds from Zimbabwe.[169] This call came despite reports that the diamond proceeds from the region were being used to

165 Kimberley Process Plenary, 'Administrative Decision on Zimbabwe Joint Work Plan', Swakopmund, Namibia, 5 November 2009 <http://www.kimberleyprocess.com/en/2009-administrative-decision-zimbabwe-jwp>.

166 Ibid.

167 Kimberley Process Plenary, 'Zimbabwe Annual Report 2010' <http://www.kimberleyprocess.com/en/zimbabwe-annual-report-2010>.

168 Kimberley Process Plenary, 'Administrative Decision on Marange (Zimbabwe)', Kinchasa Plenary Meeting, 1 November 2011 <http://www.kimberleyprocess.com/en/0012011-administrative-decision-marange-zimbabwecompendium>.

169 Kimberley Process Chair, 'Opening Address' (Speech delivered at the Kimberley Process Plenary Meeting, Johannesburg, South Africa, 22 November 2013).

fund the Zanu PF election campaign that same year, and allegations that senior government officials had plundered more than US$ 2 billion.[170]

These decisions were met with significant controversy, and they led to one of the founding NGO members of the Kimberley Process,[171] Global Witness, withdrawing from the Scheme in December 2011. The NGO declared that the 'Kimberley Process' refusal to evolve and address the clear links between diamonds, violence and tyranny has rendered it increasingly outdated' and that '[n]early nine years after the Kimberley Process was launched, the sad truth is that most consumers still cannot be sure where their diamonds come from, nor whether they are financing armed violence or abusive regimes.'[172] The criticism of the Process also echoed the words of Martin Rapaport, founder and Chairman of the Rapaport Group and the world's largest diamond trading network, the Rapaport Diamond Trading Network (RapNet).[173] Rapaport's comments condemned the Kimberley Process as a front, giving the cover of legitimacy while allowing human rights abuses to occur unfettered. The criticisms raise the question of whether the Kimberley Process is willing to face or capable of facing the current realities of human insecurity and the diamond trade.[174] It was anticipated that a new definition would be devised and agreed, following the remarks of the 2012 Chair, US Ambassador Gillian Milovanovic, at the Washington DC meeting:

> Fundamentally, we believe that carefully crafted, agreed updates to definitions, and to the procedures through which they will be invoked and applied, are central to addressing the concern of unfairness and inconsistency and also to keeping the Process relevant and effective for decades to come.[175]

However, the Plenary Meeting in 2012, and again in 2013, not only failed to come to a consensus on a new definition, but in fact failed to unanimously agree that a change in the definition was necessary.[176]

170 See, eg, Andrew Mambondiyani, 'The Curse of Marange Diamonds', *Zimbabwe Situation* (online), 4 November 2013 <http://www.zimbabwesituation.com/news/zimsit_the-curse-of-marange-diamonds/>.

171 Indeed, it was pressure from Global Witness and fellow NGO Fatal Transactions that have driven international attention and had brought the issue of Blood Diamonds to the United Nations initially, eventually leading to the negotiations which formed the Kimberley Process.

172 Global Witness, *Press Release*, 5 December 2011 <http://www.globalwitness.org/library/global-witness-leaves-kimberley-process-calls-diamond-trade-be-held-accountable>.

173 Ibid.

174 See, eg, Julie Elizabeth Nichols, 'A Conflict of Diamonds: The Kimberley Process and Zimbabwe's Marange Diamond Fields' (2011–2012) 40 *Denver Journal of International Law and Policy* 648, 651.

175 Cited in Scott Jerbi, 'Assessing the Roles of Multi-stakeholder Initiatives in Advancing the Business and Human Rights Agenda' (2012) 94(887) *International Review of the Red Cross* 1027, 1040.

176 Kimberley Process Chair, 'Final Communiqué from the Kimberley Process Plenary Meeting', Washington DC, 30 November 2012 <http://www.kimberleyprocess.com/en/2012-final-communique-plenary-washingtoncompendium>.

Martin Rapaport has offered a new definition, which has been endorsed by the PAC, the one remaining founding NGO partner of the Kimberley Process:

> Blood diamonds are diamonds involved in murder, mutilation, rape or forced servitude.[177]

PAC argues that this definition 'acknowledges the central role human rights have, and should, play in the Kimberley Process.'[178] But there are a number of problems inherent in this redefinition, which as it stands cannot provide any real guarantees for human security. The first is the limited range of activities included. At the very least, the list should be more reflective of the structure of the Responsibility to Protect. In other words, it should extend to 'genocide, war crimes, crimes against humanity and ethnic cleansing, and their incitement'.[179] This definition at least provides a wider blanket of protection against egregious human rights violations. But it also would remain focused solely on acts of direct physical violence posed by those seeking to exploit the diamonds. A concomitant issue from diamond mining is the threat of structural violence, in denying access to these resources by local populations, hindering the potential of such resources to contribute to their social and economic development and contributing to what is known as the 'paradox of plenty' or 'resource curse', and creating potentially disastrous long-term effects for the population and their environment as this predatory behaviour is engaged in an unsustainable manner. The paradox of plenty refers to the curious phenomenon recognised from the 1990s onwards, namely, that many countries rich in natural resources experience slower economic growth than countries less well-endowed.[180]

This reality is also playing out in the Chiadwza region of Zimbabwe, as a result of the Marange diamond fields. Despite the expected revenues, and despite the government having taken over the fields in 2006, in 2010 it was reported that no revenues from the fields had entered the national treasuries.[181] With the KP authorisations and sanctions being lifted, the Zimbabwe people continue to wonder 'where the revenue from diamond mining is going since the government is only receiving a tiny fraction of what the companies are getting and nothing is

177 Martin Rapaport, 'Stop Buying Blood Diamonds: The Kimberley Process is a Sham' (Rapaport Diamond Report February 2010) 1.

178 Partnership Africa Canada (PAC), 'Diamonds and Clubs: The Militarized Control of Diamonds and Power in Zimbabwe' (Report PAC, June 2010), 24.

179 UN General Assembly, *2005 World Summit Outcome Document* 60/1, UN GAOR, Sixtieth sess, Agenda Item 46 and 120, UN Doc A/RES/60/1 (24 October 2005) [138].

180 See, eg, Paul Collier, 'Laws and Codes for the Resource Curse' (2008) 11 *Yale Human Rights and Development Law Journal* 9, 11.

181 'There is nothing coming to the fiscus from Chiadzwa,' Finance Minister Tendai Biti cited in *Zimbabwe Online,* 8 March 2010 <http://www.zimonline.co.za/Article.aspx?ArticleId=5806>.

going to local communities.'[182] Local news reports are replete with commentary on the effects of the Marange fields on the local populace:

> And the unfortunate villagers continue to sink deeper into the abyss of stinking poverty. The companies which had promised to give the villagers a quarterly supply of food until they have come with income generating projects have reneged on their earlier promises. And some villagers particularly relocated by a Chinese company, last received their food supplies last year. The villagers have been reduced to worse than destitute, and today they blame their woes on the discovery of diamonds in their area, as the mining operations have uprooted them from their ancestral lands. To them the diamonds have but become a curse as malnutrition and hunger are now part of many of the relocated villagers' lives.[183]

This look at the Kimberley Process and its current challenges has revealed a number of issues that must be taken into consideration if multi-stakeholder initiatives are to effectively promote, protect and respect human security. In particular, it highlights the dangers of relying on narrow visions of human security, and the dangers of neglecting the rights-based components of security. The chapter concludes with a broader look at the interaction of human security and MSIs.

C Human security and multi-stakeholder initiatives

Examining MSIs through the lens of human security discourse reveals a number of features that need to be considered both to increase their effectiveness in reducing insecurity and to prevent these initiatives from causing unintended harmful consequences. The 2006 UN General Assembly partnership resolution is a place to start.[184] It states that all interaction between the organs and institutions of the UN and private actors should be based on the following set of underlying principles. Partnerships must:

182 G R Chimonyo, Solomon Mungure and Paul D Scott, 'The Social, Economic and Environmental Implications of Diamond Mining in Chiadzwa' (Study conducted by Centre for Research and Development 2013) 17.

183 Andrew Mambondiyani, 'The Curse of Marange Diamonds', *Zimbabwe Situation* (online), 4 November 2013 <http://www.zimbabwesituation.com/news/zimsit_the-curse-of-marange-diamonds/>. See also Charles Mangongera, 'Zimbabwe's Diamond Curse', *The Independent* (Zimbabwe), 22 November 2013 <http://www.theindependent.co.zw/2013/11/22/zimbabwes-diamond-curse/>; Hazel Ndebele, 'Opacity haunts diamond mining's Treasury remittances', *The Independent* (Zimbabwe), 15 November 2013 <http://www.theindependent.co.zw/2013/11/15/opacity-haunts-diamond-mining s-treasury- remittances/>; Andrew Mambondiyani, 'The curse of Marange diamonds…as relocated villagers wallow in poverty' *Bulawayo24* (online), 4 November 2013 <http://bulawayo24.com/index-id-opinion-sc-columnist-byo-38359.html>.

184 UN General Assembly, Resolution 60/215, UN GAOR, UN Doc A/RES/60/215 (29 March 2006).

- serve the purposes and principles embodied in the Charter of the United Nations;
- make concrete contributions to the realization of the Millennium Development Goals and the other goals contained in the Millennium Declaration, as well as in the outcomes of major United Nations conferences and summits and their reviews;
- be undertaken in a manner that maintains the integrity, impartiality and independence of the Organization.[185]

The first two components here are essential for the realisation of human security, as has been seen by previous discussion of the relationship of human security to the UN Charter, and the three interconnected pillars of rights, development and security.

(i) People-centred security

One of the lessons to be learnt from the above examination is that the initiatives seeking to redress human insecurity must be genuinely people-centred in substance and language. The above discussion revealed that while the Kimberley Process was ostensibly created to reduce human suffering, the Core Document is in fact more concerned with the preservation of national sovereignty and thus evidences a narrow concern for state security. Reframing issues around a human rather than state security focus would more efficiently attend to concerns about human suffering. The Marange example illustrates how the hidden emphasis on state security has the potential to undermine the goods that the initiative seeks to deliver.

It is also important for such initiatives to be based in or at least demonstrate consideration of international human rights law. Again, the Marange example effectively demonstrates how the lack of an explicitly rights-based approach has greatly hamstrung the KPCS's capacity to respond to serious human rights abuses and has rendered the process increasingly outdated. Such schemes should also recognise the indivisible nature of civil and political rights and economic, social and cultural rights.[186] Such recognition would assist with promoting a more comprehensive vision of security.

(ii) Comprehensive, preventative rights-based security

Another aspect of these initiatives is that they tend to be very specific in nature, not unlike the human security treaties discussed in the previous chapter. Such focus is important, allowing for specific threats to human security to be addressed

185 Ibid.

186 A required component of human security, General Assembly, *Follow-up to Paragraph 143 on Human Security of the 2005 World Summit Outcome*, 66/290, Sixty-sixth sess, Agenda Item 14 and 117, UN Doc A/RES/66/290 (25 October 2012) [3].

by context-based solutions. More problematically, however, there does appear to be a trend that MSIs tend to be developed with the aim of concentrating on aspects of broader issues with short-term solutions.[187] Structural violence and broader consideration of preventing human insecurity are given little attention. Governance gaps thus remain, which MSIs have not yet been able to fill. This is, however, beginning to be acknowledged by some MSIs, which are developing new strategies that better reflect a broader vision. One such example is the Roll Back Malaria Partnership (RBM), which was launched in 1998 and currently comprises over 500 partners from malaria-endemic countries, donor governments, corporations, nongovernmental and community-based organisations, and research and academic institutions.[188] In 2013, in collaboration with the UNDP (which, it should be remembered, was the original architect of human security discourse), RBM launched a new 'Multisectoral Action Framework' aimed at addressing the root causes of community and individuals' vulnerability to malaria, and recognising that these problems extend well beyond the health sector.[189] The action framework is intended to be implemented across all sectors of society and places particular emphasis on the socio-economic factors that contribute to the spread of malaria, such as living conditions, agricultural practices and gender inequality, environmental factors, in particular climate change and its effect on the malaria parasite, and population movements, where people with low immunity are moving to areas of high risk of transmission.

Another example centred on the health dimensions of human security is the Global Fund to Fight AIDS, Tuberculosis and Malaria.[190] The Fund's stated vision and mission statement create the impression that the Fund is prevention-orientated, as it envisions '[a] world free of the burden of HIV/AIDs, tuberculosis and malaria with better health for all', and aims to 'attract, manage and disburse additional resources to make a sustainable and significant contribution in the fight against AIDS, tuberculosis and malaria in countries in need, and contributing to poverty reduction as part of the MDGs'. These goals are unquestionably human security aligned. Moreover, the new strategic plan has introduced the issue of developing better rights-based approaches to the Fund's work, invoking human rights principles such as due diligence and non-discrimination into its practices, and mainstreaming human rights considerations into its practices.[191] However, in the development of this strategic goal, caution was advised that the Fund should not lose its focus on health.[192] This shows the difficulties for human security approaches in balancing a narrow focus against the need for a comprehensive

187 See, eg, Jens Martens, 'Multistakeholder Partnerships – Future Models of Multilateralism' (Occasional Paper No 29, Dialogue on Globalization, January 2007) 49.

188 Roll Back Malaria, <http://www.rollbackmalaria.org/>.

189 Roll Back Malaria, *A Multisectoral Action Framework for Malaria* (RBM, 2013)

190 Global Fund to Fight AIDS, Tuberculosis and Malaria <http://www.theglobalfund.org/>.

191 Global Fund to Fight AIDS, Tuberculosis and Malaria, *The Global Fund Strategy 2012–2016: Investing for Impact* (Global Fund, 2012).

192 Ibid.

vision of security. It also shows the remaining political challenges in mainstreaming human security discourse, where attention to human rights was seen to detract from the focus, rather than as a necessary ingredient for true health security.

A closely related problem of the narrow foci of MSIs is the accompanying proliferation of such partnerships, which are rarely coordinated with one another. This point was acknowledged in the *OECD Paris Declaration on Aid Effectiveness*, which commented on 'the insufficient integration of global programmes and initiatives into partner countries' broader development agendas, including in critical areas such as HIV/AIDS'.[193] This fragmentation of global resources and attention could ultimately hinder rather than complement the pursuit of comprehensive security. The proliferation of MSIs also often occurs in areas where the political will for international legal obligations is lacking, and rather than being utilised as a complement to legal efforts, MSIs operate as replacements. Just as some human security treaties discussed in Chapter Seven were framed in a way to avoid issues of state responsibility, as will be discussed, MSIs can operate in a similar fashion. As part of a comprehensive human security strategy, MSIs should be seen as only one part of a wider machinery establishing norms and producing change.[194] The Kimberley Process demonstrates an example where rather than a proliferation in the development of a comprehensive response, instead the Certification Scheme has had a chilling effect, where further action from the international community was deemed unnecessary. This has produced an overreliance on the Scheme to protect the legitimacy of the diamond industry, despite the increased criticism that it is now outdated, and as seen, has ceased to respond to the current challenges facing the diamond industry.

(iii) Participatory security

At first blush, MSIs could be considered the ultimate framework for participatory human security. But this can only be true if the partnerships involved are genuinely representative. While there are MSIs that effectively ensure representation not only of corporate and civil society partners, but also affected communities and/or individuals, Martens states that '[e]xperience and research thus far point instead to deficits in the representativeness of partnerships.'[195] He concludes that:

> With a few positive exceptions, multistakeholder partnerships reproduce precisely the power relationships and asymmetries that exist in the international system. In some senses they even intensify them by strengthening the dominance of a few powerful governments, multinationals, private foundations, and well-organised international organisations from the North, while

193 OECD, *Paris Declaration on Aid Effectiveness* (2 March 2005) [4][iv].

194 See, eg, Mariëtte van Huijstee, 'Multi-stakeholder Initiatives: A Guide for Civil Society Organisations' (Report SOMO, March 2012) 19.

195 Jens Martens, 'Multistakeholder Partnerships – Future Models of Multilateralism' (Occasional Paper No 29, Dialogue on Globalization, January 2007) 40.

governments and civil society organisations from the South often play only a token role.[196]

In terms of the deficits in representativeness from the South, a number of issues have been noted. The first is that the vast majority of MSIs originate from the North, targeting issues in the South.[197] Southern counterparts (civil, corporate and governmental) may thus feel a lack of ownership in the process. Hujitsee also notes that civil society and business in the South tend to be more distrustful towards one another.[198] The same is sometimes true of the relationship between civil society and governments in certain countries. This undermines the core principle of local ownership contained in human security.[199]

Another issue in relation to participation was demonstrated by the Kimberley Process. As noted above, one of the key NGO participants of the Scheme, Global Witness, condemned the Process and withdrew from its representation on the KPCS Board. This is not the only instance of a NGO withdrawing from an MSI. Perhaps most recently, Oxfam announced its intention to leave the Voluntary Principles for Security and Human Rights, citing frustration with the lack of meaningful progress in key areas of the implementation of the principles.[200] The loss of key NGO participants is a significant blow to the operations and perceived legitimacy of such MSIs. Furthermore, these withdrawals point to more serious problems in relation to the power balances and necessary will on the part of participants to work together and produce effective solutions. It highlights that even in informal forms of international law-making, states still retain most of the power, and that participation by non-state actors can only go so far. This demonstrates a serious impediment in international law's capacity to truly embrace human security in its current structure.

Another issue, as previously discussed, is that in some MSIs, while NGOs may be involved, there are few or no mechanisms in place ensuring the participation of affected communities or vulnerable persons. Again, however, some MSIs have in recent times developed procedures and guidelines to ensure that the programmes are responsive to the needs of actual human insecurity. One such example is the previously mentioned Global Fund to Fight AIDS, Tuberculosis and Malaria. Governance of the Fund at the local level is mainly conducted through the Country Coordinating Mechanisms (CCMs), which develop and submit grant proposals to the Global Fund based on priority needs at the national level. These mechanisms are intended to be constructed as multi-stakeholder partnerships, and

196 Ibid 41.

197 Mariëtte van Huijstee, 'Multi-stakeholder Initiatives: A guide for civil society organisations' (Report SOMO, March 2012) 41.

198 Ibid.

199 General Assembly, *Follow-up to Paragraph 143 on Human Security of the 2005 World Summit Outcome*, 66/290, Sixty-sixth sess, Agenda Item 14 and 117, UN Doc A/RES/66/290 (25 October 2012) [3].

200 Oxfam, *Press Release*, 17 April 2013 <http://www.oxfamamerica.org/press/oxfam-leaves-voluntary-principles-for-security-and-human-rights-multi-stakeholder-initiative/>.

are described by the Fund as 'central to the Global Fund's commitment to local ownership and participatory decision-making'.[201] However, many problems have been identified with the processes. Many governments proved unwilling to work with NSAs and NGOs, and thus CCMs lacked significant representation, or only included organisations that aligned themselves with the interests of the state.[202] Of particular concern was the fact that people living with the diseases (who were often stigmatised in their local communities) were not represented at all.[203] Other challenges relating to sufficient geographic representation, language barriers, resources and education were also obstacles to effective or genuine participation in these so-called partnerships. Stricter guidelines were called for again and again by NGOs at the board level, to be met with the state response that if these were to be local projects, they should have complete control over the internal operations.[204] This attracted significant criticism with a distinctly human security flavour: country ownership should not be confused with government ownership.[205] This brought about significant change in the minimum standards required in the eligibility requirements. Now applications require

> all CCMs to show evidence of membership of people that are both living with and representing people living with HIV, and of people affected by and representing people affected by Tuberculosis and Malaria as well as people from and representing Key Affected Populations, based on epidemiological as well as human rights and gender considerations.[206]

This shows the flexibility available in these kinds of initiatives, which is less possible at the level of formal international law development. Human security interests are clearly benefited by programmes that can learn, grow, and change without drawn out processes and negotiations.

V Conclusion

Human security, by its very nature, requires decision-making processes that engage with stakeholders and allow for open participation. Non-state actors, particularly NGOs, have proven invaluable as norm entrepreneurs in the field of human

201 Global Fund, CCMs <http://www.theglobalfund.org/en/ccm/>.

202 See, eg, Sonja Bartsch, 'The Global Fund to Fight AIDS, Tuberculosis and Malaria: Establishment, Current Issues and Future Challenges' (Paper presented at the Salzburg Seminar on the Governance of Health, Schloss Arenberg, Salzburg, Austria, 5–8 December 2005).

203 Ibid 8.

204 Global Fund, Eighth Board Meeting, Geneva, 28–30 June 2004 <http://www.theglobalfund.org/en/board/meetings/eighth/>.

205 Global Fund, *Report of the Executive Director,* Tenth Board Meeting, Geneva 21–22 April 2005, Doc GF/B10/2 <http://www.theglobalfund.org/documents/board/10/BM10_03ExecutiveDirector_Report_en/>.

206 Global Fund, Updated CCM Requirements <http://www.theglobalfund.org/documents/ccm/CCM_Requirements_Guidelines_en/>.

security. However, while the processes of international law-making have engaged with NSAs both in relation to human security and more broadly, the reality remains that these processes are invariably state-centric, and that participation by other actors is only possible with the permission of states. Thus while human security discourse needs NGOs to effectively plant the seeds for norm development, it is doomed to failure without commitment and leadership from states. The problem here is that this leaves human security largely to the vicissitudes of governmental changes and politics within states, such as occurred in Canada, which no longer flies the flag for the advancement of human security. Even multi-stakeholder initiatives, which are intended to offer a more level playing field in the interactions between actors, are often co-opted by the concerns of state partners, as demonstrated by the case of the Kimberley Process. Nonetheless, there are many benefits for the development of human security within such initiatives, provided that the framework and principles of human security discourse are explicitly invoked to ensure a balanced consideration of the different dimensions to providing for and promoting human security.

7 'Human security treaties' so-called

An examination of the content of human security discourse in international treaties

Security can be obtained in many ways. The normal plea is that armies protect security. This is only partly true; it is equally true that security is protected by policies.[1]

I Introduction

The preceding chapter examined how human security discourse has had an influence on international law-making processes and procedures, and demonstrated the template for the development of human security treaties. This chapter examines the language of the treaties themselves to assess influence of human security discourse on the content, and not just development, of treaties.

A number of international agreements in recent years have been affirmed as successes of human security discourse. These so-called 'human security treaties' include the *Ottawa Convention*,[2] the *Convention on Cluster Munitions* ('CCM'),[3] the *Rome Statute establishing the International Criminal Court*,[4] the *Optional Protocol to the Convention on the Rights of the Child on involvement of children in armed conflict* ('Optional Protocol'),[5] and most recently, the *Arms Trade Treaty* ('ATT').[6] These treaties have been described as human security treaties both in relation to their substantive content and the processes of their creation.[7] This

1 Jawaharlal Nehru, *India's Foreign Policy: Selected Speeches*, September 1946–April 1961 (Government of India Press, 1961).

2 *Convention on the Prohibition of the Use, Stockpiling, Production and Transfer of Anti-Personnel Mines and on their Destruction*, opened for signature 18 September 1997, 2056 UNTS 241 (entered into force 1 March 1999)('Ottawa Convention').

3 *Convention on Cluster Munitions* opened for signature 4 December 2008, 2688 UNTS 35 (entered into force 1 August 2010) ('CCM').

4 *Rome Statute of the International Criminal Court*, opened for signature 17 July 1998, 2187 UNTS 90 (entered into force 1 July 2002)('*Rome Statute*').

5 *Optional Protocol to the Convention on the Rights of the Child on the Involvement of Children in Armed Conflicts*, opened for signature 25 March 2000, 39 ILM 1285 (entered into force 2 December 2002) ('Optional Protocol').

6 *Arms Trade Treaty*, opened for signature 3 June 2013, 52 ILM 988 (entered into force 24 December 2014) ('*ATT*').

7 See, eg, Gerd Oberleitner, 'Human Security: A Challenge to International Law?' (2005) 11 *Global Governance* 185. Claudia F Fuentes Julio and Hans Günter Brauch, 'The Human Security Network: A Global North-South Coalition' in Hans Günter

chapter examines what the label 'human security treaty' might mean, how accurate the description is, and how human security might influence international treaty-making in the future.

The chapter then goes on to examine how the principles of human security manifest within these treaties, and the trends that become apparent as a result of the influence of human security. It must be noted that these treaties are not examined in light of their functional elements or their effectiveness in achieving their goals. Rather the examination aims purely to determine the degree to which human security discourse has penetrated the language and structure of international treaties.

II The human security treaties: in search of human security principles

A Treaty language

The first observation which must be made is that none of the aforementioned treaties nor any other binding international instrument actually employs the term 'human security'. This exclusion is perhaps particularly striking in the *Ottawa Convention*, given its roots. As noted earlier, the creation of this treaty was spear-headed by Canada's Foreign Minister of the time, Lloyd Axworthy, who has been one of the greatest political champions of human security from its inception.[8] However, the *Ottawa Convention*, which was developed between 1997 and 1998, came into being in the very early stages of human security discourse, prior to the Commission on Human Security's Report, and when considerable confusion still surrounded the concept. Indeed, the Thematic Debates on Human Security held by the General Assembly demonstrate that even in 2010 states remained tentative and unsure about human security and its definition.[9] Since then, however, the Reports of the Secretary General and the General Assembly Resolution on Human Security have emerged. The *Arms Trade Treaty*, whose final text was developed in 2013, came after these developments, and despite drawing strongly on these documents in the language of its preamble and elsewhere in its text,[10] also fails to actually use the term 'human security'.

However, the *Compilation of Views on the Elements of the Arms Trade Treaty* reveals that a number of states raised the issue of human security.[11] Indeed, a

Brauch et al (eds), *Facing Global Environmental Change* (Springer Berlin Heidelberg, 2009) vol 4, 991.

8 For Axworthy's endorsement of human security, see, eg, Lloyd Axworthy, 'Canada and Human Security: The Need for Leadership' (1997) 52(2) *International Journal* 183. See also Lloyd Axworthy, 'Towards a New Multilateralism' in Maxwell A Cameron, Robert J Lawson and Brian W Tomlin (eds), *To Walk Without Fear: The Global Movement to Ban Landmines* (Oxford University Press, 1998) 448.

9 The debates can be located at Human Security Unit, 'Human Security at a Glance' <http://unocha.org/humansecurity/humansecurity/resources/publications-and-products/Human-Security-At-The-General-Assembly>.

10 As will be explored below.

11 United Nations Conference on the Arms Trade Treaty, *Compilation of Views on the Elements of the Arms Trade Treaty: Background Document Prepared by the Secretariat*,

number of states called for inclusion in the preamble of an explicit clause 'to recognize that there is a clear link between the absence of commonly agreed international standards for the transfer of conventional arms and a range of negative consequences for human security and development.'[12] This was called for not only by members of the Human Security Network (Costa Rica[13] and Switzerland[14]), but by a number of other states as well.[15] Japan, in a similar vein, made note of the relationship between the rule of law and human security in its discussion:

> Strengthening the rule of law relating to control of arms transfers plays a significant role in promoting the safety of citizens and contributes to enhancing human security.[16]

Bulgaria went a step further and proposed that human security should be included as part of the assessment criteria and basic standards for import evaluations, which are ultimately found in Article 7 of the adopted treaty text, proposing that the criteria should be presented as:

> Internal, regional and international security and stability;
> International humanitarian law and international human rights law, including *human security* and development;
> Arms control and non-proliferation.[17]

This reveals that while human security has started to penetrate the language used at treaty discussions, there seems to be a continued reluctance to commit to the term in legal documentation, much like the similar reticence of the Security Council to use the language of human security in its Resolutions noted in Chapter Five. The reluctance is perhaps particularly relevant for Article 7 of the *ATT*, which employs the phrase 'peace and security' without further clarification of what form this security takes. This is uncommon in an international legal document, which would more normally state 'national security', 'international peace and security' or 'collective security'. There is thus ambiguity in the language, allowing for treaty interpretation principles under the *Vienna Convention on the Law of Treaties* to be applied.[18] The combination of discussion of human security in the

UN GAOR, UN Doc A/CONF/217/2 (10 May 2012). Other materials surrounding the conference (and preparatory committees), including draft texts, statements and background documents can be found at <http://www.un.org/disarmament/ATT/documents/>.

12 See ibid 106 (United Kingdom).

13 Ibid 20.

14 Ibid 88–9.

15 The United Kingdom, New Zealand and Zambia also called for the inclusion of such a clause; see ibid 106 (United Kingdom); 66 (New Zealand); 114 (Zambia).

16 Ibid 45.

17 Ibid 14 (emphasis added).

18 *Vienna Convention on the Law of Treaties,* opened for signature 23 May 1969, 1155 UNTS 331 (entered into force 27 January 1980) arts 31 and 32.

travaux préparatoires, and the people-centred objects and purposes discussed below, give weight to an argument that this section can be read as including human security as a consideration. On the other hand, however, it also gives rise to counter-arguments that the term 'human security' was deliberately omitted from the treaty text, and that it therefore should not be interpreted in accordance with human security principles. This uncertainty depicts the need for a clearer construction of what is currently meant by 'security' within international law.

(i) People-centred objects and purposes

Despite the reluctance to use the term 'human security' itself, the discourse is nonetheless evident in the language of these treaties, and sits at the core of the objects and purposes of each. All of the noted agreements explicitly derive their purpose from a desire to put an end to human suffering or, to put it in other words, to ensure human security. This is spelt out most explicitly in the *Arms Trade Treaty*. The *Arms Trade Treaty* has the object of establishing minimum standards in the regulation of the international arms trade. This object, as Article 1 of the Convention concisely asserts, exists for the twin purposes of '[c]ontributing to international and regional peace, security and stability' and '[r]educing human suffering'.[19] While clearly influenced by human security, it should be noted here that the two concepts of peace and security, on the one hand, and human suffering on the other, are all acknowledged, but as separate arguably isolated considerations. The *Optional Protocol*, established with the primary purpose of curbing international use of child soldiers, better reflects human security by recognising the merging and interconnected nature of the two components:

> Disturbed by the harmful and widespread impact of armed conflict on children and the long-term consequences this has for durable peace, security and development ...[20]

Where human security discourse has been most successful in the development of international norms is the shift to a people-centred approach to issues that have been traditionally treated from a purely state-centric perspective. This is evident in both the *Ottawa Convention* and the *Convention on Cluster Munitions*. Both treaties impose comprehensive bans on the use, stockpiling, production and transfer of their respective weapons. In both of these cases, the issues had originally been conceived purely in the field of disarmament, which not only led to a detachment from humanitarian considerations, but in both cases produced few results, as noted above.[21] Reconceived in the light of human security, the purposes of the Conventions became driven by the determination

19 *Arms Trade Treaty*, art 1.
20 *Optional Protocol*, Preamble.
21 See, eg, Jody Williams and Stephen Goose, 'The International Campaign to Ban Landmines' in Maxwell A Cameron, Robert J Lawson and Brian W Tomlin (eds), *To*

> to put an end to the suffering and casualties caused by anti-personnel mines ...[22]

And:

> [s]tressing the role of public conscience in furthering the principles of humanity as evidenced by the global call for an end to civilian suffering caused by cluster munitions.[23]

Similarly, the establishment of the International Criminal Court, which reflected the idea that there was a global responsibility and interest in the prosecution and punishment of perpetrators of 'such grave crimes [that] threaten the peace, security and well-being of the world',[24] also placed a heavy emphasis on human suffering as the reason for its existence:

> Mindful that during this century millions of children, women and men have been victims of unimaginable atrocities that deeply shock the conscience of humanity.[25]

It can therefore be seen that the objects and purposes of a small but increasing number of international treaties reflect the fundamental people-centred nature of human security, shifting subject matter traditionally viewed as state-centric, despite the reluctance to invoke the concept of human security explicitly. Of course, people-centred objectives are not a new phenomenon in international law, and humanitarian law and human rights law far predate the existence of human security.[26] But human security has brought this people-centred focus to topics that were once the exclusive domain of state sovereignty-based considerations, and a human security framework allows for the intersection of humanitarian, human rights and developmental concerns to coexist and act in concert, as discussed below, something that the fragmented nature of international law has rarely allowed.

(ii) Comprehensive security

The people-centred nature of human security is of course not the only facet of the discourse, and does not reflect the only incorporation of the concept into conventional international law. Another component of human security that can be

Walk Without Fear: The Global Movement to Ban Landmines (Oxford University Press, 1998) 20.

22 *Ottawa Convention*, Preamble.

23 *Convention on Cluster Munitions*, Preamble.

24 *Rome Statute*, Preamble.

25 Ibid.

26 See, eg, Theodor Meron, *The Humanization of International Law* (Martinus Nijhoff, 2006); Antônio Augusto Cançado Trindade, *International Law for Humankind: Towards a New Jus Gentium* (Martinus Nijhoff, 2010) vol 6.

evidenced in these treaties, though to a more limited extent, is an acknowledgement of the comprehensive nature of human security. This manifests in two ways: the recognition of the 'big picture' of security, from root causes to reconstruction, and a recognition of the varying forms which human insecurity can take.

Across the various treaties, there is little recognition of the root causes of human insecurity.[27] An exception to this can, however, be found in the *Optional Protocol*, the Preamble to which asserts that State Parties are

> Mindful of the necessity of taking into consideration the economic, social and political root causes of the involvement of children in armed conflicts.[28]

However, it must be stressed that this recognition finds little expression outside the Preamble, and as such no concrete obligations or genuine attempts to alter these conditions are imposed by the agreement. While the root causes of human insecurity in this sense are underrepresented in these agreements, they are all, with the obvious exception of the *Rome Statute*,[29] prevention-oriented. The three weapons-related treaties are concerned with prevention of civilian suffering through the use of the prohibited devices – in the case of antipersonnel mines and cluster munitions through comprehensive bans, and in the case of small arms a set of standards for exporting states. The other end of the spectrum is represented through provisions concerned with reconstruction and victim rehabilitation, as will be discussed below.

Moreover, the treaties reflect an understanding of the many dimensions of human security, and the impacts of their respective foci on creating insecurity. For example, the impact of antipersonnel mines is outlined by the *Ottawa Convention* as follows:

> ... antipersonnel mines ... kill or maim hundreds of people, every week, mostly innocent and defenceless civilians and especially children, obstruct economic development and reconstruction, inhibit the repatriation of refugees and internally displaced persons, and have other severe consequences from years after emplacement.[30]

The Preamble to the *CCM* contains a very similar proclamation, though it refines it further, adding social development, the loss of livelihoods, and the impact on

27 Although see below, on recognition of conditions of vulnerability.

28 *Optional Protocol*, Preamble.

29 However, here the traditional deterrence effect of criminal law should be noted; see, eg, *Kambanda (Sentencing Judgment)* (International Criminal Tribunal for Rwanda, Case No ICTR-97-23-S, 4 September 1998) [28] which discussed the purposes of sentencing as including 'deterrence, namely dissuading for good those who will attempt in future to perpetrate such atrocities by showing them that the international community was not ready to tolerate the serious violations of international humanitarian law and human rights'.

30 *Ottawa Convention*, Preamble.

international peacebuilding and humanitarian assistance.[31] The *ATT*, more succinctly, recognises 'the security, social, economic and humanitarian consequences of the illicit and unregulated trade in conventional arms'.[32] Though these clauses are progressive in their coverage, they still fail to adequately capture the full picture of human security. For example, economic and social development are highlighted, rather than the more expansive and more appropriate concept of sustainable development. Despite the fact that the environmental impact of such weapons was raised during the campaigning and negotiation of both these treaties, no mention of this impact made it into the final texts, and only vague references to existing environmental standards are made in their provisions.[33]

(iii) The three pillars of security, development and human rights

Closely related to the comprehensive account of security, there is also increased mention in such international instruments of the interconnected nature of security, development and human rights, closely reflecting the Report of the Secretary-General on Human Security and the consequent General Assembly Resolution. Both documents put this trinity at the centre of recognition of human security:

> Recognizing that development, human rights and peace and security, which are the three pillars of the United Nations, are interlinked and mutually reinforcing ...[34]
>
> For no country can enjoy development without security, security without development, and neither without respect for human rights. This triangular relationship heightens the recognition that poverty, conflict and societal grievances can feed on one another in a vicious cycle.[35]

31 *CCM*, Preamble: '*Concerned* that cluster munition remnants kill or maim civilians, including women and children, obstruct economic and social development, including through the loss of livelihood, impede post-conflict rehabilitation and reconstruction, delay or prevent the return of refugees and internally displaced persons, can negatively impact on national and international peace-building and humanitarian assistance efforts, and have other severe consequences that can persist for many years after use'.

32 *ATT*, Preamble.

33 *CCM*, Art 4(6)(h) and *Ottawa Convention* art 5(4)(c) require requests for extensions of destruction deadlines to provide accounts of the humanitarian, social, economic and environmental implications of the proposed extension, while *CCM* art 3(2) requires stockpile destruction to comply with 'international standards for protecting public health and the environment'.

34 General Assembly, *Follow-up to Paragraph 143 on Human Security of the 2005 World Summit Outcome*, 66/290, Sixty-sixth sess, Agenda Item 14 and 117, UN Doc A/RES/66/290 (25 October 2012) Preamble.

35 United Nations General Assembly, *Report of the Secretary-General on Human Security*, UN GAOR, Sixty-fourth sess, Agenda Item 48 and 114, UN Doc A/64/701 (8 March 2010) [10].

As mentioned previously, this three pillar approach can be traced back to Kofi Annan's Report, *In Larger Freedom.*[36] But it is rapidly becoming a core tenet of human security, finding its way into all authoritative accounts of the discourse within the UN as has been discussed. Thus it is significant that it finds expression in the *ATT*:

> Acknowledging that peace and security, development and human rights are pillars of the UN system and foundations for collective security and recognizing that development, peace and security, and human rights are interlinked and mutually reinforcing ...[37]

The influence of the General Assembly Resolution is immediately apparent here, as the language is almost identical. Even before this Resolution, the relationship of security, human rights and the UN Charter found its way into the language of the *Optional Protocol*, which asserts that conditions for peace and security are based upon 'full respect of the purposes and principles contained in the Charter and observance of applicable human rights instruments are indispensable.'[38] However, as will be seen below, beyond the Preambles of these instruments, the recognition of this relationship has not had a major impact on the content of these treaties.

(iv) Principle of vulnerability – leave no one behind

A final point to note in relation to the language of these treaties is the recognition given to the needs of the most vulnerable groups. This closely reflects the use of human security by the High Level Panel of Eminent Persons on the Post-2015 Development Agenda,[39] as discussed in Chapter Five. Thus human security is also closely attached to the idea of a bare minimum standard, and the need to provide attention specifically to vulnerable groups. This attention is expressed explicitly in the language in the treaties:

> Recognizing the need to provide age- and gender-sensitive assistance to cluster munitions victims and to address the special needs of vulnerable groups.[40]

It is also expressed in more subtle forms, such as in the deliberate order reversal in the *Rome Statute* where it refers to the impact of violence on 'children, women

36 Kofi Annan, *In Larger Freedom: Towards development, security and human rights for all*, UN GAOR, Fifty-ninth sess, Agenda Item 45 and 55, UN Doc A/59/2005/Add.3 (26 May 2005).
37 *ATT*, Preamble.
38 *Optional Protocol*, Preamble.
39 The Report of the High-Level Panel of Eminent Persons on the Post-2015 Development Agenda, *A New Global Partnership: Eradicate Poverty and Transform Economies through Sustainable Development*, (United Nations, 2013).
40 *CCM*, Preamble.

and men' – in that order rather than in that of the traditional phrasing 'men, women and children'.

Non-discrimination clauses are also an important facet of human security treaties, and an important way to ensure that the vulnerable are protected and accounted for in the provisions of the treaty. The *CCM* notes in its Preamble that there should be no discrimination between types of disability. However, with the exception of the *ATT*, there are no provisions in these treaties creating binding obligations of non-discrimination. The *ATT* does not contain a specific non-discrimination provision, but opens Article 5, on the question of its general implementation, with the requirement that '[e]ach State Party shall implement this Treaty in a consistent, objective and ***non-discriminatory*** manner, bearing in mind the principles referred to in this Treaty'.[41] However, future human security-related treaties should consider non-discrimination clauses, and, specifically, attention to the vulnerable, as an essential component of their make-up, going beyond developments to date.

Where the *ATT* is particularly innovative in terms of vulnerability, however, is in Article 7(4) and its explicit requirement that states conduct assessments of the risks of exported arms being used to commit serious acts of gender-based violence or violence against women and children. This provision is significant for a number of reasons. While there is a growing body of international declarations and resolutions calling upon states to take action to eliminate violence against women, Article 7(4) represents the first explicit reference to gender-based violence in a legally binding multilateral treaty.[42] It was the result of significant campaigning and widespread recognition of the need for strong language on the issue to find expression in the treaty. At the end of the 2013 negotiations, 100 states had signed on to a joint statement to this effect.[43] It represents a major shift towards a more inclusive, gender-sensitive and people-centred approach to security, as noted by Danish Ambassador Uffe Balslev during the First Committee Thematic Debate on Other Disarmament Measures, Non-Proliferation and Arms Control:

> It is our hope that we have put those years behind us where the gender perspective was largely absent from disarmament, arms control and non-proliferation processes. Men and women are affected differently by weapons and armed conflict and their contribution to disarmament efforts will be different and complementary. UN Security Council resolution 1325 recognizes this and obliges us to take it into account … There may be small pockets of opinion in this committee who still argue that these issues belong elsewhere and are not part of the core occupation of the United Nations Committee responsible for Disarmament and International Security. They must have been

41 *ATT*, art 5 (emphasis added).
42 This is a point also made by Caroline Green et al, 'Gender-based Violence and the Arms Trade Treaty: Reflections from a Campaigning and Legal Perspective' (2013) 21(3) *Gender & Development* 551, 552.
43 Ibid.

living on Mars. Nothing could be more wrong. It is about time it is reflected in our work.[44]

Gender and childhood are the two most frequently recognised forms of vulnerability, and the *Optional Protocol* recognises the intersection of vulnerabilities when it highlights children who are particularly vulnerable 'owing to their economic or social status or gender.' Intersectionality of forms of vulnerability is a core issue of human insecurity, but generally is little acknowledged.[45] There is also an emphasis in all the treaties on victims and victim assistance is a vital component of their human security makeup.

B Victim assistance

A significant and vital feature of human security treaties is the inclusion of provisions for assisting victims. As has been noted, '[t]raditionally, international law has not paid sufficient attention to victims',[46] largely as a result of its traditional inter-state structure. Human security, by shifting the focus away from states, requires due regard of the effects of violence on the human populations of those states. Recognition of the need to address the rehabilitation and social integration of victims finds expression in all of the cited treaties, but the most significant innovations have found expression in the *CCM*, which is the first to include a dedicated provision on victim assistance. As such, the *CCM* will receive particular attention in this section.

The inclusion of Article 5 in the *CCM*, dedicated specifically to victim assistance, has been described as 'revolutionary'[47] and 'groundbreaking'.[48] The *Ottawa Convention* did provide for assistance to victims, and has been cited as the first weapons-related treaty to have done so.[49] However, while the *Ottawa*

44 Statement by HE Ambassador Uffe A Balslev, Undersecretary for Disarmament, Non-Proliferation and Arms Control, Sixty-eighth Session of the United Nations General Assembly, First Committee Thematic Debate on Other Disarmament Measures, Non-Proliferation and Arms Control, New York, 30 October 2013 <http://www.reachingcriticalwill.org/images/documents/Disarmament-fora/1com/1com13/statements/30Oct_Denmark.pdf>.

45 See, eg, Aili Mari Tripp, 'Toward a Gender Perspective on Human Security' in Aili Mari Tripp, Myra Marx Ferree and Christina Ewig (eds), *Gender, Violence and Human Security: Critical Feminist Perspectives* (New York University Press, 2013) 11.

46 Carlos Fernández de Casadevante Romani, *International Law of Victims* (Springer Press, 2012) 13.

47 Bonnie Docherty, 'Breaking New Ground: The Convention on Cluster Munitions and the Evolution of International Humanitarian Law' (2009) 31 *Human Rights Quarterly* 934, 935.

48 Jessica Corsi, 'Towards Peace through Legal Innovation: The Process and the Promise of the 2008 Cluster Munitions Convention' (2009) 22 *Harvard Human Rights Journal* 145.

49 See, eg, Bonnie Docherty, 'Breaking New Ground: The Convention on Cluster Munitions and the Evolution of International Humanitarian Law' (2009) 31 *Human Rights Quarterly* 934, 950.

Convention recognised the need for victim assistance in its Preamble, it does not impose any obligations on affected states for victim rehabilitation, with this concern only appearing in Article 6 in relation to international cooperation. Though not as developed as the *CCM* obligations, the *Optional Protocol* does require State Parties to provide 'all appropriate assistance' to victims, albeit qualified by the words 'when necessary'.[50] The vague and broadly framed language employed in the *Optional Protocol* limits the potential value of this clause for victims.

The *CCM* provides a comprehensive definition of cluster munition victims in Article 2(1):

> 'Cluster munition victims' means all persons who have been killed or suffered physical or psychological injury, economic loss, social marginalization or substantial impairment of the realization of their rights caused by the use of cluster munitions. They include those persons directly impacted by cluster munitions as well as their affected families and communities.

This comprehensive definition of victims is an important reflection of human security discourse. It recognises a variety of forms of human insecurity, from physical and psychological harm, to the impact on communities of socio-economic forms of insecurity. Five of the seven components of human security highlighted by the original construction of the UNDP – personal, economic, health, political and community security[51] – are clearly represented by this definition of a cluster munitions victim. The two that are missing, and that ideally should be represented, are environmental and food security, both which could be impacted by cluster munitions. Both could, however, be convincingly argued to be incorporated into the definition through 'substantial impairment of the realization of their rights'.[52]

This definition has been derived from the definition of a victim found in the Declaration of Basic Principles of Justice for Victims of Crime and Abuse of Power, adopted on 29 November 1985. This Declaration defines victims of crime and abuses of power as persons

> who, individually or collectively, have suffered harm, including physical or mental injury, emotional suffering, economic loss or substantial impairment of their fundamental rights … The term 'victim' also includes, where appropriate the immediate family or dependents of the direct victim and persons who have suffered harm in intervening to assist victims in distress or to prevent victimization.[53]

50 *Optional Protocol*, art 6(3).

51 United Nations Development Programme (UNDP), *Human Development Report 1994* (UNDP, 1994).

52 *CCM*, art 2(1).

53 UN Declaration of Basic Principles of Justice for Victims of Crime and Abuse of Power, UN GA Res 40/34, UN GAOR, UN Doc A/RES/40/34 (29 November 1985).

The *CCM* definition, as can be seen, is clearly patterned off this definition, but there are two important modifications made. The first is the inclusion of 'communities' as a class of victim. Secondly, and related to this, there is no distinction in the *CCM* definition between 'direct' and 'indirect'. Once this is added, the conditional phrase 'where appropriate' is replaced by the clearer connection of 'affected' families and communities.

Support for, and recognition of, victims is found spread across the provisions of the *CCM*. The Preamble dedicates five separate paragraphs to emphasising the centrality of redressing human insecurity as the core focus of the treaty. As mentioned above, Article 2 provides a comprehensive definition of cluster munitions victims. This is the first definition provided in the treaty, explained even before the definition of cluster munitions themselves. Articles 6 and 7 also acknowledge victims, in relation to international cooperation and transparency, respectively. However, it is Article 5 which represents the most important contribution, with its sole focus on victim assistance. Its significance lies in its existence as a separate dedicated provision creating clear state obligations for victim assistance, but even more importantly, in its level of detail.[54]

Paragraph 1 of Article 5 of the *CCM* requires states to provide adequate 'age- and gender-sensitive assistance'. This assistance is to cover medical needs, rehabilitation (including psychological support), and social and economic inclusion. The paragraph also requires the collection of data on victims, an essential element for the development of human security indices.[55] Paragraph 2 sets out a clear plan for how these goals are to be achieved:

> 2 In fulfilling its obligations under paragraph 1 of this Article each State Party shall:
>
> (a) Assess the needs of cluster munition victims;
> (b) Develop, implement and enforce any necessary national laws and policies;
> (c) Develop a national plan and budget, including timeframes to carry out these activities, with a view to incorporating them within the existing national disability, development and human rights frameworks and mechanisms, while respecting the specific role and contribution of relevant actors;
> (d) Take steps to mobilise national and international resources;
> (e) Not discriminate against or among cluster munition victims, or between cluster munition victims and those who have suffered injuries or disabilities from other causes; differences in treatment should be based only on medical, rehabilitative, psychological or socio-economic needs;

54 See, eg, Bonnie Docherty, 'Breaking New Ground: The Convention on Cluster Munitions and the Evolution of International Humanitarian Law' (2009) 31 *Human Rights Quarterly* 934, 950.

55 For example, the Human Security Index <http://www.humansecurityindex.org/>. See also Taylor Owen, 'Human Security Mapping' in Mary Martin and Taylor Owen (eds), *Routledge Handbook of Human Security* (Routledge, 2014) 308.

(f) Closely consult with and actively involve cluster munition victims and their representative organisations;
(g) Designate a focal point within the government for coordination of matters relating to the implementation of this Article; and
(h) Strive to incorporate relevant guidelines and good practices including in the areas of medical care, rehabilitation and psychological support, as well as social and economic inclusion.

This clear, detailed plan for victim assistance can serve as a model for future instruments dedicated to human security. It is a plan that can readily be translated to other forms of threat. It also provides a useful blueprint of the necessary elements of assistance provisions. Assessment of needs allows flexibility and provides for the context-specific nature of human security, while development of national plans and strategies ensures national ownership over solutions.[56] Incorporation into existing development and human rights frameworks recognises the interconnections of the three pillars, and provides for sustainable and rights-based security. Anti-discrimination clauses ensure that no one is left behind, and the development of guidelines and good practices promotes effective, rule-based security. Perhaps the most important provision in this entire catalogue of obligations, though, is (f), involving victims as an inherent part of victim assistance strategies, going beyond protection to empowerment.

C The second dimension of human security: beyond protection to empowerment

An essential feature of the human security discourse as previously discussed are the twin goals of protection and empowerment.[57] International law's role is most obvious in fulfilling the protection component. But to most effectively produce a human security framework, provisions promoting the empowerment of individuals generally, and victims of human insecurity and the most vulnerable, more specifically, should be developed where possible. The structure of the law of treaties limits this, focused as it is on the roles and obligations of states. However, there are a few, though limited, examples of empowering provisions to be found. The *Optional Protocol*'s Preamble includes

> [e]ncouraging the participation of the community, and in particular, children and child victims in the dissemination of informational and educational programmes concerning the implementation of the Protocol.

However, there are no concrete obligations ventured in relation to this participation in the *Optional Protocol*'s provisions. As noted above, Article 5 (2)(f) of the *CCM* requires all State Parties to

56 *Human Security Resolution*, UN Doc A/RES/66/290, [3].
57 See, eg, Commission on Human Security, *Human Security Now* (United Nations, 2003).

> (f) Closely consult with and actively involve cluster munition victims and their representative organisations …

Here is a binding obligation to actively involve victims. Such clauses need to be developed further, come with binding obligations, as the *CCM* does, and be considered a necessary element in all human security-related treaties. Full engagement with human security discourse, especially its preventative dimension, requires such clauses to extend beyond victims to vulnerable groups and communities. Risk reduction education is one such mode of engagement, as provided by Article 4(2)(e) of the *CCM*:

> Lastly, each State Party shall conduct risk reduction education to ensure awareness among civilians living in or around contaminated areas of the risks posed by such remnants.[58]

As noted by Ogata and Cels, '[e]mpowerment strategies require a secure environment in which people's capacity to act on behalf of themselves and their community is fostered.'[59] The secure environment dimension is addressed by the *Rome Statute* which guarantees protection for victims and witnesses during their participation in proceedings.[60] Recognition of international civil society and increased engagement with NGOs can also foster an increased sense of empowerment, and this engagement in relation to international cooperation is addressed below. It is important to note that coalition building (between government, international organisations and representatives of civil society) and NGO advocacy were key elements in their construction, as discussed in the previous chapter.[61] Participatory approaches to international law-making must be considered a vital cog in the development of human security-related international law, and absolutely essential to the empowerment pillar of human security discourse.

D Principle of universality and mutual responsibility

(i) International cooperation and assistance

Provisions for international cooperation and assistance are not a new innovation of the human security discourse, but must be noted, as they are a necessary element of effectively providing human security. Moreover, such provisions promote a multilateral vision of security, emphasising the principles of universality and mutual

58 See also *Ottawa Convention*, art 6(7)(d).
59 Sadako Ogata and Johan Cels, 'Human Security – Protecting and Empowering the People' (2003) 9 *Global Governance* 273, 274.
60 *Rome Statute*, art 68.
61 See, eg, Don Hubert, 'The Landmine Ban: A Case Study in Humanitarian Advocacy' (Occasional Paper No 42, Institute for International Studies, Brown University, 2000) Chapter 5 – NGOs – Advocates, Assests, Critics and Goads; Benjamin N Schiff, *Building the International Criminal Court* (Cambridge University Press, 2008).

responsibility in human security discourse. Importantly, these provisions also acknowledge a range of actors who can assist with the realisation of human security, invoking not just state parties but also acknowledging the role of international institutions, regional organisations and NGOs.[62] The provisions emphasise that the role of international cooperation should be to assist from the stage of prevention[63] through to technical and financial assistance for the rehabilitation and support of victims and vulnerable groups.[64] The provisions of the *Ottawa Convention* and *CCM* are particularly comprehensive in this respect. Also significant in the *CCM* is Article 21, which creates legal obligations for norm promotion, encouraging the universalisation of the treaty and its principles.

On the other hand, there is a lack of concrete obligations established by these provisions. The provisions are vague, requiring assistance to be provided by each 'State Party *in a position to do so*'.[65] The language is even more watered down in the most recent example, the *ATT*, where states are 'encouraged' to cooperate, and the provisions for assistance are significantly less developed than those found in the *Ottawa Convention* and the *CCM*.[66] Hortatory language in relation to international cooperation misses the thrust of human security discourse. It fails to acknowledge the mutual vulnerability and principle of universality which should be a driving force for human security – that 'a threat to one is a threat to all'.[67]

All of the discussed treaties recognise and emphasise the roles of intergovernmental and non-governmental organisations as sources of assistance for state parties, in both preambular statements and the provisions for international assistance.[68] This, it has been noted, aligns with the principle of subsidiarity,[69] or put differently, the comparative advantages of the different actors.[70] On the other hand, of course, this endorsement of the pluralism of actors only goes so far. It is important to note that the limits of pluralism in these treaties is imposed by the traditional framework of the law of treaties – that only States are capable of being parties to these treaties,[71] and that the obligations of these treaties can only extend to state parties and not to other actors.

62 See, eg, *CCM*, art 6(7), *Ottawa Convention* art 6(7).
63 See, eg, *Optional Protocol* art 7(1).
64 Ibid; *CCM* art 6(7).
65 *Optional Protocol* art 7; *CCM* art 6; *Ottawa Convention* art 6; *ATT* art 16 (with the added requirement of request).
66 *ATT* art 16.
67 UN High Level Panel on Threats, Challenges and Change, *A More Secure World* (UN, 2004) 22[30], [17]. For further discussion of this principle see Chapters One and Two.
68 See, eg, *ATT*, art 16(2); *CCM*, art 6(7); *Ottawa Convention*, art 6; *Optional Protocol*, art 7, which it should be noted includes only international organisations, not NGOs.
69 Tommaso di Ruzza, 'The Convention on Cluster Munitions: Towards a Balance between Humanitarian and Military Considerations?' (2008) 47 *Military Law and the Law of War Review* 405, 431.
70 Sabine Alkire, 'A Conceptual Framework for Human Security' (Working Paper No 2, Centre for Research on Inequality, Human Security and Ethnicity (CRISE) 2003) 2.
71 *VCLT*, art 2(1)(a).

In recognition that the formal nature of treaty law prevented addressing the roles of other actors, and that the forms of human insecurity that are the focus of these treaties are most often perpetuated by armed non-state actors (ANSAs), Geneva Call was launched in 2000, created by NGO coalitions that drove the Ottawa Process (discussed in the previous chapter).[72] Geneva Call was created to produce an inclusive approach to the ban on APMs, and since expanded to other areas human security, such as gender violence and the protection of children from armed conflict. It engages in dialogue with ANSAs and provides them with the opportunity to commit to the principles of the relevant treaties through Deeds of Commitment. To date 52 ANSAs, spread across the world, have signed such Deeds of Commitment, and many are also assisting with proactive activities such as landmine removals.[73] This is a significant step forward in recognising the universality of human security.

(ii) State responsibility

The impact of human security discourse on international treaties has had one significant and disturbing consequence. One of the most effective elements of the campaign to ban landmines was the focus on casting landmines as the enemy.[74] The casting of landmines themselves as the focus of the discourse was an essential component of the Ottawa Process[75] and its success. But with landmines cast as the villain, and the focus of the treaty on the victims and the felt effects of landmines, the idea of state responsibility for the laying of mines was an issue that was effectively swept under the rug. Article 5 of the *Ottawa Convention* treats the issue of responsibility for the destruction of landmines as an issue of jurisdiction, rather than as a form of accountability by those who lay the mines. As Kitchen outlines, 'landmines themselves become the problem, rather than the States or other actors that produce and use them. Landmines become the "machine" acting against humanity, a dichotomy that not only reinforces the humanitarian discourse but also effectively forecloses the question of state responsibility for the production and use of landmines.'[76] In a way, this is a reversal of a trend observed by de Casadevante Romani, namely, that international law always ignores the victim 'because its approaches on the matter of responsibility have always focused upon the author of the wrongful act.'[77] It must be stressed, however, that a move away

72 For general information see Geneva Call <www.genevacall.org>.
73 See, eg, Geneva Call, *Annual Report 2013* (Geneva Call, 2013).
74 See, eg, Miguel de Larrinaga and Claire Turenne Sjolander, '(Re)presenting Landmines from Protector to Enemy: The Discursive Framing of a New Multilateralism' in Maxwell A Cameron, Robert J Lawson and Brian W Tomlin (eds), *To Walk Without Fear: The Global Movement to Ban Landmines* (Oxford University Press, 1998).
75 Ibid.
76 Veronica Kitchen, 'From Rhetoric to Reality – Canada, the United States, and the Ottawa Process to Ban Landmines' (2001–2002) 57 *International Journal* 39.
77 Carlos Fernández de Casadevante Romani, *International Law of Victims* (Springer Press, 2012) 15.

from state responsibility is not in keeping with the spirit or the emergent principles of human security discourse.

There is some recognition of the issue of user state responsibility in the *CCM*. The *CCM* acknowledges the culpability of user states in Article 4(4), and this is significant, as it is a retrospective provision, applying to actions states had taken prior to the conception of the *CCM*. This provision is a noted part of the Convention, remarked on by a number of commentators.[78] However, it is important not to overstate the significance of the provision, as the language of Article 4(4) is important. State Parties are 'strongly encouraged to provide, *inter alia*, technical, financial, material or human resources assistance'. This assistance includes information about the precise location of cluster munition strikes and information on the cluster munitions employed. Thus no binding obligations are created by Article 4(4); no more than forceful urging is employed. This is problematic on two significant grounds. The first is that it remains the primary responsibility of affected states to bear the costs and burdens of redressing the effects of cluster munitions. In truth, Article 4(4) is not dissimilar from the general provisions of international cooperation and assistance, failing to capture the unique responsibility of user states, other than by singling them out. Secondly, accurate information about cluster munitions is also no more than a matter of 'strong encouragement',[79] rather than mandatory. This ignores the fundamental importance of accurate information in the processes of clearing mines and risk reduction awareness for civilians. The failure to provide accurate information is thus arguably contrary to the object and purposes of the Convention, and yet is framed only in hortatory language.

The retroactivity of the provision should not be taken as a justification for failing to create binding obligations on user states. The existing obligations in both the law of treaties and state responsibility establish the viability of retroactive provisions, where express intent is demonstrated.[80] Under the *Vienna Convention on the Law of Treaties*, treaties may be retroactive if 'a different intention appears from the treaty or is otherwise established', contrary to the general presumption that a treaty does not have retroactive effect.[81] Likewise, the commentary to Draft Article 13 of the Draft Articles on State Responsibility establishes that '[a] State may agree to compensate for damage caused as a result of conduct which was not at the time a breach of any international obligation in force for that State.'[82]

78 Jessica Corsi, 'Towards Peace through Legal Innovation: The Process and the Promise of the 2008 Cluster Munitions Convention' (2009) 22 *Harvard Human Rights Journal* 145, 152. Bonnie Docherty, 'Breaking New Ground: The Convention on Cluster Munitions and the Evolution of International Humanitarian Law' (2009) 31 *Human Rights Quarterly* 934, 952.

79 CCM, art 4(4).

80 This is a point made by Bonnie Docherty, 'Breaking New Ground: The Convention on Cluster Munitions and the Evolution of International Humanitarian Law' (2009) 31 *Human Rights Quarterly* 934, 953.

81 *VCLT*, art 28.

82 ILC, *Commentary to Draft Articles of State Responsibility*, Article 13, Commentary [6].

The *ATT* also fails to include any provisions dedicated to user state responsibility. However, the very structure of the *ATT* is recognition of the idea of global mutual responsibility in relation to prevention. The *ATT* requires exporting State Parties to establish national standards establishing guidelines for the trade of conventional weapons and ammunition, and prohibits trade if there is knowledge that those weapons would be used to commit grave breaches of international human rights or humanitarian law.[83] It also requires State Parties (importing and exporting) to take steps to prevent the diversion of conventional arms and to share information with other states to assist in preventing such diversion.[84] Such steps recognise a sense of responsibility that extends beyond the end user or the affected state, and positively contributes to the universal responsibility espoused by human security discourse. This finds expression in the Preamble of the *ATT*, which refers to

> [t]he responsibility of all States, in accordance with their respective international obligations, to effectively regulate the international trade in conventional arms, and to prevent their diversion, as well as the primary responsibility of all States in establishing and implementing their respective national control systems...

Where it fails, however, is in the lack of accountability measures for states that fail to uphold these obligations. It also fails to link the responsibility to the core principles of interest in preserving human security and preventing human suffering. The language, it should be mentioned, is also very cautious: it talks only of 'respective international obligations', ie, building on existing legal obligations rather than creating any itself. However, this is in keeping with human security as conceived in the General Assembly Resolution, which, as has been discussed, stressed that human security does not impose additional legal obligations on states.

E Principle of integration – acting as a nexus for international law

An essential element of the effective utilisation of human security discourse will be through an emphasis on its integrative dimension – the way in which human security cuts across and draws on the various fields of international law. There is little evidence of such engagement in the *Ottawa Convention*, but the other treaties all demonstrate varying levels of integration, or at least acknowledge the relevance of varying fields of international law. The *Rome Statute* builds international criminal law upon serious violations of international human rights law and humanitarian law. Likewise, the *CCM* refers to 'applicable international human rights and humanitarian law' in relation to victim assistance (Article 5), acting, as di Ruzza notes, as 'a point of contact' between the two branches of international law.[85]

83 *ATT* arts 6 and 7.
84 *ATT* art 11.
85 Tommaso di Ruzza, 'The Convention on Cluster Munitions: Towards a Balance between Humanitarian and Military Considerations?' (2008) 47 *Military Law and the Law or War Review* 405, 433.

The *ATT* requires states exporting small arms to assess the possibility that those weapons

> (a) would contribute to or undermine peace and security;
> (b) could be used to:
>
> > (i) commit or facilitate a serious violation of international humanitarian law;
> > (ii) commit or facilitate a serious violation of international human rights law;
> > (iii) commit or facilitate an act constituting an offence under international conventions or protocols relating to terrorism to which the exporting State is a Party; or
> > (iv) commit or facilitate an act constituting an offence under international
>
> conventions or protocols relating to transnational organized crime to which the exporting State is a Party.[86]

The *ATT* thus draws on a wide range of pre-existing instruments and obligations, with small arms as one possible common thread. The *Optional Protocol* also draws on a wealth of pre-existing law from a range of fields. The *Optional Protocol* draws on its parent convention, the *Convention on the Rights of the Child*,[87] repeatedly. It also, however, makes references to relevant international humanitarian law, the *Rome Statute*, human rights instruments, and – uniquely – the prohibition on Child Labour established by the International Labour Organization.[88] The *Optional Protocol* also takes the additional step of ensuring that the interpretation of its provisions cannot be used to narrow the existing scope of international legal obligations:

> Nothing in the present Protocol shall be construed as precluding provisions in the law of a State Party or in international instruments and international humanitarian law that are more conducive to the realization of the rights of the child.[89]

Acting as a framework for the integration of the various pre-existing legal obligations and norms from varying branches of international law is one of the most significant elements that human security can bring to existing international law. Drawing on pre-existing obligations rather than creating new legal obligations can make the introduction of human security into international law more palatable for

86 *ATT* art 7.
87 *Convention on the Rights of the Child*, opened for signature 20 November 1989, 1577 UNTS 3 (entered into force 2 September 1990).
88 *Optional Protocol*, Preamble, art 3, art 5.
89 Ibid art 5.

states. However, as can be seen by the examples provided, there is a tendency towards vague language, and a lack of specific or deliberate integration of the principles and elements of the various threads of international law. This lack of clarity weakens the strength of the inclusion of human rights in security considerations, and does not make the nexus between the fields of international law clear: if there are conflicts it is not clear which norms prevail or how they should be evaluated. As such, the relationship between national security and human security – an unresolved dimension of human security discourse – is not made clear. What it does do, however, is merge the existing fields on international law into one regime, requiring that the varying norms be read together and harmonised as they relate to the respective treaties. This in itself is significant for a field of fragmented regimes, norms and authority.

III Two steps forward, three steps back – the current position of human security discourse

A From Ottawa *to* ATT *(and beyond) in norm production*

It is apparent from the analysis above that the impact of human security discourse on treaty law remains in a process of ongoing development. Advancements can be seen in particular in the *CCM* as compared to its predecessor, the *Ottawa Convention*. These advancements, as have been outlined in the preceding discussion, have been made particularly in the fields of victim assistance, in the framing of security as a comprehensive concept, merging prevention and remediation, and, to a lesser extent, in the fields of international cooperation and user state responsibility. However, the *ATT*, while an important and remarkable achievement in its very existence,[90] demonstrates a failure to engage more with human security discourse, and in fact takes several steps backwards. As mentioned earlier, the *ATT* is the first treaty that could be classified a human security treaty to emerge since the General Assembly issued its first determinative resolution on human security. As such, the limited engagement with human security discourse is disappointing, but not altogether surprising.

The watered-down language in the *ATT* in relation to international cooperation has already been noted. Moreover, the *ATT* is a very different creature from the *Ottawa Convention* and the *CCM*. In the case of both landmines and cluster munitions, the human security argument was straightforward – the indiscriminate nature of the weapons made it possible to argue for a comprehensive ban since they were a direct and incontrovertible threat to human security. The relationship between human security and small arms on the other hand is far more complex.[91]

90 See, eg, Barry Kellman, 'Controlling the Arms Trade: One Important Stride for Humankind' (2013–2014) 37 *Fordham International Law Journal* 687. See also Barbara von Tigerstrom, *Human Security and International Law: Prospects and Problems* (Hart Publishing, 2007). Chapter 6, in which she discusses the challenges of successfully moving towards a human security-centred approach to small arms.

91 See, eg, ibid.

It is little disputed that small arms can serve as a threat to human security, and during the Final Conference a number of statistics were presented in relation to the approximately 2,000 deaths per day caused by conventional weapons, and the US$18 billion dollars a year that conventional weapons fuelling conflict are estimated to cost Africa alone per year.[92] On the other hand, such weapons are also deemed to have legitimate use and, of course, a central role in any national security and military strategy. This close relationship with concerns of national security made it far more difficult for human security to gain traction in the debates surrounding the creation of the *ATT*. It shows the true challenges of human security discourse making headway in an atmosphere where the principles of state sovereignty and military necessity continue to prevail.

One of the most noteworthy retreats from the developments made in the preceding treaties is that the *ATT* contains no measures providing for victim assistance. The word 'victim' makes a single appearance in the Preamble of the *ATT*, in stark contrast to the extensive treatment in the *CCM*. Victim assistance had been discussed throughout the presentations of NGOs during the preparatory committees preceding the final conference on the *ATT*.[93] A compelling case was made for inclusion of victim assistance by one of the speakers for the Control Arms Coalition, Suela Lala, a victim herself of armed conflict. She argued that

> it is imperative that this treaty prioritize potential humanitarian gains. The reason for the existence of this treaty are people like me. Recognizing our foundational role in the existence of this treaty and committing to assisting us in recovery and as we work to maximize our life's potential is within reach with the proper amount of political will.[94]

Strong support for the inclusion of victim assistance had been indicated by European and African states, but Asian states were silent on the topic, and the United States, the single largest arms exporter in the world, actively opposed any such inclusion.[95] At the final conference for negotiating the *ATT*, victim assistance was abandoned in the interests of pursuing consensus, and none of the NGO statements presented at the conference raised the issue, instead choosing to focus on areas where consensus was still deemed possible, such as the inclusion of ammunition and provisions committed to preventing diversion of armed exports.[96] The opportunity to consolidate the progress made in the *CCM* and to solidify victim assistance as a component of the new human security framework for treaties was lost.

92 See, eg, Australia's National Statement, 3 July 2012 <http://www.un.org/disarmament/ATT/statements/>.

93 *ATT*, Prep Com III, 'NGO Presentations', 11–15 July 2011, <http://www.iansa.org/resource/2011/07/a_-prepcom -11-15-july-2011-ngo-presentations>.

94 Ibid.

95 For a visual representation of the support, see <http://armstreaty.org/issue/victim-assistance/>.

96 See statements by Control Arms, ICRC and others, <http://www.un.org/disarmament/ATT/statements/>.

B The narrow vision of human security

The *ATT* also tells a broader story about the scope of human security discourse in these treaties. In the draft text of the *ATT*, drawn from the unsuccessful conference in July 2012, the list of factors to be considered by exporting states had not only included the factors considered above in Article 7. It had also included '[a]dversely impacting the development of the importing State' as a consideration to be factored into the decision-making of exporting state parties. It represented a rare example of the broad approach to human security in treaty development. The provision did not, however, survive the final conference of the *ATT* and was lost with little fanfare.

This represents a broader trend that can be observed with the development of so-called human security treaties. While all of the treaties thus classed are of undeniable significance to the concerns of human security, they also all fit into the narrow conception of the discourse. While human security discourse may have provided the added impetus needed for treaties to come into existence addressing such concerns as the use of landmines and cluster munitions, the regulation of the arms trade and the prohibition of the use of child soldiers, it has not had the same effect in relation to issues that are of equal concern from the perspective of human security. Issues such as poverty, internally displaced persons and those displaced by climate change, the spread of HIV/AIDS (and other diseases such as Ebola, malaria, typhoid and polio) remain issues subject to foreign aid budgets and policy considerations, relegated (at best) to soft law rather than hard law. This 'normative chauvinism', to use the words of Simma and Alston,[97] is precisely what broad-based human security discourse seeks to expose.

IV Conclusion

Though there remains only a limited engagement with human security discourse in international legal scholarship, the practical effects of the discourse have had an impact on international law, as demonstrated in this chapter through the influence on the international treaties. However, the failure to explicitly engage with the discourse, and the reluctance to directly implement the concept, have limited the extent of its realisation. As demonstrated in the above analysis, what presence human security has in treaties has largely been relegated to the preambles, and to hortatory, rather than binding language. Nonetheless, the objects and purposes of these treaties do reflect a vision of comprehensive, people-centred security. There is also evidence of an emergence of a new vision of the international order built on three interconnected pillars: rights, development and security, centred on humanity. It is important, however, that this realignment to people-centred provisions does not come at the cost of strong commitments to state responsibility or lead to a weakening of the language and impact of international treaties dedicated to

97 Bruno Simma and Philip Alston, 'The Sources of Human Rights Law: Custom, Jus Cogens, and General Principles' (1988–1989) 12 *Australian Yearbook of International Law* 82, 94.

promoting international peace and security. Likewise, while human security-driven law should continue to integrate the various fields of law, and most particularly international human rights law, with security, these commitments need to be more clearly outlined.

Despite the demonstrated limits to the impact of human security on international treaties, the commonalities outlined are important, pointing in the direction of a human security framework promoting protection and empowerment, and founded on principles of mutual responsibility, integration, participatory decision-making, victim assistance and rights-based, rules-based people-centred security. Greater engagement with human security discourse would allow this framework to be developed further and refined. Finally, greater engagement with human security discourse is important to open up the scope of treaty-making in this field. So far the impact of human security has been felt in the areas of disarmament, arms control and armed conflict. However, human security threats broadly construed extend to other threats to human survival and well-being, including poverty, climate change and the proliferation of HIV/AIDS and other serious diseases. It is important for human security discourse to infiltrate legal discussions of these issues as well as those connected to armed violence if the international community is serious about its commitment to the realisation of human security.

8 Conclusion – the relationship between human security discourse and international law

The time for engagement

Human security is a child who did not die, a disease that did not spread, a job that was not cut, an ethnic tension that did not explode in violence, a dissident who was not silenced. Human security is not a concern with weapons – it is a concern with human life and dignity.[1]

I Introduction

Having only recently passed the anniversary of the second decade of the existence of the discourse of human security, it seems fair to state that rumours of its demise seem to have been greatly exaggerated. In some ways it is only just beginning to come into its own. From the perspective of international legal scholarship, we may in fact be witnessing the birth of human security discourse within legal analysis, though the engagement remains extremely limited, and it remains to be seen whether the recent growth in attention in the past few years will maintain any momentum. Fundamental to this will be overcoming the resistance of international legal scholarship, which is largely unfounded, and both international legal scholarship and human security discourse would be benefited by greater engagement with each other.

In the past two decades, there has been a broadening, a deepening and an opening of constructions of 'security'. As discussed in Chapter One, 'broadening' refers to the acknowledgment of a wider range of potential threats to security. Discussions began to take place about environmental security, health security and food security, and the word 'security' ceased to be synonymous with militaries and the use of force. 'Deepening', on the other hand, refers to moving the notion of security down to the individual and upward to the level of global security. Finally, 'opening' security is about the examination of the deeper meanings of the term 'security' – the critical analysis and problematising of its components, examining its normative underpinnings and ethical dimensions. Human security discourse is a reflection of all three of these phenomena, though sometimes the broadening and

1 United Nations Development Programme (UNDP), *Human Development Report 1994* (UNDP, 1994) 22.

opening dimensions of the discourse have been lost to a sole focus on the people-centred component.

While conceptualisations and definitions of human security have proliferated over its two decades of existence, there remains little agreement on a concrete definition of what human security means. However, again and again we can observe a return to the original approach taken by the UNDP in 1994, and the four core elements of human security. Human security is people-centred, of universal concern, interconnected and prevention-oriented. A large part of the resistance of international legal scholarship towards human security is the absence of a clear definition. However, these four elements offer principles and a valuable framework through which to evaluate the current structures of international law, and to provide a normative structure through which to shape the future direction of both international norm creation and international law-making. The four elements also reflect current trends already visible in existing international law.

II 'Human security' – that which shall not be named

The first general conclusion that can be drawn from the analysis of this study is that while human security as a concept is becoming increasingly used within the work of the United Nations, in the foreign policies of states, in regional institutions, in multidisciplinary academic scholarship, and by the media and civil society, 'human security' is not a term used in any binding international legal instrument. While the term has been used even by judges of the International Court of Justice, it has been used extremely sparingly and in isolation. Furthermore, the references to human security do not demonstrate any real engagement with the discourse and are used largely devoid of any broader meaning.

The treaties discussed in Chapter Seven were all developed under the auspices of the human security discourse. The Ottawa Treaty in particular, largely engineered by Lloyd Axworthy, has always been expressly accredited to the emergence of human security discourse.[2] However, all five treaties can be traced to the efforts of advocates of human security within states, international institutions and most especially NGOs.[3] The Arms Trade Treaty, concluded a year after the first comprehensive General Assembly Resolution on human security,[4] draws explicitly from the language of that Resolution:

2 See, eg, Lloyd Axworthy, 'Towards a New Multilateralism' in Maxwell A Cameron, Robert J Lawson and Brian W Tomlin (eds), *To Walk Without Fear: The Global Movement to Ban Landmines* (Oxford University Press, 1998) 448.

3 Claudia F Fuentes Julio and Hans Günter Brauch, 'The Human Security Network: A Global North–South Coalition' in Hans Günter Brauch et al (eds), *Facing Global Environmental Change* (Springer Berlin Heidelberg, 2009) vol 4, 991.

4 United Nations General Assembly, *Follow-up to Paragraph 143 on Human Security of the 2005 World Summit Outcome*, UN Res 66/290, UN GAOR, Sixty-sixth sess, Agenda Item 14 and 117, UN Doc A/RES/66/290 (25 October 2012).

> *Acknowledging* that peace and security, development and human rights are pillars of the United Nations system and foundations for collective security and recognizing that development, peace and security and human rights are interlinked and mutually reinforcing ...[5]

However, despite this inclusion, and despite human security being discussed during the negotiation process, the final text does not invoke human security explicitly. Likewise, human security is a term invoked with increasing regularity in the debates of the Security Council. The Human Security Network has formed a bloc for discussing relevant issues at the Council, but yet again this use of human security in the discussions has never translated into its inclusion in any Security Council Resolution. Even in less formal settings of norm generation, such as the Kimberley Process Certification Scheme or the Voluntary Principles for Security and Human Rights, states have shown a reluctance to commit to human security in writing. We have also recently witnessed a downward trend in the use of human security within the General Assembly. It remains to be seen whether this sudden silence will signal the end of engagement at this level of the United Nations.

This reluctance to utilise the term can be understood on several fronts. Firstly, it must be remembered that when the General Assembly acknowledged the concept in the 2012 Resolution, it simultaneously asserted that '[h]uman security does not entail additional legal obligations on the part of States'.[6] This was further elucidated in the UN Secretary-General's 2012 Report on Human Security, in which he highlighted 'that assigning a legal definition to human security would be counterproductive since the notion is both an operational and a policy framework'.[7] This, however, ignores the complexities of the current relationship between human security discourse and international law, to say nothing of future developments. Human security, as can be seen in Chapters Five, Six and Seven is being used as both a normative and operational framework for international legal instruments and their negotiation. Human security discourse then necessarily informs the content and interpretation of such instruments, and as such needs to be understood from a legal perspective. Moreover, from the other side of the issue, international law is a means for the operationalisation of human security,[8] and so again the relationship cannot be ignored. Finally, much of human security discourse already finds its place in existing trends in international law. The shift in

5 *Arms Trade Treaty*, opened for signature 3 June 2013, 52 ILM 988 (entered into force 24 December 2014) ('*ATT*') Preamble.

6 United Nations General Assembly, *Follow-up to Paragraph 143 on Human Security of the 2005 World Summit Outcome*, UN Res 66/290, UN GAOR, Sixty-sixth sess, Agenda Item 14 and 117, UN Doc A/RES/66/290 (25 October 2012) [3].

7 United Nations General Assembly, *Report of the Secretary General: Follow-up to General Assembly Resolution 64/291 on Human Security*, Sixty-sixth sess, Agenda Item 14 and 117, UN Doc A/68/685 (5 April 2012) [14].

8 See, eg, Math Noortmann and Cedric Ryngaert, 'Towards a (New) Human Security-Based Agenda for International Law and Non-State Actors?' in Math Noortmann and Cedric Ryngaert (eds), *Human Security and International Law: The Challenge of Non-State Actors* (Intersentia, 2014) 195.

focus away from states to people (in the case of international law, primarily to individuals) is reflected in the general trend of the 'humanisation' of international law.[9] The integrative principle of human security reflects current debate and analysis related to overcoming the fragmentation of international law, most notably the work of the ILC in this regard.[10] The development and increased recognition of the Responsibility to Protect is one area that demonstrates an appreciation that human security is an issue of universal concern, as is increasing recognition of the role to be played by non-state actors. All law is dedicated to the prevention of future harm, though the idea of international law as 'a discipline of crisis'[11] remains difficult to shake. But these developments have all developed in piecemeal, ad hoc ways, and generally in isolation from each other. Human security discourse offers a normative framework for future development and a critical lens through which to examine the current state of international law.

Another facet of the reluctance to explicitly recognise 'human security' is that, despite two decades of development, uncertainty about what human security means, its scope and its limits lingers, making decision-makers understandably reluctant to commit it to binding text. Indeed, the thematic debates on human security held within the General Assembly made it clear that this has been one of the primary concerns states have had since the inception of the concept. However, now that the General Assembly has committed itself to recognition of human security (albeit without an explicit definition of the concept, it must be noted), it will be interesting to see if this has an impact on formal recognition of the term in other circles. It did not appear in the Arms Trade Treaty that came after this Resolution, nor yet in Security Council Resolutions, but it remains too early to tell if the General Assembly adoption of the term will have ramifications for international law in the future.

Failure to explicitly employ the term in international legal instruments despite drawing on its principles is problematic. The *travaux préparatoires* of the relevant treaties and the verbatim records of the Security Council do not shed light on what seems to be the deliberate exclusion of the term in treaty text and resolutions. This creates an operational, normative and interpretational quandary: on the one hand there is the presence of human security discourse in the debates and negotiations, and deliberate employment of the principles and language of the discourse, while on the other there is deliberate evasion of the discourse and a failure to invoke the concept specifically. Where does that leave the discourse in international law? Should provisions be construed in accordance with human

9 Antônio Augusto Cançado Trindade, *International Law for Humankind: Towards a New Jus Gentium* (Martinus Nijhoff, 2010) vol 6. See also, Theodor Meron, *The Humanization of International Law* (Martinus Nijhoff, 2006).

10 International Law Commission (ILC), *Fragmentation of International Law: Difficulties Arising from the Diversification and Expansion of International Law, Report of the Study Group of the International Law Commission* UN GAOR, Fifty-eighth sess, UN Doc A/CN.4/L.682 (18 July 2006).

11 Hilary Charlesworth, 'International Law: A Discipline of Crisis' (2002) 65(3) *Modern Law Review* 377.

security, or were they deliberately worded to avoid such constructions? As yet, there are no clear answers to these questions.

III The impact of human security discourse on international law – a narrow path

Human security was intended to be, and has the potential to be, a transformative project. It is about bringing issues previously left in the background to the foreground, and asserting that they should be accorded the same attention and sense of urgency as more traditional security issues. The ultimate goal of human security discourse, it can be argued, is not only to deconstruct and problematise the traditional state-centric security paradigm, but to challenge some of the commonly held assumptions that are embedded in international relations (and international law), addressing the imbalances and lacunae present in the current system.

Human security is an idea that seeks to reopen analysis of the world's priorities, to produce new integrated methodologies in analysing the most complex and pressing global problems, and to give greater voice to individuals and communities in searching for solutions. But the transformative potential of human security is not being utilised, or at least not maximised, and certainly not in the case of how international law contributes to its promotion. Human security discourse has thus been applied, to date, in such a way as to only minimally challenge the current ordering of the legal system, and a focus on a narrow approach to human security only reinforces long-standing trends that treat structural violence as less serious and less urgent than the threats of armed conflict, terrorism and organised violence.

This is not to discredit the importance of what can be achieved (and has thus far already been achieved) using a narrow construction of human security. It has provided a normative framework that has allowed for development in the field of peacebuilding, addressing the effects of internal conflict and promoting protection of civilians, and it has also addressed the use of weapons such as landmines, cluster munitions and even small arms. These developments are, of course, of considerable importance. However, human security cannot be genuinely secured by addressing only some of the threats that face humankind.

This was a major topic of discussion in Chapter Four. The broad approach to human security is seen to be too encompassing, as mentioned previously – the idea that by prioritising everything, it prioritises nothing.[12] It is certainly true that the narrow approach is the 'easier' approach for international law. It has clearer boundaries, and negative constructions of peace and security are easier to legislate for than areas of positive obligation.[13] However, the narrow approach ignores a number of fundamental elements. The first, often acknowledged by proponents of

12 Roland Paris, 'Human Security: Paradigm Shift or Hot Air?' (2001) 26(2) *International Security* 87, 91.

13 This debate often plays out in the distinctions between civil and political rights (as predominately negative rights) and economic, social and cultural rights (more often positive rights), see, eg, Katharine G Young, 'Minimum Core of Economic and Social Rights: A Concept in Search of Content' (2008) 33 *Yale Journal of International Law* 113.

the narrow approach,[14] is that there is no normative justification for the distinction – no reason why deaths caused by armed conflict should be a higher priority than deaths caused by a pandemic (as one example). The narrow approach also ignores one of the fundamental principles of human security – the interconnected nature of threats. There is a nexus between security, human rights and development, as highlighted by the three-pillar approach increasingly invoked by the United Nations in relation to human security,[15] and between direct physical violence and other forms of harm. Human security issues are commonly complex issues with a range of threat multipliers, and comprehensive solutions are necessary to adequately ensure human security. Furthermore, social and economic inequalities can enhance an individual's (or a community's) vulnerability to security threats (both traditional and non-traditional). So be it under normative, ethical or pragmatic considerations, a broad approach to human security discourse is the only construction that can meaningfully contribute to the pursuit of genuine international peace and security.

This understanding of human security, however, has not been reflected in international law to date. Instead, treaty development driven by human security has focused entirely in areas of disarmament and armed conflict, and similar initiatives have not been produced to seek similar international agreement on other less traditional forms of insecurity. The Security Council has extensively adjusted its understanding of international peace and security since the end of the Cold War, albeit in a piecemeal and inconsistent way. But it has shown reluctance to recognise any threat that does not directly relate to traditional constructions of security. Thus, while the Security Council has addressed repeatedly the harm and destabilising effect of the HIV/AIDS pandemic, it has done so exclusively within the context of its effects in armed conflict and on peacekeepers. Even the Kimberley Process, an example of informal law-making, has adopted a narrow construction of human security.

However, the content of the previous chapters has also unearthed some small progressions away from a strictly narrow approach. For example, while the Arms Trade Treaty maintains a focus on direct violence, it does expand out from the traditional purview of armed conflict to more pervasive threats, including gender-based violence. On the other hand, the decision at the final conference to remove both impediments to social and economic development and corruption as criteria for limiting small arms exports showed a reluctance to genuinely expand recognition of security threats in a comprehensive way. More striking, however, was Resolution 2177 (2014), recognising the outbreak of Ebola in West Africa as a threat to international peace and security. At its core, this Resolution was groundbreaking. For the first time, it was explicitly acknowledged that a health crisis

14 See, eg, S Neil MacFarlane, 'A Useful Concept that Risks Losing Its Political Salience' (2004) 35 *Security Dialogue* 368, 369.

15 See, eg, United Nations General Assembly, *Report of the Secretary General: Follow-up to General Assembly Resolution 66/290 on Human Security*, Sixty-eighth sess, Agenda Item 14 and 118, UN Doc A/68/685 (23 December 2013).

posed a threat to international peace and security. While in the past an increasingly broader range of issues had been acknowledged by the Security Council, prior to this resolution only issues with an immediate connection to armed conflict (or organised terrorism) had been acknowledged. But here, too, optimism must be tempered. The Resolution is remarkably state-centric for a threat of such obvious human dimensions. While the Council has been increasingly acknowledging human suffering in its Resolutions, Resolution 2177 retreated to firmly state-centric concerns, perhaps as a counterweight to its otherwise innovative subject matter. It is also a response to an existing unparalleled crisis, thus showing the inadequacies of the Security Council as an instrument for the preventative dimensions of human security.

A truly meaningful relationship between human security discourse and international law requires an embrace of the broader dimensions of human security. Yet it is unlikely that a monumental shift will occur recognising the broad approach to human security in the international legal sphere, at least not in the near future. Conceptual disagreement about human security, the reluctance of legal scholarship to truly engage with the discourse, and the absence of political will combine to make a nigh impenetrable barrier for a real and meaningful relationship between human security and international law, at least for now.

IV The paradox of human security and international law

The fundamental paradox of human security discourse also plays out in its relationship to international law. Human security discourse straddles a difficult line of trying to simultaneously produce what Newman refers to as 'problem solving' and 'critical' dimensions, which were discussed in Chapter Two.[16] This, however, is problematic. The critical role of human security discourse is to challenge existing structures and normative assumptions, such as the role of the state, sovereignty and prevailing power structures. The problem-solving dimension, on the other hand, requires an acceptance of the current international order as the platform for delivering required solutions. These two functions cannot peacefully coexist, therein creating a paradox as human security discourse strives to serve two masters.

This is well demonstrated by the relationship of human security discourse and international law. Thus, for example, human security seeks to create a 'new multilateralism',[17] using the discourse and its universal concern principle to generate a new space for non-state actors in international law-making. But, while the participation of non-state actors is essential for productive and legitimate creation of human security norms, this so-called new multilateralism is still very much fixed in

16 Edward Newman, 'The United Nations and Human Security: Between Solidarism and Pluralism' in Mary Martin and Taylor Owen (eds), *Routledge Handbook of Human Security* (Routledge, 2014) 225, 231.

17 Lloyd Axworthy, 'Towards a New Multilateralism' in Maxwell A Cameron, Robert J Lawson and Brian W Tomlin (eds), *To Walk Without Fear: The Global Movement to Ban Landmines* (Oxford University Press, 1998) 448.

traditional frameworks. Such participation is only possible with the right political will of states, and the participatory rights of non-state actors can be revoked or undermined at the behest of state actors. This plays out in both formal international law-making, and less formalised multi-stakeholder initiatives, as highlighted in Chapter Six.

It has also played out in the so-called human security treaties, where human security discourse's impact on content has had a disturbing consequence where shifting the focus of the treaties to the threat of human security has created a vacuum in relation to principles of state responsibility. It is important that human security treaties do not get bogged downed by detail and transformed into technical regimes. It was highlighted that one of the key successes of human security discourse is in generating simple messages of significant normative force. But part of the message of human security should entail notions of responsibility. This is a central principle of the universality of human security. It is important that human security discourse does not allow for a disjunct between security and justice, and that human security is not then coopted by states seeking to create international legal instruments that are no more than paper tigers.

Unsurprisingly, the approach of the UN has shown an unwillingness to embrace the more critical approach of human security which challenges the role of state:

> Human security must be implemented with full respect for the purposes and principles enshrined in the Charter of the United Nations, including full respect for the sovereignty of States, territorial integrity and non-interference in matters that are essentially within the domestic jurisdiction of States.[18]

The problem-solving aspect of human security discourse is arguably vital for allowing human security to contribute positively to the creation of international law and policy. But the critical aspect is equally vital for international law. Human security discourse offers a lens through which to examine and rethink traditional constructions of the state, the role of non-state actors, sovereignty and international priorities. It also promotes integrative responses to current complex global problems, providing a holistic framework to combat the fragmentation of international law. It provides a lens for analysing the comparative advantages of not only different actors but also different fields of law for producing solutions, and it places the human being (as an individual but also as a socially embedded entity) at the centre of this analysis. It emphasises cooperation and mutual responsibility and the need for genuinely global solutions for global problems.

V Human security as a multifaceted discourse

The transformative potential of human security does not lie solely in its shift in the focus of security from the state to the individual. It is vital that the multifaceted approach of human security discourse is not lost to reductionist approaches that

18 *Human Security Resolution,* UN Doc A/RES/66/290, [4].

focus purely on its people-centric nature, and dismiss it as incapable of challenging existing power structures and the preserve of state sovereignty. It has four central components, all of which must be met in attempts to redress human security, if those attempts are to truly address the promotion of human security.

First, human security is about producing integrated solutions to interconnected threats. In this way, properly used, human security can provide a meaningful framework to the future development of international law that can overcome the existing fragmented nature of international law. It has already made some moves in this direction, by refocusing law related to disarmament and arms regulation into a more human-centric framework that takes into consideration issues of international human rights and humanitarian law. However, as has also been seen, the recognition of the interconnected nature of threats has only been minimally addressed so far by human security regulatory efforts. More genuine attempts to bridge the gaps between specialisations of international law are necessary in future attempts to produce human security norms and regulatory frameworks. In particular the relationship between security, development and rights, the three pillars increasingly emphasised as the cornerstones of the UN,[19] must be meaningfully addressed in human security efforts.

Human security is prevention oriented. As noted, human security has thus far struggled to overcome the crisis orientation noted by Charlesworth. While the Security Council has broadened its understanding of security, it has thus far only been able to do so when events have already reached a critical stage, such as in the case of the threats of the Ebola epidemic. But when challenged to address threats that have not yet demonstrated their full destructive capacity (such as in the case of climate change), the Security Council has been unwilling to act, and in such cases, arguments of state sovereignty and traditional security constructions have been able to drown out people-centric concerns. This has also been demonstrated in the cases of treaty development and the example provided of the Kimberley Process. Each of the treaties that has developed to respond to human security has only been possible because of serious levels of harm that each of the addressed issues has already produced. And the Kimberley Process has remained locked into a structure and a definition of security that no longer reflects the primary challenges to human security, incapable of preventing new abuses of diamond mining. It is also easy for the prevention-orientation to be lost, as has been demonstrated by the experiences of the Responsibility to Protect doctrine (noted in Chapter Four). However, this preventative focus is an important aspect of human security which needs to be retained, and international law is a core tool in providing regulatory frameworks that will prevent future threats to human security from being felt.

Finally, human security is a universal concern. This requires a rethink of issues of responsibility for redressing human insecurity. On the one hand this means opening up the range of actors who can contribute meaningfully to the production of human security norms, and produce human security solutions. Providing a critical lens, human security discourse highlights the existing trends that continue

19 See, eg, ibid [3].

to prioritise the interests of state, and restrict the capacity of non-state actors to participate in international law-making efforts, while simultaneously illustrating their importance to these processes. This has been demonstrated in relation to both formal and informal law making. Human security needs to be participatory, to fulfil its goal of empowerment. Thus one future area that should be focused on in future engagement with human security is how the discourse may be utilised to push for reform in the structures for participation in international law making. On the other hand, the universality of human security highlights vulnerability.

VI Human security and the principle of vulnerability

Human security emphasises the need for all persons to be able to 'enjoy all their rights and fully develop their potential'.[20] Vulnerability has been identified as central to the idea of security. It is receiving particular attention in human security discourse, and vulnerability, or more specifically the need to place vulnerability at the centre of analysis and action, is an increasingly emphasised principle of human security. The most recent recognition of vulnerability perhaps comes in the form of discussion of the post-2015 Development Agenda, where human security was raised in connection to the idea of 'leaving no one behind'.[21] It has also been one of the core focuses of the human security norms embedded in the human security treaties discussed, and in the thematic resolutions of the Security Council, recognising the unique vulnerabilities of civilians, and more specifically of women and of children in armed conflicts. Vulnerability must thus be central to future engagement between human security discourse and international law. This is one area where human security can contribute the most to existing structures of international law. Of course, vulnerability is already an issue covered extensively by international human rights law.[22] But where human rights law has traditionally focused primarily on the relationship between state and citizen, human security emphasises the global responsibilities to address such concerns. And if the moral imperative of preventing human suffering does not suffice, human security calls on the pragmatic argument of mutual vulnerability. Notions of mutual vulnerability, emphasising the fact that global threats are not stopped by national borders, have been used as a means of generating political will to respond to issues of human security, highlighted in work previously discussed, such as *In Larger Freedom*.[23] Contemporary global challenges no longer respect national borders, and that is why constructions of security that extend beyond the role of the state must be the way forward.

20 *Human Security Resolution,* UN Doc A/Res/66/290, [3].
21 The Report of the High-Level Panel of Eminent Persons on the Post-2015 Development Agenda, *A New Global Partnership: Eradicate Poverty and Transform Economies through Sustainable Development* (United Nations, 2013) 4.
22 See, eg, Bryan S Turner, *Vulnerability and Human Rights* (Penn State University Press, 2006).
23 Kofi Annan, *In Larger Freedom: Towards development, security and human rights for all,* UN GAOR, Fifty-ninth sess, Agenda Items 45 and 55, UN Doc A/59/2005/Add.3 (26 May 2005) [81].

VII Conclusion

Human security now holds a central (though perhaps waning) role in modern constructions of 'security'. As such, if international law is to remain relevant to the field of international peace and security, further engagement needs to made, and another two decades must not go by before international legal scholars start reflecting on the role of human security in international law. In turn, international legal analysis has been the missing voice in human security discourse, and could have much to contribute. This study has not advocated an uncritical adoption of human security into the lexicon of international law. Instead, it calls for a critical, comprehensive engagement with human security discourse. The analysis has shown that there have already emerged a basic model for the negotiation of human security treaties and the beginnings of a normative framework for international legal instruments, be they formal or informal. Further study and a genuine dialogue between human security discourse and international legal analysis could generate a meaningful relationship that advances the causes of both.

International legal developments such as those discussed across this volume have made some headway in advancing the cause of human security. But as has been discussed, these developments have occurred in a fragmented, piecemeal way with little certainty or predictability about future development. Human security offers a normative framework for the development of international law, the reform of international law-making, and an organising principle for current human-centric trends in international law. Ultimately human security seeks to place people at the centre of decision-making and human suffering as the primary concern for the global community. These goals should act as a clarion call for the international community and international law.

Bibliography

International legal instruments

African Charter on the Rights and Welfare of the Child, opened for signature 11 July 1990, OAU Doc CAB/LEG/24.9/49 (1990) (entered into force 29 November 1999).

Arms Trade Treaty, opened for signature 3 June 2013, 52 ILM 988 (entered into force 24 December 2014) ('*ATT*').

Charter of the United Nations.

Convention on Cluster Munitions, opened for signature 4 December 2008, 2688 UNTS 35 (entered into force 1 August 2010) ('CCM').

Convention on Prohibitions or Restrictions on the Use of Certain Conventional Weapons Which May Be Deemed to be Excessively Injurious or to Have Indiscriminate Effects, opened for signature 10 October 1980, 1342 UNTS 137 (entered into force 2 December 1983).

Convention on the Prohibition of the Use, Stockpiling, Production and Transfer of Anti-Personnel Mines and on their Destruction, opened for signature 18 September 1997, 2056 UNTS 241 (entered into force 1 March 1999) ('*Ottawa Convention*').

Geneva Convention for the Amelioration of the Condition of the Wounded and Sick in Armed Forces in the Field (First Geneva Convention), opened for signature 12 August 1949, 75 UNTS 31 (entered into force 21 October 1950).

Geneva Convention for the Amelioration of the Condition of Wounded, Sick and Shipwrecked Members of Armed Forces at Sea (Second Geneva Convention), opened for signature 12 August 1949, 75 UNTS 85 (entered into force 21 October 1950).

Geneva Convention relative to the Treatment of Prisoners of War (Third Geneva Convention), opened for signature 12 August 1949, 75 UNTS 135 (entered into force 21 October 1950).

Geneva Convention Relative to the Protection of Civilian Persons in Time of War (Fourth Geneva Convention), opened for signature 12 August 1949, 75 UNTS 287 (entered into force 21 October 1950).

Hague Convention (IV) respecting the Laws and Customs of War on Land, opened for signature 18 October 1907, 205 CTS 299 (entered into force 26 January 1910).

International Covenant on Civil and Political Rights, opened for signature 16 December 1966, 999 UNTS 171 (entered into force 3 January 1976) ('ICCPR').

International Covenant on Economic, Social and Cultural Rights, opened for signature 16 December 1966, 993 UNTS 3 (entered into force 3 November 1976) ('ICESCR').

Optional Protocol to the Convention on the Rights of the Child on the Involvement of Children in Armed Conflicts, opened for signature 25 March 2000, 39 ILM 1285 (entered into force 2 December 2002).

Protocol on Prohibitions or Restrictions on the Use of Mines, Booby-Traps and Other Devices as amended on 3 May 1996, opened for signature 5 March 1996, 2048 UNTS 133 (entered into force 12 March 1998) ('*Amended Protocol II*').
Rome Statute of the International Criminal Court, opened for signature 17 July 1998, 2187 UNTS 90 (entered into force 1 July 2002).
Statute of the International Court of Justice.
Treaty of Peace of Münster and Treaty of Peace of Osnabrück (1648) 1 Parry 271; 1 Parry 119 (Peace of Westphalia).
Vienna Convention on the Law of Treaties, opened for signature 23 May 1969, 1155 UNTS 331 (entered into force 27 January 1980).

Case law

Accordance with International Law of the Unilateral Declaration of Independence in Respect of Kosovo (Advisory Opinion) [2010] ICJ Rep 150.
Armed Activities (Democratic Republic of Congo v Uganda) (Judgment) [2005] ICJ Rep 116.
Compagnie des Phosphates et du Chemin de Fer de Gafsa v Weschler (1967) 48 ILR 171 (France, Parisian Court of Appeal).
Corfu Channel (United Kingdom v Albania) (Merits) [1949] ICJ Rep 4.
Interpretation of the American Declaration of the Rights and Duties of Man Within the Framework of Article 64 of the American Convention on Human Rights (Advisory Opinion) (1990) 29 ILM 379.
Kambanda (Sentencing Judgment) (International Criminal Tribunal for Rwanda, Case No ICTR-97-23-S, 4 September 1998).
Legal Consequences of the Construction of a Wall in the Occupied Palestinian Territory (Advisory Opinion) [2004] ICJ Rep 136.
Legality of the Use by a State of Nuclear Weapons in Armed Conflict (Request by WHO) *(Advisory Opinion)* [1996] ICJ Rep 66.
Legality of the Threat or Use of Nuclear Weapons (Advisory Opinion) [1996] ICJ Rep 226.
Lotus Case (France v Turkey) (Judgement) [1927] PCIJ (ser A) No 10 (Judgment of 7 September 1927).
Military and Paramilitary Activities in and against Nicaragua (Nicaragua v United States) (Merits) [1986] ICJ Rep 14.
M/V Saiga (No 2) (Saint Vincent and the Grenadines v Guinea) (1999) ITLS Case No 2, ICGJ 336.
Namibia (Legal Consequences of the Continued Presence of South Africa) (Advisory Opinion) [1971] ICJ Rep 16.
North Sea Continental Shelf Cases (Federal Republic of Germany v Denmark; FRG v The Netherlands) (Judgment) [1969] ICJ Rep 3.
Packer v Packer [1953] 2 AER 127.
Prosecutor v Erdemovic (Sentencing Judgment) (International Criminal Tribunal for Former Yugoslavia (ICTY), Trial Chamber, Case No IT-96-22-T, 29 November 1996).
Prosecutor v Issa Sesay, Morris Kallon and Augustine Gbao, (Proceedings) (Special Court for Sierra Leone, Case No SCSL-2004-2015-PT, 5 July 2004).
Prosecutor v Tadíc (Interlocutory Appeal) (International Criminal Tribunal for Former Yugoslavia, Appeals Chamber, Case No 94-91, 2 October 1995).
South West Africa (Ethiopia v South Africa) (Second Phase) [1966] ICJ Rep 6.

Security Council Resolutions

Security Council Resolution 161 (1961) UN SCOR, UN Doc S/Res/161 (21 February 1961).
Security Council Resolution 169 (1961) UN SCOR, UN Doc S/Res/169 (24 November 1961).
Security Council Resolution 181 UN SCOR, UN Doc S/Res/181 (7 August 1963).
Security Council Resolution 182 (1963) UN SCOR, UN Doc S/Res/182 (4 December 1963).
Security Council Resolution 221 (1966) UN SCOR, UN Doc S/Res/221 (9 April 1966).
Security Council Resolution 417 (1077) UN SCOR, UN Doc S/RES/417 (31 October 1977).
Security Council Resolution 418 (1977) UN SCOR, UN Doc S/RES/418 (4 November 1977).
Security Council Resolution 688 (1991) UN SCOR, UN Doc S/RES/688 (5 April 1991).
Security Council Resolution 770 (1992) UN SCOR, UN Doc S/RES/770 (13 August 1992).
Security Council Resolution 787 (1992) UN SCOR, UN Doc S/RES/787 (16 November 1992).
Security Council Resolution 794 (1992) UN SCOR, UN Doc S/RES/794 (3 December 1992).
Security Council Resolution 841 (1993) UN SCOR, UN Doc S/Res/841 (16 June 1993).
Security Council Resolutions 912 (1994) UN SCOR, UN Doc S/RES/912 (21 April 1994).
Security Council Resolution 917 (1994) UN SCOR, UN Doc S/RES/917 (6 May 1994).
Security Council Resolution 925 (1994) UN SCOR, UN Doc S/RES/925 (8 June 1994).
Security Council Resolution 940 (1994) UN SCOR, UN Doc S/RES/940 (31 July 1994).
Security Council Resolution 1158 (1998) UN SCOR, UN Doc S/RES/1158 (27 March 1998).
Security Council Resolution 1172 (1998) UN SCOR, UN Doc S/RES/1172 (6 June 1998)
Security Council Resolutions 1261 (1999) UN SCOR, UN Doc S/RES/1261 (25 August 1999).
Security Council Resolution 1264 (1999) UN SCOR, UN Doc S/RES/1264 (15 September 1999).
Security Council Resolution 1265 (1999) UN SCOR, UN Doc S/RES/1265 (17 September 1999).
Security Council Resolution 1296 (2000) UN SCOR, UN Doc S/RES/1296 (19 April 2000).
Security Council Resolution 1308 (2000) UN SCOR, UN Doc S/RES/1308 (17 July 2000).
Security Council Resolution 1314 (2000) UN SCOR, UN Doc S/RES/1314 (11 August 2000).
Security Council Resolution 1325 (2000) UN SCOR, UN Doc S/RES/1325 (31 October 2000).
Security Council Resolution 1373 (2001) UN SCOR, UN Doc S/RES/1373 (28 September 2001).

Security Council Resolution 1379 (2001) UN SCOR, UN Doc S/RES/1379 (20 November 2001).
Security Council Resolution 1450 (2002) UN SCOR, UN Doc S/RES/1450 (13 December 2002)
Security Council Resolution 1459 (2003) UN SCOR, UN Doc S/RES/1459 (28 January 2003).
Security Council Resolution 1460 (2003) UN SCOR, UN Doc S/RES/1460 (30 January 2003).
Security Council Resolution 1502 (2003) UN SCOR UN Doc S/RES/1502 (26 August 2003).
Security Council Resolution 1539 (2004) UN SCOR, UN Doc S/RES/1539 (22 April 2004).
Security Council Resolution 1556 (2004) UN SCOR, UN Doc S/RES/1556 (30 July 2004).
Security Council Resolution 1612 (2005) UN SCOR, UN Doc S/RES/1612 (26 July 2005)
Security Council Resolution 1624 (2005) UN SCOR, UN Doc S/RES/1624 (14 September 2005)
Security Council Resolution 1674 (2006) UN SCOR, UN Doc S/2006/1674 (28 April 2006).
Security Council Resolution 1696 (2006) UN SCOR, UN Doc S/RES/1696 (31 July 2006)
Security Council Resolution 1706 (2006) UN SCOR, UN Doc S/RES/1706 (31 August 2006).
Security Council Resolution 1769 (2007) UN SCOR, UN Doc S/RES/1769 (31 July 2007).
Security Council Resolution 1803 (2008) UN SCOR, UN Doc S/RES/1803 (3 March 2008)
Security Council Resolution 1820 (2008) UN SCOR, UN Doc S/RES/1820 (19 June 2008).
Security Council Resolution 1882 (2009) UN SCOR, UN Doc S/RES/1882 (4 August 2009).
Security Council Resolution 1888 (2009) UN SCOR, UN Doc S/RES/1888 (30 September 2009).
Security Council Resolution 1889 (2009) UN SCOR, UN Doc S/RES/1889 (5 October 2009).
Security Council Resolution 1894 (2009) UN SCOR, UN Doc S/RES/1894 (11 November 2009).
Security Council Resolution 1916 (2010) UN SCOR, UN Doc S/RES/1916 (19 March 2010).
Security Council Resolution 1929 (2010) UN SCOR, UN Doc S/RES/1929 (9 June 2010)
Security Council Resolution 1970 (2011) UN SCOR, UN Doc S/RES/1970 (26 February 2011).
Security Council Resolution 1973 (2011) UN SCOR, UN Doc S/RES/1973 (17 March 2011).
Security Council Resolution 1975 (2011) UN SCOR, UN Doc S/RES/1975 (30 March 2011).
Security Council Resolution 1998 (2011) UN SCOR, UN Doc S/RES/1998 (12 July 2011).

Security Council Resolution 2049 (2012) UN SCOR, UN Doc S/RES/2049 (7 June 2012)
Security Council Resolution 2068 (2012) UN SCOR, UN Doc S/RES/2068 (19 September 2012)
Security Council Resolution 2082 (2012) UN SCOR, UN Doc S/RES/2082 (17 December 2012)
Security Council Resolution 2122 (2013) UN SCOR, UN Doc S/RES/ 2122 (18 October 2013).
Security Council Resolution 2143 (2014) UN SCOR, UN Doc S/2014/2143 (7 March 2014).
Security Council Resolution 2165 (2014) UN SCOR, UN Doc S/Res/2165 (14 July 2014).
Security Council Resolution 2177 (2014) UN SCOR, UN Doc S/Res/2177 (18 September 2014).
Security Council Resolution 2258 (2015) UN SCOR, UN Doc S/RES/2258 (22 December 2015).
Security Council Resolution 2331 (2016) UN SCOR, UN Doc S/Res/2331 (20 December 2016).
Security Council Resolution 2332 (2016) UN SCOR, UN Doc S/RES/2332 (21 December 2016).

Security Council verbatim records, presidential statements and press releases

UN Security Council Press Release, Security Council Fails to Adopt Draft Resolution on Myanmar, Owing to Negative Votes by China, Russian Federation, UN SCOR, 5619th mtg, UN Doc SC/8939 (12 January 2007).
UN Security Council, Statement by the President of the Security Council, UN SCOR, UN Doc S/23500 (31 January 1992).
UN Security Council President, Peace-building: towards a comprehensive approach, UN SCOR, UN Doc S/PRST/2001/5 (20 February 2001).
UN Security Council, Statement of the President, UN SCOR, UN Doc S/PRST/1998/29 (24 September 1998).
UN Security Council, Statement of the President, UN SCOR, UN Doc S/PRST/2002/31 (31 October 2002).
UNSC Verbatim Record, UN SCOR, UN Doc S/PV/3980 (Resumption 1) (22 February 1999).
UNSC Verbatim Record, UN SCOR, UN Doc S/PV/4087 (Resumption 1) (10 January 2000).
UNSC Verbatim Record, UN SCOR, UN Doc S/PV/5220 (30 June 2005).
UNSC Verbatim Record, UN SCOR, UN Doc S/PV/5225 (12 July 2005).
UNSC Verbatim Record, UN SCOR, UN Doc S/PV/5663 (17 April 2007).
UNSC Verbatim Record, UN SCOR, UN Doc S/PV/5663 (Resumption 1) (17 April 2007).
UNSC Verbatim Record, UN SCOR, UN Doc S/PV/5766 (23 October 2007).
UNSC Verbatim Record, UN SCOR, UN Doc S/PV/6587 (20 July 2011).
UNSC Verbatim Record, UN SCOR, UN Doc S/PV/6587 (Resumption 1) (20 July 2011).
UNSC Verbatim Record, UN SCOR, UN Doc S/PV/6668 (23 November 2011).
UNSC Verbatim Record, UN SCOR, UN Doc S/PV/7015 (Resumption 1) (6 August 2013).

UNSC Verbatim Record, UN SCOR, UN Doc S/PV/7019 (19 September 2013).
UNSC Verbatim Record, UN SCOR, UN Doc S/PV/7213 (8 July 2014).
UNSC Verbatim Record, UN SCOR, UN Doc S/PV/7268 (18 September 2014).
UN Security Council, Statement by the President of the Security Council on Inclusive Development, UN SCOR, UN Doc S/PRST/2015/3 (19 January 2015).

UN documents

Agenda 21: Programme of Action for Sustainable Development, UN GAOR, 46th sess, Agenda Item 21, UN Doc A/Conf.151/26 (14 June 1992).
Annan, Kofi, *In Larger Freedom: Towards development, security and human rights for all*, UN GAOR, Fifty-ninth sess, Agenda Items 45 and 55, UN Doc A/59/2005/Add.3 (26 May 2005).
Commission on Human Security (CHS), *Human Security Now* (UN, 2003).
Commission on Sustainable Development, Rio Declaration on Environment and Development, UN ESCOR, Fifth sess, UN Doc E/CN.17/1997/8 (10 February 1997).
Declaration on Principles of International Law Concerning Friendly Relations and Co-operation Among States in Accordance with the Charter of the United Nations, GA Res 2625 (XXV) UN GAOR, 25th sess, Agenda item 85, UN Doc A/RES/25/2625 (24 October 1970).
de Cuellar, Javier Pérez, Report of the Secretary-General on the Work of the Organisation, UN GAOR, Forty-sixth sess, UN Doc GA/46/404 (23 September 1991) reprinted in [1991] 45 *UN Yearbook* 7, 13–14.
Diplomatic Conference for the Adoption of a Convention on Cluster Munitions, UN Doc CCM/77 (30 May 2008) <http://www.clustermunitionsdublin.ie/pdf/ENGLISHfinaltext.pdf>.
Final Document of the Third Review Conference of the Conventional Weapons Convention, UN Doc CCW/CONF.III/I (15 December 2006) 1 (Part 1) [19].
Follow-up to Paragraph 143 on Human Security of the 2005 World Summit Outcome, GA Res 66/290, UN GAOR, Sixty-sixth sess, Agenda Item 14 and 117, UN Doc A/RES/66/290 (25 October 2012).
International Law Commission (ILC), Fragmentation of International Law: Difficulties Arising from the Diversification and Expansion of International Law, Report of the Study Group of the International Law Commission UN GAOR, Fifty-eighth sess, UN Doc UN Doc. A/CN.4/L.682 (18 July 2006).
Office of the Global Compact, *Enabling Economies of Peace: Public Policy for Conflict-Sensitive Business* (United Nations, 2005).
The Report of the High-Level Panel of Eminent Persons on the Post-2015 Development Agenda, *A New Global Partnership: Eradicate Poverty and Transform Economies through Sustainable Development* (United Nations, 2013).
United Nations Inter-Agency Standing Committee, *Sanctions Assessment Handbook: Assessing the Humanitarian Implications of Sanctions* (OCHA, October 2004).
Press Release, Deputy Secretary-General, 'Deputy Secretary-General, Hailing Historic Adoption of Arms Trade Treaty During High-level Event, Urges Its Early Ratification, Entry into Force', UN Doc DSG/SM/704-DC/3453 (25 September 2013) <http://www.un.org/press/en/2013/dsgsm704.doc.htm>.
Press Release, Secretary-General, 'Secretary-General Defends, Clarifies "Responsibility to Protect" at Berlin Event on "Responsible Sovereignty: International Cooperation for a

Changed World"', UN Doc SG/SM/1 1701 (15 July 2008) <http://www.un.org/News/Press/docs/2008/sgsml1701.doc.htm>.

Special Representative of the Secretary-General (SRSG) on the issue of human rights and transnational corporations and other business enterprises, UN GAOR, Human Rights Council Comm, Fourth sess, Agenda Item 2, UN Doc A/HRC/4/035 (9 February 2007).

Statement by HE Ambassador Uffe A Balslev, Undersecretary for Disarmament, Non-Proliferation and Arms Control, 68th Session of the United Nations General Assembly, First Committee Thematic Debate on Other Disarmament Measures, Non-Proliferation and Arms Control New York, 30 October 2013 <http://www.reachingcriticalwill.org/images/documents/Disarmament-fora/1com/1com13/statements/30Oct_Denmark.pdf>.

United Nations Conference on the Arms Trade Treaty, Compilation of Views on the Elements of the Arms Trade Treaty: Background Document Prepared by the Secretariat, UN GAOR, UN Doc A/CONF/217/2 (10 May 2012).

UN Declaration of Basic Principles of Justice for Victims of Crime and Abuse of Power, GA Res 40/34, UN GAOR, UN Doc A/RES/40/34 (29 November 1985).

United Nations Department of Economic and Social Affairs (DESA), *The Inequality Predicament: Report on the World Social Situation 2005* (United Nations, 2005).

United Nations Development Programme (UNDP), *Human Development Report 1994* (UNDP, 1994).

United Nations Diplomatic Conference of Plenipotentiaries on the Establishment of an International Criminal Court, Non-governmental organizations accredited to participate in the Conference: note by the Secretary-General, Official Records of the United Nations Diplomatic Conference of Plenipotentiaries on the Establishment of an International Criminal Court (Reports and other documents), Vol III, UN Doc A/CONF/183/INF/3 (5 June 1998).

United Nations Diplomatic Conference of Plenipotentiaries on the Establishment of an International Criminal Court, Official Record, Rome, Italy, 15–17 June 1998, UN Doc A/CONR183/13 (Vol II) (15–17 June 1998).

United Nations General Assembly, Resolution 60/215, UN GAOR, UN Doc A/RES/60/215 (29 March 2006).

United Nations General Assembly, Implementing the Responsibility to Protect, Report of the Secretary General, UN GAOR, Sixty-third sess, Agenda Item 44 and 107, UN Doc A/63/677 (12 January 2009).

United Nations General Assembly, Report of the Secretary-General on Human Security, UN GAOR, Sixty-fourth sess, Agenda Item 48 and 114, UN Doc A/64/701 (8 March 2010).

United Nations General Assembly, Report of the Secretary General: Follow-up to General Assembly Resolution 64/291 on Human Security, 66th sess, Agenda Item 14 and 117, UN Doc A/68/685 (5 April 2012).

United NationsGeneral Assembly, Report of the Secretary-General: Follow-up to General Assembly Resolution 66/290 on Human Security, Sixty-eighth sess, Agenda Item 14 and 118, UN Doc A/68/685 (23 December 2013).

United Nations General Assembly, The Role of Diamonds in Fuelling Conflict, General Assembly Resolution 55/56, UN GAOR, Agenda Item 175, UN Doc A/RES/55/56 (29 January 2001).

United Nations General Assembly, *The Role of Diamonds in Fueling Conflict*, GA Res 56/263, UN GAOR, Agenda Item 37, UN Doc A/RES/56/263 (13 March 2002).

UN High Level Panel on Threats, Challenges and Change, *A More Secure World* (UN, 2004).

UN Human Rights Council, *Report of the Human Rights Council Advisory Committee on the Right of Peoples to Peace*, UN GAOR, Twentieth sess, Agenda Item 5, UN Doc A/HRC/20/31 (16 April 2012) Article 2.

UN Human Security Unit, *Strategic Plan 2014–2017* (United Nations, 2014).

United Nations Millennium Declaration, UN GA Res 55/2, Fifty-fifth sess, Agenda Item 60(b), UN Doc A/RES/55/2 (18 September 2000).

United Nations Trust Fund for Human Security, *Human Security in Theory and Practice* (United Nations, 2009).

Universal Declaration of Human Rights, GA Res 217A (III), UN GAOR, 3rd sess, 183rd plen mtg, UN Doc A/810 (10 December 1948).

Vienna Declaration and Programme of Action: Report of the World Conference on Human Rights, UN GAOR, UN Doc A/CONF.157/23 (25 June 1993).

World Summit Outcome Document GA Res 60/1, UN GAOR, Sixtieth sess, Agenda Item 46 and 120, UN Doc A/RES/60/1 (24 October 2005).

Books and book chapters

Abass, Ademola, 'African Peace and Security Architecture and Protection of Human Security' in Ademola Abass (ed), *Protecting Human Security in Africa* (Oxford University Press, 2010) 247.

Adler, Emmanuel and Michael Barnett (eds), *Security Communities* (Cambridge University Press, 1998).

Agamben, Giorgio, *State of Exception* (University of Chicago Press, 2005).

Al Haq, Mahbub, *Reflections on Human Development* (Oxford University Press, 2nd edn, 1999).

Arends, J and M Frederik, 'From Homer to Hobbes and Beyond – Aspects of "Security" in the European Tradition' in Hans Günter Brauch et al (eds), *Globalization and Environmental Challenges* (Springer Berlin Heidelberg, 2008) vol 3, 263.

d'Aspremont, Jean, 'International Law-Making by Non-State Actors: Changing the Model or Putting the Phenomenon into Perspective' in Math Noortman and Cedric Ryngaert (eds), *Non-State Actor Dynamics in International Law: From Law Takers to Law Makers* (Ashgate, 2010).

Axworthy, Lloyd, 'Towards a New Multilateralism' in Maxwell A Cameron, Robert J Lawson and Brian W Tomlin (eds), *To Walk Without Fear: The Global Movement to Ban Landmines* (Oxford University Press, 1998) 448.

Bacon, Paul and Christopher Hobson, 'Incorporating Natural Disasters into the Human Security Agenda' in Paul Bacon, Christopher Hobson and Robin Cameron (eds), *Human Security and Natural Disasters* (Routledge, 2014) 1.

Bain, William, *The Empire of Safety and the Safety of the People* (Routledge, 2006).

Balzacq, Thierry (ed), *Understanding Securitization Theory: How Security Problems Emerge and Dissolve* (Routledge, 2010).

Baylis, John, 'The Concept of Security in International Relations' in Hans Günter Brauch et al (eds), *Globalization and Environmental Challenges* (Springer Berlin Heidelberg, 2008) vol 3, 495.

Beebe, Shannon D and Mary Kaldor, *The Ultimate Weapon is No Weapon: Human Security and the New Rules of War and Peace* (PublicAffairs, 2010).

Benesch, Susan, Cristina Rodriguez and Robert Sloane, 'International Customary Law and Antipersonnel Landmines: Emergence of a New Customary Norm' in Landmine Monitor (ed), *Landmine Monitor Report 1999: Toward a Mine-Free World* (Human Rights Watch, 1999) 1020.

Bennoune, Karima, 'Productive Tensions: Women's Rights NGOs, the "Mainstream" Human Rights Movement, and International Lawmaking' in Cecilia M Bailliet (ed), *Non-State Actors, Soft Law and Protective Regimes: From the Margins* (Cambridge University Press, 2012) 125.

Bentham, Jeremy, *The Theory of Legislation* (Elibron Classics, Reprint, 1896).

Booth, Ken, 'Security and Self: Reflections of a Fallen Realist' in Keith Krause and Michael Williams (eds), *Critical Security Studies: Concepts and Cases* (UCL Press, 1997) 83.

Booth, Ken, 'Beyond Critical Security Studies' in Ken Booth (ed), *Critical Security Studies and World Politics* (Lynne Rienner, 2005) 264.

Booth, Ken, *Theory of World Security* (Cambridge University Press, 2007).

Bothe, Michael, 'Security in International Law Since 1990' in Hans Günter Brauch et al (eds), *Globalization and Environmental Challenges* (Springer Berlin Heidelberg, 2008) vol 3, 475.

Bourantonis, Dimitris, *The History and Politics of UN Security Council Reform* (Routledge, 2005).

Boutros-Ghali, Boutros, *An Agenda for Peace* (United Nations, 1992).

Boutros-Ghali, Boutros, *An Agenda for Democratization* (United Nations, 1996).

Boyle, Alan and Christine Chinkin, *The Making of International Law* (Oxford University Press, 2007).

Boyle, Francis Anthony, *Foundations of World Order: The Legalist Approach to International Relations* (Duke University Press, 1999).

Brauch, Hans Günter, 'From a Security towards a Survival Dilemma' in Hans Günter Brauch et al (eds), *Globalization and Environmental Challenges* (Springer Berlin, Heidelberg, 2008) vol 3, 537.

Brauch, Hans Günter, 'Conceptual Quartet: Security and its Linkages with Peace, Development, and Environment' in Hans Günter Brauch et al (eds), *Globalization and Environmental Challenges* (Springer Berlin Heidelberg, 2008) vol 3, 65.

Brecher, Michael and Frank P Harvey (eds), *Realism and Institutionalism in International Studies* (The University of Michigan Press, 2002).

Brölmann, Catherine, 'Specialized Rules of Treaty Interpretation: International Organizations' in Duncan B Hollis (ed) *The Oxford Guide to Treaties* (Oxford University Press, 2012) 507.

Brunnée, Jutta and Stephen J. Toope, *Legitimacy and Legality in International Law: An Interactional Account* (Cambridge University Press, 2010).

Burgess, J Peter, 'The Ethical Challenges of Human Security in the Age of Globalisation' in Moufida Goucha and John Crowley (eds), *Rethinking Human Security* (Wiley-Blackwell, 2008) 49.

Buzan, Barry, *People, States and Fear: An Agenda for International Security Studies in the Post-Cold War Era* (Harvester Wheatsheaf, 2nd edn, 1991).

Buzan, Barry, Ole Wæver and Jaap de Wilde, *Security: A New Framework for Analysis* (Lynne Rienner Publications, 1998).

Callabero-Anthony, Mely and Rolf Emmers, 'Understanding the Dynamics of Securitising Non-Traditional Security' in Mely Callabero-Anthony, Rolf Emmers and Amitav Acharya (eds), *Non-Traditional Security in Asia: Dilemmas in Securitisation* (Ashgate, 2006) 1.

Chandler, David and Nik Hynek (eds), *Critical Perspectives on Human Security: Rethinking Emancipation and Power in International Relations* (Routledge, 2011).

Charlesworth, Hilary, 'Law-making and Sources' in James Crawford and Martti Koskenniemi (eds), *The Cambridge Companion to International Law* (Cambridge University Press, 2012) 187.

Charlesworth, Hilary and Christine Chinkin, *The Boundaries of International Law: A Feminist Analysis* (Manchester University Press, 2000).

Clausewitz, Carl von, *On War* (Col JJ Graham trans, Kegan Paul, Trench, Trubner & Co, 1918) vol 1.

Combacau, Jean, 'Le Chapitre VII de la Charte des Nations Unies: resurrection ou metamorphoses?' in RB Archour and S Laghmi (eds), *Les Nouveaux Aspects du Droit International* (Pedone, 1994) 139.

Crawford, James and Penelope Nevill, 'Relations between International Courts and Tribunals: The "Regime Problem"' in Margaret A Young (ed), *Regime Interaction in International Law: Facing Fragmentation* (Cambridge University Press, 2012) 235.

Deng, Francis M et al, *Sovereignty as Responsibility: Conflict Management in Africa* (Brookings Institution Press, 1996).

Dijkzeul, Dennis, *The Management of Multilateral Organizations* (Kluwer Law International, 1997).

Dörr, Oliver and Kirsten Schmalenbach, *The Vienna Convention of the Law of Treaties: A Commentary* (Springer Science & Business Media, 2011).

Dunne, Tim and Nicholas J Wheeler, '"We the Peoples": Contending Discourses of Security in Human Rights Theory and Practice' in David Chandler and Nik Hynek (eds), *Critical Perspectives on Human Security: Rethinking Emancipation and Power in International Relations* (Routledge, 2011) 13.

Edwards, Alice and Carla Ferstman (eds), *Human Security and Non-Citizens: Law, Policy and International Affairs* (Cambridge University Press, 2010).

Edwards, Alice and Carla Ferstman, 'Humanising Non-Citizens: The Convergence of Human Rights and Human Security' in Alice Edwards and Carla Ferstman (eds), *Human Security and Non-Citizens: Law, Policy and International Affairs* (Cambridge University Press, 2010) 3.

Enarson, Elaine, 'Human Security and Disasters: What a Gender Lens Offers' in Christopher Hobson, Paul Bacon and Robin Cameron (eds), *Human Security and Natural Disasters* (Routledge, 2014) 37.

Estrada-Tanck, Dorothy, *Human Security and Human Rights under International Law: The Protections Offered to Persons Confronting Structural Vulnerability* (Bloomsbury, 2016).

Evans, Paul, 'Human Security and East Asia' in Mary Martin and Taylor Owen (eds), *The Routledge Handbook of Human Security* (Routledge, 2014) 272.

Fassbender, Bardo, *UN Security Council Reform and the Right of Veto: A Constitutional Perspective* (Martinus Nijhoff Publishers, 1998) vol 32.

Franck, Thomas, *The Power of Legitimacy Among Nations* (Oxford University Press, 1990).

Fraser, Nancy, *Scales of Justice: Reimagining Political Space in a Globalizing World* (Polity Press, 2008).

Frerks, Georg and Berma Klein Goldewijk, 'Human Security and International Insecurity: The Quest for Humane Global Governance' in Georg Frerks and Berma Klein Goldewijk (eds), *Human Security and International Insecurity* (Wageningen Academic Publishers, 2007) 21.

Frowein, Jochen Abr., 'Article 39. Chapter VII. Action with Respect to Threats to the Peace, Breaches of Peace and Acts of Aggression' in Bruno Simma et al (eds), *The United Nations Charter: A Commentary* (Oxford University Press, 2nd edn, 2002) vol I.

Fuller, Lon L, *The Morality of Law* (Yale University Press, revised edition, 1969).

Gasper, Des, 'Human Security: From Definitions to Investigating a Discourse' in Mary Martin and Taylor Owen (eds), *Routledge Handbook of Human Security* (Routledge, 2014) 28.

Glasius, Marlies, *The International Criminal Court: A Global Civil Society Achievement* (Routledge, 2006).

Goldewijk, Berma Klein, '"New Wars" and the State: The Nexus Religion-Human Security' in Georg Frerks and Berma Klein Goldewijk (eds), *Human Security and International Insecurity* (Wageningen Academic, 2007) 65.

Goucha, Moufida and John Crowley (eds), *Rethinking Human Security* (Wiley-Blackwell, 2008).

Gross, Oren and Fionnula Ní Aoláin, *Law in Times of Crisis: Emergency Powers in Theory and Practice* (Cambridge University Press, 2006).

Grotius, *On the Rights of War and Peace* (Jean Barbeyrac trans, Nabu Press, 2010) [Trans of *De Jure Belli ac Pacis*, (first published 1625)].

Guzzini, Stefano, *Realism in International Relations and International Political Economy: The Continuing Story of a Death Foretold* (Routledge, 2013).

Hammer, Leonard M, *A Foucauldian Approach to International Law* (Ashgate, 2007).

Hans, Asha and Betty A Reardon, *The Gender Imperative: Human Security vs State Security* (Routledge, 2012).

Harris, JW, *Legal Philosophies* (Butterworths, 2nd edn, 1997).

Hart, HLA, *The Concept of Law* (Clarendon Press, 1994).

Henckaerts, Jean-Marie and Louise Doswald-Beck, *Customary International Humanitarian Law* vol I: *Rules* (ICRC and Cambridge, 2005).

Henkin, Louis, *How Nations Behave: Law and Foreign Policy* (Council on Foreign Relations, 1979).

Higgins, Rosalyn, *Problems and Process: International Law and How We Use It* (Clarendon Press, 1994).

Hobbes, Thomas, *Leviathan or the Matter, Forme & Power of a Common-Wealth Ecclesiastical and Civil* (Oxford Classics, republished 1998, originally published 1651).

Hough, Peter, *Understanding Global Security* (Routledge, 2nd edn, 2008).

Jackson, Robert '"The Safety of the People is the Supreme Law": Beyond Hobbes but not as far as Kant' in William Bain (ed), *The Empire of Security and the Safety of the People* (Routledge, 2006) 15.

Jenks, CW, 'Unanimity, the Veto, Weighted Voting, Special and Simple Majorities and Consensus as Modes of Decisions in International Organizations' in Arnold Duncan McNair Baron McNair (ed), *Cambridge Essays in International Law: Essays in Honour of Lord McNair* (Stevens Publishing Company, 1965) 48.

Julio, Claudia F Fuentes and Hans Günter Brauch, 'The Human Security Network: A Global North–South Coalition' in Hans Günter Brauch et al (eds), *Facing Global Environmental Change* (Springer Berlin Heidelberg, 2009) vol 4, 991.

Kaldor, Mary, *New and Old Wars: Organised Violence in a Global Era* (Polity Press, 1999).

Kamminga, Menno T, 'The Evolving Status of NGOs under International Law: A Threat to the Inter-State System?' in Philip Alston (ed), *Non-State Actors and Human Rights* (Oxford University Press, 2005) 93.

Kant, Immanuel, *Perpetual Peace*, 1795 republished in *Kant's Political Writings* (HB Nisbet trans, Cambridge University Press, 1970).

Kelsen, Hans, *The Law of the United Nations* (Stevens, 1950).

Klabbers, Jan, 'Intervention, Armed Intervention, Armed Attack, Threat to Peace, Act of Aggression, and Threat or Use of Force: What's the Difference?' in Marc Weller (ed), *The Oxford Handbook of the Use of Force in International Law* (Oxford University Press, 2015) 1729.

Kooijmans, PJ, 'The Enlargement of the Concept Threat to the Peace' in RJ Dupuy (ed), *The Development of the Role of the Security Council* (Nijhoff, 1993) 111.

Koskenniemi, Martti, *The Gentle Civiliser of Nations: The Rise and Fall of International Law 1870–1960* (Cambridge University Press, 2001).

Koskenniemi, Martti, *From Apology to Utopia: The Structure of International Legal Argument* (Cambridge, 2nd edn, 2005).

Krause, Keith, 'Is Human Security More Than Just a Good Idea?' in M Brzoska and PJ Croll (eds), *Promoting Security: But How and for Whom?* (Bonn International Center for Conversion, 2004) 43.

Ku, Charlotte, 'Collective Security and the Personalization of Peace' in Steve Charnovitz, Debra P Steger and Peter Van Den Bossche (eds), *Law in the Service of Human Dignity* (Cambridge University Press, 2005) 336.

Larrinaga, Miguelde and Claire Turenne Sjolander, '(Re)Presenting Landmines from Protector to Enemy: The Discursive Framing of a New Multilateralism' in Maxwell A Cameron, Robert J Lawson and Brian W Tomlin (eds), *To Walk Without Fear: The Global Movement to Ban Landmines* (Oxford University Press, 1998) 392.

Lasswell, H and M McDonald, *Jurisprudence for a Free Society: Studies in Law, Science and Policy* (New Haven Press, 1992).

Lauterpacht, Hersch, 'The Reality of the Law of Nations' in E Lauterpacht (ed), *International Law, being the Collected Papers of Hersch Lauterpacht* (Cambridge University Press, 2004) vol V, 26.

Lawson, Robert J, Mark Gwozdecky, Jill Sinclair and Ralph Lysyshyn, 'The Ottawa Process and the International Movement to Ban Anti-Personnel Mines' in Maxwell A Cameron, Robert J Lawson and Brian W Tomlin (eds) *To Walk Without Fear: The Global Movement to Ban Landmines* (Oxford University Press, 1998) 160.

Lester, Eve, 'Socio-economic Rights, Human Security and Survival Migrants: Whose Rights? Whose Security?' in Alice Edwards and Carla Ferstman (eds), *Human Security and Non-Citizens: Law, Policy and International Affairs* (Cambridge University Press, 2010) 314.

Liotta, PH and James F Miskel, 'Towards an Ethical Framework for Security' in Hans Günter Brauch et al (eds), *Globalization and Environmental Challenges* (Springer Berlin Heidelberg, 2008) vol 3, 879.

MacFarlane, S Neil and Yuen Foong Khong, *Human Security and the UN: A Critical History* (Indiana University Press, 2006).

Maguire, Amy, '"Security Starts with the Law": The Role of International Law in the Protection of Women's Security Post-Conflict' in Brett Bowden, Hilary Charlesworth and Jeremy Farrall (eds), *The Role of International Law in Rebuilding Societies After Conflict: Great Expectations* (Cambridge University Press, 2009) 218.

Maslen, Stuart and P Herby, 'An International Ban on Anti-personnel Mines: History and Negotiation of the "Ottawa Treaty"' in Louis Maresca and Stuart Maslen (eds), *The Banning of Anti-Personnel Landmines: The Legal Contribution of the International Committee of the Red Cross 1955–1999* (Cambridge University Press, 2000) 606.

Matheson, Michael J, *Council Unbound: The Growth of UN Decision Making on Conflict and Post-conflict Issues after the Cold War* (United States Institute of Peace Press, 2006).

May, Larry, *Crimes Against Humanity: A Normative Account* (Cambridge University Press, 2005).

Mearsheimer, John J, 'Realism, the Real World and the Academy' in Michael Brecher and Frank P Harvey (eds), *Realism and Institutionalism in International Studies* (The University of Michigan Press, 2002) 23.

Mégret, Frédéric, 'International Law as Law' in James Crawford and Martti Koskenniemi (eds), *The Cambridge Companion to International Law* (Cambridge University Press, 2012) 64.

Meron, Theodor, *Bloody Constraint, War and Chivalry in Shakespeare* (Oxford University Press, 1998).

Meron, Theodor, *The Humanization of International Law* (Martinus Nijhoff, 2006).

Morgenthau, Hans, *Politics Among Nations* (A Knopf, 5th edn, 1972).

Moser, Susanne C, 'Individual and Community Empowerment for Human Security' in Linda Sygna, Karen O'Brien and Johanna Wolf (eds), *A Changing Environment for Human Security: Transformative Approaches to Research, Policy and Action* (Routledge, 2013) 279.

Nef, Jorge, *Human Security and Mutual Vulnerability* (IDRC, 1999).

Newman, Edward, 'The United Nations and Human Security: Between Solidarism and Pluralism' in Mary Martin and Taylor Owen (eds), *Routledge Handbook of Human Security* (Routledge, 2014) 225.

Noll, Gregor, 'Securitising Sovereignty? States, Refugees and the Regionalization of International Law' in Edward Newman and Joanne van Selm (eds), *Refugees and Forced Displacement: International Security, Human Vulnerability and the State* (United Nations University, 2003) 277.

Nolte, Greg, 'The Limits of the Security Council's Powers and Its Functions in the International Legal System: Some Reflections' in Michael Byers (ed), *The Role of Law in International Politics: Essays in International Relations and International Law* (Oxford University Press, 2000) 315.

Noortmann, Math, 'Human Securities, International Laws and Non-State Actors: Bringing Complexity Back In' in Cedric Ryngaert and Math Noortmann (eds), *Human Security and International Law: The Challenge of Non-State Actors* (Intersentia, 2014) 13.

Noortmann, Math and Cedric Ryngaert, 'Towards a (New) Human Security-Based Agenda for International Law and Non-State Actors?' in Math Noortmann and Cedric Ryngaert (eds), *Human Security and International Law: The Challenge of Non-State Actors* (Intersentia, 2014) 195.

Nussbaum, Martha C, *Frontiers of Justice: Disability, Nationality, Species Membership* (The Belknap Press, 2006).

Oberleitner, Gerd, 'Human Security: Idea, Policy and Law' in Mary Martin and Taylor Owen (eds), *Routledge Handbook of Human Security* (Routledge, 2014) 319.

Oquist, Paul, 'Basic Elements of a Policy Framework for Human Security' in Moufida Goucha and John Crowley (eds), *Rethinking Human Security* (Wiley-Blackwell, 2008) 101.

Owen, Taylor, 'In All but Name: The Uncertain Future of Human Security in the UN' in Moufida Goucha and John Crowley (eds), *Rethinking Human Security* (Wiley-Blackwell, 2008) 113.

Owen, Taylor, 'Human Security Thresholds' in Mary Martin and Taylor Owen (eds), *Routledge Handbook of Human Security* (Routledge, 2014) 58.

Owen, Taylor, 'Human Security Mapping' in Mary Martin and Taylor Owen (eds), *Routledge Handbook of Human Security* (Routledge, 2014) 308.

Paris, Roland, 'Understanding the "Coordination Problem" in Postwar Statebuilding' in Roland Paris and Timothy D Sisk (eds) *The Dilemmas of Statebuilding: Confronting the Contradictions of Postwar Peace Operations* (Routledge 2009) 53.

Pauwelyn, Joost, *Conflict of Norms in Public International Law: How WTO Law Relates to other Rules of International Law* (Cambridge University Press, 2003).

Peters, Anne, Till Förster and Lucy Koechlin, 'Towards Non-State Actors as Effective, Legitimate and Accountable Standard Setters' in Anne Peters et al (eds), *Non-State Actors as Standard Setters* (Cambridge University Press, 2009) 492.

Price, Richard, 'Emerging Customary Norms and Anti-Personnel Landmines' in Christian Reus-Smit (ed), *The Politics of International Law* (Cambridge University Press, 2004) 106.

Rawls, John, *A Theory of Justice* (Harvard University Press, 1971).

Renner, Michael, 'Security Redefined' in Michael Renner (ed), *The State of the World 2005: Redefining Global Security* (Worldwatch Institute, 2005) 3.

Renner, Michael, 'State of the World 2005: Redefining Security' in M Mwagiru (ed), *Rethinking Global Security: An African Perspective?* (Heinrich Böll Foundation, 2006).

Reus-Smit, Christian, *The Politics of International Law* (Cambridge University Press, 2004).

Roberts, Shawn and Jody Williams, *After the Guns Fall Silent: The Enduring Legacy of Landmines* (ICBL, 1995).

Romani, Carlos Fernándezde Casadevante, *International Law of Victims* (Springer Press, 2012).

Russett, Bruce, 'A Neo-Kantian Perspective: Democracy, Interdependence, and International Organizations in Building Security Communities' in Emanuel Adler and Michael Barnett (eds), *Security Communities* (Cambridge University Press, 1998).

Ryngaert, Cedric and Math Noortmann (eds), *Human Security and International Law: The Challenge of Non-State Actors* (Intersentia, 2014).

Schiff, Benjamin N, *Building the International Criminal Court* (Cambridge University Press, 2008).

Sen, Amartya, *Development as Freedom* (Oxford University Press, 1999).

Sen, Amartya, 'Birth of a Discourse' in Mary Martin and Taylor Owen (eds), *Routledge Handbook of Human Security* (Routledge, 2014) 17.

Shani, Giorgio, 'Securitising "Bare Life": Critical Perspectives on Human Security Discourse' in David Chandler and Nik Hynek (eds), *Critical Perspectives on Human Security: Rethinking Emancipation and Power in International Relations* (Routledge, 2011) 56.

Shepherd, Laura J and Jutta Weldes, 'Security: The State (of) Being Free From Danger?' in Hans Günter Brauch et al (eds), *Globalization and Environmental Challenges* (Springer Berlin Heidelberg, 2008) vol 3, 529.

Slaughter, Anne-Marie, 'A Grand Strategy of Network Centrality' in Richard Fontain and Kristin Lord (eds), *America's Path: Grand Strategy for the Next Administration* (Center for American Security, 2012) 43.

Smith, Steve 'The Concept of Security in a Globalizing World' in Robert G Patman (ed), *Globalization and Conflict: National Security in a 'New' Strategic Era* (Routledge, 2006) 33.

Solana, Javier, 'The European Union and Human Security' in Mary Martin and Taylor Owen (eds), *The Routledge Handbook of Human Security* (Routledge, 2014) 251.

Sorel, JM, 'L'élargissement de la Notion de Menace contre la Paix' in Société Française pour le Droit International (ed) *Le Chapitre VII de la Charte des Nations Unies* (Pedone, 1996) 3.

St Clair, Asuncion, 'The Role of Ideas in the United Nations Development Programme' in M Boas and D McNeill (eds) *Global Institutions and Development: Framing the World?* (Routledge, 2004) 178.

Stohl, Rachel, 'Armed and Dangerous: Stopping the Use of Child Soldiers' in Ken Rutherford, Stefan Brem, and Richard Anthony Matthew, *Reframing the Agenda: The Impact of NGO and Middle Power Cooperation in International Security Policy* (Greenwood, 2003) 60.

Stromseth, Jane E, David Wippman and Rosa Brooks, *Can Might Make Rights? Building the Rule of Law after Military Interventions* (Cambridge University Press, 2006).

Sukma, Rizma, 'Indonesia' in Pranee Thiparat (ed) *The Quest for Human Security: The Next Phase of ASEAN?* (Institute of Security and International Studies, 2001) 62.

Tadjbakhsh, Shahrbanou and Anuradha M Chenoy, *Human Security: Concepts and Implications* (Routledge, 2007).

Tadjbakhsh, Shahrbanou, 'In Defense of the Broad View of Human Security' in Mary Martin and Taylor Owen (eds), *Routledge Handbook of Human Security* (Routledge, 2014) 43.

Takasu, Yukio, 'Japan and Networked Human Security' in Mary Martin and Taylor Owen (eds), *The Routledge Handbook of Human Security* (Routledge, 2014) 239.

Thakur, Ramesh, 'From National Security to Human Security' in Stuart Harris and Andrew Mack (eds) *Asia-Pacific Security: The Economics–Politics Nexus* (Allen & Unwin, 1997) 52.

Thakur, Ramesh, *The United Nations, Peace and Security: From Collective Security to the Responsibility to Protect* (Cambridge University Press, 2006).

Thakur, Ramesh and Edward Newman, 'Introduction: Non-Traditional Security in Asia' in Ramesh Thakur and Edward Newman (eds), *Broadening Asia's Security Discourse and Agenda: Political, Social and Environmental Perspectives* (United Nations University Press, 2004) 1.

Tickner, J Ann, *Gender in International Relations: Feminist Perspectives on Achieving Global Security* (Columbia University Press, 1992).

Tigerstrom, Barbaravon, *Human Security and International Law: Prospects and Problems* (Hart Publishing, 2007).

Tomlin, Brian W, 'On a Fast Track to a Ban: The Canadian Policy Process' in Maxwell A Cameron, Robert J Lawson and Brian W Tomlin (eds), *To Walk Without Fear: The Global Movement to Ban Landmines* (Oxford University Press, 1998).

Trindade, Antônio Augusto Cançado, *International Law for Humankind: Towards a New Jus Gentium* (Martinus Nijhoff, 2010) vol 6.

Tripp, Aili Mari, 'Toward a Gender Perspective on Human Security' in Aili Mari Tripp, Myra Marx Ferree and Christina Ewig (eds), *Gender, Violence and Human Security: Critical Feminist Perspectives* (New York University Press, 2013) 11.

Tripp, Aili Mari, Myra Marx Ferree and Christina Ewig (eds), *Gender, Violence and Human Security: Critical Feminist Perspectives* (New York University Press, 2013).

Turner, Bryan S, *Vulnerability and Human Rights* (Penn State University Press, 2006).

Turner, Mandy, Neil Cooper and Michael Pugh, 'Institutionalised and Co-opted: Why Human Security Has Lost Its Way' in David Chandler and Nik Hynek (eds), *Critical Perspectives on Human Security: Rethinking Emancipation and Power in International Relations* (Routledge, 2011) 83.

Vattel, Emmerich de, *The Law of Nations, or the Principles of Natural Law, Applied to the Conduct and to the Affairs of Nations and of Sovereigns* (Charles G Fenwick, trans 1916 edn).

Vidal, Victoria, 'Informal International Lawmaking: The Kimberley Process' Mechanism of Accountability' in Ayelet Bermanet al (ed), *Informal International Lawmaking: Case Studies* (Torkel Opsahl Academic EPublisher, 2012).

Voight, Christine, *Sustainable Development as a Principle of International Law: Resolving Conflicts between Climate Measures and WTO Law* (BRILL, 2009).

Wall, Kristen, Jenny Aulin and Gabriëlla Vogelaar (eds), *Empowerment and Protection: Stories of Human Security* (Global Partnership for the Prevention of Armed Conflict, 2014).

Waltz, Kenneth, *Theory of International Politics* (McGraw-Hill, 1979).

Wæver, Ole, *Securitization and Desecuritization* (Centre for Peace and Conflict Research, 1993).

Wæver, Ole, 'Peace and Security: Two Evolving Concepts and Their Changing Relationship' in Hans Günter Brauch et al (eds), *Globalization and Environmental Challenges* (Springer Berlin Heidelberg, 2008) vol 3, 99.

de Wet, Erika, *The Chapter VII Powers of the United Nations Security Council* (Hart Publishing, 2004).

Wessels, Michael, *Child Soldiers: From Violence to Protection* (Harvard University Press, 2007).

Wheatley, Steven, 'Democratic Governance Beyond the State: The Legitimacy of Non-state Actors as Standard Setters' in Anne Peters et al (eds), *Non-State Actors as Standard Setters* (Cambridge University Press, 2009) 214.

White, Nigel D, 'The Security Council, the Security Imperative and International Law' in Matthew Happold (ed) *International Law in a Multipolar World* (Routledge, 2012) 4.

Williams, Jody and Stephen Goose, 'The International Campaign to Ban Landmines' in Maxwell A Cameron, Robert J Lawson and Brian W Tomlin (eds), *To Walk Without Fear: The Global Movement to Ban Landmines* (Oxford University Press, 1998) 20.

Wolfers, Arnold, 'National Security as an Ambiguous Symbol' (1962) republished in Christopher W Hughes and Lai Yew Meng (eds) *Security Studies: A Reader* (Routledge, 2011) 5.

Wolfrum, Rüdiger, 'Article 1' in Bruno Simma (ed), *The United Nations Charter: A Commentary* (Oxford University Press, 2nd edn, 2002) vol I.

Wolfrum, Rüdiger and Jakob Pichon, 'Consensus' in Rüdiger Wolfrum (ed), *Max Planck Encyclopedia of Public International Law* (online edn).

Yihdego, Zarey, 'The Arms Trade Treaty and Human Security: What Role for NSAs?' in Cedric Ryngaert and Math Noortmann (ed), *Human Security and International Law: The Challenge of Non-State Actors* (Routledge, 2014) 135.

Zagor, Matthew, 'Elementary Considerations of Humanity' in Karine Bannelier, Theodore Christakis and Sarah Heathcote (eds), *The ICJ and the Evolution of International Law: The Enduring Impact of the Corfu Channel Case* (Routledge, 2012) 264.

Zwitter, Andrej, *Human Security, Law and the Prevention of Terrorism* (Routledge, 2011).

Journal articles

Abbott, Kenneth W, 'Modern International Relations Theory: A Prospectus for International Lawyers' (1989) 14 *Yale Journal of International Law* 335.

Acharya, Amitav, 'A Holistic Paradigm' (2004) 35 *Security Dialogue* 355.

Anderson, Kenneth, 'The Ottawa Convention Banning Landmines, the Role of International Non-Governmental Organizations and the Idea of International Civil Society' (2000) 11(1) *European Journal of International Law* 91.

Arbour, Louise, 'The Responsibility to Protect as a Duty of Care in International Law and Practice' (2008) 3 *Review of International Studies* 445.

Axworthy, Lloyd, 'Canada and Human Security: The Need for Leadership' (1997) 52(2) *International Journal* 183.

Axworthy, Lloyd, 'Human Security and Global Governance: Putting People First' (2001) 7 *Global Governance* 19.

Axworthy, Lloyd and Allan Rock, 'R2P: A New and Unfinished Agenda' (2009) 1 *Global Responsibility to Protect* 54.

Bajpai, Kanti, 'An Expression of Threats Versus Capabilities Across Time and Space' (2004) 35 *Security Dialogue* 360.

Balcik, Burcu et al, 'Coordination in Humanitarian Relief Chains: Practices, Challenges and Opportunities' (2010) 126 *International Journal of Production Economics* 22.

Baldwin, David A 'Security Studies and the End of the Cold War' (1995) 48 *World Politics* 117.

Baldwin, David A, 'The Concept of Security' (1997) 23 *Review of International Studies* 5.

Barber, Rebecca, 'The Responsibility to Protect the Survivors of Natural Disaster: Cyclone Nargis, A Case Study' (2009) 14(1) *Journal of Conflict and Security Law* 3.

Barthwal-Datta, Monica, 'Securitising Threats without the State: A Case Study of Misgovernance as a Security Threat in Bangladesh' (2009) 35(02) *Review of International Studies* 277.

Bartlett, Katharine, 'Feminist Legal Methods' (1990) 103 *Harvard Law Review* 829.

Bederman, David J, 'Constructivism, Positivism, and Empiricism in International Law' (2000) 89 *Georgetown Law Journal* 469.

Bellamy, Alex J, 'The Responsibility to Protect and the Problem of Military Intervention' (2008) 84 *International Affairs* 615.

Bellamy, Alex J and Matt McDonald, '"The Utility of Human Security": Which Humans? What Security? A Reply to Thomas & Tow' (2002) 33(3) *Security Dialogue* 373.

Benedek, Wolfgang, 'Human Security and Human Rights Interaction' (2008) 59 *International Social Science Journal* 7.

Biermann, Frank et al, 'The Fragmentation of Global Governance Architectures: A Framework for Analysis' (2009) 9(4) *Global Environmental Politics* 14.

Broude, Tomer, 'Principles of Normative Integration and the Allocation of International Authority: The WTO, the Vienna Convention on the Law of Treaties and the Rio Declaration' (2008–2009) 6 *Loyola University Chicago International Law Review* 173.

Brunnée, Jutta and Stephen J Toope, 'International Law and Constructivism: Elements of an Interactional Theory of International Law' (2000) 39 *Columbia Journal of Transnational Law* 19.

Bunch, Charlotte, 'Feminism, Peace, Human Rights and Human Security' (2003) 22 *Canadian Woman Studies* 6.

Buergenthal, Thomas, 'International Human Rights Law and Institutions: Accomplishments and Prospects' (1988) 63 *Washington Law Review* 1.

Burke, Anthony, 'Aporias of Security' (2002) 27 *Alternatives: Global, Local, Political* 1.

Burkhalter, Holly, 'Between the Lines: A Diamond Agreement in the Rough' (2003) 135 *Foreign Policy* 72.

Burley, Anne-Marie Slaughter, 'International Law and International Relations Theory: A Duel Agenda' (1993) 87 *American Journal of International Law* 205.

Buzan, Barry, 'Negotiating by Consensus: Developments in Technique at the United Nations Conference on the Law of the Sea' (1981) 75 *American Journal of International Law* 324.

Chandler, David, 'Human Security: The Dog that Didn't Bark' (2008) 39(4) *Security Dialogue* 427.

Chandler, David, 'Human Security II: Waiting for the Tail to Wag the Dog: Rejoinder to Ambrosetti, Owen and Wibben' (2008) 39(4) *Security Dialogue* 463.

Chandler, David, 'Rethinking the Conflict–Poverty Nexus: From Securitising Intervention to Resilience' (2015) 4 *Stability: International Journal of Security and Development* 13.

Charlesworth, Hilary, 'International Law: A Discipline of Crisis' (2002) 65(3) *Modern Law Review* 377.

Chataway, Teresa, 'Towards Normative Consensus on Responsibility to Protect' (2007) 16 *Griffith Law Review* 193.
Christie, Ryerson, 'Critical Voices and Human Security: To Endure, to Engage or to Critique?' (2010) 41(2) *Security Dialogue* 169.
Collier, Paul, 'Laws and Codes for the Resource Curse' (2008) 11 *Yale Human Rights and Development Law Journal* 9.
Corsi, Jessica, 'Towards Peace Through Legal Innovation: The Process and the Promise of the 2008 Cluster Munitions Convention' (2009) 22 *Harvard Human Rights Journal* 145.
Coupland, Robin, 'Humanity: What Is It and Does It Influence International Law?' (2001) 83(844) *International Review of the Red Cross* 969.
De Wet, Erika and Jure Vidmar, 'Conflicts between International Paradigms: Hierarchy versus Systemic Integration' (2013) 2 *Global Constitutionalism* 196.
Deng, Francis, 'Frontiers of Sovereignty: A Framework of Protection, Assistance and Development for the Internally Displaced' (1995) 8 *Leiden Journal of International Law* 249.
Deudney, Daniel H, 'Regrounding Realism: Anarchy, Security, and Changing Material Contexts' (2000) 10 *Security Studies* 1.
Deva, Surya, 'Human Rights Violations by Multinational Corporations and International Law: Where from Here?' (2003–2004) 19 *Connecticut Journal of International Law* 1.
Docherty, Bonnie, 'Breaking New Ground: The Convention on Cluster Munitions and the Evolution of International Humanitarian Law' (2009) 31 *Human Rights Quarterly* 934.
Doswald-Beck, Louise, 'Human Security: Can It Be Attained?' (2003) 97 *American Society International Legal Procedure* 93.
Dupuy, Pierre-Marie, 'International Law: Torn between Coexistence, Cooperation and Globalisation. General Conclusions' (1998) 9 *European Journal of International Law* 278.
Eberlein, Burkard and Abraham L Newman, 'Escaping the International Governance Dilemma? Incorporated Transgovernmental Networks in the European Union' (2008) 21(1) *Governance* 25.
Ewan, Pauline, 'Deepening the Human Security Debate: Beyond the Politics of Conceptual Clarification' (2007) 27(3) *Politics* 182.
Fabra Mata, Javier, 'Who Can Make Security? Competition over Securitisation between the State and Non-state Actors in Colombia' (2008) 4 *Journal of Human Security* 37.
Fastenrath, Ulrich, 'Relative Normativity in International Law' (1993) 4 *European Journal of International Law* 305.
Feldman, Daniel L, 'Conflict Diamonds, International Trade Regulation and the Nature of Law' (2003) 24 *University of Pennsylvania Journal of International Economic Law* 835.
Fidler, David P, 'Caught between Traditions: The Security Council in Philosophical Conundrum' (1996) 17 *Michigan Journal of International Law* 411.
Fidler, David P, 'Governing Catastrophes: Security, Health and Humanitarian Assistance' (2007) 89(866) *International Review of the Red Cross* 247.
Fielding, Lois E, 'Taking a Closer Look at Threats to Peace: The Power of the Security Council to Address Humanitarian Crises' (1995) 73 *University of Detroit Mercy Law Review* 551.
Finnemore, Martha and Kathryn Sikkink, 'International Norm Dynamics and Political Change' (1998) 52 *International Organization* 887.
Fischer-Lescano, Andreas and Gunther Teubner, 'Regime-Collisions: The Vain Search for Legal Unity in the Fragmentation of Global Law' (2004) 25 *Michigan Journal of International Law* 999.

Floyd, Rita, 'Human Security and the Copenhagen School's Securitization Approach: Conceptualizing Human Security as a Securitizing Move' (2007) 5 *Human Security Journal* 38.

Floyd, Rita, 'Can Securitization Theory Be Used in Normative Analysis? Towards a Just Securitization Theory' (2011) 42 *Security Dialogue* 427.

Franck, Thomas M, 'The Power of Legitimacy and the Legitimacy of Power: International Law in an Age of Power Disequilibrium' (2006) 100 *American Journal of International Law* 88.

Fraser, Nancy, 'Who Counts? Dilemmas of Justice in a Post-Westphalian World' (2009) 41 *Antipode* 281.

Frerks, Georg, 'Human Security as a Discourse and Counter-discourse' (2008) 19 *Security & Human Rights* 8.

Freudenschauß, Helmut, 'Article 39 of the UN Charter Revisited: Threats to the Peace and the Recent Practice of the UN Security Council' (1993) 46 *Austrian Journal of Public and International Law* 1.

Fujioka, Mieko, 'Japan's Human Rights Policy at Domestic and International Levels: Disconnecting Human Rights from Human Security' (2003) 15(2) *Japan Forum* 287.

Galtung, Johan, 'Violence, Peace and Peace Research' (1969) 6 *Journal of Peace Research* 170.

Galtung, Johan, 'The Palme Commission Report on Disarmament and Security: a Critical Comment' (1983) 14(2) *Security Dialogue* 147.

Gasper, Des, 'Securing Humanity: Situating "Human Security" as Concept and Discourse' (2005) 6(2) *Journal of Human Development* 221.

Giddings, Bob, Bill Hopwood and Geoff O'Brien, 'Environment, Economy and Society: Fitting Them Together into Sustainable Development' (2002) 10(4) *Sustainable Development* 187.

Glasius, Marlies, '"We Ourselves, We Are Part of the Functioning": The ICC, Victims, and Civil Society in the Central African Republic' (2009) 108(430) *African Affairs* 49.

Goldewijk, Berma Klein, 'Why Human? The Interlinkages Between Security, Rights and Development' (2008) 1 *Security and Human Rights* 24.

Grayson, Kyle, 'A Challenge to the Power over Knowledge of Traditional Security Studies' (2004) 35 *Security Dialogue* 357.

Grayson, Kyle, 'Human Security as Power/Knowledge: The Biopolitics of a Definitional Debate' (2008) 21(3) *Cambridge Review of International Affairs* 383.

Green, Caroline et al, 'Gender-based Violence and the Arms Trade Treaty: Reflections from a Campaigning and Legal Perspective' (2013) 21(3) *Gender & Development* 551.

Haacke, Jürgen, 'Myanmar, the Responsibility to Protect and the Need for Practical Assistance' (2009) 1 *Global Responsibility to Protect* 156.

Haas, PM, 'Introduction: Epistemic Communities and International Policy Coordination' (1992) 46 *International Organization* 1.

Hampson, Fen Osler and Holly Reid, 'Coalition Diversity and Normative Legitimacy in Human Security Negotiations' (2003) 8(1) *International Negotiation* 7.

Hampson, Fen Olser, 'A Concept in Need of a Global Policy Response' (2004) 35 *Security Dialogue* 349.

Hayden, Patrick, 'Constraining War: Human Security and the Human Right to Peace' (2004) October–December 2004 *Human Rights Review* 35.

Henckaerts, Jean-Marie, 'Assessing the Laws and Customs of War: The Publication of Customary International Humanitarian Law' (2006) 13 *Human Rights Brief* 8.

Henk, Dan, 'Human Security: Relevance and Implications' (2005) Summer 2005 *Parameters* 91.

Henkin, Louis, 'Conceptualizing Violence – Present and Future Developments in International Law' (1997) 60 *Alberta Law Review* 575.

Ho, Satomi, 'Japan's Human Security Policy: A Critical Review of its Limits and Failures' (2008) 28(1) *Japanese Studies* 101.

Holmes, Jamila D 'The Kimberley Process: Evidence of Change in International Law' (2006–2007) 3 *International Law and Management Review* 213

Hoogensen, Gunhild and Kirsti Stuvøy, 'Gender, Resistance and Human Security' (2006) 37(2) *Security Dialogue* 207.

Howard-Hassmann, Rhoda E, 'Human Security: Undermining Human Rights?' (February 2012) 34(1) *Human Rights Quarterly* 88.

Hsien-Li, Tan, 'Not Just Global Rhetoric: Japan's Substantive Actualization of its Human Security Foreign Policy' (2010) 10 *International Relations of the Asia-Pacific* 159.

Hubert, Don, 'An Idea that Works in Practice' (2004) 35 *Security Dialogue* 351.

Hudson, Heidi, '"Doing" Security As Though Humans Matter: A Feminist Perspective on Gender and the Politics of Human Security' (2005) 36 *Security Dialogue* 155.

Ikejiaku, Brian-Vincent, 'Poverty–Conflict Nexus: The Contentious Issue Revisited' (2012) 1(2) *European Journal of Sustainable Development* 127.

Ipinyomi, Foluke, 'Is Côte d'Ivoire a Test Case for R2P? Democratization as Fulfilment of the International Community's Responsibility to Prevent' (2012) 56(2) *Journal of African Law* 151.

Jerbi, Scott, 'Assessing the Roles of Multi-stakeholder Initiatives in Advancing the Business and Human Rights Agenda' (2012) 94(887) *International Review of the Red Cross* 1027.

Johnstone, Ian, 'Security Council Deliberations: The Power of the Better Argument' (2003) 14 *European Journal of International Law* 437.

Johnstone, Ian, 'Legislation and Adjudication in the UN Security Council: Bringing Down the Deliberative Deficit' (2008) 102 *American Journal of International Law* 275.

Jouannet, Emmanuelle, 'What Is the Use of International Law? International Law as a 21st Century Guardian of Welfare' (2006–2007) 28 *Michigan Journal of International Law* 815.

Kahgan, Carin, 'Table of Content. Jus Cogens and the Inherent Right to Self Defence' (1997) 3 *ILSA Journal of International and Comparative Law* 767.

Kaldor, Mary, Mary Martin and Sabine Selchow, 'Human Security: A New Strategic Narrative for Europe' (2007) 83(2) *International Affairs* 273.

Kammerhofer, Jörg, 'Systemic Integration, Legal Theory and the ILC' (2009) 19 *Finnish Yearbook of International Law* 157.

Kaplan, Margo, 'Carats and Sticks: Pursuing War and Peace through the Diamond Trade' (2003) 35 *International Law and Politics* 559.

Kellman, Barry, 'Controlling the Arms Trade: One Important Stride for Humankind' (2013–14) 37 *Fordham International Law Journal* 687.

Keohane, Robert O, 'International Relations and International Law: Interests, Reputations, Institutions' (1999) 93 *American Society International Legal Procedure* 375.

Kettemann, Matthias C, 'The Conceptual Debate on Human Security and its Relevance for the Development of International Law' (2006) 1(3) *Human Security Perspectives* 39.

Khagram, Sanjeev, William C, Clark and Dana Firas Raad, 'From the Environment and Human Security to Sustainable Security and Development' (2003) 4 *Journal of Human Development* 289.

Khong, Yuen Foong, 'Human Security: A Shotgun Approach to Alleviating Human Misery?' (2001) 7 *Global Governance* 231.

Kirgis, F, 'Custom on a Sliding Scale' (1987) 81 *American Journal of International Law* 147.

Kim, Sung Won, 'Human Security with an Asian Face?' (2010) 17 *Indiana Journal of Global Legal Studies* 83.

King, Gary and Christopher Murray, 'Rethinking Human Security' (2001) 116(4) *Political Science Quarterly* 585.

Kitchen, Veronica, 'From Rhetoric to Reality – Canada, the United States, and the Ottawa Process to Ban Landmines' (2001–2002) 57 *International Journal* 39.

Klabbers, Jan 'The Bridge Crack'd: A Critical Look at Interdisciplinary Relations' (2009) 23 *International Relations* 119.

Knutsen, Björn Olav, 'The EU's Security and Defense Policy (ESDP) and the Challenges of Civil–Military Coordination (CMCO): The Case of the Democratic Republic of Congo (DRC)' (2009) 18(4) *European Security* 441.

Koh, Harold Hongju, 'Transnational Legal Process' (1996) 75 *Nebraska Law Review* 181.

Koh, Harold Hongju, '1998 Frankel Lecture: Bringing International Law Home' (1998) 35 *Houston Law Review* 623.

Koskenniemi, Martti, 'The Place of Law in Collective Security' (1996) 17 *Michigan Journal of International Law* 45.

Krasner, Stephen D, 'International Law and International Relations: Together, Apart, Together?' (2000) 1 *Chicago Journal of International Law* 93.

Krause, Keith and Michael C Williams, 'Broadening the Agenda of Security Studies: Politics and Methods' (1996) 40 *Mershon International Studies Review* 229.

Krause, Keith, 'The Key to a Powerful Agenda, If Properly Defined' (2004) 35 *Security Dialogue* 367.

Langmore, John and Ashley McLachlan-Bent, 'A Crime against Humanity? Implications and Prospects of the Responsibility to Protect in the Wake of Cyclone Nargis' (2011) 3 *Global Responsibility to Protect* 37.

Lasswell, Harold, 'The Political Science of Science: An Inquiry into the Possible Reconciliation of Mastery and Freedom' (1956) 50 *American Political Science Review* 961.

Leaning, Jennifer, 'Psychosocial Well-Being over Time' (2004) 35 *Security Dialogue* 354.

Linderfalk, Ulf, 'Who Are "The Parties"? Article 31, Paragraph 3(C) of the 1969 Vienna Convention and the "Principle of Systemic Integration" Revisited' (2008) 55(03) *Netherlands International Law Review* 343.

Liotta, PH and Taylor Owen, 'Why Human Security' (2006) 7 *Whitehead Journal of Diplomacy and International Relations* 37.

MacArthur, Julie, 'A Responsibility to Rethink? Challenging Paradigms in Human Security' (2007–2008) 63 *International Journal* 422.

MacFarlane, S Neil, 'A Useful Concept that Risks Losing Its Political Salience' (2004) 35 *Security Dialogue* 368.

Mack, Andrew, 'A Signifier of Shared Values' (2004) 35 *Security Dialogue* 366.

Martin, Mary and Taylor Owen, 'The Second Generation of Human Security: Lessons from the UN and EU Experience' (2010) 86(1) *International Affairs* 211.

McClean, Emma, 'The Responsibility to Protect: The Role of International Human Rights Law' (2008) 13 *Journal of Conflict and Security Law* 123.

McDonald, Matt, 'Human Security and the Construction of Security' (2002) 16(3) *Global Society* 277.

McLachlan, Campbell, 'The Principle of Systemic Integration and Article 31(3)(c) of the Vienna Convention' (2005) 54(2) *International & Comparative Law Quarterly* 279.

Mearsheimer, John J, 'Back to the Future: Instability in Europe After the Cold War' (1990) 15(4) *International Security* 5.

Mearsheimer, John J, 'The False Promise of International Institutions' (1994) 19(3) *International Security* 5.
Merkouris, Panos, 'Debating the Ouroboros of International Law: The Drafting History of Article 31(3)(c)' (2007) 9(1) *International Community Law Review* 1.
Meron, Theodor, 'The Marten's Clause, Principles of Humanity and Dictates of Public Conscience' (2001) 94(1) *The American Journal of International Law* 78.
Milanovic, Marko, 'Norm Conflict in International Law: Whither Human Rights' (2009) 20 *Duke Journal of Comparative and International Law* 69.
Moreno-Lax, Violeta, 'Systematising Systemic Integration: "War Refugees", Regime Relations, and a Proposal for a Cumulative Approach to International Commitments' (2014) 12(5) *Journal of International Criminal Justice* 907.
Moussa, Ghada, 'Gender Aspects of Human Security' (2008) 59 *International Social Science Journal* 81.
Nanda, Ved P, 'Human Rights Must be at the Core of Post-2015 International Development Agenda' (April 2014) 75 *Montana Law Review* 1.
Nasu, Hitoshi, 'The Place of Human Security in Collective Security' (2012) 18 *Journal of Conflict and Security Law* 95.
Nef, Jorge, 'Human Security, Mutual Vulnerability and Sustainable Development: A Critical View' (2006) 7 *Whitehead Journal of Diplomacy and International Relations* 55.
Newman, Dwight, 'A Human Security Council? Applying a "Human Security" Agenda to Security Council Reform' (1999–2000) 31 *Ottawa Law Review* 213.
Newman, Edward, 'Human Security and Constructivism' (2001) 2(3) *International Studies Perspectives* 239.
Newman, Edward, 'A Normatively Attractive but Analytically Weak Concept' (2004) 35 *Security Dialogue* 358.
Newman, Edward, 'Critical Human Security Studies' (2010) 36 *Review of International Studies* 77.
Ng, Trina, 'Safeguarding Peace and Security in our Warming World: A Role for the Security Council' (2010) 15(2) *Journal of Conflict and Security Law* 275.
Aoláin, Fionnula Ní and Oren Gross, 'A Skeptical View of Deference to the Executive in Times of Crisis' (2008) 41 *Israel Law Review* 545.
Nichols, Julie Elizabeth, 'A Conflict of Diamonds: The Kimberley Process and Zimbabwe's Marange Diamond Fields' (2011–2012) 40 *Denver Journal of International Law and Policy* 648.
Norheim-Martinsen, Per Martin, 'Managing the Civil–Military Interface in the EU: Creating an Organisation Fit for Purpose' (2010) 14(10) *European Integration online Papers (EIoP)*.
Oberleitner, Gerd, 'Porcupines in Love: The Intricate Convergence of Human Rights and Human Security' (2005) 6 *European Human Rights Law Review* 588.
Oberleitner, Gerd, 'Human Security: A Challenge to International Law?' (2005) 11 *Global Governance* 185.
O'Connell, Mary Ellen, 'Appraising the Methods of International Law: A Prospectus for Readers' (1999) 93 *American Journal of International Law* 291.
Ogata, Sadako and Johan Cels, 'Human Security – Protecting and Empowering the People' (2003) 9 *Global Governance* 273.
Oman, Natalie, 'The "Responsibility to Prevent": A Remit for Intervention?' (2009) 22(2) *Canadian Journal of Law and Jurisprudence* 355.
Owen, Taylor, 'Human Security – Conflict, Critique and Consensus: Colloquium Remarks and a Proposal for a Threshold-Based Definition' (2004) 35(3) *Security Dialogue* 373.

Özerdem, Alpaslan, 'The "Responsibility to Protect" in Natural Disasters: Another Excuse for Interventionism? Nargis Cyclone, Myanmar' (2010) 10(5) *Conflict, Security & Development* 693.

Paris, Roland, 'Human Security: Paradigm Shift or Hot Air?' (2001) 26(2) *International Security* 87.

Paris, Roland, 'Still an Inscrutable Concept' (2004) 35(3) *Security Dialogue* 370.

Paris, Roland, 'Rational and Irrational Approaches to Human Security: A Reply to Ralph Pettman' (2005) 18(3) *Cambridge Review of International Affairs* 479.

Petrasek, David, 'Human Rights "Lite"? Thoughts on Human Security' (2004) 3 *Disarmament Forum* 59

Pirozzi, Nicoletta and Sammi Sandawi, 'Military and Civilian ESDP Missions: Ever Growing and Effective' (2009) *Istituto Affari Internazionali* 1.

Price, Richard, 'Emerging Customary Norms and Anti-personnel Landmines' (2004) 96 *Cambridge Studies in International Relations* 106.

Purvis, N, 'Critical Legal Studies in Public International Law' (1991) 32 *Harvard International Law Journal* 81

Rajamani, L, 'The Cancun Climate Agreements: Reading the Text, Subtext and Tea Leaves' (2011) 60 *International & Comparative Law Quarterly* 499.

Reisman, W Michael, 'Sovereignty and Human Rights in Contemporary International Law' (1990) 84 *American Journal of International Law* 866.

Ripsman, Norrin M, 'The Political Economy of Security: A Research and Teaching Agenda' (2009) 3(1) *Journal of Military and Strategic Studies* 1.

Ritchie, Cyril, 'Coordinate? Cooperate? Harmonise? NGO Policy and Operational Coalitions' (1995) 16(3) *Third World Quarterly* 513.

Roberts, David, 'Empowering the Human Security Debate: Making It Coherent and Meaningful' (2005) XXII(4) *International Journal on World Peace* 3.

Roberts, David, 'Human Security or Human Insecurity? Moving the Debate Forward' (2006) 37 *Security Dialogue* 249.

Rosenberg, Sheri P, 'Responsibility to Protect: A Framework for Prevention' (2009) 1 *Global Responsibility to Protect* 442.

Rothschild, Emma, 'What Is Security?' (1995) 124(3) *Daedalus* 53.

Rutherford, Ken, 'The Hague and Ottawa Conventions: A Model for Future Weapons Ban Regimes' (1999) Spring–Summer *The Nonproliferation Review* 36.

Ruzza, Tommasodi, 'The Convention on Cluster Munitions: Towards a Balance between Humanitarian and Military Considerations?' (2008) 47 *Military Law and the Law of War Review* 405.

Sarigiannidis, Miltiadis, 'Legal Discourses on Peacemaking/Peacekeeping/Peacebuilding: International Law as a New Topos for Human Security' (2007) 62 *International Journal* 519.

Saul, Ben, 'The Dangers of the United Nations' "New Security Agenda": "Human Security" in the Asia-Pacific Region' (2006) 1(1) *Asian Journal of Comparative Law* 1.

Schachter, Oscar, 'International Law in Theory and Practice: General Course in Public International Law' (1982) 178 *Recueil des Cours* 21.

Schachter, Oscar, 'United Nations Law' (1994) 88 *American Journal of International Law* 1.

Schlichtmann, Klaus, 'An Enduring Concept for Security Council Reform' (2011) 2 *Beijing Law Review* 97.

Schwindt, Constance Jean, 'Interpreting the United Nations Charter: From Treaty to World Constitution' (2000) 6 *UC Davis Journal of International Law and Policy* 193.

Scott, Shirley V, 'The Securitization of Climate Change in World Politics: How Close Have we Come and Would Full Securitization Enhance the Efficacy of Global Climate Change Policy?' (2012) 21(3) *Review of European Community & International Environmental Law* 220.

Watson, J Shand 'A Realistic Jurisprudence of International Law' (1980) 30 *Year Book of World Affairs* 265.

Short, Nicola, 'The Role of NGOs in the Ottawa Process to Ban Landmines' (1999) 4(3) *International Negotiation* 483.

Simma, Bruno and Philip Alston, 'The Sources of Human Rights Law: Custom, Jus Cogens, and General Principles' (1988–1989) 12 *Australian Yearbook of International Law* 82.

Simma, Bruno and Andreas Paulus, 'Appraising the Methods of International Law: A Prospectus for Readers' (1999) 93 *American Journal of International Law* 291.

Simma, Bruno and Dirk Pulkowski, 'Of Planets and the Universe: Self-contained Regimes in International Law' (2006) 17 *European Journal of International Law* 483.

Simmons, Beth, 'International Law and International Relations: Scholarship at the Intersection of Principles and Politics' (2001) 95 *American Society International Legal Procedure* 271.

Slaughter, Anne-Marie, 'Security, Solidarity, and Sovereignty: the Grand Themes of UN Reform' (2005) 99 *American Journal of International Law* 619.

Sloan, Blaine, 'The United Nations Charter as a Constitution' (1989) 1 *Pace International Law Review* 61.

Sohn, Louis B, 'United Nations Decision-making, Confrontation of Consensus?' (1974) 15 *Harvard International Law Journal* 438.

Sohn, Louis, 'Voting Procedures in United Nations Conferences for the Codification of International Law' (1975) 69 *American Journal of International Law* 310.

Sohn, Louis B, 'The New International Law: Protection of the Rights of Individuals.

Rather Than States' (1982) 32 *American University Law Review* 1.

Stahn, Carsten, 'Responsibility to Protect: Political Rhetoric or Emerging Legal Norm?' (2007) 101 *American Journal of International Law* 99.

Stern, Maria and Joakim Öjendal, 'Mapping the Security–Development Nexus: Conflict, Complexity, Cacophony, Convergence?' (2010) 41 *Security Dialogue* 5.

Stockburger, Peter, 'The Responsibility to Protect Doctrine: Customary International Law, an Emerging Legal Norm or Just Wishful Thinking' (2010) 5 *Intercultural Human Rights Law Review* 365.

Suhrke, Astri, 'Human Security and the Interests of States' (1999) 30(3) *Security Dialogue* 265.

Sunstein, Cass R, 'Social Norms and Social Roles' (1996) 96 *Columbia Law Review* 903.

Suzuki, Eisuke, 'The New Haven School of International Law: An Invitation to a Policy-Oriented Jurisprudence' (1974) 1 *Yale Journal of International Law* 1

Tasioulas, J, 'Opinio Juris and the Genesis of Custom: A Solution to the "Paradox"' (2007) 26 *Australian Yearbook of International Law* 199.

Tesón, Fernando, 'The Kantian Theory of International Law' (1992) 92 *Columbia Law Review* 53.

Thakur, Ramesh, 'A Political Worldview' (2004) 35 *Security Dialogue* 347.

Thakur, Ramesh, 'United Nations Security Council Reform' (2004) 13(3) *African Security Studies* 66.

Thérien, Jean-Phillipe, 'Human Security: The Making of a UN Ideology' (2012) 26(2) *Global Society* 191.

Thomas, Caroline, 'Global Governance, Development and Human Security: Exploring the Links' (2001) 22(2) *Third World Quarterly* 150.

Thomas, Caroline, 'A Bridge Between the Interconnected Challenges Confronting the World' (2004) 35 *Security Dialogue* 353.

Toope, Stephen J, 'Fallout from "9-11": Will a Security Culture Undermine Human Rights' (2002) 65 *Saskatchewan Law Review* 281.

True-Frost, C Cora, 'The Security Council and Norm Consumption' (2007–2008) 40 *NYU Journal of International Law & Politics* 115.

Tzevelekos, Vassilis P, 'The Use of Article 31(3)(c) of the VCLT in the Case Law of the ECtHR: An Effective Anti-fragmentation Tool or a Selective Loophole for the Reinforcement of Human Rights Teleology? Between Evolution and Systemic Integration. (Vienna Convention on the Law of Treaties, European Court of Human Rights)' (2010) 31(3) *Michigan Journal of International Law* 621.

Ullman, Richard, 'Redefining Security' (1983) 8(1) *International Security* 129.

Uvin, Peter, 'A Field of Overlaps and Interactions' (2004) 35 *Security Dialogue* 352.

van Aaken, Anne, 'Defragmentation of Public International Law Through Interpretation: A Methodological Proposal' (2009) 16 *Indiana Journal of Global Legal Studies* 483.

Vásquez, Carlos M, 'Direct v Indirect Obligations of Corporations under International Law' (2005) 43 *Columbia Journal of Transnational Law* 927.

Vignes, Daniel, 'Will the Third Conference on the Law of the Sea Work According to the Consensus Rule?' (1975) 69(1) *The American Journal of International Law* 119.

Voigt, Christina, 'Sustainable Security' (2009) 19(1) *Yearbook of International Environmental Law* 163.

Wallis, Ann C, 'Data Mining: Lessons from the Kimberley Process for the United Nations' Development of Human Rights Norms for Transnational Corporations' (2005) 4 *Northwestern Journal of International Human Rights* 388.

Walt, Stephen, 'The Renaissance of Security Studies' (1991) 35 *International Studies Quarterly* 211.

Watson, Scott, 'The "Human" as Referent Object: Humanitarianism as Securitization?' (2011) 42 *Security Dialogue* 3.

Weiss, Thomas G, 'The Illusion of UN Security Council Reform' (2003) 26(4) *Washington Quarterly* 147.

Weiss, Thomas G and Karen E Young, 'Compromise and Credibility: Security Council Reform?' (2005) 36(2) *Security Dialogue* 131.

Wellens, Karel, 'The UN Security Council and New Threats to the Peace: Back to the Future' (2003) 8 *Journal of Conflict and Security Law* 15.

Wendt, Alexander, 'Anarchy Is What States Make of It: The Social Construction of Power Politics' (Spring 1992) 46(2) *International Organization* 391.

Wexler, Lesley, 'The International Deployment of Shame, Second-Best Responses and Norm Entrepeneurship: The Campaign to Ban Landmines and the Landmine Ban Treaty' (2003) 20(3) *Arizona Journal of International and Comparative Law* 561.

Wibben, Annick TR, 'Human Security: Towards an Opening' (2008) 39 *Security Dialogue* 455.

Wiessner, Siegfried and Andrew R Willard in Symposium on Method in International Law, 'Appraising the Methods of International Law: A Prospectus for Readers' (1999) 93 *American Journal of International Law* 291.

Wiessner, Siegfried and Andrew R Willard, 'Policy-Oriented Jurisprudence and Human Rights Abuses in Internal Conflict: Toward a World Public Order of Human Dignity' (1999) 93 *American Journal of International Law* 316.

Winslow, Donna and Thomas Hylland Eriksen, 'A Broad Concept that Encourages Interdisciplinary Thinking' (2004) 35 *Security Dialogue* 361.

Wong, Jarrod, 'Reconstructing the Responsibility to Protect in the Wake of Cyclones and Separatism' (2009) 84 *Tulane Law Review* 219.

Yanacopulos, Helen, 'The Strategies that Bind: NGO Coalitions and their Influence' (2005) 5(1) *Global Networks* 93.

Yanacopulos, Helen, 'Patterns of Governance: The Rise of Transnational Coalitions of NGOs' (2005) 19(3) *Global Society* 247.

Young, Katharine G, 'Minimum Core of Economic and Social Rights: A Concept in Search of Content' (2008) 33 *Yale Journal of International Law* 113.

Zahar, Marie-Joelle, 'Intervention, Prevention and the "Responsibility to Protect"' (2005) 60 *International Journal* 723.

Reports, working papers

Alkire, Sabine, 'A Conceptual Framework for Human Security' (Working Paper No 2, Centre for Research on Inequality, Human Security and Ethnicity (CRISE) 2003).

Bruderlein, Claude, 'The Role of Non State Actors in Building Human Security' (Working Paper, Centre for Humanitarian Dialogue, May 2000).

Chimonyo, GR, Solomon Mungure and Paul D Scott, 'The Social, Economic and Environmental Implications of Diamond Mining in Chiadzwa' (Study conducted by Centre for Research and Development 2013).

Coalition to Stop the Use of Child Soldiers, *Global Report 2008* (CICC, 2008).

Control Arms, *Finishing the Job: Delivering a Bullet-Proof ATT* (Control Arms, 2012).

Council of the EU, 'Report on the Implementation of the European Security Strategy – Providing Security in a Changing World' Brussels, EU Doc S407/08 (11 December 2008).

Dunhoff, Jeffrey L and Mark A Pollack, 'International Law and International Relations: Introducing an Interdisciplinary Dialogue' (Legal Studies Research Paper No 2012–18, Temple University Beasley School of Law, 2012).

EU-Russia Human Security Study Group, 'Helsinki Plus: Towards a Human Security Architecture for Europe' (First Report, May 2010).

Fioramonti, Lorenzo, 'Human Security? The Weaknesses of the EU's Involvement in Human Rights Crises' (EU-Grasp Policy Brief, March 2012).

Dabe, Gugu, 'Negotiating the Convention on Cluster Munitions: The Role of African States' ISS Paper 187 (June 2009).

Geneva Call, *Annual Report 2013* (Geneva Call, 2013).

Global Environmental Change and Human Security Project, 'Global Environmental Change and Human Security Science Plan' (IHDP Report International Human Dimensions Programme on Global Environmental Change, 1999).

Global Fund to Fight AIDS, Tuberculosis and Malaria, *The Global Fund Strategy 2012–2016: Investing for Impact* (Global Fund, 2012).

Global Witness, 'Return of the Blood Diamond: The Deadly Race to Control Zimbabwe's New Found Diamond Wealth' (14 June 2010).

Hanssen, Måns, 'Civil–Military Interaction in the European Union: Applying a Comprehensive Approach to CSDP Operations' (Working Paper FOI, 2010).

Hubert, Don, 'The Landmine Ban: A Case Study in Humanitarian Advocacy' (Occasional Paper No 42, Institute for International Studies, Brown University, 2000).

Huijstee, Mariëttevan, 'Multi-stakeholder Initiatives: A Guide for Civil Society Organisations' (SOMO, March 2012).

Human Rights Watch, *Hidden Death: Land Mines and Civilian Casualties in Iraqi Kurdistan* (HRW, 1992).

Human Rights Watch, *Diamonds in the Rough: Human Rights Abuses in the Marange Diamond Fields of Zimbabwe* (HRW, 2009).

Human Rights Watch, *Deliberate Chaos: Ongoing Human Rights Abuses in the Marange Diamond Fields of Zimbabwe* (HRW, 2010).

Human Security Report Project, *Human Security Report 2009–2010* (Simon Fraser University, 2010).

Human Security Study Group, 'A European Way of Security' (The Madrid Report of the Human Security Study Group comprising a Proposal and Background Report 8th November, 2007)

Independent Commission on International Development Issues, *North–South: A Program for Survival* (MIT Press, 1980).

Institute for International Cooperation, 'Poverty Reduction and Human Security' (Report No 05–15, Japan International Cooperation Agency, March 2006).

Independent Commission on Disarmament and Security Issues, *Common Security: A Blueprint for Survival* (Simon and Schuster, 1982).

Independent Commission on International Development Issues, *North–South: A Program for Survival* (MIT Press, 1980).

International Commission on Intervention and State Sovereignty (ICISS), *The Responsibility to Protect* (International Development Research Centre, December 2001).

International Committee of the Red Cross, *Anti-Personnel Mines – Friend or Foe? A Study of the Military Use and Effectiveness of Anti-personnel Mines* (ICRC, 1997).

International Committee of the Red Cross, *Arms Availability and the Situation of Civilians in Armed Conflict* (Geneva, June 1999).

James, Stephen, 'Human Security: Key Drivers, Antecedents and Conceptualisation' (Working Paper No 1, Institute for Human Security, La Trobe University, 2010).

Jodoin, Sébastien, 'The Principle of Integration and Interrelationship in Relation to Human Rights and Social, Economic and Environmental Objectives' (A Legal Working Paper in the CISDL Recent Developments in International Law Related to Sustainable Development Series, March 2005).

Jolly, R and DB Ray, *The Human Security Framework and National Human Development Report: A Review of Experiences and Current Debates* (2008) <http://hdr.undp.org/docs/nhdr/thematic_reviews/Human_Security_Guidance_Note.pdf>.

Kerr, Pauline, 'The Evolving Dialectic between State-Centric and Human-Centric Security' (Working Paper No 2003/2, Australian National University, 2003).

Kimberley Process Plenary, 'Administrative Decision on Zimbabwe Joint Work Plan', Swakopmund, Namibia, 5 November 2009 <http://www.kimberleyprocess.com/en/2009-administrative-decision-zimbabwe-jwp>.

Kimberley Process Plenary, 'Zimbabwe Annual Report 2010' <http://www.kimberleyprocess.com/en/zimbabwe-annual-report-2010>.

Kimberley Process Plenary, 'Administrative Decision on Marange (Zimbabwe)', Kinchasa Plenary Meeting, 1 November 2011 <http://www.kimberleyprocess.com/en/0012011-administrative-decision-marange-zimbabwecompendium>.

Koehler, Gabriele, et al, 'Human Security and the Next Generation of Comprehensive Hum Dev Goals' (Research Paper Institute of Development Studies, April 2012).

Koskenniemi, Martti, 'International Law: between Fragmentation and Constitutionalism' (unpublished paper, ANU, Canberra, 27 November 2006)

KP Civil Society Coalition, *A Guide to the Kimberley Process* (PAC, September 2013).

Krause, Keith, 'Towards a Practical Human Security Agenda' (Policy Paper No 26, Geneva Centre for the Democratic Control of Armed Forces (DCAF), 2007).

Lamb, Guy, 'African States and the ATT Negotiations' (Arms Control Today 2012) <http://www.armscontrol.org/act/2012_09/African-States-And-the-ATT-Negotiations>.

Lunde, Leiv and Mark Taylor, 'Commerce or Crime? Regulating Economies of Conflict' (Report No 424, FAFO Institute, 2003).

Making Targeted Sanctions More Effective: Guidelines for the Implementation of UN Policy Options, Final Report of the Stockholm Process on the Implementation of Targeted Sanctions, (Department of Peace and Conflict Research, Uppsala University, February 2003).

Martens, Jens, 'Multistakeholder Partnerships – Future Models of Multilateralism' (Occasional Paper No 29, Dialogue on Globalization, January 2007).

McGrath, Rae, 'The Reality of the Present Use of Mines by Military Forces' in ICRC (ed), *ICRC Report of the Symposium on Anti-Personnel Landmines* (ICRC, 1993) 7.

Mikulaschek, Christoph, 'The United Nations Security Council and the Responsibility to Protect: Policy, Process, and Practice' (Favorita Papers No 1/2010, 39th IPI Vienna Seminar, 15 January 2010).

Norheim-Martinsen, Per Martin, 'Matching Ambition with Institutional Innovation: The EU's Comprehensive Approach and Civil–Military Organisation' (Report for the Norwegian Defence Research Establishment (FFI), 3 July 2009).

OECD, *Paris Declaration on Aid Effectiveness* (2 March 2005).

Organisation of African Unity (OAU), 'The Kampala Document: Towards a Conference on Security, Stability, Development and Co-operation in Africa' adopted at the Kampala Summit, 19–22 May 1991.

Organisation for Security and Cooperation in Europe (OSCE), *Human Dimension Commitments: Volume 1, Thematic Compilation* (OSCE, 3rd edn, 2012).

OSCE Study Group, *Barcelona Report of the Study Group on Europe's Security Capabilities: A Human Security Doctrine for Europe*, presented to EU High Representative for Common Foreign and Security Policy (15 September 2004).

Partnership Africa Canada, 'Killing Kimberley? Conflict Diamonds and Paper Tigers' (Occasional Paper No 15, PAC, November 2006).

Partnership Africa Canada (PAC), 'Diamonds and Clubs: The Militarized Control of Diamonds and Power in Zimbabwe' (Report PAC, June 2010).

Physicians for Human Rights, *Hidden Enemies: Landmines in Northern Somalia* (PHR, 1992)

Quilligan, JB, 'The Brandt Equation: 21st Century Blueprint for the New Global Economy', *Brandt 21 Forum*, (2002) <http://www.brandt21forum.info/BrandtEquation-19Sept04.pdf>.

Rapaport, Martin, 'Stop Buying Blood Diamonds: The Kimberley Process is a Sham' (Rapaport Diamond Report February 2010)

Roll Back Malaria, *A Multisectoral Action Framework for Malaria* (RBM, 2013).

Saul, Ben 'The Dangers of the United Nations' "New Security Agenda": "Human Security" in the Asia-Pacific Region' (Sydney Law School Research Paper No. 08/114, 2006).

Schefer, Krista 'Chilling the Protection of Human Rights: What the Kimberley Process Waiver Can Tell Us about the WTO's Effect on International Law', (Working Paper No 2007/03, NCCR Trade Regulation: Swiss National Centre of Competence in Research, January 2007).

Sending, J, 'The Political Dynamics of the Security–Development Nexus' (Working Paper for the Standing Group for International Relations of the European Consortium for Political Research, 9–11 September 2004).

St Clair, Asuncion, 'Ideas in Action: Hum Dev and Capability as Boundary Objects' (Working Paper, University of Bergen, 2004).

Stewart, Frances, 'Development and Security' (Working Paper No 3, Centre for Research on Inequality, Human Security and Ethnicity [CRISE] 2003).

Symposium, Ministry of Foreign Affairs (Japan) ('MOFA'), *Summary Conclusion of the Symposium on Human Security*, 15 July 2010, Okuma Auditorium, Waseda University <http://www.mofa.go.jp/policy/human_secu/pdfs/sympo1007_con.pdf>.

Waiver Concerning the Kimberley Process Certification Scheme for Rough Diamonds, Decision of 15 May 2003, WTO Doc WT/L/518 (27 May 2003).

World Bank, Conflict, Crime and Violence Team, *Making Societies More Resilient to Violence: A Conceptual Framework for the Conflict, Crime And Violence Agenda* (World Bank, 2008).

World Commission on Environment and Development, *Our Common Future* (Oxford University Press, 1987).

World Commission on the Social Dimension of Globalization, *A Fair Globalization: Creating Opportunities for All* (International Labour Organization, February 2004).

Speeches and conference proceedings

Axworthy, Lloyd, 'Notes for an Address by the Honourable Lloyd Axworthy, Minister of Foreign Affairs, to the Oslo NGO Forum on Banning Anti-Personnel Landmines', DFAIT (Canada) Statement, Oslo, Norway, 10 September 1997.

Axworthy, Lloyd, 'Notes for an Address by the Honourable Lloyd Axworthy, Minister of Foreign Affairs, Canada' (Speech delivered at the Woodrow Wilson International Center for Scholars, Washington, DC, United States of America, 16 June 2000) <http://www.peace.ca/axworthyaddresstwoodrow.htm>.

Bartsch, Sonja, 'The Global Fund to Fight AIDS, Tuberculosis and Malaria: Establishment, Current Issues and Future Challenges' (Paper presented at the Salzburg Seminar on the Governance of Health, Schloss Arenberg, Salzburg, Austria, 5–8 December 2005).

Buzan, Barry, 'Human Security in International Perspective' (Paper presented at the 14th Asia-Pacific Roundtable, Kuala Lumpur, Malaysia, 3–7 June 2000).

Dongyan, Li, 'China's Approach to Non-Traditional Security (NTS)' (conference report, Institute of East Asian Studies, Berkeley, CA, 8 March 2007).

Lake, Anthony 'Address at High Level Human Security Symposium', TICAD V: Tokyo International Conference on African Development High Level Human Security Symposium (2 June 2013) (Tokyo, Japan) <http://www.mofa.go.jp/policy/oda/sector/security/pdfs/sympo1306_unicef.pdf>.

Lodgaard, Sverre, 'Human Security: Concept and Operationalization' (Paper prepared for Expert Seminar on Human Rights and Peace, Geneva, 8–9 December 2000) <http://www.hsph.harvard.edu/hpcr/events/hsworkshop/lodgaard.pdf>.

Kimberley Process Chair, 'Final Communiqué from the Kimberley Process Plenary Meeting' Washington, DC, 30 November 2012 <http://www.kimberleyprocess.com/en/2012-final-communique-plenary-washingtoncompendium>.

Kongstad, Ambassador Steffen, Opening Statement by Norway at the Belgrade Conference of States Affected by Cluster Munitions, the Way Ahead: Achieving an Effective International Response to the Problem of Cluster Munitions', 3–4 October 2007, <http://www.w3c.org/TR/1999/REC-html401-19991224/>.

Latham, Andrew, 'The Politics of Stigmatization: Global Cultural Changes and the Transnational Campaign to Ban Antipersonnel Landmines', Address Before the International Studies Association, *Columbia International Affairs Online* <www.ciaonet.org/isa/laa01/>.

Pitsuwan, Surin, Keynote Address on Regional Cooperation for Human Security, International Development Studies Conference on Mainstreaming Human Security: The Asian Contribution (10 October 2007) (Bangkok, Thailand).

Roosevelt, Franklin D, 'State of the Union Address ("Four Freedoms Speech")' (Speech delivered at the Joint Session of Congress, Washington, DC, United States of America, 6 January 1941) <http://www.fdrlibrary.marist.edu/pdfs/fftext.pdf>.

Saliba-Couture, Charles, 'The Security–Development Nexus: From Obviousness to Ambiguity' (Paper presented at the International Studies Association Annual Conference Global Governance: Political Authority in Transition, Montreal, Canada, 16 March 2011) <http://www.allacademic.com/meta/p502091_index.html>.

Sen, Amartya, 'Why Human Security?', International Symposium on Human Security (28 July 2000) (Toyko, Japan).

Tadjbakhsh, Shahrbanou, 'Human Security: The Seven Challenges of Operationalizing the Concept' (Speech delivered at the Human Security: 60 Minutes to Convince, Paris, France, 13 September 2005).

Antonio Tete on behalf of Ramtane Lamamra Commissioner for Peace and Security of the African Union, 'Relevance and Added Value of Human Security: Regional Perspective' (Speech delivered at the High-Level Event on Human Security, United Nations, New York, 8 May 2013) <https://docs.unocha.org/sites/dms/HSU/Statement%20by%20Amb%20Antonio%20Tete,%20African%20Union.pdf>.

Media reports

'Blood diamonds watchdog washes its hands', *Independent Online*, 29 August 2009 <http://www.iol.co.za/news/africa/blood-diamonds-watchdog-washes-its-hands-1.456713>.

Annan, Kofi, 'Two Concepts of Sovereignty', *The Economist* (London), 18 September 1999 <http://www.un.org/News/ossg/sg/stories/kaecon.html>.

Mangongera, Charles, 'Zimbabwe's Diamond Curse', *The Independent* (Zimbabwe) 22 November 2013 <http://www.theindependent.co.zw/2013/11/22/zimbabwes-diamond-curse/>.

Mambondiyani, Andrew, 'The curse of Marange diamonds … as relocated villagers wallow in poverty' *Bulawayo24* (online), 4 November 2013 <http://bulawayo24.com/index-id-opinion-sc-columnist-byo-38359.html>.

Mambondiyani, Andrew, 'The Curse of Marange Diamonds', *Zimbabwe Situation* (online), 4 November 2013 <http://www.zimbabwesituation.com/news/zimsit_the-curse-of-marange-diamonds/>.

Ndebele, Hazel, 'Opacity haunts diamond mining's Treasury remittances', *The Independent* (Zimbabwe), 15 November 2013 <http://www.theindependent.co.zw/2013/11/15/opacity-haunts-diamond-minings-treasury-remittances/>.

UN Department of Public Information, 'Sanctions and War: General Assembly adopts resolution on conflict diamonds' (2002), <http://www.un.org/peace/africa/Diamond.html>.

Winslow, Phillip S, 'Canadians taking lead in mine fight: United States "miffed" as nation to north forms coalition against weapon', *Baltimore Sun* (Baltimore, Maryland), 10 August 1997 <http://articles.baltimoresun.com/1997-08-10/news/1997222014_1_anti-personnel-mines-ban-on-anti-personnel-campaign-to-ban>.

'Zimbabwe to lead diamond producers: Report', *NewsDay* (Zimbabwe), 2 September 2013 <https://www.newsday.co.zw/2013/09/02/zimbabwe-lead-diamond-producers-report/>.

Index

For Product Safety Concerns and Information please contact our EU
representative GPSR@taylorandfrancis.com
Taylor & Francis Verlag GmbH, Kaufingerstraße 24, 80331 München, Germany

www.ingramcontent.com/pod-product-compliance
Ingram Content Group UK Ltd.
Pitfield, Milton Keynes, MK11 3LW, UK
UKHW020014200926
475702UK00014B/1879
9780367884383